WJEC/Eduqas

Media Studies

Revised Edition

for A Level Year 2 & A2

Christine Bell • Lucas Johnson

Published in 2023 by Illuminate Publishing Limited, an imprint of Hodder Education, an Hachette UK Company, Carmelite House, 50 Victoria Embankment, London EC4Y 0DZ

Orders: Please visit www.illuminatepublishing.com or email sales@illuminatepublishing.com

British Library Cataloguing-in-Publication Data

A catalogue record for this book is available from the British Library
ISBN 978-1-913963-29-3

Produced by DZS Grafik, Printed in Slovenia

Editor: Dawn Booth
Design and layout: Kamae Design
Cover design: Nigel Harriss
Cover image: Only Background/Shutterstock.com

Authors' acknowledgements
A big thank you to Dawn, Eve and Tania for all their hard work in putting the book together. Thanks, too, to Jo Johnson for all that she's done for Media Studies during her time at WJEC.

Thanks to the following students who allowed their work to be used: Rachel Wells of Heaton Manor School, Sophie Johnston of Varndean College, Scott Maxwell of Keswick School, Kelly Joves, George Francis, Amber Bishop, Diana Zaletova, Isabella Miles-Hardt and Mati Granica of Peter Symonds College, Michael Shenton of Oldham Sixth Form College and Sophie Burman of St Cyres School.

Dedication
In memory of my mum – LJ

For Nic, Oliver and Lucy – CB

Contents

How to Use this Book

The contents of this student book are primarily designed for those learners following the linear Eduqas Media Studies specification in England and Northern Ireland. However, some of the content is also relevant to those following the modular WJEC specification in Wales and Northern Ireland. For the WJEC specification, there are helpful indicators at key points throughout this book showing you the sections of the Eduqas content that are relevant to the WJEC specification.

This book has been written specifically for the Eduqas A Level course and includes useful information to help you perform well in the examinations and the internally assessed unit. It is designed to be used in conjunction with the Year 1 book, where the aspects of the theoretical framework that are common to both the AS and the A Level specification were introduced. This book builds on that material, introducing the additional set products, topics and theories that are specific to the A Level.

The book is split into chapters related to different aspects of the specification. Chapters 1 and 2 provide an overview of the theoretical framework and the different components within the A Level specification. Chapters 3 and 4 are concerned with the media forms and products studied in Component 1, while Component 2 is covered in Chapters 5 and 6. Component 3 (the non-examination assessment) is discussed in Chapters 7 and 8, while Chapter 9 offers tips and guidance on examination preparation. A quick guide to theoretical approaches and the named theorists you are required to study is provided in Chapter 10. A glossary of key terms is also included towards the end of the book.

Each chapter includes the following elements:

- Examples of how to analyse a range of media forms and products, using relevant critical approaches and subject-specific terminology.
- Definitions of **Key Terms** to help you in your study and revision.
- **Quickfire** questions designed to test your knowledge and understanding of the theoretical framework and the media forms and products studied in each of the components.
- **Rapid Recall** questions to check your knowledge and understanding of the topics covered in the Year 1 book.
- **Stretch and Challenge** tasks to encourage your independent learning, and to broaden your knowledge and understanding.
- **Links** directing you to relevant pages or sections in this book and in the Year 1 book.
- **Tips** to help you apply what you have learned and improve your examination technique.
- Details of the **Named Theorists** that are listed in the specification and whose theories you need to be familiar with.
- Information about other **Key Figures** related to the subject, to broaden your knowledge and understanding.

Answers to the Rapid Recall and Quickfire questions plus a list of references can be downloaded from:

bit.ly/3r1d7at.

WJEC

Overview

The following table shows the overlap in forms, products and theories between the WJEC and Eduqas A Level specifications. It also indicates where these areas are covered in this book.

Media form common to WJEC and Eduqas	Media product common to WJEC and Eduqas	Media theories common to WJEC and Eduqas	Relevant unit or component	Relevant sections of the book
Television	*The Bridge*	Narratology (Todorov) Genre (Neale) Structuralism (Lévi-Strauss) Postmodernism (Baudrillard) Feminist theories (bell hooks and van Zoonen) Representation (Hall) Reception theory (Hall)	**WJEC Unit 3:** Media in the Global Age. Section A: Television in the Global Age **Eduqas:** Component 2: Section A: Television in the Global Age	See Chapter 5, Section A: pages 151–187 See also the *Media Studies for A Level Year 1* book
Magazines	*Vogue* *Woman* *Woman's Realm* *Huck* *Adbusters*	Semiotics (Barthes) Structuralism (Lévi-Strauss) Feminist theories (bell hooks and van Zoonen) Theories of identity (Gauntlett) Reception theory (Hall)	**WJEC Unit 3:** Media in the Global Age. Section A: Magazines – Changing Representations Eduqas: Component 2: Section B: Magazines: Mainstream and Alternative Media	See Chapter 5, Section B: pages 188–215 See also the *Media Studies for A Level Year 1* book
Video games	*Assassin's Creed* franchise	Media effects (Bandura) Fandom (Jenkins)	**WJEC Unit 3:** Media in the Global Age Section C: Media in the Digital Age – Video Games Eduqas: Component 1: Section B	See Chapter 3: pages 140–146

1 Applying the Media Studies Framework

Link

The theoretical Media Studies framework is explored in detail in Chapter 1 of the Year 1 book.

Tip

All of the work you have done and the skills you have acquired in Year 1 of the course will be used and developed in the second year. Revising the Year 1 work will be essential as you embark upon Year 2.

Tip

When you are exploring the techniques used in media products to communicate meaning, remember to discuss the purpose and the effect on the audience.

Rapid Recall 1.1

What is a media platform?

Rapid Recall 1.2

What term is used to describe audience members who make their own media content?

Tip

You will need to use the Year 1 book in conjunction with this book and revise the work done in the first year of the course.

The Theoretical Framework: A Reminder

You will have gained an understanding of the theoretical framework in Year 1 of the course and used it to support your analysis of the set products. This framework continues to be the focus of your understanding in Year 2. It will provide you with the tools to engage in critical understanding and analysis of the media. The framework consists of four inter-related areas:

- **Media Language**: how the media communicates meaning through their forms, codes, conventions and techniques
- **Representation**: how the media portray events, issues, individuals and social groups
- **Media Industries**: how the processes of production, distribution and circulation engaged in by the media affect media forms and platforms
- **Audiences**: how media forms target, reach and address audiences. How audiences respond to media forms and how audience members become producers themselves

The theoretical framework is explored in detail in Chapter 1 of the Year 1 book, what follows is a brief recap of the key elements. The additional aspects of theory and the theoretical perspectives required for the second year of the A Level course will also be briefly dealt with in this chapter; they will be explored and applied to specific media products in more detail in the relevant chapters of this book.

Media Language

In developing your ability to critically analyse the media and its products you will need to use your 'Analysis Toolkit', which will equip you to engage in complex analysis both inside the classroom and when conducting your own independent research. You will need to understand how products constructed with encoded messages are decoded by the audience.

What follows is a brief reminder of the aspects of media language which will be relevant to your A Level studies: the 'Toolkit'.

Technical Codes

Technical codes contribute to the construction of media products and communicate messages to the audience. Technical codes are important in the analysis of both audio-visual and print products.

Technical Codes in Audio-Visual Products

Technical codes help to construct meaning.

Camera Shots

A range of camera shots are selected by the creators of products to communicate meanings and elicit responses from an audience. These may include:

- **Close-ups**: create emotion and tension and involve the audience. The way they may be edited with other shots helps to establish the narrative. Close-ups help to establish a connection between the character or the action on the screen and the audience. They also position the audience emotionally within the world of the product.
- **Extreme close-ups**: used to focus specifically on one element of the mise-en-scène.
- **Long shots**: give the audience more information about characters and setting.
- **Point-of-view shots**: place the audience in a particular position, for example as a character in the action, and therefore enhance involvement.
- **Establishing shots**: show the audience where a scene is taking place, allowing them to anticipate the subsequent plot developments.

Establishing shot setting the scene.

Rapid Recall 1.3

What is the purpose and effect of the technical codes used in this image from the *Super. Human.* trailer?

Camera Angles

- **High angle**: makes the subject seem vulnerable.
- **Low angle**: creates power and dominance in the mise-en-scène.

Camera Movement

This technique is used primarily to engage and involve the audience in the audio-visual product and to develop the narrative. Camera movement manipulates time and space for the audience and takes them through the story arc. Camera movements can position the audience, restrict the narrative and introduce surprises; they are linked to character movement within the mise-en-scène and encourage the audience to be more active participants in the action. The main techniques are:

- **Tracking**: this is a shot that moves the camera through the scene. The camera glides on a dolly (a type of wheeled cart use to transport the camera) and can track towards, away from or alongside the subject. A steadicam is also used to ensure smooth filming. Tracking can sometimes involve a single take to establish realism and involve the audience. This is often used instead of a close-up shot to move towards or away from the subject.

Link

The different shots, angles and movement are explored in greater detail in Chapter 1 of the Year 1 book, page 15.

Tip

The theoretical framework 'Toolkit' will enable you to effectively analyse the set products and prepare you for the unseen stimulus in the exam.

Tip

Exploring the technical codes used by the creators of products will also equip you for creating your own media products in Component 3.

Quickfire 1.1

How are camera shots related to genre?

Quickfire 1.2

What is the purpose and effect of a bird's-eye view camera angle?

Rapid Recall 1.4

What would be the purpose and effect of using a handheld camera to film a scene?

Key Term

Whip pan
When the camera pivots across a scene at speed creating a blurred shot. It is used to show passages of time, movement between locations and to suggest frenetic action.

Rapid Recall 1.5

What are transitions and how are they used in the editing of a sequence?

Rapid Recall 1.6

Give an example of non-diegetic sound and when it might be used in a media product.

Quickfire 1.3

How might technical and visual codes communicate the ideology of newspapers through their front pages?

Tip

Technical codes are an important element of media language and as such communicate messages to the audience. Being aware of the different technical codes in print and moving-image forms will enable you to engage in detailed analysis.

- **Panning**: this involves movement across the scene. This rotating camera movement can be related to pace as well as time and space. A **whip pan** can cause the audience to feel disorientated and give the effect of speed and panic.
- **Tilting**: this is where a stationary camera pivots vertically down to up or vice versa and is used to restrict the narrative by slowly revealing the subject.

Tilting from the feet up to introduce a character creates suspense.

Editing

The combination of camera shots, movement and angles all work together to construct a narrative and create meanings for the audience to decode. The way in which the audio-visual product is edited can also indicate the genre of the product. Editing can also offer visceral pleasures for the audience by selecting shots, creating enigmas and restricting the narrative to create tension and suspense.

Audio Codes

There is a range of audio codes used across different products and platforms to communicate messages to audiences. Particular audio codes are related to forms and genres, and audiences have expectations of the diegetic and non-diegetic sounds that will be heard in certain media products. Audio codes are an integral part of the construction and mediation of the product and may encompass the following:

- dialogue
- ambient sound
- sound effects
- voiceovers
- music.

Technical Codes in Print Products

As you will be aware from studying the set products and related examples in Year 1 of the course, magazines, advertisements and other print products also employ a range of technical codes to construct a narrative, convey the genre and transmit meaning. These include:

- **Layout and design**: how the product is constructed to communicate meanings.
- **Camera shots and angles**: for example, close-up shots show more detail and the choice of the image may reflect the ideology of the product. This is true of newspaper front pages where images are carefully selected, cropped and constructed in order to communicate meanings to the reader.
- **Lighting**: choices made about lighting contribute to the construction of messages within the product.
- **Colour**: the visual codes of colour transmit meanings and these meanings are recognised and accepted by audiences as they have been established over time.
- **Graphics**: splashes highlight key selling points, and graphs and maps exemplify stories.

Quickfire 1.4

Give an example of how lighting can communicate messages in a print media product.

- **Post-production techniques**: photographs are often edited and manipulated to create an effect. In November 2017, *Grazia* magazine caused controversy by Photo-shopping the hair of actor Lupita Nyong'o to make it shorter and sleeker. The suggestion was that this was done in order to 'fit a more Eurocentric notion of what beautiful hair looks like'. Nyong'o stated on social media that she was disappointed *Grazia* had edited and smoothed her hair to fit its notion of what beautiful hair should look like. In the same week, Solange Knowles complained to the *London Evening Standard* when it digitally altered her hair for its magazine front cover. The digital manipulation of images in print products is much more prevalent now and while audiences are aware that it happens, they may still be influenced by the unrealistic images of perfection that are created.

Stretch and Challenge 1.1

Find the front cover of the November 2017 *Grazia* magazine online and consider how the decisions made by the product to manipulate the image reflect its ideology.

Quickfire 1.5

How can the use of post-production techniques reflect the ideology of the magazine?

Theoretical Framework: Roland Barthes

You will have studied Roland Barthes' theory of semiotics in Year 1 of the course. Barthes is one of the theorists you must study and understand. You will be required to apply his theoretical perspective to the set products you will study in Year 2 of the course and to develop your understanding further. The Media Studies A Level specification states that you must know the following in relation to Barthes:

- the idea that texts communicate their meanings through a process of signification
- the idea that signs can function at the level of denotation, which involves the 'literal' or common-sense meaning of the sign, and at the level of connotation, which involves the meanings associated with or suggested by the sign
- the idea that constructed meanings can come to seem self-evident, achieving the status of myth through a process of naturalisation.

Link

For more on Barthes see the Year 1 book, page 19.

Barthes and other theorists of the time originally centred their ideas on language and linguistics; however, their theoretical perspectives can now be applied to a range of media forms and products, as these are the most effective forms of modern communication. Signs function at three levels:

- **the sign**: something that stands in for, or represents something, to communicate meaning
- **the signifier**: the physical form a sign takes – a sound, word or image (the denotation)
- **the signified**: the concept or meaning that is portrayed, which is then interpreted by the audience (the connotation).

One of Barthes' key ideas with regard to semiotics is his exploration of **myths** and how signs that are regularly reinforced across media forms take on the role of a myth and become accepted as natural, when in fact they are a **social construct**. For example, the sign of the rose has only come to be associated with romance and Valentine's Day through reinforcement over time, this is also a cultural construct as it only has meaning for certain cultures. The rose in this context has now become a symbol of love and romance when in fact, at its simplest level of denotation, it is a flower. This is a good example of how signs and their meanings are learned and become accepted over time. Barthes asserted that signs have historical and cultural links that will change over time: '*signs and codes are not universally given, but are historically and socially specific to the particular interests that lie behind them*' (Strinati, 1995).

Rapid Recall 1.7

What is meant by denotation and connotation in relation to Barthes' theory of semiotics?

Key Terms

Myth
Dominant ideas and beliefs that are not necessarily true but have been accepted by a culture.

Social construct
An idea or concept that is created, developed and accepted by society. These ideas are reinforced through repetition and practice.

Quickfire 1.6

Give another example of a myth that is in fact a social construct.

Tip

Engaging in independent research around the key theories and theorists will allow you to develop a more detailed knowledge and understanding.

Quickfire 1.7

How might a red rose be interpreted in different ways?

Stretch and Challenge 1.2

Research semiotics, including Barthes' theory, in greater detail to develop your understanding. A useful resource is a paper written by a media theorist, Daniel Chandler called 'Semiotics for Beginners' in his 2017 book *Semiotics: The Basics.*

Key Figure

Charles Saunders Peirce
American philosopher whose research extended into semiotics. Although he is not a set theorist, his ideas are useful to the understanding of semiotics.

Key Terms

Iconic representation
A sign that has a physical resemblance to the thing that it stands in for or represents. For example, marketing materials often feature iconic representations of the products they advertise or promote.

Arbitrary signs
Signs that bear no obvious resemblance to the thing signified, the meanings of which have been accepted through repetition over time.

Barthes also believed that the theory of semiology proves that reality is always constructed through signs, codes and recognisable conventions. This theoretical perspective is obviously important when discussing the meanings encoded in media products.

He also suggested that all signs are polysemic and, when encoded into media products, mean different things to different people. He asserted that a text is:

> *a galaxy of signifiers, not a structure of signifieds; it has no beginning; it is reversible; we gain access to it by several entrances …* (Barthes, 2009)

Charles Saunders Peirce

Charles Saunders Peirce formulated the triadic model related to semiotics. This, like Barthes' theory, incorporated the sign or object, the signifier, and he also referred to a third stage which he named the 'interpretant', meaning how a particular audience may perceive or understand the sign. He essentially defined the sign by its effect on the interpreter. He also divided signs into the following groups:

- **Icons**: these are signs that bear a resemblance to what is represented. Iconic signs have a physical similarity to the objects they 'signify', for example a bottle of perfume in an advertisement or a road sign with a car/bike on it. The sign is therefore easily recognisable. This **iconic representation** is important in certain forms of advertising to enable the easy purchase of the product.
- **Indexical signs**: these are signs that have a direct link to what they represent, they cannot exist in isolation as there is a physical connection, for example thunder and a storm. Thunder is the sound signifier and the storm is the signified.
- **Symbols**: these are signs with a symbolic link to what is represented. The sign may not actually resemble the thing to which it refers – the understanding is built up over years of habitual use and becomes part of a shared communal understanding. A symbolic sign is one that represents an object or concepts solely by agreement of the people who come into contact with it. These **arbitrary signs** have a variety of meanings, for example Big Ben, depending on where it is used, can take on a symbolic importance related to tradition and London being the centre of power. Similarly, the Nike 'tick' meant nothing on its own but has come to mean high-end sports clothing.

Quickfire 1.8

Can the perfume bottle pictured on the right also function as a symbol?

Tip

A useful infogram, explaining semiotics, can be found on the Behance website: https://www.behance.net/gallery/9474813/Explaining-Semiotics-Infographic.

The Nike logo is an example of an arbitrary sign.

The perfume bottle is an icon.

Theoretical Framework: Claude Lévi-Strauss

One of the theorists related to media language that you will study in Year 2 of the course is **Claude Lévi-Strauss** and his ideas regarding **structuralism**. You will be required to apply your understanding to the set products you studied in Year 1 and the new set products you will be introduced to in Year 2 of the course. The main elements of this theory you must study are:

- the idea that texts can best be understood through an examination of their underlying structure
- the idea that meaning is dependent upon (and produced through) pairs of oppositions
- the idea that the way in which these binary oppositions are resolved can have particular ideological significance.

Binary Opposites

Lévi-Strauss' theory of structuralism is relevant to the set products studied. His theoretical perspective focuses on the fact that all media products have a structure which encompasses a set of rules that are accepted by audiences. Lévi-Strauss first identified **binary opposites** in literature but they can be applied to media products. They are concepts or forces that are set against each other, which then can produce a dynamic that may work in, for example, a music video narrative.

Lévi-Strauss suggested narratives emerge through conflict and are another way in which signs and their meanings are created. With binary opposites, signs are contrasted with opposite meanings to make them more powerful. Basic binary oppositions tend to be between good and evil or male and female, and audiences are then positioned to respond in a certain way. Stereotypes are then constructed through the other attributes we give to the binary oppositions.

Another common binary opposite is between villains and heroes. A further aspect of this theory is that the understanding of one element of the conflict is dependent on awareness of the other: an audience needs to be able to recognise the villain in order to understand the role of the hero and to anticipate the progression of the narrative. Binary opposites are not necessarily natural; they are cultural and are used by media producers to communicate simple and, at times, more complex meanings. They often contribute to stereotypes and also create myths.

For example, crime dramas often establish the narrative through the creation of a structure of oppositions including good and evil, gender, race and class.

Binary opposites can be used by media products to help define what they want to represent. For example, in a charity campaign about Africa, the product may play on the binary opposites of developing versus developed world, as audiences understand these 'opposites'. Some media products, for example newspapers, will represent one side as positive and another as negative in a political story, in order to make their point.

The narrative of *The Bridge* is structured around a series of binary oppositions.

Named Theorist

Claude Lévi-Strauss
A French social anthropologist whose work was important to the theory of structuralism.

Key Terms

Structuralism
A critical approach used to analyse the underlying structures or patterns of meaning within a text or culture.

Binary opposites
When people, ideas, concepts or values are set up in conflict with one another.

Quickfire 1.9

How do the binary opposites used in crime dramas have an ideological significance?

Quickfire 1.10

What binary oppositions are established in the set television product *The Bridge*?

Rapid Recall 1.8

How can media products be said to be polysemic?

Link

For more on visual codes see the Year 1 book, pages 19–20.

Visual Codes

As you will recall from your Year 1 work, visual codes are an intrinsic aspect of semiology and are one of the ways in which media products combine elements of media language to communicate meanings to the audience. Visual codes are used to encode messages to be decoded by the consumer of the product; they contain signs, the connotations of which will be read differently by different audiences. Following is a reminder of the main visual codes:

- **Code of clothing**: the costume choices made by the creator of the product communicate messages to an audience.
- **Code of expression**: this rapidly communicates meanings and advances the narrative.
- **Code of gesture**: this is another example of a non-verbal communicator that transmits messages to an audience.
- **Code of technique**: the manipulation of the image or audio-visual piece can convey meanings.
- **Images**: the selection of images to be used in a media product will construct a preferred meaning for the audience.
- **Colour**: due to the fact that certain colours have specific connotations and take on the role of signs, they can be used to establish meanings in certain media forms.
- **Iconography**: the meanings attached to the objects, settings and backgrounds.
- **Graphics**: the visual representations that are part of the construction of the media product, for example drawings, diagrams and typography.

Consider how visual codes that construct meaning are used to construct the image below from the TV drama *Peaky Blinders*:

Visual codes are used to construct meanings for the audience to decode in this image from *Peaky Blinders*.

- The code of clothing of the men in the image places the drama in the past, the choice of clothing, including the caps, will be a key element of character construction and marketing for the programme. The similarity in the mens' clothing establishes them as part of a group with a common purpose.
- The code of expression of the characters is serious, intimidating and purposeful. They are looking directly at the audience and the still suggests it is taken from a shot tracking backwards, the effect being to make the audience feel threatened.
- The scene is shot at night, the colours are therefore muted and dull, suggesting the darker narrative themes of the drama and creating a sinister aesthetic. The iconography of the bleak setting and the weapons foreshadows the violent plot of the drama.

Paradigms and Syntagms

These form another aspect of semiotics related to how the combination of elements of media language, including visual codes, influence meaning. When they encode messages, the creators of media products must ensure they choose the right combination of signs, including language, graphics, colour and iconography, to communicate messages to the audience.

There is a set of options available to the producer depending on the product they want to create. This set of options is called a **paradigm**. The paradigm must work for the product and subsequently the audience if the meanings are to be successfully transmitted.

The paradigmatic choices made about a media product are important in communicating messages to the audience and include:

- **lexis**
- images
- graphics including font styles
- technical codes
- audio codes
- colours.

The encoder chooses one sign rather than another, making a paradigmatic choice that will influence the product's meaning.

In relation to these paradigmatic choices, the producer must ensure that the different signs chosen combine to create an overall effect. This combination of signs that are linked together in particular ways is called a **syntagm**. The combination has to be successful in order to create meanings for the audience. For example, in an advert the typography has to work with the image, the choice of colours, the layout and the lexis in order to communicate meanings effectively.

Consider the paradigmatic choices that have been made in the advert on the right for the Miss Dior fragrance. The colour signifier is important: the natural skin tones and the use of pink for the bottle and the floral headband, signify the femininity of the fragrance. The construction of a natural image is reinforced by the inclusion of bare shoulders and wind-blown hair signifying a sense of freedom and romance echoed in the slogan '#WAKEUPFORLOVE'. The name of the fragrance 'Miss Dior' is written in cursive writing, that and the silver bow on the bottle add to the connotations of romance and are part of the brand identity of the product. The signs all work together to construct the syntagm that suggests the fragrance without actually being able to smell it.

Language and Mode of Address

The term 'language' used here is different from the 'media language' that is part of the theoretical framework. Here it refers to the choices made regarding the written and spoken language used in a media product and how they communicate meanings to an audience. The linguistic choices made by the creators of media products may affect the meaning.

Language

The language incorporated in a media product may include:

- the imperative to create a dramatic effect
- **ellipsis** to establish enigmas
- slang and colloquialisms to appeal to a specific audience demographic
- direct quotations to establish realism and credibility

Quickfire 1.11

How could you apply Lévi-Strauss's theory of binary opposites to the image from *The Bridge* on page 11?

Key Terms

Paradigm
A set of related signs from which the encoder can choose. In choosing one sign rather than another, the encoder of the product makes a paradigmatic choice.

Lexis
The specific words used in a product which may relate to the genre of the product and include terminology that is understood by the target audience.

Syntagm
A combination of signs that, when linked together in a particular way, produce meanings.

Rapid Recall 1.9

Give an example of how specific lexis communicates meanings in a media product and the effect this may have upon an audience.

Rapid Recall 1.10

Give an example of a media product that uses ellipsis.

Key Term

Ellipsis
The use of three dots at the beginning, middle or end of a sentence to attract attention and interest through the withholding of information.

Quickfire 1.12

How do the language choices made on *The Sun*'s front page reflect its ideology?

Quickfire 1.13

Which other language devices are used on *The Sun*'s front page?

Tip

Awareness of a range of different language devices and their use will prepare you for the analysis of the unseen products in Component 1.

Rapid Recall 1.11

What is meant by hyperbole and how is it used in a media product?

Tip

Always consider the choices that have been made by the creators of the product with regards to the language techniques chosen. These choices often reflect the ideology of the product.

Link

A more detailed explanation of these key language points can be found in the Year 1 book, pages 21–22.

Key Terms

Idiom
A well-known phrase with a figurative, not literal, meaning.

Repertoire of elements
The key features or conventions that are recognisable to an audience and as such distinguish one genre or sub-genre from another.

- idiomatic phrases are universally recognised by audiences and frequently are used by the tabloid press for humour and to make fun of people they don't like or approve of. The famous front page of *The Sun* with a headline about bacon (seen at: https://www.thesun.co.uk/news/8969124/bacon-sandwich-loving-ed-miliband-says-brits-should-eat-less-meat-to-tackle-climate-change/) was said to have seriously damaged Ed Miliband's credibility in the run-up to the General Election in 2015. It uses two **idioms**: 'making a pig's ear' and 'saving the bacon'. This manipulation of recognisable idioms, combined with the choice of image, creates a negative representation of the politician and makes him a figure of fun, showing the power of language and images to create meaning.

Other language features used include:

- puns and alliteration for effect
- hyperbole to persuade.

Mode of Address: A Reminder

Mode of address refers to the way in which the media product communicates to the audience through the written and spoken language and style used:

- **Informal mode of address**: is used to communicate in a more casual way with an audience, using, for example, slang and abbreviations.
- **Formal mode of address**: including complex vocabulary and a serious code of expression, is employed by certain media products that want to engender a more serious approach.
- **Direct mode of address**: the product communicates directly with the audience through the positioning of the characters, the selection of the central image and language choices, for example the use of personal pronouns.
- **Indirect mode of address**: is used more commonly by products that aim to create a storyworld that does not involve the audience directly.

Genre

You will have developed your understanding of the concept of genre in Year 1 of the course and will continue to apply that understanding in Year 2 in a more sophisticated way to aid you in the analysis of the set products. Genre is an important element of media language, it is only assessed specifically in relation to the set products in Component 2 but may also enhance your analysis of the products you study in Component 1.

Here is a reminder of the key points related to a study of genre:

- genre is a way of categorising media products
- each genre has a **repertoire of elements** that are recognisable to audiences, as they have been built up over time. These established codes and conventions are useful in the marketing of the product
- some media products belong to hybrid and sub-genres. Nelson (2009) thinks that nowadays the planning of many TV drama series involves the consideration of generic hybrids.
- it has, however, recently become increasingly difficult to place some products in a specific genre, as the creators of products strive to find new forms in order to appeal to audiences.

Tip

Remember to use subject-specific lexis when discussing genre in relation to the set products.

The repertoire of elements of any genre can be divided into the following key areas:

- narrative, referring to the structure of the product
- characters
- iconography and setting
- technical and audio codes.

If you studied the sci-fi/supernatural thrillers television option, you will already have examined some of the elements above in Year 1 when studying the Component 2 set product *Black Mirror* and you will revisit them in Year 2 of your course when you study *The Returned*, considering the similarities and differences between the two genres including:

- the narratives of both genres focus on extraordinary occurrences and their effect upon the characters. However, the supernatural thriller genre usually focuses upon events that have no rational explanation and so creates unease in the characters. In contrast, the science-fiction narratives, as suggested by the name, focus on aspects of science, for example AI, robots and the effect of new technology on society
- the iconography of the sci-fi genre may include futuristic costumes and weapons in comparison to the often more everyday iconography of the supernatural thriller
- the setting of a product in the science-fiction genre may be bleak and dystopian or otherworldly, suggesting the thematic concerns of this genre. The supernatural thriller settings may be more ordinary and recognisable so making the extraordinary more frightening.

Theoretical Framework: Genre

In Year 1 of the course you will have studied Steve Neale, and applied his theory to set products. You will be required to develop your understanding of this theoretical perspective further and apply it to the products studied in Year 2. You will recall that the main elements of this theory you must study are:

- the idea that genres may be dominated by repetition, but are also marked by difference, variation and change
- the idea that genres change, develop and vary, as they borrow from and overlap with one another
- the idea that genres exist within specific economic, institutional and industrial contexts.

However, it is also useful to broaden your understanding of this central media concept by being aware of other theoretical perspectives related to the study of genre. Other theorists who discuss genre include:

Daniel Chandler

While the main focus of **Daniel Chandler**'s research work is semiotics, he also discusses genre and he concludes that:

- genres position audiences differently and therefore elicit different responses linked to audience expectations
- the creators of the product belonging to a specific genre will have an idea of their audience and therefore the 'preferred reading' for that product
- genres create an **interpretive community** where an audience derives pleasure from sharing their knowledge and understanding of a particular genre with others
- genres reflect society and as such genres come and go as audiences change. Audiences themselves can help to construct genres.

The rise of digital platforms means new genres are created but these new genres still tend to have their roots in pre-existing genres.

Genre Revision: Key terms checklist

You need to be confident in using the following key terms related to genre:

- hybrid genre
- sub-genre
- codes and conventions
- stock characters
- iconography
- linear narrative
- non-linear narrative
- formulaic structure
- story arc.

Key Figure

Daniel Chandler
He refers to himself as a semiotician and his book *Semiotics: The Basics* (2017) is a useful text for developing understanding of media language. Now retired, he is an Emeritus lecturer in the Theatre, Film and Television Studies department at Aberystwyth University.

Tip

Daniel Chandler's website, http://visual-memory.co.uk/daniel/, is also a useful area for research into media language.

Key Term

Interpretive communities
Initially used by Stanley Fish, a literary critic, to explain how different groups of people, i.e. readers or audiences, interpret texts similarly due to their shared social and cultural positions and their experiences.

Key Terms

Semantics
Relates to the branch of linguistics concerned with how meanings are created. In a study of the media this applies to the meanings of the words or objects contained within a product.

Syntactic
In linguistics, this refers to the way in which words are ordered in a sentence in order to create meaning. When applying this to media products, it refers to the structure of the product and how the construction of the semantic elements in any given genre create meanings.

Pragmatics
Relating to practical considerations, for example the importance of the generic elements of a media product in its marketing.

Key Figure

Rick Altman
A Professor of Cinema and Comparative Literature at the University of Iowa, USA. He has written widely on genre theory and narrative.

Tip

A useful text to broaden your understanding of genre is *The Television Genre Book*, edited by Glen Greeber, BFI, 2015 (3rd edition).

Quickfire 1.14

How does the repertoire of elements of a particular genre help in the marketing of a product?

Link

You will find a diagrammatic explanation of Todorov's narrative theory in the Year 1 book, page 24.

Rick Altman

Rick Altman is another media theorist whose theoretical perspective on genre is useful to study. He stated that:

- A genre can be identified through two different elements: **semantic** and **syntactic**. The semantics of a genre are the recognisable elements that place a product in a given genre and communicate meaning to an audience. These are not rigid but fluent and changing and may include, for example:
  - language
  - visual codes including iconography
  - stars
  - ideology.
- The syntactic elements are less obvious; they give the audience a range of physical pleasures including emotional, visceral and intellectual. They may also link the semantic elements and the narrative structure of the product.
- Altman extended his theory to include **pragmatic** elements of genre. This refers to the way in which institutions use genres and the relationship between genres and the audience. For example, film companies will produce films from a range of genres in one year but they will also be aware of rising and falling trends. According to www.the-numbers.com from 1995–2023 the adventure and action film genres controlled 26.27% and 21.94% of the market share respectively compared with the romantic comedy genre at 4.41%. Audiences will respond to genres differently and may also recreate their own genres. YouTube is full of recut versions of existing media products made by fans of a specific genre.

Theoretical Framework: Narratology

From your Year 1 studies you will remember that all media products have a narrative, which is a structure that conveys meaning and is recognisable to an audience. Narratology is a term used to describe the study of narrative in media products and as such is an integral element of media language and the theoretical framework with which you must be familiar. All media products place events or textual features in a particular order; in this way they construct meaning.

In Year 1 of the course you will have studied Tzvetan Todorov, and applied his theory to set products. You will be required to develop your understanding of this theoretical perspective further and apply it to the products studied in Year 2. You will recall that the main elements of this theory you must study are:

- the idea that all narratives share a basic structure that involves a movement from one state of equilibrium to another
- the idea that these two states of equilibrium are separated by a period of imbalance or disequilibrium
- the idea that the way in which narratives are resolved can have particular ideological significance.

Many media products use a range of different narrative techniques to hold the attention of an evermore demanding audience. In audio-visual products these may include:

- **The manipulation of time and space**: television programmes, films and music videos frequently challenge their audiences by moving the action between different timeframes. Whereas in the past the audience would be shown the time change through a range of what now seems outdated devices, including the hands of a clock moving backwards or the use of sepia, now the sophistication of the audience is such that they are expected to work this out for themselves.

- **Three-strand narratives**: a common formulaic structure used in TV dramas.
- **Flexi-narratives**: interweave and are more complex and challenging for the audience.

Narrative Conventions in Audio-Visual Products

As you will remember, narratives are constructed through the use of specific conventions which are used to convey meanings to the audience and progress the storyline. These include:

- flashbacks to move the narrative in time and space and to provide additional information
- point-of-view shots to position the audience
- apparently impossible positions, which enhance the viewing experience by showing the audience action from an unusual/impossible position
- privileged spectator position, giving the audience additional information through a specific shot, thus involving them more closely in the narrative
- voiceovers, which are used to supplement on-screen action
- enigma codes, restricting the narrative to create tension and anticipation in the audience
- action codes, which advance the narrative and create audience expectation of what will follow.

Narrative Conventions in Print Products

For media producers, narrative conventions are ways of organising random items of information into a structure that will make sense for the audience. As such, narrative is important in creating meaning, and the way in which the narrative in a particular media form is constructed will affect how audiences respond. This is true in the case of print forms, for example magazines and newspapers, where the producers are not dealing with a straightforward narrative as might be the case with a film or television programme.

With regards to a newspaper, the main story can often be a big event that has happened far away, for example a war or a natural disaster. The job of the journalist is to create a narrative around the event that will make it relatable to the target audience. This is often achieved through a focus on specific people (personalisation) or specific details that make the story seem more real to the reader. This gives the audience points of reference which they can relate to their own lives and experiences. Other elements, for example photographs, can function as mini narratives communicating aspects of a bigger story. The narrative of a front-page newspaper story is therefore constructed and creates meaning through the use of headlines, copy, photographs and captions.

The war in Ukraine in 2022 was a continuing news story, therefore using images to construct mini narratives helped to keep the focus specifically on the plight of the residents of the Ukrainian cities under bombardment. This news image of a soldier kissing a young woman was selected to personalise the distant war and make it more relatable to audiences, giving them a point of reference that is universal – the relationship between two people. The code of clothing of the soldier's uniform and her civilian dress emphasises the situation in Kyiv. Enigmas are established regarding who they are and where they are going and the audience is positioned to feel empathetic to their situation.

Rapid Recall 1.12

Todorov's theory is based on the idea of texts having a linear narrative. What does this mean?

Stretch and Challenge 1.3

Consider how time and space is manipulated in one of the set products you have studied and the effect this has on the narrative.

Narrative Revision: Key terms checklist

You need to be confident in using the following key terms related to the study of narrative:

- linear
- non-linear
- restricted
- unrestricted
- diegetic world
- self-contained narrative
- equilibrium/disequilibrium
- narrative arcs.

Quickfire 1.15

What elements make up the narrative structure of a magazine?

News photograph documenting the events in Ukraine.

Quickfire 1.16

How do news photographs construct a narrative for the reader?

Stretch and Challenge 1.4

Look at a range of front pages of newspapers and consider how they have created a narrative for their lead news story.

Key Figure

Vladimir Propp
Russian structuralist theorist who conducted research into fairy stories, establishing the range of character types found in them and their role in the narrative. He discussed his findings in his 1920 book *The Morphology of the Folk Tale.*

Key Terms

Character typology
A system that defines the characteristics of different types of people or characters across a range of different narratives, for example the hero and the villain.

Trans-historical
While some ideas and beliefs are initially relevant to a particular time period, certain ideas embody universal truths that cut across different time periods and forms of expression.

This example illustrates that the way in which the narrative is constructed in a media product, for example a newspaper, can also influence how the audience responds to the event. The narrative may contain points of view and bias, suggesting how the audience may view the event or which side to take and may reflect the ideology of the product's creators. The headlines and photographs will have been carefully chosen to position the audience emotionally. These choices about how to construct the narrative therefore limit the range of responses an audience may have.

Other narrative conventions used in print products include:

- taglines on a film poster, which give clues to the film's narrative
- headlines, which can be dramatic or informative in the way in which they communicate narrative information. They may also reflect a point of view
- cover lines on magazines, which create mini narratives and contain enigmas to entice readers to buy the product
- images and captions, which also develop the narrative, as illustrated in the example of the news photograph on the previous page. Consider what caption may have accompanied this image to anchor the narrative
- language and mode of address communicate information and may give clues to the genre of the product
- enigma codes, including teasers on film posters and DVD covers, which restrict the narrative information to attract an audience.

Additional Theories: Vladimir Propp

While Todorov's theoretical perspective largely relates to how the narrative progresses through chronological action, other theories consider different aspects of narratology. **Vladimir Propp** was a theorist who studied the importance of character in narrative. He used **character typology** to divide characters into different groups with differing characteristics and functions within the narrative.

Propp's research and subsequent theories are **trans-historical** and while his original focus was folk and fairy tales, his ideas can be transferred to more modern media products, including films and television programmes that reflect a more contemporary context. The ideas themselves, however, do not change. He divided characters into eight key roles and 31 functions.

Proppian character roles:

- the hero
- the villain
- the donor: helps the hero by providing a gift with magical properties
- the dispatcher: sends the hero on a quest
- the false hero: appears heroic but turns out not to be
- the helper: supports the hero in his quest
- the princess: the reward or prize for the hero
- the princess' father.

Proppian **character functions** are chronological events related to characters that drive the narrative, for example:

1. A command not to do something is addressed to the hero.
2. This command is ignored.
3. The hero is tested/attacked and receives a magical agent as a result.
4. The hero uses the magical gift.
5. The hero and villain join in direct combat.
6. The villain is defeated by a range of different means.
7. The false hero is exposed.
8. The villain is punished.
9. The hero is married, attaining his prize of the princess.

In character-driven narrative theory the idea is that characters influence a narrative through cause and effect, the narrative progresses as a result of their actions. All characters have motives, which are revealed during the course of the storyline; the narrative is driven through their need to achieve their goals. This may mean that characters then come into conflict with one another; this is another important element of narrative structure.

Theoretical Framework: Postmodernism

This is one of the more demanding theories you will study in Year 2 of the course. You will be required to develop your understanding of postmodernism and apply it to the products you studied in Year 1 and those you will study in Year 2. Postmodernism is only assessed in relation to the Component 2 products. The main elements of the theory are:

- the idea that in a postmodern culture the boundaries between the 'real' world and the world of the media have collapsed and that it is no longer possible to distinguish between reality and simulation
- the idea that in a postmodern age of **simulacra** we are immersed in a world of images that no longer refer to anything 'real'
- the idea that media images have come to seem more 'real' than the reality they are supposed to represent (**hyperreality**).

Key points related to postmodernism:

- Postmodernism focuses on the idea that the media no longer holds a mirror up to or manipulates reality, but instead has become that reality and as such is seen to be the only reality we have.
- The evolvement of postmodernism directly links to the modern consumerist culture that celebrates the pursuit of pleasure.
- Postmodernism also relates to technological progress, whereby the mass media have become central to all communication, thus defining what is relevant and important, for example the top 'trending' topics on Twitter and the use of Instagram to capture and share transient moments instantly. The internet, it could be said, is the ultimate postmodern form, lacking any sort of structure and offering a series of erratic, fragmented pages which may or may not have any meaning related to what we are looking for.

Key Term

Character functions
Refers to the structural reason the character is in the narrative. All characters have a key role to play in extending the plot.

Quickfire 1.17

Which of the Proppian character roles may be difficult to apply to more modern media products?

Tip

Although Propp is not a 'Named Theorist', his theory may be usefully applied to some of the products you study and may therefore enhance your analysis and understanding.

Tip

It is not possible to apply Propp's theory to all media products and you should not try to do so, it is more useful to some than others.

Key Terms

Simulacra
Postmodern concepts used to describe signs that simply refer to another sign rather than anything 'real'. Simulacra are commonly understood as copies of copies. The singular is simulacrum.

Hyperreality
A state or condition in which images or simulations may be accepted as 'real' as they come to seem more real than reality itself.

- Postmodernism as a theoretical perspective has progressed from theories such as those of Lévi-Strauss, which were focused on the idea that texts have a clear and formulaic structure. Postmodernism relates to a more collage-bricolage-like approach, postmodern texts deliberately play with meaning and use intertextuality.
- Postmodern texts are concerned with identity. This relates to Gauntlett's idea that we now have a range of different 'models' from which we can create our identities.
- Traditional references to identity anchored in 'the real', for example the family, class and community, are being eroded and replaced by hyperreality in the media.
- Postmodernism is concerned with the creation of a hyperreality where something fake and artificial becomes more definitive than the reality. Baudrillard uses Disneyland as an example, which in its immersive reality becomes more real than Los Angeles itself and as such masks the reality that surrounds Disneyland, which is also a simulation in its ideological representation of America.
- Baudrillard asserted that there then becomes an inability to distinguish reality from simulation; this is the case with regard to highly manipulated images of women in adverts and on magazine covers and in the construction of fake news images and footage. Similarly, fans of soap operas can find it difficult to distinguish between the fictional character and the actor playing the character (Baudrillard, 1984).
- Strinati (1995), in his discussion of postmodernism, asserts that **metanarratives** are being eroded as time and space become more confused. Modern technology has created a shrunken world. This was predicted by Marshall McLuhan in the 1960s, before the arrival of the internet, in his book *The Gutenberg Galaxy* (1962). McLuhan's theory posed the idea that there are four eras of human history: the acoustic age, the literary age, the print age and the electronic age that the world was then entering. He predicted that the electronic age would be characterised by a group of people brought together by technology, which he called the **global village** – this could be understood as being the internet.
- With the advent of postmodernism, metanarratives were said to be eroded as new points of reference became established, largely from the media and popular culture. Postmodernism cannot, by its very definition, be explained by universal theories related to, for example, religion, history and science.
- A key word related to Baudrillard's postmodern theory is simulacrum, which refers to the construction of signs that then masquerade as reality. This is evident in the media, for example the way in which virtual reality computer games manipulate time and space and create believably real worlds for the players.
- Postmodernism includes borrowing from other elements of popular culture in order to make something seemingly new and more 'real'. Intertextuality is often a key element of postmodern texts.

Stretch and Challenge 1.5

In order to broaden your understanding of postmodernism as a theoretical perspective, read the chapter on postmodernsim in Dominic Strinati's (1995) book, *An Introduction to Theories of Popular Culture.*

Key Terms

Metanarrative
Refers to an accepted account or interpretation of events on which people have come to base their beliefs, for example the narratives associated with historical truths and those related to religion. It is a term used for *'any theory claiming to provide universal explanations and to be universally valid'* (Sim, 2011).

Global village
This phrase was coined by Marshall McLuhan and refers to the metaphoric shrinking of the world due to advances in technology.

Advances in technology have enabled virtual reality computer games to create immersive worlds that appear real.

Applying Postmodernist Theory to Media Products

Postmodernism is evident across all media forms and products, and you will be required to apply this theoretical perspective and Baudrillard's specific theory to some of the set products you have studied for Component 2. It may also be appropriately applied to the unseen Component 1 products.

Television: this media form has become increasingly postmodern as it adopts a more playful and experimental approach to genre. One of the optional set products for Component 2 is *Black Mirror*, which contains postmodern elements as it blurs the boundaries between simulation and reality.

Although postmodernism is not one of the theories you are specifically required to study for Component 1, you may find it useful for exploring the way in which music videos, advertisements and video games create meanings and audience pleasures.

Advertising: this form is arguably most postmodern in its approach. A lot of adverts are now less focused on selling the actual product and more about constructing a visual experience for the audience in order to sell the product. Adverts very self-consciously use references from popular culture or will critique and parody existing media products. It is also true that contemporary advertising constructs a cultural representation within the advert rather than focusing on the product as it would appear in the real world. Adverts for beauty products construct a hyperreality centred on the ideology of beauty; the construction does not bear a resemblance to real life due to the use of post-production techniques.

The Guinness advert (2017), *The Compton Cowboys*, part of the *Made of More* series, demonstrates postmodern elements in its construction. The actual product does not feature in the advert and the only branding evident is the harp logo shown in the opening. While the advert uses references to popular culture through the focus on the riders of south central Los Angeles, there are also intertextual references to the western film and the documentary genre.

As with other postmodern texts, the focus of the advert is on the emotional and symbolic meaning and is not directly related to the product. This conforms to the idea that we are now a culture more concerned with superficiality.

Music videos: mix styles and genres in very obvious ways and incorporate collage, pastiche and intertextual references. While in the past the expectation would be that music videos would interpret the song lyrics in an often straightforward way, now an increasing number of music videos are more experimental, complex and challenging as a postmodern form.

Video games: offer a hyper-real experience first hand due to the interactive nature of the form. This has led to a moral panic in some areas of the media regarding the possible effect of video games on the behaviour of the players who are said to be unable to divorce the reality of the game from their own real lives.

Online media: the creators of blogs and vlogs create seemingly realistic worlds and invite the audience to become part of that hyperreality. They construct identities for themselves that are then 'sold' to audiences who may want to emulate the bloggers and use them as role models.

Quickfire 1.18

Watch *The Compton Cowboys* Guiness advertisment here: www.youtube.com/watch?v=ZRr-hE9TMdo. How does the advertisement reflect the postmodern approach?

Stretch and Challenge 1.6

Engage in independent research into further examples of postmodern adverts.

Quickfire 1.19

How do video games and online sites illustrate elements of a postmodern theoretical perspective?

Applying Theory: Media Language

The grid below summarises the main theories and theoretical perspectives that must be studied over Components 1 and 2. The key elements related to each theory have been outlined above and will also be referred to in the chapters specifically dealing with each component and their forms and products. Although you may also study and show your knowledge and understanding of other relevant theories, the ones set out below must be studied in relation to the areas of the specification indicated.

Tip

Although postmodernism as a theoretical perspective is only required to be studied in specific areas of Component 2, your knowledge and understanding can be transferred to other set products and the unseen products.

Theory/theoretical approach	Component 1 forms	Component 2 forms/products
Semiotics, including Roland Barthes	Advertising and marketing Music video Newspapers	Magazines: both products Online: both products
Genre theory, including Steve Neale		Television: both products
Structuralism, including Claude Lévi-Strauss	Advertising and marketing Music video Newspapers	Television: both products Magazines: both products Online: both products
Narratology, including Tzvetan Todorov		Television: both products
Postmodernism, including Jean Baudrillard		Television: *Peaky Blinders* or *Black Mirror* or *Killing Eve* Online: both products

The Specification: Key Statements

For each of the key areas of the theoretical framework – Media Language, Representation, Media Industries and Audiences – there is a set of statements in the specification that must be used as the basis of your studies. These statements will be used to formulate the assessment for each of the areas of the specification. It is therefore important that you are aware of them, their meaning and how they can be applied to the set products. They can also be used as a basis for questions related to the sections of the examination papers. The grid below shows the statements for Media Language and explains their meaning and the forms and examination components to which they relate.

Rapid Recall 1.13

How does the television product you studied in Year 1 demonstrate hybridity?

Key statement: Media Language	Component 1 Media forms	Component 2 Media forms	Explanation
How the different modes and language associated with different media forms communicate multiple meanings	Advertising and marketing Music video Newspapers	Television Magazines Online	Different media forms will communicate meanings in different ways through aspects of media language. This will include technical, audio and visual codes, language and mode of address. This statement also links to theoretical perspectives including Barthes (semiology) and Lévi-Strauss (structuralism). Media products are constructed using signs and codes, and as such are polysemic and include a range of meanings that will be interpreted differently by audiences. The modes and language will differ according to the media product.
How the combination of elements of media language influence meaning	Advertising and marketing Music video Newspapers	Television Magazines Online	Producers make choices and select elements of media language in order to communicate meanings. For example, the decisions a newspaper may make regarding what to put on its front page, including images, headlines and captions, and how these may influence the readers. This statement also refers to the paradigmatic choices made by the creators of the products that will affect the meaning; for example, in an advert, the choice made about colour, font style and shot type. The syntagmatic choices regarding how the product, for example a film poster, is constructed will also affect the meaning.
How developing technologies affect media language	Music video Newspapers	Online	This refers to the technological developments related to specific media forms and how these affect the meaning of the product. Developing technologies have allowed newspaper websites to combine elements of media language including audio-visual, images and text to construct meaning while computer-generated imagery (CGI) and other evolving technologies are used in music videos to enhance production. Developments in technology have also meant that there are greater opportunities for interactivity and consequently the relationship between the product and the audience has changed.
The codes and conventions of media forms and products, including the processes through which media language develops as a genre	Advertising and marketing Music video Newspapers	Television Magazines Online	This refers to the codes and conventions that place a product in a specific genre and that are common to particular media forms. This includes visual, technical and audio codes, iconography, narrative and characters. These conventions are common to all examples in a particular form, for example most television crime drama contains certain characters and has an expected narrative structure. Audiences become familiar with genre conventions, and producers will use this to market new products and to create audience expectation.

(continued)

Key statement: Media Language	Component 1 Media forms	Component 2 Media forms	Explanation
The dynamic and historically relative nature of genre	Component 2 only	Television Magazines	This is the idea that genres are constantly changing and evolving over time, reflecting historical and sociological changes. New genres appear and hybrid genres are created to address the needs of audiences and reflect changes in society. The popularity of genres also reflects society at the time. During the lockdown in 2021, according to a Vodafone poll, *Peaky Blinders*, *Downton Abbey*, *Only Fools and Horses* and *Friends* were in the top ten programmes watched, suggesting that audiences wanted escapism and comedy at this time. Genres are also important to industries in terms of marketing, playing on audience expectations. Theorists, including Steve Neale, suggested that genres were concerned with 'repetition and difference' – audiences need to recognise the genre's codes and conventions but also expect the product to offer something different.
The processes through which meanings are established through intertextuality	Advertising and marketing Music videos Newspapers	Television	Media producers use elements of media language to communicate meanings through references to other texts that are recognisable to audiences. For example, Janelle Monáe's music video for *Turntables* makes several intertextual references to communicate their message about social inequality, including news footage, documentaries, American icons, cultural codes and the protest song. Audiences will interpret this product on different levels according to their understanding of these references.
How audiences respond to and interpret the above aspects of media language	Advertising and marketing Music videos Newspapers	Television Magazines Online	How media products are constructed will affect how an audience responds to them. As stated above, media products are polysemic and will communicate more than one meaning and have more than one audience interpretation. This will also be affected by aspects of the audience themselves, e.g. their ideology.
How genre conventions are socially and historically relative, dynamic and can be used in a hybrid way	Component 2 only	Television Magazines	Genre conventions, particularly with regard to television and magazines, will evolve and reflect changes in society. This is evident, e.g., in the way in which gender is represented in magazines and how that reflects the issues and concerns related to the time in which the products were created. It is also the case that, in an attempt to attract audiences, hybrid genres are created which include elements of more than one genre, which, when combined, produce something new and innovative. According to Neale (1980), contemporary genres are examples of 'repetition and difference' – audiences need to be confident in the familiar while also being offered something new and exciting this may be relevant to the television set products.
The significance of challenging and/or subverting genre conventions	Component 2 only	Television	This statement is very relevant to the television set products in Component 2. The producers of media products will often challenge or subvert more typical genre conventions in order to produce something new that may appeal to a broader audience. An example is the episode of *Black Mirror*, 'San Junipero', which is a hybrid genre combining elements of sci-fi and romance. It is also a period piece as the plot takes place in the 1980s and 1990s.

(continued)

Key statement: Media Language	Component 1 Media forms	Component 2 Media forms	Explanation
The significance of the varieties of ways intertextuality can be used in the media	Advertising and marketing Music videos Newspapers	Television	Media products will use intertextuality in different ways for different purposes and effects. Adverts, e.g., may use intertextual references in order to target a specific audience who will understand the allusions contained in the product. Music videos, e.g. *Riptide*, will experiment with more postmodern approaches by incorporating more sophisticated cultural intertextual references to make the audience feel special when they recognise them. Other forms will use intertextuality as a quick way of communicating meanings and addressing a particular audience.
The way media language incorporates viewpoints and ideologies	Advertising and marketing Music videos Newspapers	Television Magazines Online	The way in which media products are constructed using the elements of media language will communicate messages to an audience regarding the ideology of the products. The paradigmatic choices made by the creators of newspapers in relation to the selection of images, headlines and mode of address will very often reflect their political viewpoint. The independent magazine products have clear viewpoints evident in their content. The *Daily Mirror* demonstrated its left-wing viewpoint on the refusal of Boris Johnson to resign over the lockdown party allegations through the choice of the headline 'Zero Shame'.

The Media Studies Framework: Representation

In Year 1 of the course you will have studied representation in relation to some of the set products. You will have considered how media products construct representations of social groups, including age, gender and ethnicity as well as how issues and events may be re-presented. You will have used the set products to explore:

- how all media products are constructed and present versions of reality
- how the representations reflect the **dominant ideology** of the creators of the product
- how stereotypes are used to communicate messages to an audience
- how representations are constructed in different media products in order to create meaning.

Representation is a more complex concept than it may seem at first and in Year 2 of the course you will need to develop your understanding of this important area of the theoretical framework. You will be required to apply your understanding of representation to the additional products you will study in Year 2 of the course.

In addition to the aspects of representation you studied in Year 1 of the course, in Year 2 you will explore:

- the way in which representations make claims about realism
- the impact of **industry contexts** on the choice media producers make about how to represent events, issues and social groups
- the effect of historical context on representations
- how representations invoke discourses and ideologies and position audiences
- how audiences' responses to and interpretations of media representations reflect social, cultural and historical circumstances.

Key Term

Dominant ideology
Refers to how those in positions of power present, repeat and reiterate a particular viewpoint that then appears to be 'dominant' or the norm. This is then accepted by the audience.

Industry context
Refers to elements of the production, for example the media organisation, production processes, distribution, marketing and regulation.

Key Terms

Subordinate
A group that is disadvantaged compared with other groups and may face unequal treatment or discrimination.

Ethnocentrism
The attitude that one's own ethnic group, culture or nationality is superior to others.

Tip

Although you are advised on the key aspects of the set theorists that you are required to study, familiarising yourself with their broader ideas will develop your understanding further in Year 2 of the course.

Quickfire 1.20

Give an example of a subordinate group in society which may be represented in a particular way by the media.

Quickfire 1.21

What did Stuart Hall state was the difference between representation and re-presentation?

Quickfire 1.22

How can the depiction of a rose have different meanings?

Subordinate groups are defined by how much power they have in society.

Theoretical Framework: Stuart Hall

In Year 1 of the course you will have studied the cultural theorist Stuart Hall and applied his theories to the set products. You will be required to develop your understanding of this theoretical perspective further and apply it to the products studied in Year 2. You will recall that the main elements of his theory you are required to study are:

- the idea that representation is the production of meaning through language, with language defined in its broadest sense as a system of signs
- the idea that the relationship between concepts and signs is governed by codes
- the idea that stereotyping, as a form of representation, reduces people to a few simple characteristics or traits
- the idea that stereotyping tends to occur where there are inequalities of power, as **subordinate** or excluded groups are constructed as different or 'other' (e.g. through **ethnocentrism**).

Society is divided into dominant and subordinate groups and this division is reflected in how particular social groups are represented in the media. The traits of the two groups contribute to the construction of stereotypes and may include:

Dominant groups	Subordinate groups
Have control and access to power	Lack power in society
Make decisions/rules	Adhere/adapt to rules and decisions
Define how society is organised	Have to fit into the dominant culture
Belong	Are seen to be outsiders
Have little experience of being treated differently	Are very aware of differential treatment
Control resources	Need to access resources
Seen to be 'normal' members of society	Seen to be 'different' or 'other'

The main categories of subordinate groups relate to gender, religion, race, ethnicity, age and sexual orientation.

Stuart Hall's research brought him to the conclusion that there are two ways of looking at visual representation:

- representation that is more descriptive and is a depiction of something
- re-presentation where the media, for example, re-present something that is already there. Here, there is an additional element of giving meaning to what is being represented. This meaning could involve mediation and as such could be a distortion.

However, even a depiction does not resemble real life. Hall gives the example of a picture of a rose which, although we recognise it, is not the same as a real rose in a garden. The depiction of the rose itself can also have different meanings according to where it is seen.

Hall asserted that there was then a gap between the true meaning of what is being presented (the representation) and how it is presented (re-presentation).

This theory is applicable to some of the media forms and products you will study, particularly newspapers. All newspapers have access to the same news each day, but how they decide to represent that news will be influenced by the ideology of the newspaper and the messages they want to communicate to their readers. For example, a simple depiction of the resignation of Liz Truss in 2021 would have been descriptive and straightforward, using the facts of what happened and less dramatic images and headlines. However, on the day, different newspapers re-presented this event differently, each constructing a different meaning for the story according to the ideology of the paper. This consequently affected how the readers interpreted this event, with the newspaper, through its construction and mediation, functioning as an **opinion leader**.

Hall (1997) also stated that one way in which representations are constructed is through signs and codes that, in order to be effective, must be recognised by the audience. This 'shared understanding' will allow the meanings and representations to be communicated and understood by the audience; they are 'social conventions' that we have unconsciously absorbed to enable us to be part of our culture.

As you will have explored in Year 1 of the course, signs and codes are used to communicate messages through media language in many media forms, and those messages are understood and accepted by audiences as they have been reinforced over time. A simple example of how signs work through a shared understanding is traffic lights, which are understood globally and as such has become part of a cultural language. Without this shared understanding there would be chaos on the roads.

Revision: Key Elements of Representation

Encoding and decoding: the creators of media products use elements of media language to encode messages through the way in which they construct representations of social groups. The audience then decode these messages in different ways. The response of the audience may be affected by a range of elements, including, for example, their age, gender, ethnicity and culture.

Stereotypes: stereotypes are rapid ways of communicating messages to an audience and can be both positive and negative. They reduce groups of people to a set of simple recognisable traits. They can also reflect the ideology of a society.

Construction: the creators of media products use media language to construct representations and to re-present reality. This construction of aspects of reality can appear natural and as such is unquestionably accepted as truth by some audiences. However, the construction of reality in media products is obviously selective and the focus will be decided by the producer, the audience will then be positioned by the way in which the representation is constructed. The ideas and beliefs of this producer will ultimately affect the representation presented to the audience.

Selection: this is linked to construction. The representation of events, issues and social groups, as well as self-representation, are constructed through processes of selection and combination. The producer will select what to include and what to leave out; this will affect the meaning and the audience response to the representation.

Key Term

Opinion leaders
Those in positions of power, for example newspaper owners and editors, who aim to persuade an audience of their point of view.

Quickfire 1.23

Which other theory/theoretical perspective is founded upon the idea that signs and codes communicate messages?

Quickfire 1.24

What does Hall mean by 'shared understanding'?

Quickfire 1.25

What affects how a paper chooses to represent an event?

This drawing of a rose is a representation, it is not the same as the actual flower.

Consider how stereotypes are used in the media.

Mediation: this refers to the way in which media products manipulate reality in order to communicate meanings. It is the processes the product goes through before it reaches the audience. When we view a media product we are seeing someone else's version of reality encoded with their messages and beliefs. While we are more likely to accept the mediation evident on the front cover of a women's lifestyle magazine, where airbrushing and image manipulation construct an unrealistic image of female beauty, some products seem less mediated, particularly those that purport to deliver the truth. Newspapers and documentaries are more likely to mediate reality as they often want to persuade the audience of their point of view. At times this can be more subtle and unobtrusive.

The way in which a product is mediated will encourage the audience to focus on one element of the product rather than another. The organisation of the product will foreground an aspect that may be more in keeping with the ideology of the producer. This is particularly true of newspapers where the organisation of the front page and the selection of stories from the many on offer that day, will reflect the beliefs of the paper, which they will then hope to communicate to their readers.

Context and purpose: the way in which social groups, issues and events are represented changes according to the context and purpose of the product. Beyoncé, Janelle Monáe and Alicia Keys all represent issues in their music videos; however, the product is essentially a promotional tool that functions as a marketing device for the artists as well as raising awareness of issues that may concern them. The way in which the particular issue is represented contributes in turn to the representations of the artist and their star persona and may make them seem more relatable. The way in which the issue is constructed will be controlled by the artist and be related to their opinion and viewpoint. For example, Beyoncé uses Hurricane Katrina as a starting point to address a range of systemic issues about race and ethnicity in American culture and history.

The same issue was represented differently in other contexts, for example the press at the time of Hurricane Katrina, where the focus was very specifically on the tragedy of the natural disaster and what had been done to help the people.

Stretch and Challenge 1.8

Researching the ways that different newspapers mediate the truth will broaden your understanding of how newspapers represent events and people.

Stretch and Challenge 1.7

Select a newspaper front page. Write at least three paragraphs discussing how the newspaper has re-presented the front page story for its readers. Use as many of the 'Key terms' listed on this page as you can in your analysis.

Rapid Recall 1.14

Give an example of how stereotypes can convey the ideology of a society.

Representation Revision: Key terms checklist

You need to be confident in using the following key terms related to representation:

- stereotypes
- construction
- selection
- mediation
- encoding
- decoding
- context and purpose.

Tip

Becoming familiar with the ownership and ideology of different newspapers will prepare you for the unseen element of Component 1: Section A and the industry element of Component 1: Section B.

Constructing Identity: The Representation of Self

An important aspect of representation is the way in which advances in technology have enabled people to construct representations of themselves. It has never been easier to create a version of yourself that may not be entirely true. In the same way that media products mediate and re-present reality, individuals can also selectively construct versions of themselves.

YouTube, Instagram, Facebook and other social media platforms offer opportunities for self-representation, allowing users to alter profiles and regularly update aspects of identity according to mood and circumstances. The opportunities to mediate reality by deleting photos and changing 'status' make identities in the digital world fluid and ever evolving. However, this fluidity can be restricted to being who we think others want us to be, rather than reflecting our true identity. Facebook profiles and Instagram photos could be said to be a 'presentation of self' that we want others to see. The interactive nature of these platforms allows others to comment on the identity created and may persuade us to make changes in order to conform to expectations. Even celebrity bloggers such as Zoe Sugg will react to adverse comments and may reconstruct themselves and their social media content in the light of these.

Zoe Sugg uses her YouTube channel to construct a representation of herself, this has evolved as she has changed and one section of her vlog focuses on her family life now that she is a mother. Her 'Day in The Life' vlogs allow audiences to see a glimpse of her life at home.

Another collection of vlogs shows a different aspect of the star focusing on her broader concerns and her role as an influencer for her fans, for example 'Mindfulness, Meeting, Books & Current Favourites' where she discusses the importance of mindfulness routines in managing her life.

Zoe Sugg, on her YouTube channel (https://www.youtube.com/@ZoeSugg), presents an image of herself to her audience and in doing so acts as a positive influencer for young women, highlighting issues that are of interest to the target audience.

Another way in which users of social media construct identities is through **virtue signalling** (Bartholomew, 2015). Bartholomew uses this term for the way people post certain content online to suggest how good and virtuous they are and to contribute to a sense of identity that establishes them with a strong moral compass, for example discussing key issues, re-tweeting links to charitable causes and sharing links. Others will then respond or 'like' these and in turn seem equally virtuous.

Mindfulness, Meetings, Books & Current Favourites | ad

497K views • 2 months ago

Valentines Day, Office Newness & Old Favourites

593K views • 2 months ago

Quickfire 1.26

What affects the way in which an issue or event may be represented in the media?

Key Term

Virtue signalling
The act of posting online content that suggests the person is good and virtuous.

Stretch and Challenge 1.9

Read the whole of 'Facebook and the Presentation of Self: A Structure-versus-Agency Analysis of Folk Tales' (McLaughlin, 2017) as it has a range of points that can be applied to an analysis of blogs and vlogs and the idea of self-representation in the media.

Theoretical Framework: David Gauntlett

In Year 1 of the course you will have studied the identity and audience theorist David Gauntlett and applied his theories to the set products. You will be required to develop your understanding of this theoretical perspective and apply it to the products studied in Year 2. You will recall that the main elements of his theory you are required to study are:

- the idea that the media provide us with 'tools' or resources that we use to construct our identities
- the idea that while in the past the media tended to convey singular, straightforward messages about ideal types of male and female identities, the media today offer us a more diverse range of stars, icons and characters from whom we may pick and mix different ideas.

Gauntlett asserts that, in particular, digital media gives people a range of opportunities to be **prosumers** who create their own content. His theory reinforces the more autonomous role of the audience in the digital age.

Key Term

Prosumers
Derives from the marketing term 'production by consumers' and is used to describe those individuals who comment on, create or adapt existing content and then distribute it through the internet and social media.

Tip

There are a lot of articles about social media as an evolving platform. Engaging in wider reading will expand your knowledge and understanding of this constantly changing area.

In 2017 Gauntlett revisited and updated his ideas around identity in the media to expand upon and develop those first published in 2008. These included:

- the idea of people having a route to self-expression and therefore a stronger sense of self and participation in the world, through creating and exchanging content online
- that '*media [made by all of us] … can be places of conversation, exchange, and transformation*'
- that the internet was '*a fantastically messy set of networks filled with millions of sparks – some igniting new meanings, ideas, and passions, and some just fading away*'
- the idea that people can build their own sense of identity through creativity and by becoming part of a creative community.

(Adapted from http://davidgauntlett.com/blog/)

Rapid Recall 1.15

Which media forms did you apply David Gauntlett's theory to in Year 1 of the course?

In the second edition of his book *Making is Connecting*, Gauntlett, while acknowledging the negative and worrying elements of the internet and social media, reaffirms his belief that people are enabled by the internet to:

> *connect with others, share creative projects, and be inspired by each other, in ways which were not possible before.* (Gauntlett, 2018)

Tip

You will need to regularly revisit the work you did on key theorists in Year 1 of the course and apply it to the products you study in Year 2. Your conceptual understanding should have developed to allow you to respond to the Year 2 products at a more sophisticated level.

Representations of Gender in the Media

You will already have explored how gender is represented in historical and contemporary media products and how this representation reflects the context in which the product was made. The following is a recap of the main points from Year 1 of the course:

- The way in which women are represented in the media has largely evolved to reflect changes in society.
- However, there still exist stereotypical representations of women that reinforce more outdated ideas and beliefs.
- Women still tend to be judged by how beautiful they are and the media are full of aspirational images of women that ordinary women are expected to strive to attain.
- Where women are expected to compete with men they are defined by how strong and powerful they are rather than how credible they are within the product.

Tip

David Gauntlett is a practising media theorist who regularly comments on the media and revisits his theories. You can expand your knowledge of his work by accessing his blog: http://davidgauntlett.com/blog/.

- Language of power when used to describe a woman is often derogative and gender specific, for example 'diva' and 'feisty'. Sheryl Sandberg and Beyoncé spearheaded the 'Ban Bossy' campaign to raise awareness of these anomalies in the way in which women are represented through language.
- While there are many stereotypical representations of women that still exist in the media, there are also products whose aim is to challenge those stereotypes and offer more positive, credible representations of women.

During the time in which you study A Level Media Studies there will be reports in the media regarding the continued disparity between men and women in society. This may be related to inequality of pay or a lack of fair representation. In 2023 there was an outcry and #OcarsSoMale was trending to register concern at the lack of nominations for female directors at the annual awards ceremony.

In his 1983 book, *The Media in Britain*, **Jeremy Tunstall** suggests that the presentation of women in the media is biased as it emphasises only women's domestic, sexual and marital roles depicting them as housewives, mothers, consumers and sex objects.

This was certainly true in some areas of the media, in particular advertising, and is still the case in some media forms today. In advertising during the 1950s and 1960s, as you will recall from the study of the historical advertising product *Tide*, women were seen to be frequently fulfilling the roles indicated by Tunstall.

Find the 1939 advertisement for Kellogg's PEP Vitamins *'So The Harder A Wife Works, The Cuter She Looks'* here: https://www.ghostofthedoll.co.uk/retromusings/category/food-drink/food/.

Consider how this example defines the gender roles at the time. The woman is visually represented as the housewife and homemaker, indicated by the code of clothing and iconography of the duster. She is also seen to be sexually attractive and 'cute', in both images the man is touching her as his possession. Ironically, the vitamins will help her to succeed at the multi-roles she must play. He, in contrast, is defined by his suit as the wage earner, with a single role to play.

Men

Representations of masculinity have also evolved to reflect sociological change.

- The advent of the metrosexual man has resulted in the emergence of a man who is in touch with his emotional side while also retaining his inherent masculinity, making him attractive to both sexes and a sellable commodity.
- Men as well as women are now under pressure to adhere to an expectation of how to look.
- How the media presents what it means to be male in contemporary society is constantly evolving and consequently has an effect on men's identity, how they see themselves and their place in society. As Gauntlett asserted, the contemporary world is becoming more diverse in its representation of masculinity.
- While there still exist representations of men in the media today that remain focused on what are seen to be traditional attributes, including power, body image and sexual attractiveness, there is also a growing fluidity with regard to representations of masculinity.

Rapid Recall 1.16

Which theorist explores the idea of the 'Trinity Syndrome' and what did she mean by this?

Key Figure

Jeremy Tunstall
Is a professor of Sociology who, as part of the Global Media Research Centre at City University, London, explored the areas of media sociology and international communications. He has published several books including *The Media are American* (1977), *The Media in Britain* (1983) and *The Media Were American* (2007).

Quickfire 1.27

How can Jeremy Tunstall's theory be applied to the historical *Tide* advert you studied in Year 1?

Harry Styles: the epitome of metrosexual man

- Certain genres are associated with specific representations of **masculinity**, for example advertising, while in other forms, for example music videos and crime dramas, new, more diverse representations are apparent. The **Nordic noir** television crime sub-genre features men who are 'troubled souls', invariably trailing emotional baggage and flawed in some way. The opportunity to present masculinity in this way has led to more interesting, three-dimensional characters who have credibility within the narrative.
- The music genre has always had a range of representations of masculinity and performers who actively challenged more traditional, expected roles. A modern example is Harry Styles, a performer who regularly confronts the social norms of masculinity. He appeared on the front cover of the December 2020 Vogue wearing a Gucci dress, so subverting the codes of masculinity. Read what Harry Styles has to say about barriers in clothing and Olivia Wilde's hopes for the future in the accompanying article at https://www.vogue.com/article/harry-styles-cover-december-2020, where you can also see the cover.

Ethnicity

You will have considered how **ethnicity** is represented in some of the products you studied in Year 1 of the course. You will have explored the difference between ethnicity and **race** and discussed the following points in relation to this area of the theoretical framework:

- Representations of ethnicity in the media today are generally more diverse than in the past. Just like representations of other aspects of social identity such as gender, representations of **race** and ethnicity reflect changes in society. These representations can shape and influence the way in which we see ourselves and those around us.
- However, issues of under-representation, misrepresentation and stereotyping continue to persist as people from minority ethnic groups still tend to be defined in terms of their 'otherness' in some areas of the mainstream media.
- Positive representations of black, Asian and minority ethnic groups can be found in some areas of the media, for example the music industry, which while it may still reinforce more traditional stereotypes, also offers a vehicle for many black artists to control their representations and present aspects of their cultural identity, for example Beyoncé and Janelle Monáe.

Theoretical Framework: Paul Gilroy

In Year 2 of the course you will study the **postcolonial** theorist Paul Gilroy. You will need to apply his theories to the products you studied in Year 1 and the ones you will study in Year 2. The main elements of his theory with which you must be familiar are:

- the idea that **colonial** discourses continue to inform contemporary attitudes to race and ethnicity in the postcolonial era
- the idea that **civilisationism** constructs racial hierarchies and sets up binary oppositions based on notions of otherness.

Key Terms

Masculinity
The state of 'being a man', which can change as society changes. It is essentially what being a man means to a particular generation. This will then be reflected in the contemporary media.

Nordic noir
A sub-genre constructed for marketing purposes and defines a type of Scandinavian crime drama featuring bleak, cold settings, troubled characters and dark storylines.

Ethnicity
A person's cultural identity, which may be indicated through customs, clothing or food. Your ethnicity suggests an identity that is based on a sense of place, ideology or religion.

Race
Defined by racial characteristics, for example skin colour and facial features.

Postcolonial
Refers to the time after the end of colonial rule. Postcolonial studies explore the lasting impact of colonial rule on people, countries and culture.

Colonial
Refers to the practice of acquiring political control of another country.

Civilisationism
Refers to Gilroy's idea that geopolitics will always be centred on cultural differences rather than similarities. He associated civilisationalism with ethnocentrism, as, in his opinion, it reproduces racial hierarchies and colonial attitudes by constructing certain, usually non-Western cultures as 'other'.

Rapid Recall 1.17

What is meant by tokenism in relation to the representation of ethnicity in media products?

Despite the fact that the way in which different ethnic groups are represented in the media has progressed, resulting in more positive and credible representations, there are still issues surrounding representations of race and ethnicity and the notions of power. As Gilroy states, where there are inequalities of power, racial hierarchies are constructed. Even when the representations of race or ethnicity in a product go beyond tokenism, it is often the case that white ethnic groups are seen to be the more powerful and in control.

Gilroy used his review of the Steve McQueen film *12 Years A Slave* (2014) to re-state his belief that racial division is still prevalent and not a thing of the past. It asserts his concerns over the durability and continued potency of racism in a supposedly 'post-racial' world. The title of the review reinforces this, '12 Years a Slave: In our "Post-racial" Age the Legacy of Slavery Lives On' (Gilroy, 2013). The review echoes his thoughts about civilisationalsim and the lasting effect of colonialism on modern culture and living.

Stretch and Challenge 1.10

Read the whole of Paul Gilroy's (2013) review online, which exemplifies his theoretical perspective.

Another useful theorist to study in relation to the representation of race and ethnicity is **Manuel Alvarado**. Similar to Gilroy, his theoretical perspective in relation to ethnicity is based on the idea that people from ethnic minority groups tend to be defined in terms of their difference and perceived 'otherness'. These constructed representations can focus on racial characteristics and on preconceived audience perceptions. The narrow representations are often drawn from other media products rather than from reality and therefore reinforce the stereotype. Alvarado believed that the representation of ethnic groups could be divided into four categories:

- the exotic
- the pitied
- the humorous
- dangerous.

Key Figure

Manuel Alvarado
Guatemalan-born English academic who specialised in media studies research. In his lifetime he was Head of Education at the BFI, held professorships at key universities and wrote extensively about media education.

The Exotic

This stereotype links closely to what theorist Stuart Hall called the secret fascination of 'otherness' (Hall, 1997) – this is the way in which the media represent people who are different.

This theoretical perspective can also be linked to Gilroy's theory of postcolonialism and the way in which civilisationalism reproduces racial hierarchies.

Tip

Consider how you can apply Gilroy's theoretical perspective to the products you studied in Year 1 of the course.

This sense of 'otherness' can be viewed both positively and negatively but is usually a construction by the product. The 'exotic' stereotype re-presents the individual in terms of codes and signifiers related to how they look, what they wear, what they eat and their 'different' customs that seem to make them less relatable to a specific audience. *'Difference signifies. It "speaks"'* (Hall, 1997).

The Pitied

In certain media products, people from ethnic minority groups are stereotyped as vulnerable and as victims. This is true of some newspaper and television news reports with a focus of developing countries; largely this is because the only time certain countries appear in the news is when they are linked to disasters, for example conflict, famine and earthquakes. Similar representations may be used for charity campaigns in order to shock the audience into action.

Consider the purpose and effect of using the selected image in this Oxfam advertisement.

The Humorous

In the context of certain media products, for example situation comedies and particular film genres, the audience is encouraged to laugh at the ethnic stereotypes contained within the text. These stereotypes have often been built up over time and, as with all stereotypes, they exaggerate recognisable features and traits. In the early days of sit-coms racist humour was seen as an acceptable way of making people laugh. This is no longer the case but products such as, for example, *Citizen Khan*, have attracted a range of views about the programme, which was written by British Muslim Adil Ray. Ofcom received complaints about the programme when it aired for the first time in 2012 and it divided opinion, with accusations that it stereotyped the Pakistani community in Britain. Similar criticisms of racial stereotyping have been levelled at *Bad Education* (BBC) which returned for a Christmas special in 2022.

Stuart Hall discusses the dangers of stereotyping, in particular of those who are seen to be 'different' culturally, and suggests, like Gilroy, that it reinforces racial hierarchies and that stereotyping:

> *is part of the maintenance of social and symbolic order. It sets up a symbolic frontier between … what belongs and what does not or is 'Other'…* (Hall, 1997)

Dangerous

Alvarado states that some media products represent minority ethnic groups as a threat to society and they are often blamed for social problems. Refugees are frequently represented stereotypically in certain areas of the media in the UK as 'immigrants' who have entered the country illegally. The choice of language serves to reinforce the negative stereotype and affect how an audience may view a particular social group. The **ghettoisation** of some social groups reinforces the idea of 'difference' as they become marooned communities who are seen as apart from the norm. Some newspapers, for example, manipulate the readers' fears of the unknown by grouping together individuals under the common title of 'immigrants'. This lack of personalisation makes it easier to blame them for a range of social problems. This also reinforces Hall's theory that stereotyping tends to occur where there are inequalities of power, as subordinate or excluded groups are constructed as different or 'other'.

Alvarado more recently added 'sexualised' to his list of representative ethnic groups. This highlights the way in which some media forms represent ethnic groups as sexually violent or provocative as in some films, or as sexual objects in certain music genres, for example rap and hip-hop.

All of the above ways in which Alvarado suggested ethnicity is represented across a range of media products reinforces the link between representation, difference, defined as being 'other', and power.

Issues and Events

You will have explored how issues and events are represented in some of the set products you have studied in Year 1 of the course, for example newspapers, and will have covered the following points:

- The way in which the issue or event is represented will reflect the ideology of the product.
- The issue or event will have been re-presented and constructed through the use of media language, including technical and audio codes, visual signs and signifiers, language and mode of address.
- The ways in which issues and events are represented in media products do not offer a 'window on the world'. They are mediated and may reflect particular ideas and opinions.

Quickfire 1.28

Why might the construction of humorous representations of other cultures featured in *Citizen Khan* and *Bad Education* be thought by some audiences to be problematic?

Rapid Recall 1.18

How do tabloid newspapers use aspects of media language to represent events and issues?

Tip

Remember to apply the theories and theoretical perspectives discussed in this introductory chapter to the set products you studied in Year 1 and those you will study in Year 2.

Key Term

Ghettoisation
The treatment of particular social groups as if they are different and separate from other parts of society and therefore not as important.

Tip

When exploring the way in which issues and events are represented in media products, carefully consider how the audience is being positioned by the way in which the issue or event is constructed.

- The producers of the media product will make choices regarding what to select and include in the representation. The way in which the event or issue is re-presented may affect the way in which the audience responds.
- Media products can become opinion leaders and influencers, persuading the audience to accept a particular viewpoint through the way in which the issue or event has been represented.
- The media product may focus upon a particular aspect of the issue or event, thus offering the audience only a selective perspective. Where the audience does not have the whole story it becomes more difficult to form independent judgements.
- Where issues and events are outside of the experience of the audience they have to rely on the media products and their interpretation, which may be mediated to encode a particular viewpoint or ideology.
- This particular viewpoint may be apparent across a range of issues and events, meaning that the audience only has access to one particular point of view, for example the representation of certain political stories in the right-wing press.

Stretch and Challenge 1.11

For comparison, explore how the same issue or event is represented in other forms and products. This will allow you to see different forms of mediation and highlight the ideology of the producers and how they appeal to their audience.

Tip

The grid at the bottom of this page allows you to clearly see which theory/theoretical perspective relates to which product and form. You need to familiarise yourself with these requirements. You will notice that not all the theories need to be applied to all of the products. This information will guide you when preparing for examination questions.

Applying Theory: Representation

The grid below summarises the main theories and theoretical perspectives that you are required to study across Components 1 and 2. The key elements related to some of the theories have been outlined above and these and other named theories and theorists will be referred to in the chapters specifically dealing with each component and their forms and products. Although you may also study and show your knowledge and understanding of other relevant theories, the ones set out below must be studied in relation to the areas of the specification indicated.

Note

At the time of writing *gal-dem* was the approved set product. Please make sure you double check the WJEC/Eduqas website or Illuminate (https://bit.ly/3r1d7at) for the most up-to-date information on which set products you should be studying.

Theory/theoretical approach	Component 1 Forms	Component 2 Forms/products
Theories of representation, including Stuart Hall	Advertising and marketing Music video Newspapers	Television: both products Online: all products
Theories of identity, including David Gauntlett	Advertising and marketing Music video	Magazines: both products Online: all products
Feminist theories, including Liesbet van Zoonen and bell hooks	Advertising and marketing Music video	Television: both products Magazines: both products
Theories around ethnicity and post-colonial theory, including Paul Gilroy	Advertising and marketing Music video	Online: *gal-dem* or *Attitude*
Theories of gender performativity, including Judith Butler		Television: *The Bridge* or *Black Mirror* or *Killing Eve* Online: JJ Olatunji or Zoe Sugg

The Specification: Key Statements

The grid below shows the statements for Representation and explains their meaning and the forms and examination components to which they relate.

Key statement: Representation	**Component 1 Media forms**	**Component 2 Media forms**	**Explanation**
The way events, issues, individuals (including self-representation) and social groups (including social identity) are represented through processes of selection and combination	Advertising and marketing Music video Newspapers	Television Magazines Online	The idea that all media products construct representations through the decisions made about what to include and what to leave out. The media producers will construct the representation in order to appeal to the target audience and reinforce their ideology.
The way the media, through re-presentation, construct versions of reality	Advertising and marketing Music video Newspapers	Component 1 only	The media do not construct reality; it is not a *'window on the world'* (**David Buckingham**, 2003). The media re-presents reality and mediates it for the audience. This representation may change according to the product and its purpose and ideology: *The media intervene; they provide us with selective versions of the world, rather than direct access to it.* (Buckingham, 2003)
The processes which lead media producers to make choices about how to represent events, issues, individuals and social groups	Advertising and marketing Music video Newspapers	Magazines Online	The way in which the producers of media products choose to construct representations will be influenced by a range of factors. These will include the ideology of the producers, for example the political stance of a newspaper, the target audience and their expectations and the context in which the product was created.
The effect of social and cultural context on representation	Advertising and marketing Music video Newspapers	Television Magazines Online	The way in which media products construct representations will reflect the time in which they were produced. For example, the historical magazines, *Tide* advert and *Kiss of the Vampire* film poster reflect the place of women in society in the 1950s and 1960s and aspects of the culture of the time. Some of the music videos you will study, for example Janelle Monáe's *Turnables* and Sam Fender's *Seventeen Going Under*, are commenting on contemporary society.

(continued)

Key Figure

David Buckingham
A writer and researcher specialising in media education. He is Visiting Professor at various universities and is a leading internationally recognised expert on children's and young people's interactions with electronic media, and on media literacy education.

Key statement: Representation	Component 1 Media forms	Component 2 Media forms	Explanation
How and why stereotypes can be used positively and negatively	Advertising and marketing Music video Newspapers	Television Magazines Online	Stereotypes are quick ways of communicating information and as such reduce certain social groups to a set of narrow, recognisable characteristics. Stereotypes are reinforced over time and link to the cultural/social and historical context. The thought-provoking and positive representations of disability in *Super. Human.* challenges more stereotypical representations and aims to confront the perceptions of some audiences. The music video *Turntables* uses positive and negative representations of minority ethnic groups in order to raise awareness of a social issue.
How and why particular social groups, in a national and global context, may be under-represented or misrepresented	Advertising and marketing Music video Newspapers	Television Magazines Online	As Gilroy, Hall and other theorists have stated, the way in which particular groups in society are represented links to who holds the power. Media industries are generally owned and controlled by dominant groups who reinforce stereotypical representations of minority groups, resulting in these groups being under- or misrepresented. The constant reinforcement of these stereotypes across the media results in the representation being accepted as the 'norm'. However, it is the case that some media industries and forms try to challenge the misconceptions fuelled by erroneous stereotypes. For example, the music industry, through music videos, offers a more diverse representation of ethnicity and uses the music video form to raise awareness of cultural inequalities (*Formation*, *Underdog*, *Turntables* and *Seventeen Going Under*) to a global audience. In a national context, companies such as the BBC have embedded targeting under-represented groups within their charter; *Have You Heard George's Podcast?* is an example of a programme whose aim is to broaden the Radio 4 schedule and give a voice to under-represented groups.
How media representations convey values, attitudes and beliefs about the world and how these may be systematically reinforced across a wide range of media representations	Advertising and marketing Music video Newspapers	Television Magazines Online	This also relates to the link between representation and power. The ideology of the dominant groups in society may be reinforced across a range of media products. The way in which women have been typically represented in a sexual way across a range of media products, reinforcing their perceived roles in society is one example. The largely right-wing press will also reinforce ideas about what it means to be British and will represent certain social groups as 'other' and therefore to be feared. Where audiences only receive a narrow diet of media content, particularly with regards to the internet or a particular newspaper, they may have their opinions and preconceived ideas reinforced.
How audiences respond to and interpret media representations	Advertising and marketing Music video Newspapers	Television Magazines Online	This is the idea that modern audiences are active rather than passive consumers of the media and as such will respond to the way in which media products construct representations in different ways. Hall suggested that responses may be affected by factors including, age, gender, ethnicity, demographic group, situation, and the context and purpose of the product. This will result in an acceptance of the preferred reading of the product or, alternatively, a negotiated or oppositional reading.

(continued)

Key statement: Representation	Component 1 Media forms	Component 2 Media forms	Explanation
The way in which representations make claims about realism	Newspapers	Television Magazines Online	As discussed in this chapter, media products that claim to present real life, for example newspapers and documentaries, are not 'windows on the world'. They re-present events and issues through a process of selection and mediation. The way in which they choose to represent reality will also be influenced by ideologies.
The impact of industry contexts on the choices media producers make about how to represent events, issues, individuals and social groups	Newspapers	Television Magazines	The representations constructed by the media will be influenced by organisational factors. These may include the political viewpoint of the newspaper, for example the funding model and the ownership/ control of the product. Different newspapers report political events in different ways reflecting their ideological values and viewpoints.
The effect of historical context on representations	Advertising and marketing Music videos	Television Magazines	The representations constructed in media products will reflect the social, cultural and historical context of time of production. For example, the post-war period of the *Tide* advert and the historical and contemporary representations of race in *Formation* and *Turntables.*
How representations invoke discourses and ideologies and position audiences	Advertising and marketing Music video Newspapers	Television Magazines Online	The representations of events, issues and social groups in the media are constructed in such a way as to position audiences. This may be in relation to the way in which a character is constructed through technical codes and editing, for example Saga in *The Bridge*, or through emotive headlines in newspapers. The positioning may be direct and emotional, for example in the *Super. Human.* trailer. The way in which the representation is constructed also relates to the ideology of the product and how this is debated, for example the political leanings of a newspaper or the under-representation of areas of society in *Underdog*.
How audience responses to and interpretations of media representations reflect social, cultural and historical circumstances	Advertising and marketing Music video Newspapers	Television Magazines Online	The ways in which audiences respond to media products will be influenced by contextual factors, including gender, age and ethnicity. For example, it is important when exploring the historical set products to consider how audiences of the time would have responded to them, rather than adopting a 21st-century viewpoint. Similarly, audiences of differing political viewpoints will respond to the *Daily Mirror*'s front page differently. Hall's reception theory can be applied here.

The Media Studies Framework: Industry

During Year 1 of the course you will have explored the industry context of the set products you studied. In Component 1: Section B and Component 2 you will be required to demonstrate this knowledge and understanding of industry in the examination. In Year 2 of the course you will also be introduced to new theories and theoretical perspectives related to media industries. You will already be aware of the following elements of industry in relation to your Year 1 products and must now apply this understanding to the products you will study in Year 2:

- The significance of ownership and funding in relation to media industries, for example the difference in funding between the two films you will study, *Black Panther* produced by a major film studio and *I, Daniel Blake* which is a low-budget UK/French production that received funding from the BFI and the BBC in a very different model from most mainstream films.
- In an interesting industry move, in February 2018 Trinity Mirror, the owners of the Mirror newspaper group, made a £200 million deal with Richard Desmond to buy his newspaper and magazine titles, including: the *Daily Express*, the *Star* and the celebrity gossip magazine *OK!* This expanded the Mirror group empire (renamed Reach plc) and allowed it to become more competitive in digital forums when print newspaper sales are falling.
- The distribution and circulation processes of media industries will differ and this has been affected by changes in technology related to media production. For example, it is much easier than in the past for bloggers such as Zoe Sugg to reach an audience through digital platforms. Online magazines complement the print versions and are more easily produced. They offer different opportunities for audiences, generating substantial web traffic and making them attractive to advertisers. Some larger, more powerful organisations operate a vertical integration model and have the means to distribute and circulate their products.
- Promotion and marketing is an important aspect of media industries. All media organisations use marketing devices to maintain both national and global audiences. Advances in technology have allowed producers to target audiences across a range of platforms, thus reaching a broader audience.
- Individual producers are also an important element of media industries. Ken Loach, as director of *I, Daniel Blake*, is a very significant voice in the film industry and would have been important in securing funding for the film, based on his past experience and success. Similarly, the producers of online vlogs and blogs have unprecedented control over their product, the advertisers and the fanbase they have created.
- The ways in which different media industries are regulated have a direct effect on what is produced. This may differ globally. Some areas of the media are more difficult to regulate, for example online content. The ways in which we consume media have changed dramatically over recent years, many of us are now **digital natives** and anyone can be a prosumer.
- In 2017, the Conservative government attempted to force internet companies to allow government access to the private communications of all users of the internet in order to crack down on extremist and objectionable material.

Link

More information about industry can be found on page 43 of the Year 1 book. What you have here is a brief reminder of the key points with some different illustrative examples.

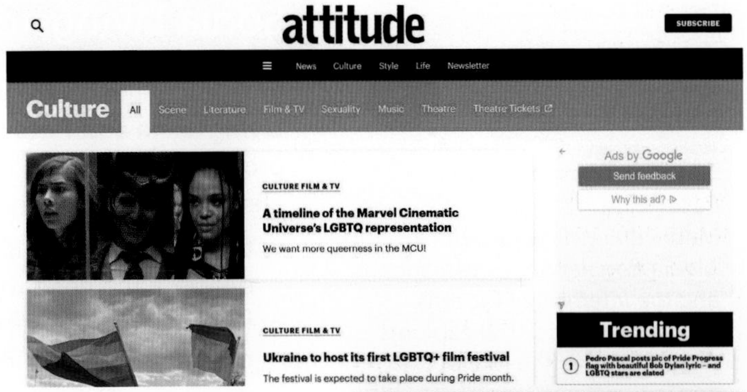

Changes in technology have enabled online magazines to thrive.

Quickfire 1.29

How might the *Daily Mirror's* takeover of the *Daily Express* affect the *Express*?

Quickfire 1.30

Give an example of distribution in the film industry.

Rapid Recall 1.19

What is vertical integration?

Key Term

Digital natives
People born or brought up during the age of digital technology who therefore have a high level of digital literacy when it comes to using computers and the internet.

Stretch and Challenge 1.12

Keep up to date with developments in the media industries by reading the 'Media' section of newspapers, for example the *Guardian*, or listening to relevant podcasts, for example *The Media Show* on Radio 4 and BBC Sounds.

Named Theorists

Sonia Livingstone and Peter Lunt
Media theorists whose book, *Media Regulation: Governance and the Interests of Citizens and Consumers* (2012) explores the history and the role of the communications regulator Ofcom.

While some think it is a good idea to protect citizens from harmful internet material, others see it as an infringement of free speech and privacy and a form of censorship. This discussion around the regulation of the internet is ongoing and in 2022 an Online Safety Bill began its way through parliament. The government worked with the regulator Ofcom to introduce a new set of laws to protect children and adults online and to make social media companies more responsible for their users' safety.

Theoretical Framework: Sonia Livingstone and Peter Lunt

In Year 2 of the course you will study the regulation theories of **Sonia Livingstone and Peter Lunt**. You will need to apply these theories to the products you studied in Year 1 and the ones you will study in Year 2. The main elements of regulation theory with which you must be familiar are:

- the idea that there is an underlying struggle in recent UK regulation policy between the need to further the interests of citizens (by offering protection from harmful or offensive material) and the need to further the interests of consumers (by ensuring choice, value for money and market competition)
- the idea that the increasing power of global media corporations, together with the rise of convergent media technologies and transformations in the production, distribution and marketing of digital media, have placed traditional approaches to media regulation at risk.

Applying Theory: Media Industries

The grid below summarises the main theories and theoretical perspectives that must be studied over Components 1 and 2. The key elements related to each theory have been outlined above and will also be referred to in the chapters specifically dealing with each component and their forms and products. Although you may also study and show your knowledge and understanding of other relevant theories, the ones set out below must be studied in relation to the areas of the specification indicated.

Theory/theoretical approach	Component 1 Forms	Component 2 Forms/products
Power and media industries, including Curran and Seaton	Film Newspapers Radio Video games	Magazines: both products
Regulation, including Livingstone and Lunt	Film Newspapers Radio Video games	Television: both products Magazines: both products Online: all products
Cultural industries, including David Hesmondhalgh	Film Newspapers Video games	Television: both products Online: all products

The Specification: Key Statements

The grid below shows the statements for Media Industries and explains their meaning and the forms and examination components to which they relate.

Key statement: Media Industries	Component 1 Media forms	Component 2 Media forms	Explanation
Processes of production, distribution and circulation by organisations, groups and individuals in a global context	Film Newspapers Radio Video games	Television Magazines Online	Media industries have different processes depending on the type of product they create. For example, the production and distribution of a magazine will be different from that of a film. In the modern, digital age it is easy for individuals, for example bloggers and vloggers, as well as large media organisations, to produce and distribute content on digital platforms.
The specialised and institutionalised nature of media production, distribution and circulation	Film Newspapers Radio Video games	Television Magazines	The media are very diverse and digital platforms facilitate more specialised processes of production and distribution. This may be particular to certain media 'institutions'. The methods of distribution will be affected by other industry elements, for example funding and ownership. The newspaper industry has addressed the falling circulation numbers of the print product by creating an online presence.
The relationship of recent technological change and media production, distribution and circulation	Film Newspapers Radio Video games	Magazines Online	Technological developments have had a huge influence on the way in which media products in different industries are produced, distributed and circulated. One of the most important is the development of online media platforms that facilitate the national and global distribution and marketing of media products. For example, radio, which is a more traditional media form, can now distribute *Woman's Hour* and *Have You Heard George's Podcast?* through BBC Sounds and other digital platforms.
The significance of patterns of ownership and control, including conglomerate ownership, vertical integration and diversification	Film Newspapers Radio Video games	Television Magazines	The different patterns of ownership across media industries will have a specific impact on what is produced. The ownership of the product will influence its ideology. Some industries, for example newspapers, are under the control of powerful groups that can therefore use the product to communicate particular ideas and beliefs. Similarly, vertically integrated industries, for example mainstream film companies, are powerful as they hold the means to produce and distribute the product. Some media industries are using advances in technology to diversify and are distributing products across a range of media platforms to widen appeal.

(continued)

Key statement: Media Industries	Component 1 Media forms	Component 2 Media forms	Explanation
The significance of economic factors, including commercial and not-for-profit public funding, to media industries and their products	Film Newspapers Radio Video games	Television Magazines Online	The funding models of different media forms will directly impact upon what is produced. For example, the BBC as a public service broadcaster is required by its Charter to produce diverse content appealing to a range of audiences (*Woman's Hour* and *Have You Heard George's Podcast?* are good examples). Models that are more driven by profit, for example the mainstream film and video games industry, are more concerned with commercial success and broad audience appeal. Independent films, with less funding, for example *I, Daniel Blake*, have to be more innovative in the way they are produced and marketed.
How media organisations maintain, including through marketing, varieties of audiences nationally and globally	Film Newspapers Radio Video games	Television	It is essential that media products continue to attract and appeal to audiences. Most creators of media products now have access to a global as well as a national market. Developments in digital convergence have facilitated a broader audience reach, including traditional marketing devices, for example posters and trailers, as well as those that make use of digital technology, for example viral and cross-platform marketing and the internet. Traditional media forms (radio and newspapers) use BBC Sounds and websites to attract both global and national audiences taking advantage of **technological convergence**. The film and gaming industries that have a global reach maintain audiences through the use of universal themes, and relatable narratives and characters in their products, ensuring global appeal.
The regulatory framework of contemporary media in the UK	Film Newspapers Radio Video games	Television Magazines	It is important that you are not only aware of how the different media forms are regulated, but also that you understand the impact of such regulation on what is produced. The main UK regulatory bodies are: • **Ofcom**: television and radio • **BBFC**: film, including theatrical, DVD and digital. Also, video games and virtual reality (independent and self-financing regulator) • **IPSO**: most of the press post-Leveson • **ASA**: regulates advertising to ensure it is 'legal, honest, decent and truthful' • **VCS**: video games regulator that applies the PEGI rating system.

(continued)

Key Term

Technological convergence
The ability to distribute content across different platforms, thus increasing commercial potential. For example, the BBC radio and television audience is no longer restricted to live watching and listening as they can access content through a range of digital platforms to suit their needs.

Link

There is more information on the individual regulators in the Year 1 book:

Ofcom page 87
IPSO page 102
BBFC page 94
VSC page 115.

Key statement: Media Industries	Component 1 Media forms	Component 2 Media forms	Explanation
The impact of 'new' digital technologies on media regulation, including the role of individual producers	Film Newspapers Video games Radio	Online	While some aspects of online content can be regulated by the existing bodies, some content, especially that produced by individuals, is at the moment very difficult to regulate. As has been discussed earlier in this chapter, there is an ongoing debate regarding how the internet should be regulated while still protecting the rights of individual citizens.
How processes of production, distribution and circulation shape media products	Film Newspapers Video games	Television	Media production will be affected by the processes related to the specific industry. For example, the owners and editors of a newspaper will shape the production of the media product. Likewise, the music industry will create the music video as a means of promoting the star and their brand image. Over time, technological developments have also shaped media products, for example the interactive potential and CGI techniques used in the film, television and video game industry.
The impact of digitally convergent media platforms on media production, distribution and circulation, including individual producers	Film Newspapers Radio Video games	Magazines Online	Due to the developments in technology and the rise in digital platforms, digital convergence operates across media industries, platforms and audiences. This flow of content across media platforms facilitates the construction of a brand identity. For example, Zoe Sugg originally reached her audience through her website, her main platform now is her YouTube channel as well as a range of merchandise and books reinforcing her brand and broadening her audience reach. As a result of digital convergence, there is greater interactivity between the product and the audience, whose migratory behaviour enables wider distribution.
The role of regulation in global production, distribution and circulation	Film Newspapers Radio Video games	Television	Regulation will be different in different countries. The global distribution of the non-English language products you study will be affected by regulation in different countries. Regulators, for example the BBFC, may make different decisions about products than those made by the country of origin.
The effect of individual producers on media industries	Film Newspapers Video games	Television Online	This refers to both individual production companies as well as people. Bloggers and vloggers have revolutionised the industry in terms of the way in which 'ordinary people' can become globally successful brands with huge, influential fanbases. Similarly, Ken Loach as an individual film director had an effect on the commercial success of *I, Daniel Blake*.

The Media Studies Framework: Audiences

From your Year 1 course you will have gained an understanding of audiences as an essential element of the theoretical framework. You will have explored:

- the changing relationship between media industries, their products and the audiences that consume them

Link

Look back at page 35 of the Year 1 book for the list of aspects of audiences you will need to cover.

Tip

As with other areas of the framework, you will need to apply the skills, terminology, theorists and theoretical framework you explored in Year 1 of the course to the products you will study in Year 2.

Rapid Recall 1.20

Give an example of the ways in which the media categorise audiences.

Named Theorist

Henry Jenkins
Is Provost Professor of Communication, Journalism, Cinematic Arts and Education at USC Annenberg School for Communication and Journalism. He has written extensively about the role of the fan in shaping modern media culture.

Key Term

Participatory culture
The opposite of consumer culture, as it is a culture in which private individuals are not only consumers but also contributors and producers (prosumers). This has been made easier by new technologies. Jenkins' research showed that members of this culture believed their contributions mattered and they felt connected to each other.

Rapid Recall 1.21

Which New York advertising company used cross-cultural consumer characteristics to categorise audiences?

- the cultural, social and historical factors that affect how audiences may respond to media products
- how media industries and individual producers target, appeal to and attract audiences
- how media industries group and categorise audiences to make them easier to target, thus ensuring the commercial success of their products
- the impact changing technologies have had on the way in which audiences access and consume media products
- how audiences become actively involved with media products
- the way in which media language creates meaning to appeal to an audience.

In addition, in Year 2 of the course you will consider:

- how different media technologies and platforms reach specialised audiences on a national and global scale
- how media organisations respond to the changing nature of audiences and reflect the needs of both mass and specialised audiences
- how audiences use the media in different ways for different purposes which may reflect demographic factors as well as aspects of personal identity and social and cultural elements
- the importance of specialised audiences, for example fan audiences, to the media
- how social, cultural and historical circumstances may affect the way in which an audience responds to a media product.

Theoretical Framework: Henry Jenkins

In Year 2 of the course you will study **Henry Jenkins** and his fandom theories. You will need to apply these theories to the products you studied in Year 1 and the ones you will study in Year 2. The main elements of Jenkins' theory with which you must be familiar are:

- the idea that fans are active participants in the construction and circulation of textual meanings
- the idea that fans appropriate texts and read them in ways that are not fully authorised by the media producers ('textual poaching')
- the idea that fans construct their social and cultural identities through borrowing and inflecting mass cultures images, and are part of a **participatory culture** that has a vital social dimension.

In Jenkins' work he asserts the importance of fans as some of the most active and socially connected consumers and prosumers of media content. Their evolvement as such illustrates how audiences have changed as media platforms have expanded to allow the creation of a participatory culture. His research also discusses the importance of the fan to the marketing and success of media products, and that fans and fan communities are examples of a new and important relationship between the media product and the audience.

Jenkins also heralds bloggers as an example of a media democracy where private individuals have become more active and migratory, engaging with and harnessing the power of a global community. He asserts that bloggers are the new, more dynamic journalists.

Stretch and Challenge 1.13

Read Jenkins' thoughts on the importance of fans in *Convergence Culture: Where Old and New Media Collide* and his assertions on bloggers in *Fans, Bloggers and Gamers: Exploring Participatory Culture.*

Key Points Related to Audiences: A Reminder

Categorising Audiences

In order to more effectively target audiences and therefore ensure the success of their product, media industries divide their audiences into categories, grouping people according to, for example, social groups (age, gender, ethnicity), income, social status and lifestyle. Two main ways in which audiences can be categorised are by:

- **Demographic profiling**: this categorises audiences according to their class, occupation and income, and, while it is seen as outdated by some media organisations, this method is still used by others to aid in audience targeting.
- **Psychographic profiling**: defines audiences by their values, attitudes and lifestyles (VALs) and is based on the motivational needs of an audience.

Another method of categorising audiences is generational advertising, based on when different audience groups were born and how this defines them:

Silent generation: born before 1945. The oldest category to target. They are loyal consumers and have long-standing relationships with products and businesses. They like simple, straightforward content.

Baby boomers: these people were born at the end of World War II up until the 1960s and are thought to be more idealistic.

Generation X: followed the baby boomers, are more cynical and are wary of change and innovation.

Generation Y/Millennials: were born between 1981–1996 and are consequently shaped by technology. They are more likely to seek out brands that support social and environmental causes.

Generation Z/'Zoomers': born 1997–2010, the most diverse and technically literate group. They hold a large amount of spending power and rely on recommendations on social media.

Generation alpha: born after 2010 in the age of the iPad. The group are still young but are the category who have been most exposed to electronic technology from an early age.

Link

More information about psychographic profiles can be found in the Year 1 book, pages 36–37.

Tip

In an examination question it is good practice to isolate the key audience word in the question and then consider this in relation to the media products you are asked to analyse.

Some audience categories relate to the year of birth.

How Media Products Target, Attract, Reach, Appeal to and Address Audiences

Media organisations use a range of techniques to attract and maintain audiences.

For example:

- **Technical and audio codes**: audio-visual and print products rely on these media language elements to attract and maintain their audiences.
- **Language and mode of address**: this is often used when targeting a niche or **specialised audience** or when trying to make the audience feel part of the community of the product, for example the lexis used in the cover lines on the front covers of lifestyle magazines.
- The way in which the product is constructed and how this in turn constructs the audience.

Key Term

Specialised audiences
An audience with specific interests and needs which requires targeting in a particular way.

Different audiences need to be targeted differently.

- The marketing and distribution methods used. Many products use cross-platform marketing to ensure that products reach a broad audience. Different platforms will be used for different audiences.
- The positioning of the audience and how this then involves them in the product.

How Audiences are Constructed by Media Products

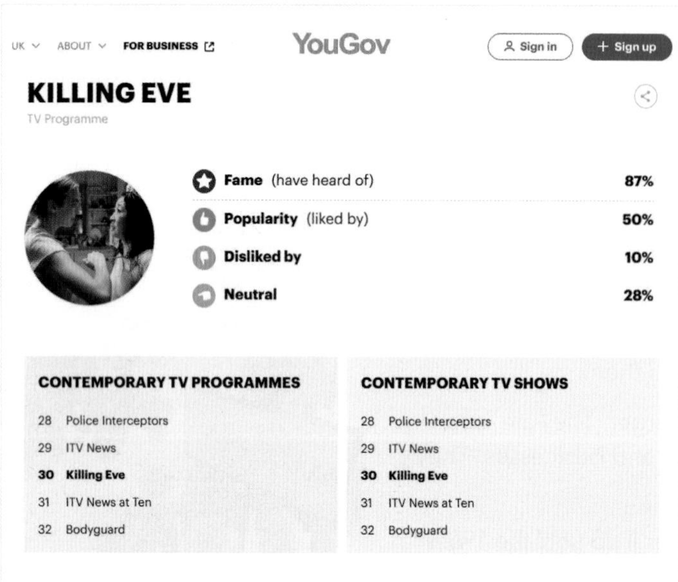

Media organisations use their research to construct an idea of their audience. The content of the product will reflect the target audience and aim to reinforce preconceived ideas about who the audience are or would like to be. Some products create media packs giving information to potential sponsors and advertisers, in which they detail actual and fictional information about their audience.

One useful source of audience data is the YouGov website. YouGov is an international research data and analytics group that regularly collates information about audiences globally. It allows users to access data about the different audiences for a range of brands and products, for example information about the audience for *Killing Eve*, part of which is shown on the left, can be found here: https://yougov.co.uk/topics/entertainment/explore/tv_programme/Killing_Eve?content=articles.

How Audiences are Positioned by Media Products

Rapid Recall 1.22

How can you apply George Gerbner's cultivation theory to the way in which newspapers position audiences?

This refers to the relationship established between the audience and the product. As a result of the positioning, different audiences may respond in different ways. Media products use a range of strategies to position audiences:

- **Technical and audio codes**: the camera can position the audience inside the storyworld and so enhance their pleasure and understanding. Similarly, audio codes can invoke an emotional response from an audience and can indicate how an audience is expected to behave, for example music building to a crescendo in a tense scene in a crime drama.
- **Language and mode of address**: producers of media products will make paradigmatic choices about the lexis to be used in a particular product in order to place the audience in a specific position. The informal mode of address used in women's lifestyle magazines with the use of personal pronouns invites the audience to be a part of the magazine's community.
- **The construction of the product**: and how the product constructs the idea of the audience. The cover lines and central image of magazines often construct an unreal but aspirational image of the reader and so may place them in the position of wanting to attain the looks and body of the cover model. This in turn helps to sell the magazine.
- **The ideology of the product**: the headlines, sub-headings and captions in newspapers, for example, position the audience to accept the ideas and beliefs of the product.

Audience Responses

Audiences respond to different media products in different ways. Modern audiences are generally active compared with the passive audiences of the past. The relationships between the audiences and the media products have changed and this reflects changes in society. The opportunities audiences have to respond to the media have developed along with the developments in technology. In an examination response you may want to discuss literal or actual audience responses as well as theoretical responses discussed by the theorists you will study. There are many opportunities for audiences to engage in actual responses, including blogs, Twitter and other social media platforms. This allows the audience to feel engaged with the product and have a sense of ownership.

Rapid Recall 1.23

Stuart Hall is one of the theorists you will have studied with regards to audience responses in Year 1 of the course. What are the three hypothetical positions from which audiences may decode messages in media products?

Theoretical Framework: Clay Shirky

In Year 2 of the course you will study Clay Shirky's 'end of audience' theories. You will need to apply these theories to the products you studied in Year 1 and the ones you will study in Year 2. The main elements of Shirky's theories with which you must be familiar are:

- the idea that the internet and digital technologies have had a profound effect on the relations between media and individuals
- the idea that the conceptualisation of audience members as passive consumers of mass media content is no longer tenable in the age of the internet, as media consumers have now become consumers who 'speak back to' the media in various ways, as well as creating and sharing content with one another.

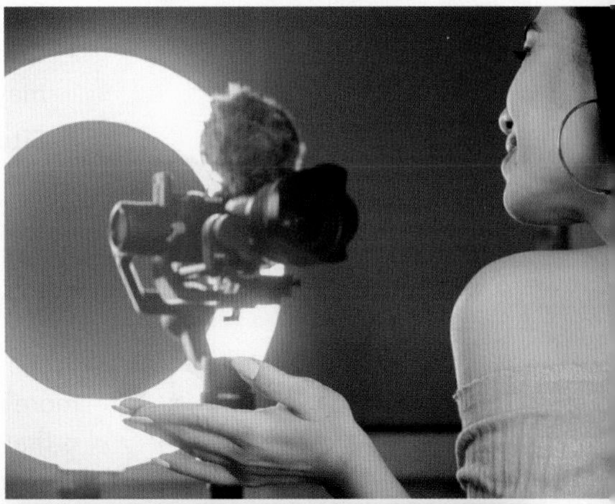

Bloggers and vloggers create and share content across digital platforms.

Citizen journalism has had a massive impact on the way in which we receive news and factual information. Digital platforms mean that the public can more easily collect, comment upon and then disseminate news and other content.

It is also the case that the receivers of media content are no longer passive consumers who accept the preferred reading intended by the producers. They will, as Clay Shirky asserted, 'speak back to' the media and in doing so may also create their own challenging content. This was the case with the Pepsi advertising campaign in April 2017 featuring Kendal Jenner as a model who takes a break from modelling to offer a Pepsi to the riot police at a demonstration and so restores peace and harmony. The advert caused a global outrage and Pepsi bowed to the pressure of the audience and removed the ad. The preferred reading, according to Pepsi, was a message of global peace, but the very literal oppositional audience reading saw it as making light of the demonstrations being held, including Black Lives Matter, to protest against social injustice, by suggesting it all could be sorted out with a Pepsi.

As well as engineering such a response that Pepsi cancelled an expensive campaign, individual audience members globally also created and disseminated their own content, including mocking memes poking fun at Pepsi's supposed ideological standpoint.

Key Term

Citizen journalism
The collection, dissemination and analysis of news by ordinary members of the public, usually via the internet.

Quickfire 1.31

How does Shirky's theory reflect changes in audience responses that have come about due to technological progress?

What Affects an Audience Response?

You will have learned that audiences are individuals, not a mass, and as such their responses may be influenced by a range of factors including:

- **Gender**: different genders may respond to different media products and indeed different genres in diverse ways. Some products may be constructed with different genders in mind and will reinforce stereotypical representations.
- **Age**: older audiences who are not digital natives may be less comfortable with the internet and social media. This also relates to the idea of cultural competence. Younger audiences are generally more desensitised and are more relaxed with content older audiences may find offensive.
- **Ethnicity**: ideas, beliefs and culture may affect how someone responds to a media product.
- **Culture and cultural experience**: how an audience responds to a media product may be influenced by culture, upbringing, experiences and key influencers.
- **Situation**: the situation of the audience, for example where they are, may affect the response. For example, watching a film in a cinema surrounded by people who want to see the film gives a particular audience pleasure.

Quickfire 1.32

How do advertisements construct representations to target specific genders?

Rapid Recall 1.24

What is meant by cultural competence?

Rapid Recall 1.25

Albert Bandura is one of the theorists that you will have studied in Year 1 of the course. What are the key points of his theory?

Tip

Remember to be aware of the focus of an audience question and plan your response accordingly.

Rapid Recall 1.26

What is meant by participatory culture?

Stretch and Challenge 1.14

Keep up to date with new types of media content to broaden your understanding of how different media forms are appealing to audiences. Reviews in online newspapers are a useful way of doing this.

Audience Interaction

In the modern world, with the advances in technology, it has never been easier or more accepted for audiences to engage interactively with products. The expectation is that audiences are active and want to engage with the media, both as consumers and prosumers. As illustrated earlier in this section, audiences now play a vital role in creating and disseminating content across a range of media platforms. As Shirky asserted: *'The media is no longer professionals broadcasting to amateurs.'* The producers of some media products actively encourage audiences to interact, as this is an effective way of maintaining their interest in the product and ensuring audience loyalty. Interactive opportunities for audiences include:

- Using social media, including Twitter, to follow and comment on media products and to share these with others. The final series of the BBC crime drama *Happy Valley* was trending on Twitter in January 2023. This helps to create a buzz around a new product, which helps in the marketing and, if successful, draws in a larger audience. This was particularly true of *Happy Valley* as each episode was broadcast on a Sunday evening and could not be watched in its entirety on iPlayer. This encouraged audiences to share their predictions about the narrative.
- Online fan communities and forums are a good example of participatory culture allowing audiences to be part of a viral community of like-minded people sharing ideas.
- Individuals can also become active creators of media content, creating blogs and vlogs from the comfort of their own bedroom. The success of YouTubers such as Zoe Sugg is a testament to this.
- Media producers are also realising the need to involve audiences more actively in their products. In 2018 Steven Soderbergh's crime drama *Mosaic*, made for HBO, was originally released as an interactive app. The programme allows the audience to experience the narrative from the point of view of different characters and to access the content on multiple platforms.

Applying Theory: Audiences

The grid below summarises the main theories and theoretical perspectives that must be studied over Components 1 and 2. The key elements related to each theory have been outlined above and will also be referred to in the chapters specifically dealing with each component and their forms and products. Although you may also study and show your knowledge and understanding of other relevant theories, the ones set out below must be studied in relation to the areas of the specification indicated.

Theory/theoretical approach	**Component 1 Forms**	**Component 2 Forms/products**
Media effects theories, including Albert Bandura	Video games	
Cultivation theory, including George Gerbner	Advertising Newspapers	Magazines: both products Online: all products
Reception theory, including Stuart Hall	Advertising Newspapers Radio Video games	Television: both products Magazines: both products
Fandom theories, including Henry Jenkins	Radio Video games	Television (*Peaky Blinders* or *Black Mirror* or *Killing Eve*) Online (JJ Olatunji or Zoe Sugg)
'End of audience' theories – Clay Shirky	Newspapers Radio Video games	Online: all products

The Specification: Key Statements

The grid below shows the statements for Audiences and explains their meaning and the forms and examination components to which they relate.

Key statement: Audiences	**Component 1 Media forms**	**Component 2 Media forms**	**Explanation**
How audiences are grouped and categorised by media industries, including by age, gender and social class, as well as by lifestyle and taste	Advertising Newspapers Radio Video games	Magazines Online	The categorising of audiences according to, for example, demographics and psychographics makes them an easier target to reach. Some media industries, for example television, advertising and newspapers, analyse audiences in terms of categories. The ability to produce specific data on target audiences also appeals to potential advertisers.
How media producers target, attract, reach, address and potentially construct audiences	Advertising Newspapers Radio Video games	Television Magazines Online	Media producers use a range of techniques specific to the media form in order to appeal to audiences. Due to advances in technology, different audiences can now be reached across a range of media platforms. The way in which the product is constructed in turn constructs an idea of the target audience, for example the use of the central image in lifestyle magazines suggests the audience.

(continued)

Key statement: Audiences	Component 1 Media forms	Component 2 Media forms	Explanation
How media industries target audiences through the content and appeal of media products and through the ways in which they are marketed, distributed and circulated	Advertising Newspapers Radio Video games	Television Magazines Online	The ways in which media producers and their products target audiences will differ according to the form. For example, television crime dramas will use narrative; blogs will use the appeal of the blogger and the diverse content. The marketing and distribution of the product relates to the target audience. *Woman's Hour* is distributed as a daily live broadcast, as a podcast and on BBC Sounds. Its diverse distribution methods and the content appeal to a range of different, largely female audiences. *I, Daniel Blake* employed a range of below-the-line marketing techniques, reflecting the economic context of the production.
The interrelationship between media technologies and patterns of consumption and response	Newspapers Radio Video games	Online	Developments in technology have broadened the ways in which audiences can consume and respond to media products giving them more involvement with the media. Many products are distributed across different platforms. Media democracy combined with technology allows audiences to respond to media products via social media platforms and to create and share their own content as prosumers.
How audiences interpret the media, including how and why audiences may interpret the same media in different ways	Advertising Newspapers Radio Video games	Television Magazines	All media products are polysemic and so audience responses to media products may differ according to how the audience interprets the meanings encoded in the product. How the product is constructed (media language and representations) and other factors including age, gender, ethnicity and cultural experience may affect how an audience interprets the product.
How audiences interact with the media and can be actively involved in media production	Newspapers Radio Video games	Online	There are various ways in which audiences can interact with media products; this is largely related to the form. For example, many newspapers, in their print and online versions, encourage audiences to contribute their opinions about stories and features, some of which are published. Audiences can also be prosumers and create their own content, for example as bloggers and vloggers and as members of fan sites.
How specialised audiences can be reached, both on a national and global scale, through different media technologies and platforms	Radio Video games	Magazines Online	The advances in media technologies have made it much easier for the creators of media products to access a range of national and global audiences. For example, *Woman's Hour* can reach its specialised global audience via BBC Sounds, while bloggers such as Zoe Sugg and JJ Olatunji use social media platforms to establish their fanbase. The niche audiences for digital magazines can be reached through online versions of the product.

(continued)

Key statement: Audiences	Component 1 Media forms	Component 2 Media forms	Explanation
How media organisations reflect the different needs of mass and specialised audiences, including through targeting	Newspapers Radio Video games	Television Magazines Online	Some large media organisations, for example the BBC, cater for both mass and specialised audiences as part of their public service remit. For example, *Woman's Hour* targets a specialised audience reflected in the content. Alternatively, most newspapers create content that targets their mass audience and reflects the ideology of the paper, for example the *Daily Mirror* reflects the needs of its left-wing audience by including stories that support liberal Labour policies.
How audiences use media in different ways, reflecting demographic factors as well as aspects of identity and cultural capital	Advertising Newspapers Radio Video games	Television Magazines Online	The uses and gratifications theory suggests that audiences use different media products to satisfy different needs. In addition, factors such as age, gender and ethnicity may affect how audiences use media products. Cultural capital, including education and intellect, may mean that only specialised audiences will 'use' a Radio 4 programme such as *Woman's Hour*. Magazines, through their content and construction, reflect aspects of the identity of the reader.
The role and significance of specialised audiences, including niche and fan, to the media	Radio Video games	Television Magazines Online	The developments in technology have contributed to the rise in the diversity of audience groups who have access to a range of media platforms. These include specialised audiences who are both consumers and prosumers, actively engaging with media products while also creating and disseminating their own content. These audiences, in some cases, have been instrumental in marketing and sharing products. The continued success of Zoe Sugg and JJ Olatunji is down to their loyal fan community. Independently produced media products, for example online magazines, exist through the support of their niche audiences.
The way in which different audience interpretations reflect social, cultural and historical circumstances	Advertising Newspapers Radio Video games	Television Magazines	The media product must always be considered in relation to the time and context in which it was made. Modern audiences will interpret the historical magazine differently from the audience for whom the product was intended. Other products, for example newspapers, will be 'of their time' and as such will reflect the social and cultural context, for example opinions of the current social and political landscape.

Contexts of Media

In Year 1 of the course you will have gained an understanding of the contexts in which the products you studied were created. In Year 2 you will continue to develop your knowledge and understanding of this aspect of the theoretical framework. In specific parts of the examination you will be required to analyse how media products reflect the social, cultural, historical, economic or political contexts in which they were produced.

Rapid Recall 1.27

How do *Woman's Realm* and *Woman* reflect a historical context?

Historical Context

- How genre conventions are historically relevant and dynamic. Genres develop and change as they reflect historical circumstances and may be interpreted differently by different audiences.
- The historical context will affect the representations in the product. This is evident in the *Tide* advert and other adverts of the time where the patriarchal role was accepted and women were defined by their domestic role. This will be viewed differently by a modern audience.
- This also refers to the way in which technological change has affected media production, distribution and circulation. The development of the internet and other cross-media and social media platforms reflects the modern context in which products are created. The historical magazines were only available in print, whereas now magazines also have an online presence.

Social and Cultural Context

- Genre conventions relate to society; particular genres will become popular at specific times. The rise in popularity of the Nordic noir genre and its darker themes reflects a mood in the society of the time.
- The ideology of the society of the time will reflect what is produced. For example, online magazines *Attitude* and *gal-dem* reflect the needs of more specialised, niche audiences who may have been under-represented in the media.
- How and why particular social groups, nationally and globally, may be under-represented or misrepresented. A specific audience is targeted by *gal-dem* who may have been marginalised and under-represented in other media forms.
- Audience responses to and interpretations of media products reflect social circumstances. The rise of vloggers and bloggers directly links to social change in which ordinary people can create and distribute content and can influence their audience.

Rapid Recall 1.28

How do JJ Olatinjii or Zoe Sugg reflect the cultural significance of online platforms?

Economic Context

How media products relate to their economic context in terms of:

- global production, distribution and circulation
- patterns of ownership and control and funding. For example, the difference in funding between a high-budget film, for example *Black Panther*, and *I, Daniel Blake*, an independent film funded by the BFI and BBC, will affect how the film is produced and distributed.

Political Context

- Media products reflect the political contexts in which they were made through elements including their representations, themes, messages and ideologies as well as through aspects including political orientation, production and distribution. This is clearly evident in newspapers that construct news stories in a way which reflects their political ideologies.

Contexts: A Summary

It is not required or relevant to apply all the areas of context to all the set products. The following grids suggest the most appropriate contexts to study for each product/form.

Component 1 Set products/forms

Media form	Set products	Suggested contexts
Advertising and marketing	*Tide* (1950s) print advertisement	Historical Social and cultural
	Super. Human. (2020) audio-visual advertisement	Social and cultural Economic Political
	Kiss of the Vampire (1963) film poster	Historical Social and cultural
Music video	**Group 1** *Formation*, Beyoncé (2016) or *Turntables*, Janelle Monáe (2020) or *Underdog*, Alicia Keys (2020)	Social and cultural
	Group 2 *Riptide*, Vance Joy (2013) or *Seventeen Going Under*, Sam Fender (2021) or *Little Bit of Love*, Tom Grennan (2021)	Social and cultural
Newspapers	**Section A** *Daily Mirror*, 1 February 2022 front page and article on 'Partygate' and *The Times*, 1 February 2022 front page	Social and cultural Economic Political
	Section B *Daily Mirror* – complete edition chosen by centre; related online and social media content and *The Times*, complete edition chosen by centre; related online and social media content	Social and cultural Economic Political
Film	*Black Panther* (2018) Cross-media study	Social and cultural Economic Political
	I, Daniel Blake (2016) Cross-media study	Social and cultural Economic Political

Media form	Set products	Suggested contexts
Radio	*Woman's Hour* or *Have You Heard George's Podcast?* Related online and social media content	Social and cultural Economic
Video games	*Assassin's Creed* franchise Related online and social media content	Social and cultural Economic

Component 2 Set products/forms

Media form	Set products	Suggested contexts
Television	*Peaky Blinders* (2013) or *Black Mirror* (2016) or *Killing Eve* (2018)	Historical Social and cultural Economic
	The Bridge (Denmark/Sweden, 2015) or *The Returned* (France, 2012) or *Tehran* (Israel, 2020)	Social and cultural Economic Political
Magazines	*Woman* (1964) or *Woman's Realm* (1965) or *Vogue* (1965)	Historical Social and cultural Economic
	Huck (2016) or *The Big Issue* (2016) or *Adbusters* (2016)	Historical Social and cultural Economic Political
Online	JJ Olatunji/KSI or Zoe Sugg	Social and cultural Economic
	gal-dem or *Attitude*	Social and cultural Economic Political

Note

At the time of writing *gal-dem* was the approved set product. Please make sure you double check the WJEC/Eduqas website or Illuminate (https://bit.ly/3r1d7at) for the most up-to-date information on which set products you should be studying.

The Media Studies A Level Specification

2

OVERVIEW

The aim of the Eduqas A Level Media Studies specification is to build upon the work started in Year 1 of the course. In addition, during the second year of your A Level course you will:

- Develop and apply your understanding of the media through both critically analysing and producing media products, demonstrating your knowledge and understanding of the theoretical framework.
- Gain a more developed understanding of key **theoretical approaches**, enabling you to question and critically explore aspects of the media.
- Engage with less familiar elements of the media, including products from different historical periods and global settings.
- Engage with elements of the media produced outside of the **commercial mainstream** and those aimed at or produced by minority groups.
- Explore the global nature of contemporary media, considering how media industries operate globally and target global audiences.
- Explore media products made outside the US and UK, including non-English language television.
- Demonstrate your understanding of the link between exploring and making media products by creating a cross-media product for an intended audience.
- Be given the opportunity to work in more than one form, so developing your practical skills, building upon those acquired at Year1/AS Level.

Key Terms

Theoretical approaches
The academic framework related to the study of a particular discipline, for example Media Studies, which underpins understanding.

Commercial mainstream
With regards to the media, refers to traditional forms of mass media with a broad audience and powerful influence.

Media Forms and Products

Similar to Year 1, you will engage with a range of forms and products, some of which you will study in breadth (Component 1) and some in depth (Component 2). These forms are:

- advertising and marketing
- music videos
- newspapers
- radio
- film
- video games
- magazines
- television
- online media.

The products studied will incorporate those included in the Year1/AS specification and those specific to Year 2/A Level. Together they will:

- have social, cultural and historical significance
- include products from a range of genres/styles, forms and audiences
- represent different historical periods and global settings
- illustrate different industrial contexts, including those outside of the commercial mainstream
- include products aimed at, or produced by, minority groups
- reflect contemporary and emerging developments in the media

Stretch and Challenge 2.1

A key to success at A Level is engaging in independent research and study. Exploring the set theories and others that interest you will expand your knowledge and understanding and inform your examination responses.

Tip

Theories and theoretical perspectives should not be studied in isolation; you should be able to apply them to support your critical analysis of your set products. They will be explored in greater detail in the chapters covering the different components and set products.

Tip

You will not be expected to apply all the theories to each set product. Information regarding which theories need to be covered for each form is in the appropriate chapters of this book.

Key Term

Cultivation theory
The idea that constant exposure to the media influences (or cultivates) particular attitudes and beliefs that shape our perception of the world around us.

Link

The Year 1/AS Level theories are covered in the appropriate sections of the Year 1 book, for example Gauntlett's theory of identity is covered in relation to the set magazine products on page 168.

- provide opportunities to engage in more complex analysis and the application of the theoretical framework
- extend your experience of the media and its output.

Theories and Theoretical Perspectives

In the second year of the A Level course you will revisit the theories and theoretical perspectives you studied in the first year and be introduced to new ones. You may also refer to other theories you have used in class or researched independently. You are required to study the following theories related to the theoretical framework.

Area of the theoretical framework	Year 1/AS Level theories	Additional A Level theories
Media Language	Semiotics, including Barthes Narratology, including Todorov Genre theory, including Neale	Structuralism, including Lévi-Strauss Postmodernism, including Baudrillard
Representation	Theories of representation, including Hall Theories of identity, including Gauntlett	Feminist theories, including van Zoonen and hooks Theories of gender performativity, including Butler Theories around ethnicity and postcolonial theories, including Gilroy
Media Industries	Power and media industries, including Curran and Seaton	Regulation, including Livingstone and Lunt Cultural industries, including Hesmondhalgh
Audiences	Media effects, including Bandura **Cultivation theory**, including Gerbner Reception theory, including Hall	Fandom theories, including Jenkins 'End of audience' theories – Shirky

You will be guided regarding which aspects of the theories and theoretical approaches you need to study for which forms and products. You will also be expected to apply the theories you studied in Year 1 of the course to the additional products you are required to study in Year 2. The expectation is that you will apply the theories in a more critical way and evaluate them where required in Year 2. There is a summary of the main points of all the theories and theorists you need to know in Chapter 10 of this book.

Contexts of Media

At A Level you will continue to develop your understanding of how the media products you study reflect relevant contexts. These contexts include:

- social contexts
- cultural contexts
- economic contexts
- political contexts
- historical contexts.

Skills

In Year 2 of the A Level Media Studies course you will continue to expand, develop and apply the skills you were introduced to in Year 1. This will prepare you for the more sophisticated analysis and creation of media products required.

In analysing media products at A Level you will:

- Use **critical analysis** to compare how media products use media language and audience response to construct and communicate meanings. This will include products created outside of the commercial mainstream.
- Use and reflect critically upon a range of complex theories to develop a more sophisticated understanding of the media.
- Use specialist subject-specific terminology in a more developed way in your discussion and analysis of a range of media products. This will include employing more sophisticated critical vocabulary as well as confidently using terminology related to the form you are studying.
- Debate critically, through discursive writing, key questions related to the social, cultural, political and economic role of the media.

In creating media products you will:

- Apply the knowledge and understanding of the theoretical framework you have gained at Year 1/AS and A Level to a **cross-media production** that you will produce.
- Apply knowledge and understanding of the **digitally convergent** nature of contemporary media through the creation of a cross-media production.
- Use your knowledge and understanding of media language across different media forms to express and communicate meanings to a specific audience.

Drawing Together Knowledge, Understanding and Skills

There are some questions in which all of the above elements will be assessed to allow you to demonstrate your ability to draw together your knowledge and understanding from across the full course of study. This opportunity will be in Component 1: Section B. In addition, Component 3 requires you to practically apply this knowledge and understanding to a media production.

The Components: An Overview

The A Level Media Studies specification is composed of three components through which you will explore the entire theoretical framework.

Component 1: Media Products, Industries and Audiences

This component at A Level is worth 35% of the qualification and 90 marks. It allows you to develop your understanding of the theoretical framework begun at Year 1/AS to enable you to analyse media products from a variety of forms produced for different audiences.

Quickfire 2.1

Give an example of how cultivation theory can be applied.

Link

Contexts are considered in more detail, in relation to the A Level Media Studies specification, in Chapter 1 of this book.

Quickfire 2.2

Give an example of a set product you studied in relation to a specific context in Year 1 of this course.

Key Terms

Critical analysis
Refers to your ability to apply your knowledge and understanding of the theoretical framework in a sophisticated way, informed by your learning. For example, exploring the relevance of a particular media theory in relation to one of the set products.

Cross-media production
At A Level your production must cover more than one form. For example, a DVD cover and poster for a film **and** online promotional material.

Digitally convergent
The ability of audiences to view multimedia content across different platforms and devices.

Tip

At A Level you are expected to be able to analyse a greater range of products in a more critical way in order to demonstrate a more complex level of understanding. You will need to practise this skill.

Quickfire 2.3

Why is being able to critically reflect upon theories important?

Quickfire 2.4

Give an example of how you could use your understanding of the theoretical framework in your own production work.

Tip

The focus of the title of Component 1: Section A at A Level is 'Analysing', suggesting a detailed and critical approach to the media products studied.

Rapid Recall 2.1

What do you understand by the term media language?

Tip

As part of your independent learning you should ensure that you have engaged in research around the set products, particularly those with which you may be less familiar.

Overview

At A Level this component develops your knowledge and understanding of:

- key aspects of the theoretical framework – media language, representation, media industries and audiences – to enable you to engage in more sophisticated analysis of media products from a broad range of forms
- products from specific media industries created for specific audiences
- how media products relate to their social, cultural, historical, political and economic contexts
- complex and challenging media theories and theoretical perspectives
- sophisticated subject-specific terminology.

Component 1 is divided into two sections – Section A and Section B – which cover different elements of the theoretical framework.

Section A: Analysing Media Language and Representation

For this section you will be required to build upon the knowledge and understanding acquired during Year 1 of the course. You will cover elements of media language and representation that will support your analysis of the set media products for Component 1 and the extended examples you study. You will:

- Analyse media language, considering how elements of media language incorporate viewpoints and ideologies and how audiences may respond to media language.
- Consider the factors that influence representations and use relevant theoretical perspectives and theories to explore how the media represents events, issues, individuals and social groups.
- Consider how representations relate to relevant contexts.

Section A: Set Products

You will be set products by Eduqas and the way in which you approach these products, for example studying some in Year 1 and others in Year 2 of the course, will be decided by your teacher. You may revisit some of the products from Year 1 and apply more complex theories to them. The set products are:

Advertising and marketing (print and audio-visual advertisements)	Music video	Newspapers
Tide print advertisement (1950s) *Super. Human.* Tokyo 2020 Paralympic Games audio-visual advertisement (2020) Film poster: *Kiss of the Vampire* (1963)	**Group 1** *Formation*, Beyoncé (2016) or *Turntables*, Janelle Monáe (2020) or *Underdog*, Alicia Keys (2020) **Group 2** *Riptide*, Vance Joy, (2013) or *Seventeen Going Under*, Sam Fender (2021) or *Little Bit of Love*, Tom Grennan (2021)	*Daily Mirror*, 1 February 2022 front page and article on 'Partygate' and *The Times*, 1 February 2022, front page

As well as the products set by Eduqas, you will also study a range of additional products related to the set forms in order to broaden and develop your understanding of the theoretical framework and to prepare you for the unseen element in the Section A assessment.

***I, Daniel Blake* is the additional film product to be studied at A Level/Year 2.**

Section B: Understanding Media Industries and Audiences

In this section you will continue to develop your knowledge and understanding of the theoretical framework with regards to media industries and audiences. This will include:

- the significance of ownership and funding
- the role of regulation in global production and distribution
- the impact of digitally convergent platforms and the effect of individual producers on media industries
- the targeting of mass and specialised audiences
- the categorisation and construction of audiences
- the exploration of how audiences' use of and responses to the media reflect identity, and social, cultural and historical circumstances.

Quickfire 2.5

Give an example of an additional product you could study to prepare you for the unseen in Component 1.

Section B: Set Products

In Year 2 you will study some additional set products as well as the ones studied in Year 1:

Advertising and marketing	Film (cross-media study, including film marketing)	Newspapers	Radio	Video games
Tide print advertisement (1950s) and *Super. Human.* Tokyo 2020 Paralympic Games audio-visual advertisement (2020)	*Black Panther* (2018) and *I, Daniel Blake* (2016)	*Daily Mirror* and *The Times*	*Woman's Hour* or *Have You Heard George's Podcast?*	*Assassin's Creed* franchise

You will see that, at A Level, an additional film has been introduced. *I, Daniel Blake* provides a contrast to *Black Panther* in terms of its production context, as it is an independent film. As with *Black Panther*, you are not required to analyse the film from a media language or representation context, but only in terms of industry. This is to avoid an overlap with the Film Studies specification. You will be expected to explore the marketing of the film through focusing on a trailer, a poster and any online marketing materials, including the website for the film.

A second newspaper has also been introduced in the form of *The Times* to offer a contrast to the *Daily Mirror*. For this form you will be expected to analyse one complete edition of each newspaper chosen by your centre and selected key pages from the newspaper's website, including the homepage and at least one other page.

Tip

As you will be aware from Year 1 of the course, advertising is only studied in relation to audiences and film is only studied in relation to media industries.

Quickfire 2.6

What do you think the reasons are for studying two different films and two different newspapers?

Tip

It would broaden your awareness of the newspaper industry, which is a detailed study form, if you developed your understanding by regularly accessing the website for the set newspaper and looking at more than the set edition.

Tip

It is important to remember that you are studying these set products in a much more detailed way than in Year 1 of the course, using more complex theories and theoretical perspectives.

Key Term

Sustained line of reasoning Refers to writing that is logically developed. Points are clearly identified and then developed using appropriate evidence. This then leads to a clear conclusion.

Tip

Careful reading of the question and planning responses will help you to structure a coherent response to ensure that you have included the relevant content.

Quickfire 2.7

What implications do stepped questions have for planning your time in the examination?

How Will I Be Assessed for Component 1 at A Level?

A reminder: this component assesses the following aspects of the theoretical framework:

- media language
- representation
- media industries
- audiences
- media contexts.

The questions may focus on any of the above forms in the relevant sections of the Component 1 examination.

You will be assessed on your use of relevant theories or theoretical perspectives and your use of subject-specific terminology.

The extended response questions will require you to construct and develop a **sustained line of reasoning** that is coherent, relevant, substantiated by specific examples and structured in a logical way.

Section A: Analysing Media Language and Representation [45 marks]

This will assess media language and representation in relation to **two** of the media forms studied for this component. You will also be required to respond to unseen media products from the set forms.

There will be two questions:

- **One question** will focus on media language and be worth 15 marks. You will be required to analyse an unseen audio-visual or print product from any of the forms studied for Section A: advertising and marketing, music videos or newspapers. You will apply the knowledge and understanding gained from analysing the set products and other related examples to enable you to effectively analyse the product.
- **One question** will assess representation and be worth 30 marks. The question will require you to compare one of the set products with an unseen audio-visual or print product from any of the forms you have studied for this section. You may be required to compare products from the same or different media forms, for example the music video set product with an unseen print advertisement. This is an extended response question.

Across Section A as a whole, there will always be one unseen audio-visual resource and one unseen print-based resource; Question 1 will relate to an audio-visual resource and Question 2 will relate to a print-based resource.

In your responses you will be expected to refer to a range of complex theories and theoretical perspectives in a developed way to support your analysis.

Section B: Understanding Media Industries and Audiences [45 marks]

This section will assess your understanding of:

- media industries
- audiences
- relevant contexts.

The examination questions will cover any of the forms studied for this section: advertising, film, newspapers, radio and video games. There will be two questions; there is no unseen product in this section.

- **Question 3** will be a stepped question that will assess your knowledge and understanding of media industries in relation to at least one of the forms you have studied.
- **Question 4** will be a stepped question assessing your knowledge and understanding of audiences. This will focus on a different media form in relation to at least one different form from that assessed in Question 3.

In one of the questions you will be rewarded for drawing together knowledge and understanding from across the full course of study, including different areas of the theoretical framework and media contexts. This information will be included in the examination paper.

Component 2: Investigating Media Forms and Products in Depth

At A Level this component is worth 90 marks and is 35% of the overall qualification. The focus is the in-depth study of media forms and products.

Overview

In this component, as at Year 1/AS, you will study three media forms in depth, covering all areas of the theoretical framework. These forms are:

- television
- magazines
- online media.

At A Level you will study websites as well as blogs. You will explore these forms through set products. Also, you will study two set products for each of these media forms. In the Year 1 book some of the key critical approaches were covered in relation to the set forms and the relevant Year 1 products were introduced.

In exploring the Year2/A Level set products through close analysis you will:

- Compare their use of media language and the representations they offer in relation to relevant social, cultural, economic, political and historical contexts.
- Study the role of media industries in shaping the products.
- Consider the way in which both mass and specialised audiences are targeted and addressed.
- Apply relevant and advanced theories.
- Reflect critically upon the theories and theoretical perspectives.
- Continue to develop your use of relevant and sophisticated subject-specific terminology.

Tip

It is important that you familiarise yourself with the structure of the examination paper so that you know what is required in each section.

Tip

You will need to be aware of the command words related to particular questions, these will guide your response.

Section A: Television in the Global Age

You will see from the title of this component that the exploration of television is broader in scope than at AS. Through an in-depth study of both of the set products for this form you will explore:

- The global nature of the television industry including the rise of international co-productions and the global reach of broadcasters.
- The dynamics that shape contemporary television production, distribution and circulation.
- The significance of the economic and industry contexts in which the set products are produced, including the role of public service broadcasting in a global marketplace.
- The way in which the television industry is regulated and how the set products are marketed.
- How national and global television audiences are defined, constructed and targeted.
- The specific audience appeal of the programmes exploring issues such as fandom and how different audiences use media products.
- The way the television products relate to broader cultural and historical contexts and the cultural and ideological significance of the representations they offer.

Tip

At A Level it is essential for success that you explore the two products chosen for each media form in detail, focusing on the key elements of the theoretical framework. The products have been selected because they raise interesting and challenging issues relating to their industry and audience contexts.

Options for Television Set Products

One option, which includes both set products, must be chosen from the following:

Option 1 Crime drama	Option 2 Sci-fi/supernatural thrillers	Option 3 Sci-fi/supernatural thrillers
Peaky Blinders (UK) Series 1, Episode 1 (2013)	*Black Mirror* (UK) Series 3, Episode 4: 'San Junipero' (2016)	*Killing Eve* (US/UK) Series 1, Episode 1 (2018)
The Bridge (Denmark/ Sweden) Season 3, Episode 1 (2015)	*The Returned* (France) Season 1, Episode 1: 'Camille' (2012)	*Tehran* (Israel) Series 1, Episode 1 (2020)

Key Term

Alternative media
Media products that differ in their content, production and distribution from more mainstream media forms.

***The Big Issue* is an interesting study in terms of its production and distribution practices.**

Section B: Magazines: Mainstream and Alternative Media

In this section, you will study two magazine products, one mainstream and one **alternative media**, including the historical example produced before 1970 that you looked at in your first year. Studying a more contemporary magazine product in addition to this will enable you to explore the effect of social, cultural and historical contexts on the representations offered by the magazines.

Through an in-depth study of both of the set products for this form you will explore:

- a commercial magazine and one produced outside the commercial mainstream
- the different contextual factors that shape the magazine's production, distribution, circulation and consumption
- how media language incorporates viewpoints and ideologies
- the historical and industry contexts in which the magazines were produced.

Rapid Recall 2.2

Give three key points you learned regarding the contexts of the pre-1970 magazine you studied in Year 1.

Options for Magazine Set Products

One option, which includes both set products, must be chosen from the following:

Option 1	Option 2	Option 3
Woman (23–29 August 1964, IPC)	*Woman's Realm* (7–13 February 1965, IPC)	*Vogue* (July 1965, Condé Nast)
Adbusters (May/June 2016, Vol. 23 No. 3, Adbusters Media Foundation)	*Huck* (February/March 2016, Issue 54, TCO London)	*The Big Issue* (17–23 October 2016, No. 1227, Dennis & The Big Issue Ltd)

Stretch and Challenge 2.2

Read 'Alternative Media' (2007) by Professor Victor Pickard, which can be found online. In it he outlines what he and other theorists think constitutes alternative media.

Link

The Year 1 book looks at the magazines produced before 1970 in Chapter 5.

Section C: Media in the Online Age

In your first year you will have studied the growing significance of online platforms and how the appeal of YouTubers Zoe Sugg or JJ Olatunji/KS reflects the contemporary media landscape and the growing importance of online, social and participatory media. In your second year, you will develop your study of online media platforms by also looking at an online magazine or magazine website.

You will develop your knowledge and understanding by exploring:

- the ways in which these convergent media platforms increasingly overlap
- the ways in which media consumers have become prosumers who regularly and actively create and disseminate online content
- how digital platforms can be used to reach specialised audiences
- how the chosen set products serve to demonstrate significant emerging developments in the media
- the ongoing impact of technology on media language and audience interaction.

Group for Online Media Products

One product from each group must be chosen for study.

Group 1	Group 2
Zoe Sugg https://www.youtube.com/channel/UCrUbqTCagwsaP2FmrOp1TsA https://zoella.co.uk/ or **JJ Olatunji/KSI** www.youtube.com/user/KSIOlajidebt HD	**gal-dem** http://gal-dem.com/ or **Attitude** http://attittude.co.uk

One of the main appeals of online media products is their immediacy; they are dynamic products that change regularly to meet the needs of their audience. For this reason, WJEC/Eduqas have not specified particular posts or entries for you to study from the set online products. Instead, you are required to study in depth the following elements of the relevant blog and website:

- the codes and conventions of the homepage, including aspects of layout and design
- examples of posts, such as specific blogs, vlogs or articles from the online products
- examples of interactivity, including links to and use of social and participatory media.

How Will I Be Assessed for Component 2 at A Level?

At A Level, this component assesses your knowledge and understanding of media language, representation, media industries, audiences and media contexts in relation to the two products studied for each media form. You will be assessed on your use of relevant theories or theoretical perspectives and relevant subject-specific terminology. In addition, at A Level you will also be required to evaluate academic theories.

The A Level paper for Component 2 consists of three sections:

- Section A: Television in the Global Age
- Section B: Magazines: Mainstream and Alternative Media
- Section C: Media in the Online Age.

There will be one two-part question **or** one extended response question based on the set products you have studied in each section. Each question is worth 30 marks.

Each part of a two-part question will be based on one set product. Extended response questions will be based on both of the set products studied for that form.

Quickfire 2.8

Which additional elements will you need to consider when studying the additional A Level magazine products?

Tip

The three media forms covered briefly here are explored in more detail in Chapter 5 of this book. The information here serves as an overview of the specification as a whole.

Note

At the time of writing *gal-dem* was the approved set product. Please make sure you double check the WJEC/Eduqas website or Illuminate (https://bit.ly/3r1d7at) for the most up-to-date information on which set products you should be studying.

Quickfire 2.9

What are the advantages of producing a web magazine compared with the print version?

Quickfire 2.10

Why do you think *gal-dem* and *Attitude* are interesting products to study in this section?

Tip

As well as studying the set products for Component 2, you will also be expected to enhance your analysis through reference to relevant theories and theoretical perspectives. These will be covered in greater detail in Chapter 5 of this book.

Component 3: Cross-Media Production

At A Level, this component is worth 30% of the overall qualification and carries 60 marks. This component is the non-exam assessment, you will have practised the skills required during the AS Year 1 course. This component is internally assessed in your centre and moderated by Eduqas.

Overview

You will be given a choice of production briefs by Eduqas which will be released on 1 March in the year prior to your assessment, allowing your teacher to commence your production work at any point from that time.

You will be required to apply the knowledge and understanding of the theoretical framework you have gained across the course in terms of Media Language, Representation, Media Industries and Audiences.

Consequently, your production must be based on **two** media forms.

The media forms indicated below will always be set but the precise requirements of the set brief will change each year and you will be required to create a production for a different intended audience and industry context. For the cross-media production you will be required to respond to the specific requirements of the chosen brief by making decisions about the genre or style of the product appropriate to the specified target audience. You will also need to address any industry contexts highlighted in the brief.

Creating a music video is part of the Advertising and Marketing: Music brief. These stills are provided courtesy of Isabella Miles-Hardt from Peter Symonds College.

A Level Cross-Media Production Briefs

Television	Create a cross-media production to include a sequence from a new television programme and related print or online products.
Advertising and marketing: music	Create a cross-media production to include an original music video for a new or local/unsigned artist or band and related print or online products.
Advertising and marketing: film	Create a cross-media production to include a print marketing campaign for a new film, and related audio-visual or online products.
Magazines	Create a cross-media production to include a new print magazine and related audio-visual or online products.

Tip

At AS, the requirement is to use and apply academic theories and theoretical perspectives. At A Level you are required to evaluate these, forming ideas regarding the importance, significance and relevance of the theories and theoretical perspectives in relation to the set products.

Link

For a reminder of the key elements of vlogs/blogs refer to Chapter 5 of the Year 1 book.

Rapid Recall 2.3

What is meant by an extended response question?

Tip

The briefs need to be studied carefully before you make your final choice. Remember, the specific details will change each year and you must ensure that what you produce addresses these requirements.

Quickfire 2.11

Give an example of an audio-visual product you could produce for the film marketing option that conforms to the requirements of the brief.

Tip

To avoid overlap with the Film Studies specification, the film marketing cross-media production must not include a complete short film, film sequence or trailer.

What Do I Need to Submit for Component 3 at A Level?

A Statement of Aims and Intentions, completed after your research and planning.

A cross-media production taken from the above briefs. Your centre may offer you all of the briefs to choose from or a selection.

A cover sheet detailing key aspects of your work, including equipment and software used, and crediting any audio you may have used and any non-assessed participants.

How Will I Be Assessed for Component 3 at A Level?

Component 3 assesses the following Assessment Objective:

> *Create media products for an intended audience by applying knowledge and understanding of the theoretical framework of media to communicate meaning.*

The assessment will be based on the Statement of Aims and Intentions and the cross-media production. This component assesses your ability to:

- Respond to the requirements set out by your chosen production brief. At A Level this means creating a cross-media production where the products are clearly inter-related.
- Complete all tasks set out in the brief effectively. This involves creating an appropriate cross-media product for the industry context specified, for example pages of a lifestyle magazine for a mainstream publisher.
- Engage the intended target audience outlined in the brief, for example a magazine for 25–44 year old affluent 'aspirers'.
- Demonstrate that you can use media language to communicate meaning, thus showing your knowledge and understanding of the theoretical framework gained from the work done for Components 1 and 2.
- Use media language to construct representations, in particular of social groups.
- The total number of marks available is 60:
  - 10 marks for the Statement of Aims and Intentions
  - 30 marks for creating media products that meet the requirements of the set brief, including suitability for the chosen form, genre, industry context and audience
  - 20 marks for creating media products which use media language to communicate meanings and construct representations.

Link

This component is covered in more detail in Chapter 7 of this book.

Tip

At A Level, you are required to create cross-media products, it is therefore important that you spend time considering how your products will be inter-related.

Quickfire 2.12

How does this magazine cover, created by a student, demonstrate knowledge and understanding of media language?

Music magazine courtesy of Isabella Miles-Hardt from Peter Symonds College

3 Component 1: Media Products, Industries and Audiences

OVERVIEW

At A Level in this component you will:

- Develop your knowledge and understanding of key aspects of the theoretical framework related to media language and representation, building on the work you have done in Year 1 of the course.
- Study products from specific media industries and for specific audiences considering the relevant industry and audience issues that they illustrate.
- Further develop your understanding of media contexts through exploring how media products relate to their social, cultural, historical, political and economic contexts.
- Develop your ability to use relevant subject-specific terminology.
- Develop your ability to apply and critically explore relevant theories and theoretical perspectives in relation to the products studied.

Rapid Recall 3.1

What is meant by subject-specific terminology?

Tip

In Year 2 of the course the expectation is that you will develop your ability to analyse media products in a more sophisticated way using all of the elements of the theoretical framework.

Component 1: Media Products, Industries and Audiences

You will remember that there are two examination components which have a different focus, different forms and products, and consequently demand different approaches. In Component 1 you will study the forms and products set by Eduqas and, in addition, examples your teacher has chosen from the different forms to prepare you for the unseen element of the examination. As you will remember from the Year 1 book, in this component the aim is to study the forms in breadth rather than in depth. The forms and products to be studied in more specific detail appear in Component 2.

Some of the products that were studied in Year 1 you will revisit in Year 2 and consider them in the light of new, more challenging aspects of the theoretical framework. You will also be introduced to new products.

The aim of this section of the Year 2 book is to develop your analytical skills and to introduce you to the more challenging elements of the theoretical framework through the study of both the set products and other relevant examples.

In Year 2 of the course you will build upon what you have learned in Year 1.

Component 1: Set Forms and Products

Media form	Section	Area of study: Section A	Area of study: Section B
Newspapers (this is the in-depth study covering all areas of the framework)	A B	Media Language Representation Media contexts	Media Industries Audiences Media contexts
Advertising and marketing	A B	Media Language Representations Media contexts	Audiences Media contexts
Music video	A	Media Language Representation Media contexts	
Radio	B		Media Industries Audiences Media contexts
Video games	B		Media Industries Audiences Media contexts
Film: cross-media study, including film marketing	B		Media Industries Media contexts

Tip

Just as in Year 1, it is important to familiarise yourself with the focus of study for the different forms and products.

Tip

You will be advised which contexts are relevant for which forms and products. You will not be required to apply all the media contexts to the products studied as this would not be appropriate.

Section A: Analysing Media Language and Representation

In this section you will:

- Analyse media language across a range of forms and products, considering how the elements of media language incorporate viewpoints and ideologies.
- Develop your understanding of the significance of genre.
- Consider how audiences may respond to media language in different media products.
- Explore representations of events, issues, individuals and social groups in the media considering the factors that influence representations.
- Use and apply relevant theories and theoretical perspectives in your analysis of media products.

Develop the ability to:

- **Analyse critically** and compare how media products construct and communicate meanings through media language.
- Analyse critically and compare a range of different products and forms.
- Use and apply a range of complex theories related to a study of the media.
- Use specialist subject-specific terminology appropriately in a developed way.

Key Term

Analyse critically
This phrase is specific to the A Level/Year 2 element of the specification, as the ability to analyse critically is an advanced skill involving expressing opinion through subjective writing. It also refers to the careful exploration and analysis of the set products.

Tip

Engaging in wider reading and using subject-specific glossaries will expand your vocabulary. There is a glossary at the end of this book and the Year 1 book to help you.

Tip

The expectation at this level is that you will be able to construct a coherent logical argument which is supported by relevant examples. Practising examination responses for the higher mark questions will develop your discursive skills.

Tip

One of the aims of this specification is to broaden your understanding of the media by introducing you to products with which you may not be familiar. You can develop this understanding by exploring different products as part of your independent learning.

Quickfire 3.1

Why are the more traditional advertising platforms proving less successful?

Key Term

Three clicks user
The three-click rule is related to website navigation and suggests that this is the optimum number of clicks to access information or make a purchase on the internet.

- Use discursive writing to debate questions relating to the social, cultural, political and economic role of the media.
- Construct and develop a sustained line of reasoning in an extended response.

Component 1: Section A Set Products

Advertising and marketing (print and audio-visual advertisements)	Music video	Newspapers
Tide, print advertisement (1950s) *Super. Human.* Tokyo 2020 Paralympic Games audio-visual advertisement (2020) *Kiss of the Vampire* film poster (1963)	One option from each group must be studied: **Group 1** *Formation*, Beyoncé (2016) or Turntables, Janelle Monáe (2020) or *Underdog*, Alicia Keys (2020) **Group 2** *Riptide*, Vance Joy (2013) or *Seventeen Going Under*, Sam Fender (2021) or *Little Bit of Love*, Tom Grennan (2021)	*Daily Mirror* (1 February 2022) front page and article on `Partygate' and *The Times* (1 February 2022) front page

Investigating the Set Forms and Products: Advertising and Marketing

The advertising industry is one of the media forms that has undergone the most amount of change in recent years. Due to the segmentation of audiences across different media platforms, it has become harder for advertisers to ensure that they reach their target audience. Where, in the past, adverts would be seen in the more traditional print form in magazines and newspapers, and on television and radio in audio-visual forms, the increase in digital platforms means advertisers have had to diversify in order to remain successful.

In 2007, Steve Jobs and the advent of the iPhone revolutionised the way in which consumers could be reached. Since then the continued technological progress of smartphones, the internet and social media have changed the way in which advertising works with and on audiences. Advertisers have never had so much access to consumer data that allows them to engage in targeted marketing. The new generation of consumers demand bite-sized content and the new challenge is to get their attention. It is the case that some consumers may be using more than one device at once and will be switching from one platform to another, so gaining their attention is difficult. For example, 79% of respondents to a recent survey by Statista said they used their mobile phone while watching television and 44% used a tablet (https://www.statista.com/statistics/961382/second-screen-usage-by-device-in-the-uk/).

Audiences want immediacy from their social media use and the younger generation has been termed the **three clicks users**. In response to this, many advertisers now incorporate a 'buy' button in their adverts.

Advertisers also have to think more carefully about brand recognition. They must ensure that their brand is instantly recognisable as users click through their social media platforms.

It is also the case that consumers themselves play a role in advertising a brand. Consider the importance of bloggers and YouTubers such as Zoe Sugg in marketing products. Their fanbase is a lucrative one for advertisers, ensuring they access a massive audience very easily. Added to this, the vlogger is also seen to be an endorser of the product and thus an influence. This will resonate with fans who want to emulate the vlogger by buying what they discuss on their YouTube channel or vlog.

Media Language and Advertising

The advertising forms you will study are both print and audio-visual and include film posters and print and television adverts. Below is a reminder of the key elements of media language related to print and audio-visual advertising, along with the key statements from the specification that relate to media language.

How the combination of elements of media language influence meaning

How the different modes and language associated with different media forms communicate multiple meanings

How do Advertisements Use Media Language?

Both audio-visual and print adverts have a limited amount of time to catch the attention of the audience and make an impact. Regardless of the advertising sub-genre, all advertisements share a repertoire of elements that establish the product. This includes:

- **Visual codes**, including colour, gesture, clothing and expression that, combined together, communicate meanings. For example, in the Dior *Homme* advertisement (www.youtube.com/watch?v=Ocjdar1yqW8) the use of the iconic New York city skyline and the name of the fragrance constructs an image of sophistication. The codes of clothing, gesture and expression create connotations of romance, for example the black tie dinner suit and the up-market restaurant, and of a more basic masculinity, for example the sweaty dance floor and the white t-shirt. The visual codes used in the advertisement create an image of the fragrance and, similar to other fragrance advertisements, link the brand to an aspirational lifestyle divorced from reality.
- **The logo** in the bottom-right corner of the frame reminds the audience of the well-known up-market brand. In advertisements, the logo is a visual code that is instantly recognisable and communicates meaning, this is particularly important when, as is the case in the Dior advertisement, the company is selling a lifestyle and there is limited or no specific reference to the product.
- **A slogan** that is memorable and has associations with the product.
- **Audio**, the choice of music and/or song can be very important and serves to make the advertisement memorable. In the Dior *Homme* advertisement the choice of *I'm Your Man* with the gravelly voice of Leonard Cohen reinforces the masculine nature of the fragrance and the romantic narrative. The lyrics reinforce the constructed representation of masculinity.
- **Language** that is used for impact, for example hyperbole, making exaggerated claims about the product.

Tip

Look back at Chapter 2 of this book where the key statements are explained in more detail. These statements will form the basis of the examination questions so it is important that you familiarise yourself with them.

Quickfire 3.2

What is meant by an influencer?

Quickfire 3.3

Give an example of an advertising sub-genre.

Quickfire 3.4

How do logos have a semiotic function?

Rapid Recall 3.2

Give an example of how advertisements use mode of address as a persuasive device.

The logo of Lloyd's Bank is recognisable to audiences and is regularly used in advertisements. In recent campaigns actual black horses are used to reinforce the brand identity.

- **A narrative**: in adverts with high production values the advertisement often resembles a short film and costs a similar amount of money to make. Like a film, the narrative will establish characters whose story will relate to the product in some way. This is true of the story world created for the Dior *Homme* campaign, which shows actor Robert Pattinson in different scenarios. Even advertisements with smaller budgets may create a recognisable 'character' and a storyline as part of the branding and product's identity. Lloyds Bank has used the black horse as its iconic symbol for many years. In its most recent advertising campaign, 'Drumbeat', it re-establishes this recognisable motif within a new narrative, illustrating how the bank is part of the lives of everyday people.

Stretch and Challenge 3.1

Study a range of examples of advertisements and consider how they use aspects of media language in order to communicate meanings. This will prepare you for the unseen element of the examination.

Other Techniques Used by Advertisers

- **Hard sell**: where the advertisers have a limited amount of time to transmit their message and the product needs to communicate essential information.
- **Soft sell**: where the aim of the advertiser is to sell a lifestyle associated with the product as means of attracting the audience.
- **Demonstrative action**: seeing someone use the product may convince the audience of its efficacy.
- **Mode of address**: the way in which the advertisement 'speaks' to its audience and establishes a relationship that may encourage them to engage with the product.
- **Intertextuality**: using references to one product within another to make the advertisement more interesting and relevant to the target audience. In the Dior *Homme* advertisement there are intertexual references that may resonate with the audience and so make the advertisement memorable. In the scenarios, Robert Patterson channels the urban heroes of American films, past and present. The use of the Leonard Cohen track, *I'm Your Man*, is a further intertextual reference.
- **Endorsement**: both celebrities as brand ambassadors and ordinary people are used to endorse a product or to raise awareness about an issue. If the audience likes or respects the celebrity then they are more likely to listen to what they have to say. The choice of Robert Pattinson as a celebrity endorser for the brand will appeal to both men and women, both of whom may buy the product. *'With an irresistible raw sex appeal, he plays a game of strength, charm and power'* (www.dior.com).
- **Unique selling point**: in the competitive world of advertising it is important that a product, new or established, makes itself seem different from its competitors by highlighting what is unique about it. Existing products will, for example, produce new flavours or ingredients while new products will make claims for what they can do. Some advertisers draw attention to their product by the uniqueness of their campaign.
- **Parody**: advertisements for well-known and long-established brands often use more interesting techniques to remind the audience of their existence in the face of competition. The 2010 campaign for Old Spice, a brand of men's toiletries associated with older men, employs humour in parodying the vintage adverts featuring a 'real man'. The slogan *'Make Sure Your Man Smells Like a Man'* attracted attention to the contemporary product by making fun of the older adverts yet reminding the audience of the longevity of the brand. The campaign went viral and won the Grand Prix at Cannes, one of the most prestigious advertising awards. During mid-2010, *Smell Like a Man*, held eight of the top 11 most popular videos on YouTube (www.thedrum.com).

Key Term

Parody
An imitation or copy of a particular product or style using deliberate exaggeration for comic or satirical effect.

- **Typography and graphics**: both print and audio-visual advertisements use font styles and graphics as part of the paradigmatic choices in order to communicate messages about the product.
- **Layout and design**: the way in which the advertisement is constructed and the syntagmatic choices made communicate messages to the audience.

These advertising strategies have been used and reinforced over time, as you will have learned in your analysis of the *Tide* set advertising product. While the techniques may be more sophisticated in some contemporary examples, the advertisements are using the same repertoire of elements that are recognisable to audiences. Consider the strategies used by these advertisements for washing powder:

- The visual codes of bright, primary colours encode positive messages about the product. The codes of expression are invariably happy smiling women, the suggestion being their lives are transformed by the washing powder. The direct mode of address talks to the woman at home, persuading her of the claims of the product.
- The iconic representation reinforces the brand and reminds the purchaser of the product.
- The endorsement of the 1950s housewife, who seemed largely like the ordinary woman, would be convincing for the average housewife struggling with the weekly wash.
- The advertisements use demonstrative action to show how effective the product is. This is combined with persuasive, hard-sell language devices, including hyperbole and superlatives. As can be seen from the examples on the right, it was clearly a competitive market and therefore important to suggest that the product was better than any others on offer.
- The advertisements make similar claims: *'no other soap gets her WHITES SO WHITE without bleaching'* and *'no other washing product known will get your wash as CLEAN as TIDE!'* The use of the personal pronoun in the *Oxydol* advert reinforces the ideology that the cleanliness of the home was the sole responsibility of the woman.
- Numbered bullet points and expansive copy are other techniques used, notice how much more information appears on these advertisements compared to modern examples.
- Enigmas are created through ellipsis in order to attract the audience, *'Now she uses the new super-soapy OXYDOL because ... '* and the multiple use of imperatives and exclamation marks dramatises the narrative of the product.

Quickfire 3.5

What do these advertisements tell us about the social and cultural context of the time in which they were made?

Tip

It is important to always consider the contexts related to the products you study. Advertisements are very good indicators of the social and cultural context of the time in which they were produced.

Advertisements for non-consumable products

You will have studied how charity and awareness-raising advertisements use media language in Year 1 of the course. At A Level you will also need to consider some of the more challenging statements from the specification. For example:

The way media language incorporates viewpoints and ideologies

The aim of advertisements and campaigns designed to raise awareness is to inform the audience of issues and injustices and, in doing so, invariably encode the ideas and values associated with the advertiser. Like advertisements for consumable products, those raising awareness of an issue or an event, for example the Paralympics, are still promotional tools associated with a brand, for example Channel 4, and often use similar techniques to those selling tangible products. However, the aims are different; for example, charity advertisements raise awareness and employ strategies to persuade the audience to support the charity by donating. As you will have learned from your analysis of the set product *Super. Human.*, this advertising sub-genre shares common codes and conventions, which include:

- Branding of the company and the campaign. The producer of the advertisement will use a recognisable logo, for example in *Super. Human.* the Channel 4 logo appears throughout the advert in the bottom left corner and full screen at the end of the advert. The focus of the campaign highlighted in the name *Super. Human.* is reinforced throughout the advertisement.
- A slogan related to the latest campaign. An advertiser, for example a charity, may run different campaigns, in this case the name of each campaign within the brand often has a different focus but includes iconography and an ideology that relate to past campaigns. For example, the 2016 Barnardo's children's charity campaign, 'Believe in Me' was a part of Barnardo's broader 'Believe in Children' campaign which was personalised to relate to the young people featured in the advertisement through the hashtag 'Believe in me' but also included the recognisable branding of the charity.

Link

There is an analysis of a charity advertisement on pages 63–64 of the Year 1 book to help prepare you for the unseen element of the examination.

Quickfire 3.6

What are the similarities in viewpoint and ideology between the Women's Euros football campaigns from Nike and EE and the *Super. Human.* advertisment?

Tip

It is useful in preparing for the examination to relate the key statements from the specification to specific examples.

Some important national and global events will attract advertisers who, as well as marketing their brand, will aim to raise awareness of a particular issue or concern. *Super. Human.*, Channel 4's advertisement for its coverage of the Paralympics, focused on reminding audiences of the Channel 4 ideology of giving a voice to the underrepresented, but also drew attention to the event itself and the specific issue of the misrepresentation of disabled athletes.

Similarly, during and after the UEFA Women's Euros in 2022 there were a range of different spin-off campaigns by companies promoting both the event, women's' football in general and issues related to it. For example, Nike and *Elle* magazine's advertisement tie-in *Never Settle. Never Done*, focusing on key female players and young aspiring women footballers, highlighting their skill and technical ability, demanding equality of coverage with the men's game (https://www.youtube.com/watch?v=PZIqV7wNyyU). EE's *It's Not Her Problem* advertisement (https://www.youtube.com/watch?v=r-ZUqZTF8Il) , whilst promoting the brand, focused on the abuse faced by women footballers. The advertisement features problems including injuries and balancing training and homelife but finishes by the problem perpetrated by men, online sexist abuse.

The codes and conventions of media forms and products, including the processes through which media language develops as genre

Certain conventions are common across forms and sub-genres, they develop and become recognisable to audiences as producers repeat and reinforce certain codes and conventions. Consequently, audiences have expectations of the product and will respond accordingly. For example, they understand that campaigns designed to raise awareness may use more shocking and emotive images in order to create an impact.

- **Technical codes**: specific sub-genres of advertisements will use particular shots, angles and editing techniques that are recognisable to audiences. For example, advertisements that focus on raising awareness of an issue or highlighting particular events typically use close-up shots positioning the audience to identify with the characters and therefore empathise with their situation. This is often combined with a direct mode of address, further reinforcing the advert's attempt to create a relationship with the audience. Establishing shots quickly communicate messages about where the advertisement is set so that audiences anticipate the narrative.
- **Visual codes**: the iconography and settings will relate to the focus of the campaign and may reinforce an issue that is being raised. In *Super. Human.*, the focus is on the athlete and the sport, for example Ellie Simmonds putting on her goggles in the pool, or training in the gym. These settings are juxtaposed with domestic scenes of everyday life as a disabled person, suggesting the normality of their situation. Gesture codes communicate frustration, competition and celebration to highlight the obstacles that need to be overcome to be successful.
- **Audio codes**: an important element of advertising campaigns. This may be the inclusion of a recognisable voiceover, the narrative voiced by someone involved in the event or issue, or the use of a particular song which will become the anthem of the campaign. In the Nike *Never Settle, Never Done*, the choice of the track *Shake It To The Ground* by DJ Blaqstarr and Rye Rye, with its pounding beat, synchronises with the rapid filming and editing, creating the idea of power and strength in the women's game. In *Super. Human.* sound effects underscore the music, emphasising the battle of training, including grunts, groans and tape being applied.

The significance of the variety of ways in which intertextuality can be used in the media

Advertisements often use intertextuality by referencing other texts with which the audience may be familiar, thus adding layers of significance to the product itself.

- The choice of audio track will resonate with audiences. The choice of the soundtrack for *Super. Human.* is *So You Want to be a Boxer* from the film *Bugsy Malone*. This is an upbeat song which, through its intertextual links to the film, effectively communicates the struggles of the disabled athletes while giving the advertisement a positive feel. The music will resonate with older and contemporary audiences and reinforce the ideology of the advertisement.
- The advert uses other codes and conventions that are familiar to adverts that aim to raise awareness, including the personalised approach to encourage the audience to examine their preconceived ideas about disability. The use of on-screen graphics with emotive language is also an intertextual reference to examples from the sub-genre.
  - **Language and mode of address** is another recognisable convention that will have an impact on the audience. This may involve the people in the advert speaking to the audience directly, as the celebrities used in the *MQ* charity campaign raising awareness of mental health illness do. This hard-hitting campaign can be found here: www.pablolondon.com/work/mq.

Tip

The focus in Year 2 is the ability to critically explore theory and theoretical perspectives in relation to the product studied. You will be expected to be able to engage in critical debate about the usefulness of specific theories and how they contribute to the understanding of the product.

Tip

In order to be able to critically explore theories and theoretical perspectives it is useful to familiarise yourself with the key theorists and their ideas through engagement in background research.

Applying Theory

One of the skills you will acquire in your study of this subject in Year 2 of the course will be:

- to use and reflect critically upon a range of complex theories of media studies.

It is important that you use relevant theories and theoretical perspectives in your analysis of the set media products and the unseen examples in the examination. This will allow you to demonstrate a more sophisticated understanding of how media products are constructed to communicate meanings to an audience.

Consider how you can apply the following media language theorists and theoretical perspectives in relation to the advertisements you study.

Barthes: Semiotics

- The idea that texts communicate meanings through a process of signification.
- The idea that signs can function at the level of denotation, the literal common-sense meaning of the sign and the level of connotation which involves the meanings associated with the sign.
- The idea that constructed meanings can become self-evident due to repetition over time.

Consider how the Paco Rabanne fragrance *Invictus* uses mythical associations with Roman games, visual codes of colour and the iconography related to success and power to rapidly communicate messages about the fragrance.

Consider the fact that advertisements as a form have very little time to arrest the attention of the audience and communicate messages. This is even truer with contemporary advertising platforms where the audience can erase the advert with the click of a button. They therefore must rely even more on the use of recognisable signs and codes that can be easily interpreted by audiences, for example visual codes including colour and iconography.

Claude Lévi-Strauss: Structuralism

Lévi-Strauss investigated the idea that texts can be understood through an examination of their underlying structure. He believed that meaning is created through pairs of oppositions, which he called binary oppositions. He suggested that the way in which these binary oppositions are resolved has ideological significance and as such communicates meanings to the audience.

Consider how structures are created through binary oppositions in *Super. Human.*

Binary oppositions create meanings throughout the *Super. Human.* advertisement. The images of gruelling training regimes are contrasted with the celebratory images at the end of the advertisement when success is achieved. A further visual binary opposition is created between the dreamlike sequences with dramatic images, music and the rich colour palette, and the everyday reality conveyed though ambient lighting and the strident audio code of the alarm clock. Animated and archive footage are included in opposition to real-life actions to introduce humour and reinforce the narrative. The on-screen graphic 'To be a Paralympian there's got to be something wrong with you' creates a conceptual binary opposition between audience perceptions of Paralympic athletes and the reality, encouraging an audience to reflect upon how language is used in relation to this social group.

Quickfire 3.7

How does iconography communicate messages in the *Invictus* advert?

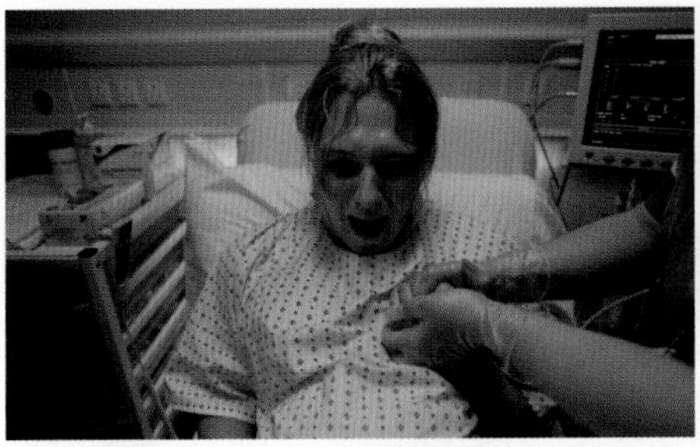

Applying Theory: Semiotics

You need to be prepared to analyse a range of examples of advertisements showing your understanding of the theoretical framework to equip you for approaching the unseen products in the examination. Roland Barthes' theory of semiotics is one that is universal and as such can be applied to all of the products you study as it essentially deals with how media products communicate messages through recognisable signs and codes.

Analysing an Example: Dior *Hypnotic Poison*

Find the advertisement for this fragrance featuring Monica Bellucci online: https://www.theperfumegirl.com/perfumes/fragrances/dior/hypnotic-poison/. There are also other advertisements for this fragrance that make the same paradigmatic choices (https://www.dior.com/en_gb/beauty/products/Y0063401-hypnotic-poison-eau-de-toilette).

This advert uses a range of signs and codes to communicate messages to the audience. The messages are delivered through the paradigmatic choices made by the encoders of the product.

- The recognisable typography of Dior is part of the branding and is used across all products. It is recognisable as a high-end fashion and beauty brand. This is echoed in the powerful typography used for the name of the fragrance and the choice of the name itself *Hypnotic Poison* signifying a heavy, night fragrance.
- The theme and motifs of the advertisement are the story of Eve and the Garden of Eden. This is the archetype of Eve as the ultimate seductress and is being used to sell the fragrance. The iconography of the serpent, the forbidden fruits and the perfume bottle shaped like an apple further reinforce the theme and the audience associations.
- The model's direct mode of address and code of expression could be said to be sexually alluring, reinforcing the stereotype of the temptress, appealing to men as well as women who may want her power.
- The colour codes of purples and deep reds are strong while still feminine and have connotations of a more powerful fragrance. It is important that, as the audience is unable to smell the perfume, the advertisement contains signifiers that suggest the fragrance.
- The iconic representation of the bottle reinforces the themed branding for this product.
- The slogan *'Dior est mon Poison'* and the text *'The Scented Salmander'* convey a sense of danger surrounding the fragrance and signify the sense of power this may bring to the wearer.
- In the more recent advertisements for the brand there is a less stereotypical depiction of the female who features as a disembodied hand but the iconography of the snake and the fruit and the strong colours signifying passion remain.

Quickfire 3.8

How does the structure of the product create meanings in the *Super. Human.* advertisement?

Tip

When you are analysing products in preparation for the unseen element of the examination, consider how they are structured and how binary oppositions are created to communicate meaning. This could be through images, characters, technical and audio codes as well as through ideological messages.

Quickfire 3.9

What paradigmatic choices have the producers of the advert for Dior *Hypnotic Poison* made?

Stretch and Challenge 3.2

Carry out a commutation test on two advertisements of your own choice, considering how meanings are constructed and changed according to the use of signs and signifiers.

Key Term

Commutation test
A structuralist, analytical technique used in the paradigmatic analysis of any text. It determines if a change of sign/signifier leads to a change in meaning.

- The syntagm of the advertisement works to convey a message. The aim is to use recognisable signs to encourage the audience to make connections between the signifiers and what the perfume could achieve for the woman if purchased.

The paradigmatic choices made by the creators of media products will encode meanings and affect the way in which audiences decode those meanings. One way of proving this is through a **commutation test**, which involves substituting one sign for another in the same paradigm and assessing how this changes the meaning of the product. For example, consider the advertisement for *Daisy* perfume. If you were to change the setting and iconography in the Dior advertisement for those in the *Daisy* advertisement, this would construct a very different representation of the fragrance and of women. This tells us that the choices made about, for example, clothing, props and mise-en-scéne effectively work together to convey messages about the fragrance. The audience will expect the *Daisy* perfume to be more floral and lighter due to the signifiers used in the advertisement. Similarly, if the colour palette in the *Daisy* advert was substituted for the one used in *Hypnotic Poison*, the audience would decode the expectations of the fragrance differently.

Analysing Film Posters: Media Language

In Year 1 of the course you will have also explored film posters as part of advertising and marketing. Film posters are part of film distribution and as such play an essential role in communicating information about the film to the audience. Film posters have been an important part of film marketing since the advent of the film industry but have changed dramatically with advances in digital technology.

Recap: The Aim of a Film Poster

- To promote a new film to an audience.
- To establish the film genre through the use of star actors, iconography and narrative clues.
- To create enigmas about the film to hook the audience. These are also established through **teaser campaigns**.
- To establish the iconic images and motifs that will create an identity for the film and be used in other promotional material.

Key Term

Teaser campaign
Posters or trailers that are part of the marketing campaign for a new film. They are released before the main campaign and their aim is to create a 'buzz' around the film through the creation of enigmas that catch the attention of the audience.

In the examples on the next page, from the film *Iron Man 3*, you can see the difference between the teaser and the movie poster and how both are important elements of the marketing campaign.

The teaser poster (left) hooks the audience through restricting information. The main movie poster (right) gives more detail about the film.

The teaser poster contains limited information, but what has been selected is iconic and creates an enigma related to the titular character. The central character is pictured in a dramatic action shot, he is seen in a vulnerable and dangerous situation, catching the attention and so, 'teasing' the audience, making them want to see the film to find out more. The teaser poster builds anticipation by only featuring the central image, the film name, the iconic branding of Marvel and 'in cinemas soon' teaser. The film poster contains much more information, including the star actors featured in hierarchical importance, the name of the film and clues to the narrative through use of the iconography of battle and conflict.

Key Conventions of Film Posters

In order to prepare for the unseen element of the examination and to effectively analyse the set product, you need to be able to discuss the key conventions of film posters. It is also essential to explore how the posters reflect the social and cultural contexts of the time in which they were made. In addition, film posters provide rich evidence of the audience of the time and the popularity of specific genres.

How the combination of elements of media language influence meaning

The codes and conventions of media forms and products, including the processes through which media language develops as genre

Despite changes over time and developments in genre and technology, film posters continue to employ a recognisable set of conventions and use elements of media language to communicate meanings quickly to audiences. In this way the genre develops as the codes and conventions of film posters will be repeated in other aspects of the marketing, for example film trailers and DVD covers. These common conventions include:

- A repertoire of elements related to the film genre. Even where a film has been re-made, as in the case of the film *IT* originally released in 1990 and re-made in 2017, the conventions are similar. The posters for both films can be found at http://www.imdb.com.

Quickfire 3.10

Why are teaser posters an important part of the marketing campaign?

Tip

It is important to familiarise yourself with different styles of film posters as this may be part of a Component 3 brief.

Link

Pages 66–67 in the Year 1 book give more information on analysing film posters and consider different, wider examples of the form.

- **Paradigmatic choices** that reflect the genre and sub-genre where appropriate, including typography and iconography reflecting the film's themes. The choice of font for *IT* in both posters suggests the horror genre. In the 2017 poster for *IT* the iconographic links to childhood are developed through the inclusion of the balloon, the yellow raincoat and the wellingtons. These add a further level of horror due to the vulnerability of the small boy.
- **Visual codes** that give clues to the genre and establish characters and setting. In the 2017 *IT* poster the primary colours of red and yellow with connotations of happiness and childhood are in binary opposition to the horrific indistinct image of the clown, which should also relate to childhood, but here is distorted to communicate a very different meaning.
- **Promises of pleasure** that enhance audience expectations of the film. The use of the term *'Master of Horror'* will resonate with the 1990 audience, who will be aware of Stephen King's novels. *'Everything you were ever afraid of'* promises fear as a pleasure.
- **Stars** that are recognisable to audiences and may be relatable to the film genre.
- **Star billing** is often used to suggest a hierarchy of importance and as such is an important marketing device.
- Where there are no recognisable stars, for example in a lower-budget, independent film, the **narrative** will be the focus of the marketing.
- The **tagline** creates an enigma and is used in all the marketing information for the film. The tagline *'You'll float too'*, used in the 2017 poster for the film *IT* creates an enigma as it suggests a personal, pleasurable experience for the audience but the other visual clues suggest the opposite.
- The **images** suggest the narrative and genre and give clues to character roles.
- The **language and mode of address** used in the poster may include personal pronouns to speak directly to the audience or may employ hyperbole as a selling technique.
- **Expert criticism** uses opinion leaders, for example film magazines, newspapers and film critics, to persuade the audience to go and see the film.
- **Marks of quality**, including references to well-known directors and past films, reinforce the credibility of the film for an audience.

Applying Theory

Semiotics: Roland Barthes

Historic Film Posters

You will be aware from your studies in Year 1 of the course that you are required to explore products from different historical periods and to consider the historical, social and cultural contexts related to those products. In Year 1 of the course you will also have explored how Roland Barthes' theory of semiotics communicates meaning in the set film poster product *Kiss of the Vampire*. Consider how this theory can also be applied to the film poster *The Brides of Dracula*, from the same period.

The structure of both these products communicates meanings to an audience through the use of media language, including the repertoire of elements expected in a film poster.

Quickfire 3.11

What are the main differences between the two film posters for *IT* (which can both be found at http://www.imdb.com)?

Quickfire 3.12

How does the 2017 film poster for *IT* appeal to a more contemporary audience?

Rapid Recall 3.3

How does the film poster for *Kiss of the Vampire* use media language to communicate messages?

Both posters use typography to suggest the genre, *Kiss of the Vampire* uses a wooden-like font style that has connotations of the coffin and the use of dripping blood suggests the stake used in this genre. In *The Brides of Dracula* the wavy font and use of the colour red has connotations of blood and horror.

Both posters include the typical iconography of the genre: the isolated setting, the castle on the hill, bats and fangs. The visual codes of the women's and the male vampires' clothing, and the code of expression, including the staring eyes of the vampire, are also typical of the genre.

The other visual signifiers include the muted, dark colour palette and the use of moonlight. In the set product the full moon is a recognisable element of the narrative in this genre, which is repeated in literature and other cinematic examples.

Recognisable characters are used in both posters. The inclusion of the 'brides' in this poster reflects the fact that the Dracula narrative was reinvented in many films, particularly by the **Hammer** film company which saw the appeal of this film genre for audiences in the 1960s and 1970s and made several versions of the popular **Bram Stoker** story.

The audience of the time would be familiar with this film genre and the associated iconography. As a less desensitised audience they would find the film poster more frightening than a modern audience, despite the fact that it is hand-drawn. The actor Peter Cushing would be recognisable to audiences for his role as Van Helsing in other horror films of the time.

Key Figures

Hammer
A British film company known for its Gothic horror films made from the mid-1950s–1970s, featuring Christopher Lee and Peter Cushing as Dracula and Van Helsing.

Bram Stoker
An author best known for his 1897 Gothic novel *Dracula*, which established the story of the vampire in popular culture and has been the inspiration for many films.

Structuralism: Claude Lévi-Strauss

In both posters binary opposites are used to create meaning. For example, there is clear opposition between the vampires and their victims. Also, in both posters the women are dressed in light and the vampires in dark clothing, the connotations of white being used as a symbol of purity and, in the second poster, associated with the idea of brides and therefore virginal. However, in *Kiss of the Vampire* there is also a binary opposite established between the two women: one is weak, vulnerable, passive and blonde, and the other is dark haired, more dominant and has her own victim in the shape of the kneeling male. She is also constructed to appear more voluptuous and sexual in her clothing, focusing on her role as a vampiric seductress, a typical character type of the genre.

There is also a binary opposite established with regards to the idea of the kiss, normally a signifier of love and romance but here the inference is that the kiss is the bite of the vampire and as such is dangerous.

The ideological significance of the binary opposites included in the posters is related to the changing gender roles of the time and will be explored in more detail in the section on representation.

Stretch and Challenge 3.3

Visit the Hammer website, www.hammerfilms.com, and research the films it created.

Rapid Recall 3.4

What does Steve Neale mean by 'repetition and difference'?

Key Term

Narrative trope
Describes commonly recurring elements in a narrative, including literary devices, clichés and conventions.

Quickfire 3.13

What is a parody?

Tip

The key statements related to a study of representation are explored in Chapter 2 of this book. Familiarising yourself with these will help to prepare you for the examination questions.

Analysing an Example: *Therapy for a Vampire* Film Poster

As stated previously, the vampire horror sub-genre has stood the test of time and continues to be popular with audiences. Film producers are very aware of the capacity the genre has to attract an audience and they have reinvented this film genre in many creative ways. As Steve Neale asserted, genres maintain audiences through the employment of 'repetition and difference'. Audiences need to understand the codes and conventions of a specific genre and these have usually been reinforced over time as is the case with the vampire horror genre.

While reinforcing recognisable conventions, filmmakers also occasionally subvert these elements to produce a film that is a bit different. This is the case in the film poster for *Therapy for a Vampire* (www.rogerebert.com/reviews/therapy-for-a-vampire-2016), which employs the main elements of a vampire horror film but uses them for comedic value. The title itself suggests a modern take on the genre through the use of the term 'therapy' while reinforcing genre recognition through the use of the 'written in blood' font for the word 'vampire'.

The character of the vampire is established through visual signifiers, for example the code of clothing and expression. In addition, the other characters are equally recognisable types from the genre: the binary opposites of the two women, one fair and one dark, one vulnerable and one more powerful, and the background character, who would conventionally have been the vampire character Van Helsing, in this example is in fact Sigmund Freud, the eminent psychoanalyst, so linking to the concept of 'therapy' in the film's narrative.

The iconography of the bats, the full moon and the graveyard tick more generic boxes to allow the audience to assume that this is a vampire horror film. However, the conventions are subverted with the inclusion of the tagline '*500 years of marriage is enough*', which, while playing on the **narrative trope** that vampires live forever, suggests that this film is a parody.

The use of intertextuality plays on the audience recognition of the codes and conventions of one genre to create a film that uses those elements for different a purpose, to create humour.

Component 1: Section A: Representation

As you will realise from your Year 1 studies, representation is one of the key areas of the theoretical framework that must be explored in relation to the set products and unseen examples. In the examination you will always be required to answer a question on representation, in which you will compare one of your set products with an unseen example from the same or a different form.

It is important that you understand representation as a concept and can use this understanding to analyse a range of media products. You will need to explore how events, issues, individuals and social groups are represented and the factors that influence those representations. To help you analyse the products in a more detailed way you will be expected to refer to relevant theories and theoretical perspectives.

Representations of Social Groups in Advertising: Gender

Advertisements as a media form are interesting as, similar to some other media products, they give us information about the society and culture of the time, particularly in relation to gender roles. They also have to communicate messages quickly, as the audience flick through a magazine or fleetingly pass a billboard, they therefore often use stereotypes to transmit information. Recognisable types have been used in advertising regardless of the decade, specifically in the case of gender where, while some adverts reflect the change in gender roles in modern society, others reinforce typicality, for example the woman as the homemaker whose responsibility is also to be beautiful. Adverts also continue to reflect what society constitutes as beautiful and while some may say that, unlike in the past, the modern woman is now wearing make-up and dressing in a particular way for herself and not for her man, this is debatable.

Women are still exposed to stereotypical notions of what is beautiful in advertising.

Applying Theory: Feminist Theory

Liesbet van Zoonen is one of the set theorists for representation. Some of the areas she explores include:

- the idea that gender is constructed through discourse, and that its meaning varies according to cultural and historical context
- the idea that the display of women's bodies as objects to be looked at is a core element of Western patriarchal culture.

It is certainly true that the debate about gender roles and what actually constitutes gender is being discussed in contemporary society more so than at any other time (van Zoonen, 1999), but is this awareness reflected in the advertisements we see around us every day?

The effect of historical perspectives on representations

Key Figure

Liesbet van Zoonen
Professor of Sociology and Dean of the Erasmus Graduate School of Social Sciences and the Humanities at Erasmus University Rotterdam. She is known for her work on gender and the media.

Link

There is more information about the set advertising products and the relevant contexts on pages 109–111 of the Year 1 book.

Stretch and Challenge 3.4

Consider how van Zoonen's theory can be applied to the advertisements you have studied in preparation for the examination.

Tip

It is important in Year 2 to consider the theories and theoretical perspectives you study and explore their relevance to the media products.

Social, Cultural and Historical Contexts: 1950s Advertising

The 1950s was an era well before the sexual revolution of the 1960s and 1970s but it was defined by a consumer boom which saw the rise in the production of new technologies, particularly in the domestic sphere. The representations of gender featured in the adverts of the time seem amusing to a modern audience and archaic, but they are an effective reflection of the society of the time:

- The stereotypical representation of gender reflects the post-war domestic role of women in the 1950s.
- While men were the target of the car industry, women were the target market for the new domestic appliances of the time. These were desirable products and reflected the status of the family in their ability to afford them.

The girl in this advertisement is sure that her mother will be delighted with the gift of a Hoover for Christmas.

- Developments in technology empowered women in the home but they were still encouraged to strive for domestic perfection. There was pressure on the woman not to let her family down through the lack of whiteness in her wash and her poor culinary skills.
- The construction of the majority of adverts through visual codes and language reflects this cultural and historical context.
- Men were invariably shown in suits as the breadwinner while women were expected to be glamorous even when doing the washing, but would usually have the signifier of the apron to reinforce their role. This role and the way in which it was represented in the media would have been disappointing for women who had taken a more active role in the war and had been given a sense of freedom. In the adverts of the time women were situated in a patriarchal world despite their more active role undertaken in the war years.

With regards to the representation of women in advertising, van Zoonen asserts:

> *Monitoring projects, consumer boycotts and other means have been employed to put pressure on advertising agencies to come up with more diverse and less traditional portrayals of women.* (van Zoonen, 1999)

Consider whether you agree with van Zoonen's statement with regards to the examples of advertisements you have studied.

With regard to the representation of men in historical advertisements, most of the time they were seen dressed formally in a suit, a visual signifier of their status in society. Even when they weren't wearing a suit, they were seen to be dominant in the patriarchal world of the 1950s, including the domestic sphere, reinforcing the idea that women had their particular place in the society of the time and men theirs. Women were often evident in advertisements aimed at men, for example shirts, cigarettes and cars, and were represented as responsible for men looking smart or in awe of their manliness, reinforcing the more subservient role of women in society. The representations in these older advertisements seem shocking to a contemporary audience, but they are a reminder of the hierarchical roles in the society of the time.

Rapid Recall 3.5

How does the *Tide* advert on page 71 reflect the historical and social context of the 1950s?

Link

On page 65 of the Year 1 book there is an analysis of a *Maybelline* advert which is a useful example to use in evaluating how far representations of women in advertising have come.

Quickfire 3.14

How far do the advertisements you have studied support or challenge Gauntlett's points about representations of gender in advertising.

It could be said that there is a greater range of representations of gender in contemporary advertising and that audiences expect to see less stereotyping and more representations of strong, successful women. However, it is also the case that certain advertising forms, for example fragrance and beauty products, still construct stereotypical representations of women. While representations of men in advertising have changed dramatically since the 1950s, women still seem to have to do more to themselves to achieve perfection while men can just look rugged and natural. According to Gauntlett (2002) women are told that natural beauty is not sufficient – make-up is required, which is an 'unequal message' as men are not expected to make as much effort.

In contemporary advertising, as in the historical examples explored, women continue to be exposed to unrealistic and unattainable representations that have been manipulated to create a version of reality:

> *And advertising regularly reinforces the desirability of particular physical looks.* (Gauntlett, 2002)

Representations of Ethnicity in Advertising

You will have explored the representations of ethnicity in Year 1 of your course in relation to the set products. Similar to the points made about the representations of gender, representations of ethnicity are constructed in order to communicate messages. The representations will change according to the context and purpose of the advertisement. With regards to charity campaigns, the aim is to raise our awareness and engage our sympathy, and this is usually done through the construction of negative images of developing countries. This reinforcement of negative stereotypes feeds into preconceived ideas about the people and places and adheres to Alvarado's theoretical perspective explored in Chapter 1 that this representation is to be pitied.

Tip

Alvarado's theory is explored in more detail in Chapter 1 of this book. He is not a named theorist but his theoretical perspective related to representations of ethnicity is relevant to your broader understanding.

How representations invoke discourses and ideologies and position audiences

The advertisement on the right for Oxfam represents ethnic minority groups in a particular way and also represents an issue: poverty. The discourse invoked, and the ideology, is clearly stated in the copy – the global disparity between rich and poor. The audience is positioned through the use of shocking statistical evidence in the headline and by the emotive image of the boy wearing the clothes he has found and standing in mud. The audience is also positioned to act by the use of personalisation, the selection of the words, *'TOGETHER'*, *'WE'* and *'JOIN US'*, suggests they can make a difference and *'EVEN IT UP'*. The construction of the advertisement makes the boy look vulnerable; a common convention of this advertising sub-genre, as he looks up at the information, is reinforcing the idea that he is a victim of such ideological circumstances that result in his situation.

This example of a charity advertisement reinforces Alvarado's theory that some media products stereotype ethnic groups as continually being in need of help and as victims. These representations are mediated in order to achieve their purpose to raise awareness and money. The advertisement invites a discourse regarding the disparity between developed and developing countries and the economic global situation.

Applying Theory

Gilroy

Consider how Gilroy's claims that colonial discourses continue to inform contemporary attitudes to race and that within society there are racial hierarchies based on notions of otherness. He stated:

> *racial difference obstructs empathy and makes ethnocentricity inescapable. It becomes impossible even to imagine what it is like to be someone else.*
> (Gilroy, 2004)

While it may be true that, as Gilroy suggests, there exist racial hierarchies that originate from past relationships between people of different ethnicities, it is also the case that many charity campaigns succeed by the very fact they encourage the audience to empathise with the plight of someone they don't know and have never met.

Link

Page 71 in the Year 1 book applies the theory of semiotics to advertising examples.

Quickfire 3.15

Why do you think charity and awareness-raising campaigns are allowed to include more shocking images?

Representation of Issues and Events in Advertising

From your study of the set advertising products *Tide* and *Super. Human.* and the wider examples of advertisements you also have studied, you will see that advertising has a range of purposes, including the marketing of consumable products as well as raising awareness of social ills and global concerns. In this respect, advertisements are often a means of representing an issue or an event but in a different way from other media platforms, for example newspapers, as their purpose is different. Often charities will respond to a particular event, for example an earthquake or other natural disaster that has devastated the lives of a community. They will also respond to ongoing issues that are of global concern, for example poverty. However, they still use a recognisable range of techniques particular to the advertising form in order to persuade. A reminder of these:

- Images whose intention is to shock or arrest the attention of the audience.
- The use of celebrities as ambassadors for the campaign or because they have personal experiences related to the issue or event.
- Audio codes, including the use of existing songs which are given a new significance when related to the campaign, as well as voiceovers giving relevant information and often using a particular mode of address.
- Information, including statistics, to support what is being said. For example, the Oxfam campaign referred to earlier uses a statistic related to wealth and poverty as a central focus of the print advert.
- Personalisation – sometimes this type of campaign avoids the use of celebrities and instead uses actual people telling their story, as this is seen to be more effective in engaging audiences. Part of the success of the *Super. Human.* advertisement in marketing the paralympics and changing the audience perception of disabled athletes was the construction of the athletes as real people with relatable stories.
- Technical codes to construct the representation, for example close-ups, direct mode of address and establishing shots to show, for example, the scale of a disaster.
- Recognisable iconography related to the issues or event, for example in the case of an earthquake appeal, ruined buildings.

Representations of Diversity in Advertising

As has been discussed earlier in relation to the range of advertising campaigns that were inspired by the football Women's Euros 2022, many companies have produced campaigns that are not just about selling their products but also demonstrating their values and social conscience by supporting and raising awareness of issues, for example addressing the lack of diversity in advertising. Channel 4 has a 'Diversity in Advertising' Award that has been running since 2016 to encourage advertisers to produce campaigns that explore the issue of under-represented and misrepresented groups in society. While there has been an increase in representations of visible and non-visible disabilities in advertising, which is more reflective of society, there are still only 4% of advertisements that feature someone with a disability and in only 1% of examples the person with the disability has a lead role (www.diversityinadvertising.co.uk/about/). The range of disabilities represented still tends to be narrow and there is a focus on the condition or disability rather than representing the disabled people as they are.

One of the previous winners of the award was the Adam&Eve advertising agency which produced an advert that was a collaboration between Lloyds Bank and the charity Mental Health UK, the aim of which was to get people talking about the taboo subject of mental health. The agency was awarded £1 million free airtime for a creative idea focused on a nonvisible disability. The #GetTheInsideOut campaign took an interesting perspective and avoided direct discussion of personal experience; instead a version of the guessing game 'Who Am I?' was invented with celebrities including Professor Green and Jeremy Paxman, young people with limited knowledge of the issues and employees of Lloyds Bank to represent the issue in a more realistic and relatable way. Like Channel 4's *Super. Human.* advertisement, the aim of this campaign was to challenge audience perceptions of who may be affected by mental health issues.

Information about the award, past winners and Channel 4's aims to encourage more authentic representations of visible and non-visible disabilities can be found here: https://www.diversityinadvertising.co.uk/about/.

Quickfire 3.16

Why do you think the techniques used by Lloyds Bank in representing this issue may be successful?

Stretch and Challenge 3.5

Watch the full audio-visual advert and read the article 'We Need to Talk About Mental Health: Behind Lloyds Bank's Campaign to Break an Advertising Taboo', on the *Campaign* magazine website, related to the Lloyds Bank and other awareness-raising campaigns.

Representation in Horror Film Posters

How audience's responses to and interpretations of media representations reflect social, cultural and historical circumstances

It may be the case that when the focus of the question is representation you may be required to compare an unseen film poster with the set product *Kiss of the Vampire*, or with a product in a different form. The most obvious areas of representation for both historical and contemporary horror film posters is gender. In relation to the historical product, the representation of women can be placed within a historical and social context and as such this reflects the changing role of women at the time. The 1960s were seen as the start of women's liberation, with campaigns for equal rights and pay. The contraceptive pill was introduced in 1961, although at first only for married women, but women could see more sexual freedom on the horizon. As a result, men were feeling more challenged and felt their historical authority was in danger. This is reflected in some of the films of the time and their marketing materials, where the changing representation of women is evident:

> *it is women's sexuality, that which renders them desirable – but also threatening – to men, which constitutes the real problem that the horror film exists to explore.* (Neale, 1980)

Stretch and Challenge 3.6

When you are exploring wider examples in class and independently, consider how film posters reflect the social and historical context of the time.

In the *Kiss of the Vampire* poster (shown on page 78), the representations of the women are binary opposites, reflecting what was happening in society at the time. One woman, stereotypically blonde, is weak and subservient, while the second is seen as powerful and in control of both men. Challenging the typical stereotype, the vampire in his code of gesture and expression appears fearful and threatened by the woman, reflecting the position of men in the 1960s some of whom were becoming increasingly worried about the changing role of women in society.

Quickfire 3.17

How does the 1960s film poster for *The Vampire and the Ballerina* reinforce the gender representations of the time?

Applying Theory

Liesbet van Zoonen

Feminist theory is a relevant perspective to consider in relation to the set film poster and van Zoonen's assertion that the meaning of gender varies according to cultural and historical context and as such is a reflection of the society of the time. In the horror film genre women were both, as van Zoonen has stated, objects to be looked at and examples of new, more emancipated women who seemed to be challenging the idea of their expected sociological roles.

David Gauntlett

It could also be said that these posters affirm Gauntlett's theory with regards to identity in that, at the time, they provided women with 'tools' or role models with which to construct their own stronger sense of identity. However, they also challenge his theory that there was less diversity of representations in the past. If you compare the 1960s film posters with the *Tide* adverts and similar domestic products, it can be seen that as women became more vocal in their demands for equality, the way in which they were represented also became more diverse. This illustrates the fact that certain media products reflect sociological change and as such are important historical artefacts.

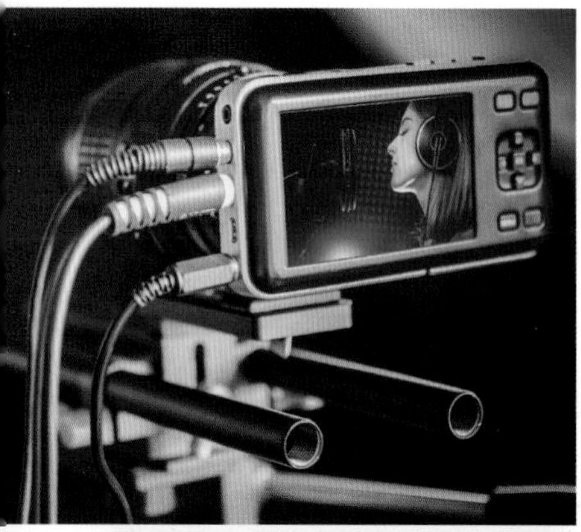

The music video can be used to establish the artist's persona.

Investigating the Set Forms and Products: Music Video

You will have explored some aspects of the music video form in Year 1 of your course and applied your understanding to the set products and the wider examples you have studied in class. In this chapter the aim is to explore the set products in greater detail, considering how media language communicates meaning and how the media represents social groups and issues. Music videos have in recent years become more complex and more reflective of the sub-genre of the artist or band than in the past. This is in part due to developments in technology. Many bands/artists allocate a large budget to music videos as part of their marketing, as they are also a means of establishing the identity of the performer and therefore creating and maintaining a fan-base. It is also increasingly the case that artists use the form to highlight issues about which they feel strongly, for example Sam Fender highlights social injustice in many of his videos.

Tip

Exploring the contexts related to the set products is an important element of the theoretical framework.

Economic Context

As the purpose of music videos extends beyond creative expression, to ensuring financial success, it is important to consider the economic context in which they may be produced. When bands and artists first start out, the music videos are understandably low budget, they then increase in budget and consequently become more ambitious with higher production values as the band or artist becomes more successful. However, the band or artist may consciously make artistic decisions about the style of the music video in order to reflect their music genre and ideology. Music videos can also contribute to the fame of the artist by winning awards, for example Beyoncé's *Formation* won several awards, including a Clio Award for Innovation and Creative Excellence in a Music Video in 2016, and was also nominated in the music video category at the Grammy's, reflecting the fact that music videos have become an art form in themselves. Sam Fender won a prestigious Ivor Novello Award in 2022 for 'Best Song Musically and Lyrically' for Seventeen Going Under.

***Formation* won the award for Best Music Video at the 2017 Grammy Awards.**

Beyoncé's marketing team also released the music video the day before her performance at the Super Bowl, this and her performance to over 100 million people was a strategic ploy and helped to launch *Formation* and ensure media coverage and economic success for the artist.

Quickfire 3.18

How can music videos also relate to a social context?

Media Language

How the different modes and language associated with different media forms communicate multiple meanings

Andrew Goodwin: Key Principles of Music Videos

Andrew Goodwin, a media practitioner and theorist, investigated how music videos as a form are structured in order to communicate messages to audiences and he established some key principles.

Links Between the Music and the Visuals

This is when there is close relationship between the musical style and what is seen on the screen. For example, the pace of the editing of the music video matches the beat of the music. In *Formation*, there are references to 'bounce', a New Orleans music and dancing style. The dancing in parts of the video is matched to the editing to reflect this music style.

Links Between the Lyrics and the Visuals

Goodwin's research suggests that this link has three purposes: to illustrate the lyrics at a more straightforward level; to amplify the lyrics in order to communicate a message more clearly to an audience; and to offer a contradictory message creating **disjuncture**. Consequently, the video may interpret the lyrics in a way not considered by the audience, so requiring them to be more active in their viewing in order to decode the meaning. It may also mean in some cases that the visuals bear no resemblance to the lyrics. In *Formation*, the lyrics on their own may seem confusing to an audience as there are several obscure references, but these are amplified for the audience through the use of visuals. However, there is still a level of cultural understanding demanded to understand all the references.

In Sam Fender's music video *Seventeen Going Under*, the narrative is non-linear, moving between the past and the present reflecting Fender's dominant message of learning from the mistakes of the past and understanding the angst of his 17 year old self. The different narrative strands are dominated by the performance of the artist who, through the lyrics and the exemplification of a significant chorus line, acts as the storyteller. The images are highly illustrative, often featuring a literal interpretation of the lyrics, this gives a greater sense of realism to the characters and his story.

Alternatively, Vance Joy's music video *Riptide* subverts typical conventions of the form: the audience expect the lyrics to be interpreted for them in some way by the visuals, but here the interpretation is overt and very literal at times, obscuring rather than amplifying the meaning. *Riptide* rejects normal narrative devices expected in a music video and instead constructs a montage of apparently disparate images that lack narrative cohesion, leaving the audience to draw their own conclusions and meanings. There is repetition of image sequences, not for amplification, but to create more disjuncture, for example the woman running to the sea which is repeated with the woman in different clothing, literally matching the lyrics but this succeeds in creating an enigma, not narrative clarification. Similarly, the shot of the two lollies being pulled apart is used as a visual for the lyrics but has no obvious place within the narrative.

Key Figure

Andrew Goodwin
Was a professor at the University of San Francisco until his accidental death in a fire in 2013. He wrote extensively on music television and cultural theory, one of his most popular books is *Dancing in the Distraction Factory: Music Television and Popular Culture* (1992).

Key Term

Disjuncture
Lacking unity, thus creating a separation or disconnection, for example between the lyrics and the visuals in a music video.

The codes and conventions of rap music are reinforced across different forms and platforms.

Quickfire 3.19

What reasons can you give for the way in which the music video for *Riptide* is constructed?

Tip

Consider the relationship between elements of media language and the way in which particular genres develop across different forms and platforms. This is a result of audience recognition of the well-established codes and conventions.

Quickfire 3.20

What is the effect of incorporating the intertextual references in *Turntables*?

The most disconcerting links between the lyrics and the visuals are the repeated shots of the woman singing into the microphone and becoming increasingly disheveled as the music video progresses. Here the wrong lyrics appear on the screen as the actual lyrics are heard and as her lip-synching becomes disjointed. This very deliberately subverts the typical conventions of music video where the 'star' would be filmed singing the correct lyrics with perfect lip-synching.

Demonstrating Genre Characteristics

The codes and conventions of media forms and products, including the processes through which media language develops as genre

Music videos are a marketing device and part of their purpose is to establish the conventions of the music sub-genre, in doing so they will include the repertoire of elements specific to that genre. As is the case with any media product, the clear recognition of the sub-genre facilitates the marketing of the product. In the music industry, conventions related to music sub-genres may be common across different platforms and this familiarity to audiences can guarantee success of a product. Audiences have preconceived ideas of what to expect from a music video based on their understanding of the genre and the star's identity. For example, rap artists create a certain 'look' through visual codes, including, clothing, gesture and expression, which will be reinforced in their live performance, vinyl sleeves and music videos, and which will establish the artist as part of this sub-genre.

Intertextual References

The significance of the varieties of ways intertextuality can be used in the media

Music videos are often influenced by other media texts and cultural references. These intertextual links are then used as symbols within the music video to communicate messages to an audience. Some of the set music video products incorporate intertextuality for a range of purposes. In Janelle Monáe's music video *Turntables* a variety of intertextual references are used to exemplify the lyrics of their protest song including:

- Direct references to the 2020 Amazon documentary *All In: The Fight for Democracy*, for which the song was originally written and which focuses on the issue of voter suppression and the fight for democracy. The film's subject is the 2018 elections for the Governor of Georgia. It drew attention to the tactics used to suppress voting rights to ensure the election of the Republican candidate at the expense of the black Democrat candidate, Stacey Adams.
- References to other political events to further highlight the under-representation of black Americans and to raise awareness of social inequalities. This takes the form of archive footage, including the voice of black American writer James Baldwin from 1968 and featured in the 2016 documentary film based on his work, *I Am Not Your Negro*.
- References to other historical events that have significance in black history and so communicate messages about contemporary issues, for example images of Muhammad Ali, who throughout his life challenged white supremacy, segregation and all forms of racism and of gestures of protest, including the iconic and globally recognised Black Power raised fists of Tommie Smith and John Carlos at the 1968 Olympics; these are then shown to be replicated in the more contemporary images of protest.
- References to contemporary issues and events, for example the protests after the killing of George Floyd and the Families Belong Together campaign, whose aim was to reunite immigrant families separated at the US–Mexican border by a policy initiated during the Trump administration.

Formation also makes many intertextual references in order to communicate messages to the audience. These demand a high level of media literacy from the audience and some references will resonate more with certain audiences. Like in *Turntables*, these references move about in time and place, suggesting the importance of the historical context on contemporary issues. These include:

- References throughout the music video to Hurricane Katrina, the New Orleans flooding and the subsequent rise in racial tensions.
- References to slavery and the relationship between plantation owners and slaves. Beyoncé subverts the typical images of the time by featuring black women dressed in antebellum dresses similar to those worn in the 1939 film *Gone With the Wind*, to make a point about how divided society was in the past and commenting also on contemporary society.
- Although *Formation* recreates a similar scene from the time, the hair of the women suggests their important cultural and racial heritage. Other intertextual references to hair and racial features also appear in the video.
- References to news footage of police confrontation with black people and to the deaths of black people. For example, the video opens with words of the YouTuber Messy Mya, who was subsequently killed in a shooting in New Orleans in 2010, asking what happened after New Orelans?
- In *Riptide* the intertextual references are used in a different way, contributing to the surreal feel of the music video and are less related to communicating an overall message than the other two examples. The main textual references to films are more literal and overt. The music video itself is constructed like a short film, as there is no representation of the artist performing and the style is instead a montage of images. There are references to the horror/thriller genre, with the repeated images of the woman's body being dragged away, the graveyard scenes, the stabbing of the hand and the progressively abused state of the woman 'performer'. These references demand that the audience engage more actively to decode meanings from the product.
- *Riptide* also has echoes of the cinematic style of the film director **Wes Anderson** whose attention to symmetry is reflected in the way that the shots are constructed in the music video and the montage style adopted by director Dmitri Basil. Vance Joy commented on the links to Wes Anderson created through the lens used by Basil and the way in which he selected the things to be included. He was particularly amazed by the objects in some of the clips including the lollipop stick to match the lyrics 'come unstuck' and the close-ups of the Romanian passport and the airline ticket (Klinger, 2014).

There are also similarities in the video with the way Anderson uses colour palettes moving from muted hues to bold splashes of colour.

Stretch and Challenge 3.8

Watch the YouTube clip of Kanye West's appearance in the 'Concert for Hurricane Relief', https://www.youtube.com/watch?v=9pVTrnxCZaQ, to gain a better understanding of the racial tensions referred to.

Key Figure

Wes Anderson
An American film director, producer, screenwriter and actor known for his distinctive visual and narrative style evident in films such as *The Grand Budapest Hotel* and *The Royal Tenenbaums*.

The 1939 film *Gone with the Wind* is set on a plantation during the American Civil War and depicts the life of Scarlett O'Hara, a privileged Southern Belle.

Stretch and Challenge 3.7

Watch the YouTube clip, https://www.youtube.com/watch?v=FZ7r2OVu1ss, from the film *Gone with the Wind* to gain a better understanding of the intertextual references used in *Formation* in relation to slavery and plantation life.

Quickfire 3.21

How does *Riptide* demonstrate the conventions of a concept-based music video?

Tip

Consider why intertextual references have been used in the music videos. Avoid just listing them; they are there to communicate messages to the audience.

Rapid Recall 3.6

Which theorist introduced the idea of the male gaze that is closely related to Goodwin's idea of 'notion of looking'?

Stretch and Challenge 3.9

Consider the other intertextual references in the music video and how they contribute to the style of it.

Notion of Looking and Voyeurism

Here, Goodwin develops the idea of the 'male gaze' theory to explore examples where music videos involve the idea of the audience as looking in on either the life of the artist or a character in the narrative of the music video. This can also involve iconography related to looking and seeing, including mirrors, cameras and screens within screens, where the act of looking is very overt. In some music videos this also encompasses the sexual objectification of the female body where the woman is reduced to a passive object to be looked at. This may also relate to the way in which the woman is filmed, where her body is fragmented so the focus is on the more sexual aspects of her body. In Lana Del Rey's music video *Ultraviolence* (which can be seen at www.youtube.com/watch?v=ZFWC4SiZBao), the audience is uncomfortably positioned behind the camera intimately filming the woman as she walks to her wedding.

At one point, the video consciously shows us the hand of a man reaching from behind the camera and touching Del Rey's face, suggesting we are the film maker and her body is also fragmented. This is even more disconcerting as the lyrics are concerned with domestic violence, which is in direct contrast to the pastoral, dream-like quality of the music video.

This representation of the artist was also used in her Madame Tussaud's waxwork, reinforcing it as an iconic image.

This concept of voyeurism has caused controversy and discussion in some music videos, for example Miley Cyrus' *Wrecking Ball* music video where she is constructed in a very sexually explicit and objectified manner. The argument centred on whether she was being exploited in an aim to reinvent her persona for a new audience, or if she was herself instrumental and complicit in constructing this representation. Regardless of which, the audience is encouraged to 'look at' the artist in a particular way. It was also said at the time that this music video was a marketing ploy to ensure the success of the launch of the new look for Cyrus and as such was very successful, attracting 19 million views on Vevo in the first 24 hours of its launch. This representation of the artist was also used in her Madame Tussaud's waxwork reinforcing it as an iconic image.

Performance, Narrative and Concept-Based Music Video

These are the three styles of music video discussed in Goodwin's theory.

Performance videos have developed from the early days of music video production where, due to restrictions in technology and the lesser demands of the audience with regards to the new form, it was enough to see the band or artist in performance. This is still used to develop the star persona and to demonstrate musical ability and therefore the credibility of the artist. Beyoncé uses the performance video to showcase her dancing ability, communicate with her fans and establish her star quality.

Music videos featuring the artist performing in concert also usually incorporate shots of the audience enjoying themselves and can make the viewer feel part of the experience.

Narrative music videos tell a story using either the artist or band themselves or actors. This style of music video also sometimes cuts between the narrative and the artist performing in order to establish the star persona of the performer in the minds of the audience. Some narrative music videos do not feature the artist at all but are instead a visual construction of the lyrics. Alicia Keys incorporates performance and dance into her music video *Underdog* alongside a narrative to construct a sense that she is part of the community that is the focus of her song and supportive of their issues.

Tip

Remember that you may be required to respond to an unseen music video in Section A of Component 1 of the examination, so it is important to explore a range of different examples.

In Tom Grennan's music video *Little Bit of Love* a narrative is constructed with the artist as a central character, acting and performing and creating a very personal viewpoint. The structure features a disruption, a climax and a resolution, and the music video is constructed as a short film featuring a title and credits. Technical codes contribute to the storytelling, for example the establishing shots of the urban milieu placing the artist at the centre of his community and the close-ups of Grennan and his brother to signify emotion. Editing cuts between the artist performing and the narrative around his brother and the money. The narrative also carries a message that although you are a product of your environment and what happens in your formative years, you can make decisions that allow you to change your course for the better. The final shot slows the pace from the frenetic early editing to a slow zoom in to the serene, slightly surreal 'family' scene.

A **concept-based** music video is a more abstract creation not based on a coherent narrative or necessarily featuring performance. It may interpret the song lyrics but in an enigmatic way that does not make the meaning clear. A concept-based video may also reference, or be inspired, by other artistic styles and may experiment with different filming and editing techniques. Its aim is to hook the audience through the unusual style and make a statement by creating a mood. An example of this style is the set product *Riptide*.

Link

On pages 72–73 of the Year 1 book, performance and narrative music videos are discussed in more detail with specific examples.

The Demands of the Record Label

The creation of the star image is an important aspect of the music video, which is in essence a promotional device for the artist or band. Goodwin (1992) asserts that music videos are essentially advertisements and so ignore common narrative:

> *As consumers, we make up our own meaning of a song in our minds: a music video can anchor meaning and gives the record company/artist a method of anchoring meaning.* (Goodwin, 1992)

The record label/company may think it important to feature the artist as much as possible in the video; this is particularly true of a new performer who needs to establish themselves in a competitive market. The use of close-ups and direct mode of address help the artist to engage with the audience, who then feel that they are being directly sung to.

Some artists will develop a **motif** or use particular iconography, which makes them easily recognisable and encourages fans to imitate their style. This visual style will then be repeated across their work: Bono from U2 has used the visual motif of his glasses for most of his music career.

Often the iconography or motif will be related to the theme of the new album and will appear on all marketing merchandise. Beyoncé regularly releases merchandise related to a single or an album.

Quickfire 3.22

How does the point Goodwin makes about the demands of the record label relate to the economic context of music videos?

Key Term

Motif
A dominant or recurring theme or idea in literary, artistic or musical work.

The use of close-ups and direct mode of address, for example Tom Grennan in *Little Bit of Love*, establishes a relationship between the artist and the audience.

Tip

Although Goodwin is not one of the theorists set for study in this specification he is relevant for this form. It is important that you consider a wider range of theorists where appropriate.

Key Term

Extended metaphor
A comparison between two dissimilar ideas in order to amplify meaning, which may extend throughout the text. For example, in *Hallelujah* the use of a religious narrative to explain the romantic relationship.

Stretch and Challenge 3.10

Broaden your understanding of the music video form by exploring a range of examples. Try to apply Goodwin's theory to the music videos as part of your independent research.

Media Language: Analysing a Music Video

Panic! At the Disco: *Hallelujah* (https://www.youtube.com/watch?v=DxYyHHR0Q1c)

How the combination of elements of media language influence meaning

Goodwin's theory can be a useful structure for analysing the wider examples of music videos you will study in preparation for the unseen element of the examination.

In the video for *Hallelujah*, the conventional elements of the music video genre combine to communicate messages to the audience. The link between the lyrics and the visuals does not clearly illustrate the meaning in a literal way but does provide an **extended metaphor** regarding the relationship between the artist and the woman he is pursuing, and as such amplifies the meaning for the audience. The links are related to the religious language and imagery and his hope to be 'saved'.

The video is performance intercut with narrative, typical of the rock-pop sub-genre. It features the band's front-man, Brendon Urie, in a dual role as performer and as characters in the story, the change being indicated by code of clothing. When he is performing he is dressed in a red suit and when he is in character his clothing is of the 'ordinary young man' stereotype.

There are several intertextual references in the video related to both language and visuals. The narrative element of the video closely resembles a video game scenario as he tries to overcome a range of obstacles in order to reach the woman. She is represented through code of clothing as part of the game, with links to, for example, the *Assassin's Creed* franchise, while in his modern clothing he is more the gamer.

The audience, too, is positioned for this aspect of the video as the player as they are shown typical gameplay shots. This may enhance the appeal of the video for the contemporary audience.

The intertextuality is closely related to the narrative, the character in the music video is confronted with a series of optical illusions in his chase after the girl, it is only when he embraces and trusts that the illusions are real that he reaches her. The maze and his inability to trust are a metaphor for the relationship. There is also intertextuality related to the Church and there is frequent and repeated use of religious imagery related to the performance aspect of the video, including the confessional box where the performer appears as both the sinner and the priest. This is reinforced by the song title, which establishes this as a gospel rock anthem.

With regards to the demands of the record label, there is a clear attempt to establish a relationship between the front man of the band and the audience. He is central to the narrative and appears performing the song using direct mode of address and close-up shots. A conscious decision has been made to feature only Brendon Urie, not the whole band, as he is the most recognisable and longest-serving member of the band.

In an interview given by Urie during the marketing of the video, he continues the religious motif in relation to his fan-base:

> *there's a little tagline in there that I throw out to our fans, I like to call them 'my sinners', and I'm a fellow sinner.* (Bagish, 2015)

This video and the single were the first by the band in two years and the first after the drummer Spencer Smith left, so in an economic context it was important to re-launch the band with a music video that includes an arresting and enigmatic narrative and also serves as a promotional vehicle for the star to remind the fan-base of his persona.

Applying Theory

Structuralism: Claude Lévi-Strauss

As music videos are short, they are therefore required to communicate the narrative and any related messages in a restricted timeframe. An exploration of their underlying structure allows the viewer to decode the messages and establish a meaning. One of the ways this is done is through the use of binary opposites. Consider how the meaning behind the music video *Seventeen Going Under* is constructed through binary oppositions, for example the personal, introspective, older Fender set in direct comparison to the angry, confused 17 year old. The binary opposites in this music video are also stylistic, communicated in cutting between the artist in the street, becoming increasingly distanced from his environment and the narrative scenarios depicting his troubled youth.

Similarly, in Tom Grennan's music video *Little Bit of Love* meaning is constructed through binary oppositions, for example the difference in the relationship between the man and his brother which is happy and at times shown to be tender and caring, and the fact that he also exists in a violent world in which he is trapped.

Both these music videos demonstrate that the resolution of opposites can have ideological significance, particularly where music videos encode social messages. Consider how *Seventeen Going Under* and *Little Bit of Love* suggest that past experiences need not define what happens in the future and how both these artist demonstrate that this media form can be used to raise awareness of social issues.

Tom Grennan's music video combines representations of toxic masculinity and vulnerability.

Representation in Music Videos

You will already have explored representation as an element of the theoretical framework in Year 1 of the course in relation to the set music video and the broader examples you have studied. Depending on the music sub-genre and the artist, videos will construct different representations of social groups. For example, rap music videos tend to construct less positive representations of women, displaying a more misogynistic attitude, reflecting the music style and the themes of the songs. Certain female artists will construct positive images of women in positions of power and use the form to challenge more typical stereotypes of gender.

Tom Grennan's music video *Little Bit of Love* features a range of representations of social groups that are often misrepresented or under-represented including age, gender and class as well as social issues. The music video constructs a version of reality based on Grennan's own situation, the representations are personal but are also constructed to have universal appeal through his use of real locations, situations and relatable `characters'.

Representations of masculinity are a key element of the music video and Grennan in previous interviews has discussed the notion of toxic masculinity. He asserts *Little Bit of Love* represents aspects of toxic masculinity as well as the unconditional love between brothers. Whilst Grennan is seen as angry and violent, he is also depicted as emotional and struggling with his mental health, evidenced in the lyrics about voices in his head, articulating the experience of young men who may feel trapped by their situation and environment. The metaphor of swimming is a recurring motif in the music video and represents freedom, a way out and a means to establish a bond with his younger sibling.

Taylor Swift has used the music video to reinvent herself, moving away from the 'girl next door' stereotype to a stronger more powerful representation. The music video *Look What You Made Me Do* is full of intertextual references to events in her life, including the symbolic dollar she was awarded in the sexual assault case against a DJ and well-documented rifts with other music stars.

At the start of the video she literally rises from the dead and then is presented in a range of different powerful personas throughout the video. One shot shows her standing above all the past representations of herself from previous music videos.

Taylor Swift uses her music videos as a means of self-representation.

Music videos are interesting documents reflecting the social and cultural context of the time in which they were made. Increasingly they are also a vehicle for the artist to represent issues about which they may feel strongly. As can be seen in *Formation*, Beyoncé constructs representations within her music videos that reflect the themes in her music at the time. Janelle Monáe, as a black, female and non-binary artist is concerned to project a positive representation of gender and, in particular, black women through their music while also representing issues about which they are concerned, for example social inequalities.

Applying Theory

Feminist Theory

In the set products, *Formation* and *Riptide*, and the wider example of Taylor Swift, there is an interesting ambiguity in how the female artists are constructed. On the one hand they are powerful and in control and yet, on the other hand, are also sexually objectified and, with reference to van Zoonen, present themselves as objects to be looked at, reinforcing Western patriarchal culture. bel hooks' assertion that feminism is a struggle to end the ideology of patriarchal oppression can be explored in relation to *Formation*: is Beyoncé embracing feminism as a political commitment or a lifestyle choice that will help to sell her music and maintain her fan-base?

bell hooks herself has raised concerns about the type of feminism that Beyoncé presents and its ideological impact on the young women who see her as a role model. hooks, speaking at a conference in 2014 in New York entitled 'Are You Still A Slave?', focusing on the representations of women of colour in the media, was responding to the front cover of *Time* magazine which featured Beyoncé as one of the world's 100 most influential people. The controversy was related to the fact that the front cover image showed Beyoncé in a very revealing outfit thus, in the eyes of many, demeaning her role as a supposed feminist and reinforcing the idea of women as objects to be looked at (van Zoonen, 1994).

It was acknowledged by hooks that the choices in how to represent the star may not have been her own, but also reinforces her idea that race as well as sex determine the extent to which individuals are exploited. As hooks said, if we take an image of a:

> *rich, very powerful black female, and let's use it in the service of imperialist, white supremacist, capitalist patriarchy, because she probably had very little control over that cover, that image.* (Sieczkowski, 2014)

However, she did go on to express her concerns about Beyoncé's assertion that she is a feminist; these concerns can be read at Sieczkowski (2014).

Janelle Monáe uses their music and celebrity profile to project positive representations

Link

Page 76 of the Year 1 book considers the application of David Gauntlett's theory of identity to music videos.

Tip

Consider how the representations in the music videos you have studied are constructed through selection and combination and how they may instigate a discourse around, for example, social issues and gender.

Stretch and Challenge 3.11

Read Nevin's (2017) article, 'Look What You Made Her Do: Decoding the Disses of Taylor Swift's New Video', on the *Guardian* website, in which he explores the representation of Swift and the intertextual references in *Look What You Made Me Do.*

Stretch and Challenge 3.12

Look at the 5 May 2014 cover of *Time* magazine online (https://time.com/magazine/us/75229/may-5th-2014-vol-183-no-17-u-s/) and consider whether you think it helps or hinders Beyoncé's claim to be feminist.

Stretch and Challenge 3.13

Read the article by Sieczkowski (2014) related to bel hooks' comments about Beyoncé and feminism and watch the video of the discussion on the *Huffington Post* website.

Quickfire 3.23

How does Beyoncé's representation in *Formation* both conform to and challenge bel hooks' feminist perspective?

Link

Page 77 of the Year 1 book applies Stuart Hall's theories of representation to music videos.

Tip

Consider how race and ethnicity is represented in the examples of music videos you have studied on the course. Be prepared to critically explore these examples in relation to theoretical perspectives.

How representations invoke discourses and ideologies and position audiences

This ambiguous representation of gender is echoed in *Riptide*, which appears to construct contradictory messages with regards to women. The video at times seems to reinforce a sense of patriarchal domination through the objectification of women. While the women in the video are not overly sexualised, the audience is at times positioned as voyeurs of women's bodies and to their seeming mis-treatment, conforming to van Zoonen's theoretical perspective of gender. The camera shows us fragmented sections of women's bodies, for example feet running and a hand being stabbed. There are also frequent shots of the woman escaping or running away, reinforcing a more typical representation of the woman as victim. At the same time, the construction of the progressively dishevelled performer seems to challenge the typical representation of women in music video, but the images are disturbing as the audience is positioned in close proximity to the woman. The dream-like and surreal atmosphere of the video distances these representations from reality and may be said to intrigue rather than disturb. The response may also differ according to the gender of the viewer.

Postcolonial Theory: Gilroy

Formation and *Turntables* conform to and challenge Gilroy's postcolonial theory. Both music videos incorporate binary opposites based on notions of difference and otherness in terms of race and ethnicity. *Formation* positions Beyoncé as the strong black woman challenging the notions of the postcolonial legacy. However, in the video, her 'otherness' is represented as a source of strength and black pride rather than a signifier of racial or cultural inferiority, as she chronicles a whole history of racial inequality and oppression, from slavery through to the Black Lives Matter movement and issues of police brutality. In this way, she is able to challenge and subvert the operation of white power that has been used to oppress black people in American society.

In *Turntables* the narrative embeds positive messages and values, constructing representations of a successful black, female and non-binary music artist to subvert negative stereotypes of ethnicity. The representations of race and ethnicity are constructed in the music video in order to challenge the under-representation and misrepresentation of particular ethnic groups that may originally stem from colonial attitudes. The representation of ethnic minority groups as victims and the notion of 'otherness' is largely avoided and replaced by more positive representations of power through protest. However, the very fact that Monáe has to address misrepresentation and under-representation in this music video, suggests, as asserted by Gilroy, that there exist racial hierarchies based on cultural binary oppositions.

Investigating the Set Forms and Products: Newspapers

As you will have discovered during Year 1 of the course, the media form that is included in Section A and Section B of Component 1 is newspapers. This form is studied in relation to all aspects of the theoretical framework: Media Language, Representation, Media Industries and Audiences. You will also be required to consider contexts in relation to this form, including social and cultural, economic and political. As can be seen, newspapers are to be studied in detail.

Economic context: newspapers are surviving in a competitive market that has been dramatically changed by developments in technology and changes in consumer habits. The circulation of the print product has fallen and newspapers have had to look to new ways of attracting and maintaining readers in order to ensure economic success.

Social and cultural context: newspapers are often viewed as a window through which we see what is happening in the world at the time; they are thought to mirror society. However, this reflection of society is one that is **mediated** in relation to the beliefs of the newspaper.

Political context: newspapers reflect the political context in which they were made through their ideology and the way they represent certain stories. This context is also evident through aspects of their ownership, political orientation and readers.

The media mediates issues and events in the news, particularly more complex stories, for example foreign conflicts. These can be defined by the newspaper through, for example, what is selected and what is left out, the sources referenced and the way in which language is used.

You will have learned from your study of this form in Year 1 that it is important to be aware of how different newspapers present their stories and their view of the world in different ways and how this may reflect an ideological viewpoint.

Archive newspapers are still used as documentary evidence of past events and as such serve to chronicle the time in which they were produced.

Newspapers, as can be seen in the set products and other front pages covering the Gray report into the then Conservative government's parties during the Covid lockdown, also serve to highlight the opinions of the creators of the product and these will vary according to the ideological stance of the publication. Newspapers are therefore powerful in their ability to persuade their readers of a particular viewpoint, particularly when it reinforces one they already hold.

For example, in 1992 *The Sun* took credit for persuading their readers to vote Neil Kinnock out of office in the General Election of that year with the headline that can be seen at https://en.wikipedia.org/wiki/It%27s_The_Sun_Wot_Won_It#/media/File:It's_The_Sun_Wot_Won_It.jpg, demonstrating the newspaper's belief in its power as an opinion leader.

Newspapers as a form are studied in relation to all aspects of the theoretical framework.

Key Term

Mediated
Refers to the way in which the media present aspects of the world to the audience. Newspapers act as a mediator constructing stories and, in the process, encoding meaning.

Link

The codes and conventions of a newspaper's front pages are developed in more detail on pages 77–78 of the Year 1 book.

Rapid Recall 3.7

Why might the coverage of an event or a particular story be different in different newspapers?

Quickfire 3.24

What strategies have newspapers employed to try to ensure economic stability?

Media Language

How the combination of elements of media language influence meaning

Similar to other media products you have studied, newspapers share a repertoire of common elements in relation to media language. These typical codes and conventions are recognisable to audiences and communicate meanings. A reminder of some of these is below:

- **The masthead**: the name of the paper, which may encode its ideology. This may also be communicated through the typography chosen for it. Some newspapers will rebrand themselves to maintain the interest of their audience. In 2018 the *Guardian* re-launched as a tabloid newspaper and redesigned its masthead, creating a bolder more arresting style. The *Guardian* explained the new headline font had more readability and the new masthead represents the *Guardian*'s place and purpose in the turbulent news agenda of today (*Guardian*, 2018b).
- **The plug/puff**: this is at the top of the front page and its purpose is to broaden the appeal of the newspaper to the reader by suggesting what else the paper can offer them. On the day of the launch of the new-look *Guardian* newspaper, *The Sun* used a plug to suggest it was better value than the new 'tabloid' *Guardian* and the *Daily Mirror*.
- **The headline**: this is used to hook the audience and may use a range of language devices, including puns, alliteration and hyperbole. For the engagement of Prince Harry to Meghan Markle, all the newspapers, apart from the *Financial Times*, covered the event using different headlines to appeal directly to their audience. Both the *Daily Mirror* and *The Times* used quotes from Prince Harry; however, as *The Times* is a quality paper which would not usually run celebrity-style stories, the main headline is not related to the engagement. This has a sub-heading instead, suggesting it is not as important to its readers as the political story that carries the main headline.

The headlines of the **popular press** tend to be more dramatic and enigmatic, while those of the **quality press** carry more information.

- **The strapline**: is usually above or below the main headline and provides more detail about the story.
- **The central image**: is what draws the eye of the reader. In the case of the royal engagement, the press were invited to the photo call for the announcement, so all the photographs are very similar but also slightly different. These images are usually taken by photographers who work for the newspapers or who are freelance. However, in this age of citizen journalism, the ordinary person can find their phone snaps being used. For instance, a photograph of the royal family at Christmas was taken on a phone by a member of the public, Karen Anvil, who managed to get a better shot than the professionals; this can be see at https://www.dailymail.co.uk/femail/article-11571511/royals.html. These images may offer a different perspective of an event which may be of interest to the reader. Some newspapers, particularly the quality press, will use **standalone images** to catch the attention of the reader.
- **A splash**: an important news story that will be the lead on the front page, for example the royal engagement, which was covered by the majority of national newspapers on the day of the announcement.

Stretch and Challenge 3.14

Read more about the *Guardian's* decisions regarding the new design for the newspaper and the economic context that influenced the change in the online Press Release '*Guardian* and *Observer* Launch New Tabloid Format and Digital Redesign' (2018a).

Key Terms

Popular press
Refers to the cheaper newspapers with a mass circulation. They are also commonly known as the tabloid press.

Quality press
Refers to newspapers that are distinguished by their seriousness. They cover the news in more detail and international stories. They were previously known as broadsheet newspapers.

Standalone images
Arresting images with no story attached. They may be used as a hook to attract an audience.

Quickfire 3.25

Why is it no longer appropriate to use the terms tabloid and broadsheet when referring to contemporary newspapers?

Analysing the Set Product: Media Language

The newspaper set product for Year 2 of the course is the front page of *The Times* newspaper. It covers the same event you explored in Year 1 with the front page and inner pages of the *Daily Mirror*: the inquiry into the parties held at Downing Street during the lockdown.

The way media language incorporates viewpoints and ideologies

The way in which this front page has been constructed employs media language to communicate messages to the reader. It is useful to apply Barthes' semiotic theory when exploring the product, as the pages communicate their meaning through a process of signification. The signs encoded in the product will be decoded by the readers. Consider the different ways in which the paradigmatic choices of media language communicate meanings on this front page:

- **The masthead**: this is bold and recognisable and effectively signifies the ideology of the paper, suggesting that it reports upon the issues of the time. The typography chosen is strong and commands the front page and is placed either side of the crest and logo. The overall aesthetic suggests tradition and reliability.
- **Layout and design**: the front page is largely text-led which is conventional for a quality newspaper, suggesting that the publication aims to give detailed information on the main stories. *The Times* usually has a large image on the front page to draw the eye of the reader and this may be a standalone or, in this case related to the main story. The text is compact and detailed; sub-headings are not generally used to split up the stories into sections, suggesting that the readers are comfortable with detailed information and analysis. The sub-heading with jump lines to the analysis of the story on the inner pages, establishes the newspaper as an opinion leader. The coloured plug promotes *Times2*, the lifestyle supplement, offering readers content that is different and lighter than the serious news stories.
- **Images**: the images that are chosen by the newspaper may reflect their viewpoint on the story. The central image is a close-up photograph of Boris Johnson with an indirect mode of address. *The Times* leans to the right politically, the image chosen displays a code of expression showing some trepidation on Boris Johnson's face as he goes to the Commons. The newspaper has selected this photograph to suggest that he does have questions to answer, while not explicitly criticising him.
- **The caption**: this is detailed, anchoring the image of Boris Johnson. Further anchorage is provided by the pull quotes taken from Sue Gray's report, the choice of these conveys implicit criticism of the events and the government.
- **Language and mode of address**: the expectation is that the language of a quality newspaper like *The Times* will be formal. *The Times* usually engages in serious news and will not demonstrate its opinions as obviously as other popular newspapers, for example the *Daily Mirror* and *The Sun*. The headline is informative rather than dramatic, see https://www.thetimes.co.uk/article/sue-gray-hands-partygate-report-to-boris-johnson-fc36wxsjd. However, there is subtle, implicit criticism through the selection and use of language on the front page, for example including the number 'four' and choosing the specific aspect of the report that comments on a 'drinking culture'.

Rapid Recall 3.8

What is the difference between the circulation and readership of a newspaper?

Tip

In order to prepare for the Component 1 Section A examination, it is important to consider how a range issues and events are covered by different newspapers.

Rapid Recall 3.9

How was the viewpoint of the *Daily Mirror* communicated more obviously on its front page?

Stretch and Challenge 3.15

Read more about how different newspapers covered the findings of the Sue Gray report into the lockdown parties here: www.independent.co.uk/news/uk/politics/sue-gray-report-newspaper-front-pages-b2087702.html.

Link

On page 79 of the Year 1 book these points are explored in more detail in relation to the newspapers produced during the Partygate scandal.

Tip

To develop your understanding of the set newspaper products, it is important to research other examples and consider how other newspapers represented the same event.

Tip

While the focus here has been on the front pages of newspapers, the inner pages can also allow you to analyse the ideology and viewpoints of the publication in relation to particular issues and groups in society.

Representation in Newspapers: Issues and Events

The way in which representations make claims about realism

All newspapers have access to the same stories each day; the choice each newspaper makes about the stories they will run in their papers will be determined by a range of factors, including the profile of the newspaper's readership and its ideology. As an audience you will read the newspaper, in print or online, that reflects your own ideas and viewpoints. We trust that publication to give us news and information about the world in which we live and, because this is a form that deals with fact not fiction, we assume that what we are seeing and reading is 'real'. However, just like fictional media forms, the press selects, constructs and mediates the news and is not a 'window on the world', although it may appear to be so.

You will recall from your exploration of newspapers in Year 1 of the course that it is important to consider the following when analysing how events and issues are represented:

- The discourse and ideology of the newspaper, including its political allegiances. This may affect the way in which the newspaper covers the event or issue and subsequently how audiences respond to its version of reality. Readers of a particular newspaper are more likely to accept the representations constructed by the publication, they will resonate with the readers who share the newspaper's ideology.
- The process of selection, construction and mediation in representing the event or issue. For example, the *Guardian* is a left-leaning newspaper with liberal views that would be less likely to support the Conservative government's policies that are in direct contradiction to the paper's ethos. This is evident in its front page for 1 February 2022 with a headline about Gray finding failure of leadership, which can be seen at https://www.theguardian.com/theguardian/2022/feb/01. Their choice of a direct quotation from the report represents Boris Johnson in a negative light and they also suggest that the Tory party is divided.
- The language and mode of address of the newspaper will contribute to the construct of the representation and convey meaning to the reader. Tabloid, popular newspapers tend to employ direct mode of address and dramatic language on their front pages. For example, see the *Daily Mirror*'s front page headline and hyperbolic sub-heading the morning after the England women's football team won the Euros: https://twitter.com/DailyMirror/status/1553860172719837187.
- The focus of the representation. The choices made by the newspaper regarding, for example, the central image and the headlines, may draw the readers' attention to a particular aspect of an event or issue. This may be different from other newspapers. The *Telegraph*'s front-page coverage of the women's football Euros win used a standalone image of the celebrations but the main headline was about Sunak pledging an income tax cut, which can be seen at https://www.pressreader.com/, suggesting this would interest their readers more than the sport story.

The impact of industry contexts on the choices media producers make about how to represent events, issues, individuals and social groups

As has been illustrated in the exploration of the front pages in this chapter, the ownership, funding, style and political ideology of the newspaper will affect the way in which events are represented. It is important to consider the industrial contexts of the newspaper set products and the other newspapers you study on the course and what impact this may have on the representations constructed in the newspaper.

Stereotyping reinforces inequalities of power.

Applying Theory: Stuart Hall

Consider how you could apply and evaluate the following aspects of Stuart Hall's theory to the examples of newspapers explored in this chapter and those you have studied in class:

- The idea that representation is the production of meaning through language defined as a system of signs. Consider how newspapers, in particular front pages, use signs and codes, the meanings of which have been established over time, to communicate messages to their readers.
- The idea that stereotyping, as a form of representation, reduces people to a few simple characteristics or traits. Consider how newspapers, in order to communicate messages rapidly, construct stereotypical representations.
- The idea that stereotyping tends to occur where there are inequalities of power, when subordinate or excluded groups are constructed as 'different' or 'other'. For example, the ways in which some newspapers represent refugees and other minority social groups. Some of the tabloid press engage in ethnocentrism, referring to refugees as 'migrants' and instilling fear in their readers based on a sense of difference. Headlines illustrating this form of representation have included several from the *Daily Mail*, including the one regarding migrants and the housing crisis at https://twitter.com/SkyNews/status/733414483222134784.

Quickfire 3.26

How does the representation of refugees demonstrated in the headlines from the *Daily Mail* reflect the newspaper's ideology?

Stretch and Challenge 3.16

Consider the way in which different newspapers invoke discourses and ideologies and position audiences.

Section B: Understanding Media Industries and Audiences

In this section you will continue to develop your understanding of key aspects of Media Industries. This will include:

- the significance of ownership and funding
- how processes of production, distribution and circulation shape media products
- the impact of **digitally convergent platforms** on media production, distribution and circulation
- the effect of individual producers on media industries.

Smartphones are an example of a digitally convergent platform.

Key Terms

Digitally convergent platforms
Where different media platforms merge with one another as a result of advances in technology. For example, the smartphone brings together different functions in one device: users can make phone calls, browse the internet, facetime, play games, watch films and listen to music. All of these would have previously existed on separate platforms.

Mass audiences
Large groups of people that are targeted by media products. This is made much easier due to technological progress.

Contemporary and emerging media
Refers to all types of communications based on digital technology, including those platforms that facilitate communication, disseminate information and include interactive elements.

Tip

Remember that advertising is only studied in relation to audiences and film is only studied in relation to industry.

You will also develop your understanding of media audiences considering:

- the targeting of **mass audiences** and specialised audiences
- how a specialised audience scan be reached through different technologies and platforms
- how the way in which audiences use and respond to the media reflects identity and social, cultural and historical circumstances
- the role and significance of specialised audiences, including niche and fan, to the media.

In Year 2 of the course you will study media products in addition to those studied in Year 1. The media forms and products are set by Eduqas and are as follows:

Advertising	Film (cross-media study including film marketing)	Newspapers
Tide print advertisement (1950s) and *Super. Human.* Tokyo 2020 Paralympic Games audio-visual advertisement (2020)	*Black Panther* (2018) and *I, Daniel Blake* (2016)	*Daily Mirror* and *The Times*

Radio	Video games
Woman's Hour or *Have You Heard George's Podcast?*	*Assassin's Creed* franchise

The focus of this section is different from that of Section A. Here you will explore the set products as examples of the related industries and in relation to audiences. You will not be required to engage in the analysis of the textual features of the set products as you did in Section A, but you should study them in order to consider how they illustrate industry and audience issues. To broaden your understanding in relation to industry and audience you will also study the **contemporary and emerging media** related to the set products.

Before the advent of television, radio was an important part of daily life.

Investigating the Set Forms and Products: Radio

Industry

Similar to other media industries, radio has been affected by changes in technology and the demands of the audience. As a result, the radio industry has had to address how it reaches audiences across a range of platforms in order to maintain interest in its output. However, while some critics heralded the end of the radio medium due to the advances in digital technology, it has risen to the challenge and found a place and an audience in modern media communication.

According to RAJAR figures in October 2022, 33 million people tuned into live radio output. On BBC Sounds there were 178 million plays of podcasts and on-demand programmes and 2.7 million plays of music mixes, demonstrating the continued expansion of radio content across media platforms (BBC, 2022b).

The specialised and institutionalised nature of media production

To cater for the range of audiences, each radio station, including both commercial and public service broadcasters, has a distinct profile that is demonstrated through, for example, the content, presenters and mode of address. Some presenters become synonymous with the profile of the station, for example Nick Robinson and Mishal Husain from the *Today* programme for Radio 4 and Greg James, Radio 1. Concern is often expressed when a popular presenter who is a significant part of the BBC branding leaves a station, for example the departure of Radio 2's Ken Bruce after 31 years for rival commercial station Greatest Hits Radio. Audiences have clear expectations of what they will get when they listen to a particular radio station; this has been built up over time and becomes part of the branding of the station.

The significance of economic factors, including commercial and not-for-profit public funding, to media industries and their products

For radio, just as for any other media form, the nature of the funding and other economic factors has an impact upon what is produced. Radio, unlike many other forms, has a range of different formats and funding profiles:

- **The BBC**: a public service broadcaster. In 2022, according to the BBC Annual Report (BBC, 2022), there were ten wider radio networks, two national radio services in each of Scotland, Wales and Northern Ireland, and 39 local radio stations.
- **National commercial radio stations**.
- **National brands**: a major national commercial radio operator is Bauer Media, which launched a new radio brand in June 2018. Hits Radio is a new station for Bauer, which also owns market-leading networks Absolute Radio, Magic Radio and KISS. Hits Radio became the first national commercial station to broadcast outside of London, a major economic decision for the company.

  The group managing director of Bauer Radio, Dee Ford, highlighted the importance of targeting the right audience in order to ensure economic success:

  > *Hits Radio has been informed by audience insight, which combined with our talented programming instinct unearthed a need for a fresh, exciting national radio brand.* (Bauer, 2018)

- **Independent local radio.**
- **Community radio.**
- **Hospital radio.**

As can be seen by the logo for Hits Radio, the distinctive identity of each station will be communicated through the content, the presenters and the marketing devices employed. Audiences will then know what to expect from a particular station and often become loyal listeners to a station or even to a particular presenter.

Link

Pages 83–85 of the Year 1 book give more information on the radio industry, which is summarised briefly in this section.

Quickfire 3.27

Why do people still continue to listen to radio?

Stretch and Challenge 3.17

Conduct some independent research into the popularity of different radio platforms with regards to a range of audiences.

Rapid Recall 3.10

What is meant by a station profile?

Key Term

Commercial radio station
A station that generates revenue through advertising and sponsorship. This is particularly true of local commercial stations that will provide a platform for local business advertising.

Rapid Recall 3.11

Give an example of a national commercial radio station.

Hits Radio is the fourth station for the Bauer Media company.

Radio content is now available across a range of platforms.

Quickfire 3.28

How has the radio form adapted to technological change?

Key Term

Royal Charter
This initially established the BBC and is its constitutional basis. Until 2016 it was reviewed before renewal, every ten years, by the government. Since 2016 it is every 11 years. The Charter sets out the public purpose of the BBC, guarantees its independence and outlines the duties of the BBC Trust.

Key Figure

Lord Reith
He was the founder of the BBC in 1922 and became the first General Manager of the British Broadcasting Corporation. He created the pattern for public service broadcasting that we see today in Britain.

The relationship of recent technological change and media production, distribution and circulation

Radio, similar to other media forms, has developed as a result of changes in technology. These changes have facilitated the distribution and circulation of radio products. Online media platforms have become particularly important in the distribution and circulation of media content nationally and also for a wider global audience. Radio programmes can now be accessed through a range of digital and online platforms, for example BBC Sounds, apps and podcasts, giving audiences a range of listening opportunities to suit their lifestyle. There were 1.54 billion UK plays of radio, music and podcasts on BBC Sounds in 2021/2022, up 23% on the previous year (*BBC Annual Report 2021/22*). The advent of Digital Audio Broadcasting (DAB), a way of broadcasting digitally rather than through an analogue signal, has improved sound quality and dramatically improved the problems with interference and reception, making listening to the radio a more pleasurable experience.

Set Product Industry Focus: The BBC

The significance of patterns of ownership and control, including conglomerate ownership, vertical integration and diversification

The BBC is a public service broadcaster whose output spans across national and local services. In addition, the BBC World Service broadcasts globally in over 28 languages. The advances in digital technology have ensured the continued expansion of the BBC Radio network.

The BBC does not carry advertising and at the time of writing is funded by the licence fee, giving it some freedom from competition and allowing it to produce programmes to target a range of audiences across its channels and digital platforms, not just the mainstream. Every 11 years the government sets out its vision for the BBC in the **Royal Charter**. The aim of the BBC Royal Charter of 2016 was to reinvent public service broadcasting for a new generation. The BBC announced a new mission that it would serve audiences with impartial, high-quality and distinctive content and services in order to educate and entertain the public (BBC, 2016).

This echoes the aim of **Lord Reith**, the founder of the BBC, who first said that the role of a public broadcaster was to inform, educate and entertain. Part of the 2016 mission statement included the need to reach a younger audience.

How did the BBC spend its money 2021/2022?

Television	Radio
BBC One £1.2 million	Radio 1 £36 million
BBC Two £327 million	Radio 2 £47 million
BBC Four £22 million	Radio 3 £35 million
CBBC and CBeebies £98 million	Radio 4 £85 million
	Radio 5 Live £50 million

Source: www.statista.com

Quickfire 3.29

Why do you think more money is spent on Radio 4 than the other radio stations?

In response to the new Charter in 2016, the BBC and its Director-General Tony Hall set out their mission to inform, educate and entertain in a speech to staff, which can be read at https://www.bbc.co.uk/mediacentre/speeches/2017/tony-hall-ny-message.

However, there was some controversy over the 2016 Charter as there was seen by many to be government interference and threatened the loss of the publicly funded and autonomous nature of the BBC.

Every year the BBC publishes a report on its performance. The main points underpinning recent BBC Annual Reports are:

- To provide impartial news and information to help people understand and engage with the world around them.
- To support learning for all ages.
- To show the most creative, highest quality and distinctive output and services.
- To reflect, represent and serve the direct communities of all the UK's nations and regions, and in doing so support the creative economy across the UK.
- To reflect the UK, its culture and values to the world.

The role and funding of the BBC continues to be debated; in a world where fewer people watch live television the licence fee is seen by many to be an outdated economic concept. However, many people are supportive of the BBC as an impartial broadcaster that is free from commercial constraints and is there to provide a 'public service'. In 2022 the current Conservative government froze the licence fee at £159 for two years. The licence fee makes up a major part of the BBC's income and in exchange the BBC must provide public service broadcasting. After the announcement of the licence fee freeze and the statement from the then Culture Secretary Nadine Dorries, who inferred that the licence fee would be scrapped, many celebrities voiced their support for the BBC and for the licence fee which amounts to 43p a day, citing the wealth of content available:

> *I'm often struck by how many who say they don't consume BBC output in fact do, in one form or another – the FA Cup, local radio, CBeebies, online, the news etc. – and it costs them per day about an eighth of the cost of a cappuccino at Costa. I think that's good value.* (Richard Coles, Twitter)

In its 2021/2022 Annual Report the BBC stated that there was an opportunity, in the highly competitive market of today, for the BBC to secure world-class public service content and services that are freely available and for the good of all.

The BBC World Service is a global provider of radio content.

Stretch and Challenge 3.18

Read a defence of the BBC and its funding here: https://www.independent.co.uk/news/media/tv-radio/bbc-reforms-is-the-new-royal-charter-ideologically-driven-meddling-or-a-clear-pathway-for-the-future-a7026781.html. Consider the arguments for and against the retention of the BBC as a public service broadcaster.

BBC Radio

The specialised and institutionalised nature of media production, distribution and circulation

BBC Radio is also governed by the Royal Charter and by the BBC mission statement as summarised above.

Marketing

It is important, as with all media forms, that the radio station markets itself to the potential audience. Radio uses some of the following strategies:

- cross-platform marketing
- websites linked to a specific station
- **BBC Taster**: allows audiences to sample new programmes and interact with the BBC
- **the schedule**: the station's output will be marketed regularly throughout the day on the radio with trailers. The schedule is also published and particular programmes may be covered in more detail in articles in the press, for example in the *Radio Times*.

Rapid Recall 3.12

Give an example of cross-platform marketing.

Link

The conventions of speech-based radio are covered in more detail, with alternative examples, on pages 84–85 of the Year 1 book.

As part of their branding, radio stations create a specialised profile that will become recognisable to their audiences and be established over time. Radio 4 is a speech-based station, which has a repertoire of recognisable elements including:

- **Presenters**: these are part of the branding of the programmes and, in some cases, the station itself. As it is a non-visual medium, the voice and mode of address of the presenter will also be synonymous with the station. In speech-led programmes, the presenter is the anchor, guiding the audience through the programme's content. Some presenters have been a part of the programmes they front for many years, for example Jenni Murray was one of the presenters of Radio 4's *Woman's Hour* for 32 years until 2020. Others move about stations and forms, for example Lauren Laverne is a television presenter who is also the voice of *Six Music*, presented *Late Night Woman's Hour* and is the host of *Desert Island Discs*.
- **Discussion-focused programmes**: the format of many speech-based programmes is a group of people talking about a series of topics or one specific topic, led by a presenter.
- **Contributors**: can be a range of different people brought onto the programme to add to its content and can include: experts in a particular topic, news correspondents and location reporters. The public can also be participants in radio programmes through phone-ins where they are encouraged to give their ideas and opinions related to events and issues.
- **Dramas**: part of Radio 4's speech-led output is its dramas, which include works from new writers, a soap opera and adaptations of novels.
- **Documentaries**: cover a range of topics and are an important feature of the Radio 4 schedule.
- **Outside broadcasts**: the versatility of the radio medium allows programmes to be easily broadcast from different national and global locations. For example, The Listening Project is a partnership between BBC Radio 4, BBC local and national radio stations, and the British Library. Since 2012 the project has invited people in different locations around the country to have their conversations on a range of topics recorded. These would then be archived in the British Library's permanent audio archive.

Quickfire 3.30

Which long-running radio soap opera is broadcast on Radio 4?

Quickfire 3.31

How does The Listening Project fit into the mission of the BBC as highlighted in its Annual Report?

Stretch and Challenge 3.19

Study Radio 4's schedule for an average week and consider the diversity of programming on offer to the audience.

Link

Page 87 of the Year 1 book provides more detailed information about the role and power of Ofcom.

Industry: Regulation

The BBC is regulated internally by the Royal Charter, which dictates the way in which the BBC is governed and funded. The 2017 Charter introduced a significant change to the governance and regulation of the BBC. A single BBC Board replaced the Executive Board and the BBC Trust. The BBC is also regulated externally by Ofcom, but it is the initial responsibility of the BBC to regulate its output to avoid intervention by the external regulator.

Industry: Set Products *Woman's Hour and Have You Heard George's Podcast?*

Woman's Hour

The specialised and institutionalised nature of media production, distribution and circulation

Woman's Hour is an interesting example of how Radio 4 has maintained and developed a long-running programme that is a key element of the Radio 4 schedule and has continued to make it relevant for a modern audience.

Consider how *Woman's Hour* fulfils the remit of the BBC to inform, educate and entertain. It is a programme that is produced with the aim of targeting a specific audience. The fact that the BBC is funded by the licence fee allows the channel greater freedom to be more creative and experimental with its programming content. The programme has low production values, no music, limited location reporting or clever editing; the focus is the engaging presenters, the calibre of the guests and their discussion topics that are explored using intellectual and specialised vocabulary. This style of programme may be deemed too risky for more commercial channels that have to attract advertisers by securing audience numbers.

Part of the continued success of *Woman's Hour* and *Have You Heard George's Podcast?* is the fact that they are both products that are distributed across different platforms, which suits the listening patterns of a broad audience including those who may be less familiar with listening to live radio programmes.

The launch of BBC Sounds is a good example of technological convergence, enabling a range of opportunities for audiences to access radio content. BBC Sounds is available on PCs, laptops, tablets and phones reflecting the changing way in which the BBC distributes its content to address developments in technology and audience consumption.

> **How media organisations maintain varieties of audiences**
> The relationship of recent technological change and media production, distribution and circulation and the impact of digitally convergent media platforms

Consider how *Woman's Hour* fits a specialised profile of Radio 4 and how it conforms to the codes and conventions of speech-led broadcasts and engages the target audience:

- **The presenters**: the programme has had many presenters over the years, but in 2020 there was a significant change when long-running presenters Jenni Murray (33 years) and Jane Garvey (13 years) left to be replaced by Emma Barnett and Anita Rani, clearly signalling that the BBC intended to broaden the audience for the programme by including younger presenters from more diverse backgrounds.
- **Discussion**: the whole premise of the programme is based on discussion around a particular topic. While the audience is largely female, the topics are not solely based around female experiences but aim to offer a female perspective on a range of issues that will interest a broad range of listeners. Topics covered in January 2023 included *Happy Valley* and kinship care and speaking to children about Andrew Tate.
- **Contributors**: the guests and contributors reflect the focus of the programme and the highbrow style of the station, illustrating its appeal to a specialised audience. Guests in 2022/23 included Janelle Monáe, Baroness Kidron and Chantha Chandran.
- **Production and distribution**: the programme is broadcast daily at 10am for one hour, there is also an omnibus/best bits edition on a Saturday at 4pm. As has been stated earlier in this section, the distribution relates to reaching the target audience and there is no longer an assumption that the audience will be listening live at that time, there are also opportunities for audiences to access the programme on the digital platform that best suits them.

Tip

You are required to study extracts from at least two episodes of *Woman's Hour*, but it will broaden your understanding of the programme and how it reflects the BBC's ideas and ethos if you listen to other episodes and engage in independent research.

Quickfire 3.32

What can you say about *Woman's Hour* in relation to an economic context?

Anita Rani is a presenter of *Woman's Hour*.

Link

On page 87 of the Year 1 book there is a section applying Curran and Seaton's theories to *Woman's Hour*.

The ability to listen to radio programmes via podcasts and other digitally convergent platforms is of significant importance to the industry.

Named Theorists

Livingstone and Lunt
These academic theorists are specific to Year 2 of the A Level course. One of Sonia Livingstone's areas of research concerns the opportunities and risks related to the advances in digital and online technology. Peter Lunt has written on the media and public participation in popular culture and media regulation.

They have both written widely on the media and its relationship with consumers.

Key Term

Watershed
The time when it becomes permissible to broadcast programmes that are unsuitable for younger audiences. In the UK this is after 9pm.

Have You Heard George's Podcast?

How processes of production, distribution and circulation shape media products and the significance of economic factors to media industries and their products

Consider how the fact that the BBC is a public service broadcaster, funded by the licence fee, facilitates the production of programmes like *Have You Heard George's Podcast?*, which would be seen to be much more of a risk for more commercial organisations. The style of the product suggests it is more specialised, there are elements that reflect those of BBC productions, for example the use of specialised highbrow vocabulary and an expectation that audiences will be familiar with and interested in the topics covered. However, the topics covered are eclectic and experimental, illustrating the willingness of the BBC to take a risk with new and innovative content.

The podcast is a relatively new format and is different from the radio broadcast, this distribution method allows the BBC to give more autonomy and creative control to the podcaster, allowing it to experiment with themes, content and style, creating, in this case, a production that mixes music, speech and storytelling to convey ideas and messages. A product like *Have You Heard George's Podcast?*, which is a very different addition to the BBC output, also enables the BBC to fulfil one of its aims, to reflect diversity. As stated in the 2022 Annual Report, the BBC aims to ensure that the voices heard on radio reflect the diverse make-up of the BBC (www.bbc.co.uk/annualreport202122).

The podcast format is also relatively cheap to produce with low production values. The digital distribution contributes to the lower costs and, consequently, the BBC may be more willing to take chances when the economic loss will be less if the product is unsuccessful. The fact that the podcast is available across a range of different digital platforms means the reach will be broader and this will contribute to the marketing and branding of BBC content.

Applying Theory

Regulation: Livingstone and Lunt

Consider how you could apply and critically explore the following aspects of **Livingstone and Lunt**'s theory to *Woman's Hour* and *Have You Heard George's Podcast?*:

- The idea that there is an underlying struggle in recent UK regulation policy between the need to further the interests of the citizens (by offering protection from harmful or offensive material) and the need to further the interests of consumers (by ensuring choice, value for money and market competition).

BBC Television and Radio is self-regulatory in the first instance. As a media organisation it is responsible for working with production companies to ensure that it does not breach regulatory codes. The new unitary BBC Board is responsible for ensuring that the BBC fulfils its mission as set out in the 2017 Charter. The Board is accountable for all the BBC's activities. Where there are concerns the BBC has the option to give pre-programme warnings and to schedule programmes after the **watershed**. The BBC is also externally regulated by Ofcom who can act in response to audience complaints.

As a public service broadcaster, the BBC has strict guidelines about what content can be broadcast. The developments in technology mean that content is distributed across different digital platforms, this has made regulation more complex. However, the BBC's role as a self-regulator seemingly challenges Livingston and Lunt's assumption that 'new media' is harder to regulate. The BBC includes written and verbal warnings about the the language and content of *Have You Heard George's Podcast?*, illustrating that the organisation has considered audience access to the podcast and employed relevant self-regulatory measures to protect audiences.

Audiences

Radio as a form has adapted to technological change in order to ensure its survival. It is in competition for audiences with a range of forms, including the rise of streaming services Netflix and Amazon, therefore effectively targeting and maintaining its audience has never been more important (BBC, 2022).

Radio and podcasts have retained an appeal for audiences for the following reasons:

- They are both undemanding forms, they do not ask for complete concentration from listeners, allowing them to do other things while listening, for example driving.
- They distribute content on other platforms to broaden access to the content. In 2021/22 on BBC Sounds there were 11.54 billion plays of radio, music and podcasts, this was an increase of 23% on 2020/21. Seven hundred million hours of content were played through Sounds (BBC, 2022).
- Radio is referred to as a companion medium because of its intimacy with audiences. Many programmes also offer opportunities for the audience to interact. The form also encourages intimacy, with the direct mode of address adopted.

The Set Products: *Woman's Hour*

Audiences: Social and Cultural Context

It is important to consider the role of *Woman's Hour* in reflecting the changing roles of women in the UK over the past 70 years. *Woman's Hour* was originally broadcast in the 1940s, so it is relevant to consider the role of the programme in documenting the evolving place of women in society and the demands of this audience to have programmes on both radio and television that cater for their interests and concerns. Some audiences may question the need to produce a programme with a specific audience of women. The continued production of *Woman's Hour* and the change in presenters designed to reach an even broader audience, sends a positive message to listeners about how the BBC is actively considering the way in which women are represented by the institution.

> How audiences are grouped and categorised by media industries, including by age, gender and social class, as well as by lifestyle and taste

- *Woman's Hour* is a good example of how a media product and organisation can group an audience. This makes the programme easier to market for the BBC as the target audience is clearly defined. The audience group is suggested by the programme's content, reflecting gender, age, lifestyle and taste. The programme appeals to a specialised audience and as such contributes to the aim of the BBC to cater for diverse audiences.
- In one week in February 2023, the topics covered included: conditions in women's prisons, Beyoncé, tidying vs mess, women playing male roles in Shakespeare, and alcohol, sexual assault and recall, highlighting the aim of the programme to target a broad female audience.

Link

Page 81 in the Year 1 book gives more information about the role of Ofcom.

Listening to the radio can fit into the daily routine of the audience.

Rapid Recall 3.13

Why is the radio form sometimes called the blind medium?

Rapid Recall 3.14

What is audio streaming and what impact has it had on the radio audience?

Link

Pages 90–91 of the Year 1 book explore how these two set products appeal to audiences.

Quickfire 3.33

How does *Woman's Hour* reflect social and cultural contexts?

Key Term

BBC World Service
This is the largest international broadcaster, distributing content in over 40 languages.

- There is an expectation that the female listener will have a historical understanding or a wish to learn about how women's roles have changed since the 1950s and to consider contemporary events and issues from a female perspective. There is also an assumption that the women listening are largely professional and independent and have a particular set of values.
- The contributors, the presenter and the topics therefore clearly target the middle class, intelligent, female audience. However, men also feature in the programme and male listeners regularly respond to the topics covered.
- The live programme is one hour long and is focused totally on discussion of key topics of interest to the target audience. This demands a level of concentration and interest in the topics and guests that will sustain the listener for the duration of the programme, suggesting the audience profile.

How specialised audiences can be reached, both on a national and global scale, through different media technologies and platforms

- BBC Radio as a media organisation has historically provided content for national and global audiences, the latter through the BBC World Service. This service has taken advantage of developments in technology and now has a website, podcasts, newsletters and a Facebook page.
- Radio content generally is now easily distributed globally due to the progress of digital technology. Radio continues to be a portable medium and can be accessed in a range of locations via a series of digital platforms. The diverse lifestyles of the *Woman's Hour* audience are catered for by the ability to access content across a range of digital platforms to suit their needs. Some audiences will loyally listen to the daily programme, this allows them to interact directly through social media platforms and be a part of the programme's community. Others will 'catch-up', selecting the episodes that match their interests and concerns. Audiences can subscribe to the podcast *Woman's Hour Daily* to catch-up on episodes and be notified when new ones are released. The programme also has its own website offering additional linked content that can be accessed by a national and global audience.
- The choice of Emma Barnett and Anita Rani as the main presenters has particular resonance for the target audience. Their status and persona, established through other media products, means that their personalities are integral to the programme and its target audience. Both women have a large Twitter following and a fanbase including young aspirational women, this broadens the national and global reach of the programme. Emma Barnett won Best Speech Presenter for *Woman's Hour* at the Audio and Radio Industry Awards in 2022. Mohit Bakaya, Controller of Radio 4, said of the programme and Anita Rani's appointment: '*I want Radio 4 to continue to seek ways to better reflect and be relevant to the audience across the UK, and* Woman's Hour *has a special role in this*' (RadioToday, 2021).

The Set Products: *Have You Heard George's Podcast?*

Audiences: Social and Cultural Context

Issues of diversity and misrepresentation of ethnic minority groups have become a significant talking point in contemporary society. In this podcast George the Poet covers social and cultural issues across the podcast 'chapters' reflecting the concerns of black communities. One event covered is the Grenfell Tower fire of 2017 which became a focal point of the debate around society's treatment of vulnerable social groups.

How specialised audiences can be reached, both on a national and global scale, through different media technologies and platforms

- Podcasts have been a major development in distributing content to specialised audiences. Minority groups who have traditionally been excluded from mainstream radio have used podcasts to find a voice. George's unique and experimental approach and his evocation of young black British life might never have been commissioned to appear in a conventional radio schedule.
- Podcasts are also available across a range of platforms broadening the access for a range of audiences and their needs. The podcast format also allows broadcasters and individuals to reach smaller more niche audiences, an opportunity that is not always available on other formats where there are economic constraints and the aim is to cater for a wider audience. Sean Glynn from the podcast company Novel asserted that while the big, award-winning podcasts continue to be popular, there is a growing demand for 'better-researched', even 'niche' content and that authenticity is key to success. Kate Taylor, the founder of Feast Collective that supports freelance podcasters stated that niche content is a market strength and that people want to make their own specialised shows (*Observer*, 2023).
- While there is not usually an interactive element in podcasts as there is with many conventional radio programmes, George has addressed this by creating Common Ground, a social media forum where audiences can interact with the podcaster and respond to the issues covered in the podcasts, which takes them:

> *on a journey where we can listen, share, and understand each other. We'll then play these thoughts back to you in visual form and show you what unites us.* (Common Ground, 2021)

How audiences are grouped and categorised by media industries, including by age, gender and social class, as well as by lifestyle and taste

- The content of *Have You Heard George's Podcast?* suggests that it is targeting specific audiences with an interest in the topics covered and the particular eclectic style of delivery.
- One of the key aims of the BBC as an organisation is to cater for more diverse audiences. Radio 5 Live's target audience are middle-aged ABC1/C2DE. Broadcasting the podcast might be seen as an attempt to diversify Radio 5 Live's audience and attract younger listeners through the use of the conventions of talk radio.
- The topics covered combine personal introspection and more global issues suggesting the possible target audience and fulfilling the BBC remit to inform, educate and entertain.

Applying Theory

'End of Audience' Theory: Clay Shirky

Shirky (2009) suggested that the internet and digital technologies have had a profound effect on the relations between media and individuals. In his theory he puts forward the idea that audiences have changed as the ways in which they can access media products have revolutionised access and ability to interact with and respond to media products.

Consider how advances in digital technologies, as outlined by Shirky, have allowed radio and podcasts to exist as viable platforms with a distinct relationship with their listeners.

Stretch and Challenge 3.20

To broaden your understanding of *Woman's Hour* **or** *Have You Heard George's Podcast?* and their audience, research the podcasts and the guests from previous editions of the programmes.

Quickfire 3.34

Why are Emma Barnett and Anita Rani suitable presenters for *Woman's Hour*?

Quickfire 3.35

Why is the podcast a suitable format for *Have You Heard George's Podcast?*

Link

Page 89 of the Year 1 book considers the application of Stuart Hall's reception theory to *Woman's Hour* and *Have You Hear George's Podcast?*

Radio can be listened to across a range of digital platforms.

Rapid Recall 3.15

What is meant by convergence?

Link

The set film product *Black Panther* is covered in detail in the Year 1 book.

Quickfire 3.36

What extracts from the films would help to exemplify elements of the film industry?

Tip

In Section B of the examination you will be required to demonstrate your knowledge and understanding of key aspects of the film industry. The lower mark questions may ask you to specifically refer to factual information about the industry.

Rapid Recall 3.16

Give an example of an element of the film that indicates high production values.

Investigating the Set Forms and Products: Film

As you will be aware from your study of this form in Year 1, film is studied in relation to industry only. You will study the two film set products, exploring the convergence of media platforms and technologies.

In Year 1 you will have studied the film *Black Panther*, an example of a high-concept mainstream film. In order to study contrasting aspects of the film industry, the Year 2 set product is *I, Daniel Blake* which is an independent production. In order to further develop your understanding of the film industry and its marketing strategies you are required to study:

- at least one trailer for each film
- at least one poster for each film
- online marketing where relevant
- selected extracts from each film that can be used to exempify elements of the film industry in relation to this product.

For both the set products it is important to explore a range of industry elements including:

- how processes of production, distribution and circulation shape the film products
- the significance of economic factors to the films
- the effect of individual producers on the way in which the film is created and its distribution and circulation
- how global and national audiences are maintained through marketing
- the regulatory framework of the film industry.

The different types of production contexts evident in the film industry are illustrated through the two set products. In your study of *Black Panther* in Year 1 you will have established the key indicators of a mainstream film, which include:

- high production values
- high-profile stars often associated with the film genre
- elements that can be used in the marketing of the film and become part of the film's branding, for example the soundtrack and the logo
- visually attractive elements, for example sets and special effects
- a narrative that can be easily marketed and is indicative of the genre
- characters that are stereotypical of the genre, including key, recognisable protagonists.

***Black Panther* is an example of a mainstream film with high production values.**

Economic contexts

The significance of patterns of ownership and control, including conglomerate ownership, vertical integration and diversification

The different production contexts apparent in the film industry are largely defined by financial concerns. Mainstream, high-concept films have a greater level of funding as they are produced by the major film studios that are media conglomerates. Their financial strength allows them to invest in big projects. Major production companies often operate through **vertical integration** and **horizontal integration**, which gives them more control in the production, promotion and distribution of the films.

Independent Films

As you will have explored in Year 1 of the course, the production and economic contexts of independent films are different. An independent film:

- is usually made outside the financial and artistic control of a major film company
- is privately created and financed
- is made by smaller film companies or individual producers with a lower budget. This is often evident through the absence of high-profile stars and the use of everyday settings
- is defined by a distinguishable style often related to the genre, the social message or the filmmaker
- may have a different filming style, for example the use of handheld cameras and ambient lighting to establish realism and the credibility of the film's themes
- often focuses on the narrative related to the theme, which is used in the marketing material because the usually unknown actors are not marketable
- may have a different distribution model, for example viral and word-of-mouth marketing, screenings at smaller, independent cinemas and a shorter run.

Set Product: *I, Daniel Blake*

This is the second set film product at the time of writing. The requirement is that you explore the film in relation to its industry context; there is no requirement to engage in textual analysis of the actual film in this section, as you will not be assessed on this in Section B of the examination.

Industry Context

I, Daniel Blake is an independent film in the **socialist realist genre**. It was directed by Ken Loach, who has long been associated with this film genre. One of the most famous and influential television plays he directed was *Cathy Come Home*, a drama focusing on the story of a young mother, a victim of a social system that breaks up her marriage, takes away her children and leaves her homeless. *Cathy Come Home* resulted in a parliamentary debate and raised awareness of homelessness in a pre-welfare state society. Similarly, several years on, *I, Daniel Blake* shocked its audience and brought about discussion related to the need for social change.

Key Figure

BFI
The British Film Institute (BFI) is the UK's leading organisation for film and moving image and curates the world's largest film and television archive. It delivers UK and global moving image products through an extensive and diverse programme and a range of festivals throughout the year. Find out more about the organisation here: https://www.bfi.org.uk/about-bfi.

Key Terms

Vertical integration
In terms of the film industry, this refers to a film company that owns other companies across different stages of the process, for example a production company that owns a distributor. This facilitates their ability to distribute and exhibit their films.

Horizontal integration
When different companies producing and selling similar products join together.

Social realist genre
Refers to films that give an indication of what life is really like. Often explore wider social issues through the creation of emotional personal stories.

Link

Pages 92–94 of the Year 1 book have information on distribution and regulation in the film industry.

Rapid Recall 3.17

What is meant by a media conglomerate?

Rapid Recall 3.18

What is word-of-mouth marketing?

Stretch and Challenge 3.21

Engage in research into the social realist genre and its place in the history of the film industry. The **BFI** has a useful brief history placing Ken Loach in the overview of the genre: 'Social Realism', BFI (2014).

Quickfire 3.37

Why would the BFI fund *I, Daniel Blake*?

Stretch and Challenge 3.22

Research the BFI and its support for independent filmmakers: www.bfi.org.uk.

Key Terms

Grassroots campaign
A marketing strategy that targets a smaller, niche group, often a particular community, in the hope that they will spread the word to a broader audience.

Disruptive-display advertising
Advertising content that appears in unexpected places, for example in the plug of a daily newspaper, which arrests attention because it challenges expectations of what is typical.

Stretch and Challenge 3.23

Read this article in the *Daily Mirror* about the social importance of *I, Daniel Blake*, https://www.mirror.co.uk/lifestyle/going-out/film/9-reasons-i-daniel-blake-8971379.

The significance of economic factors to media industries and their products

I, Daniel Blake is a UK/French production, which was also funded by BBC Films and the BFI awarding National Lottery funding. This type of multi-company financial support is a typical model for independent film productions. The film became Ken Loach's largest grossing film, making over $8 million and gaining much critical acclaim including winning the Palme D'Or at Cannes. It was also nominated for several BAFTAs. The remits of both the BFI and the BBC as a public service broadcaster are committed to finding and developing new talent and collaborating with established directors and writers.

BBC Films

This is the feature-making branch of the BBC, which is at the forefront of independent filmmaking in the UK. It co-produces approximately 12 films a year. In 2023 these included, *Aftersun* with Oscar nominated Paul Mescal, *Triangle of Sadness* and *The Lost King*.

How processes of production, distribution and circulation shape media products

The distribution company for *I, Daniel Blake* was eOne, an independent Canadian company that had previous success with *The BFG* (2016, Spielberg) and *The Girl On the Train* (2016, Taylor). The marketing strategy for *I, Daniel Blake* was devised by British executive Alex Hamilton, who initially saw the film at Cannes.

Hamilton decided to go with a **grassroots campaign** and with this in mind he opted for Newcastle instead of London for the premiere of the film. eOne organised several community screenings to ensure maximum reach in the region.

eOne also worked with Trinity Mirror and Zenith to promote the film, gaining the producers an estimated £15 million in editorial campaign value.

In the *Daily Mirror*, Daniel Blake the character was given a one-off column, 'My Britain', based on the *Daily Mirror*'s weekly series 'Real Britain', dealing with social issues dealt with in the film that also affect the left-wing readership. The newspaper carried a plug on its front page asking readers for their attention and to look at Daniel Blake's column (see https://www.thepaperboy.com/uk/daily-mirror/front-pages-today.cfm?frontpage=48231).

Disruptive-display advertising, including masthead and front cover takeovers, were also used across the Trinity titles and platforms.

Trinity Mirror was approached by eOne to collaborate in the marketing of the film. The company felt that there were clear links between the narrative and themes of the film and the ideology of the *Daily Mirror*. Trinity Mirror stated that their creative solution was to give Daniel Blake the voice that he doesn't have in the story by handing over their platforms to him (cited in Newsworks, 2015a)

David Johns, who played Daniel Blake, delivers a speech during the 'Real Britain' meeting co-organised by the *Daily Mirror*.

As a result of this marketing campaign, 59% of readers recalled seeing the feature and 57% said it made them want to go and see the film (Newsworks, 2015a).

The distribution company employed other innovative strategies to draw the attention of audiences to the film and its pertinent themes. The actors stood outside the West End premiere holding placards to raise awareness of the issues covered in the film. The coverage of this in the press helped to market *I, Daniel Blake* to a wider audience.

The film was also shaped by the way in which it was produced. It is a low-budget social realist film with low production values.

It was filmed on location in Newcastle in real settings, for example the job centre, the food bank and the hospital. The understated style is typical of Loach and the use of real locations establishes the credibility of the characters and their narrative.

Some of the extras in the job centres were the actual people who work there. All the actors were largely unknown and, as is typical of independent films, the product was sold on the strength of its narrative and the issues it addresses – in this case the flaws in the benefit system and the effect of this on the individual. There is no use of special effects and no soundtrack, reinforcing verisimilitude.

As part of your study of this film and how it highlights aspects of the film industry, you will be required to study the trailer, the poster and the website that are all part of the marketing campaign. The trailer establishes the film as an independent social realist film from the start, watch the *I, Daniel Blake* official trailer https://www.youtube.com/watch?v=ahWgxw9E_h4. The aim of any trailer is to hook the audience, establish an interest and in so doing persuade them to come and see the film. The trailer for *I, Daniel Blake* does this by:

- Establishing the credibility and critical success of the film through shots of awards and the funding partners of the BBC and BFI.
- Using on-screen graphics to suggest to the audience that 'pleasure' is to be gained by watching the film and to give clues to the narrative.
- Using marks of quality, for example the director Ken Loach, to suggest the artistic validity of the film. Audiences who know Loach's previous work will know what to expect.
- Enigma codes are established to hook the audience.
- The use of on-screen graphics to establish the narrative and themes of the film.
- The selection and construction of visual codes, including clothing and expression, reinforce the film's place in the social realist sub-genre.
- Fade to black editing, the use of ambient lighting and the music creates the mood and pace of the film.
- The characters and their story are introduced and the audience are encouraged to identify with them. Their relationship is intriguing as it develops through the trailer, and the empathy established between the characters and the audience encourages them to watch the film in order to find out more.
- The final shots of the trailer establish a sense of community and hope for the outcome that may appeal to an audience as they may be relatable to many.

The style of the writing on the wall at the end of the trailer becomes part of the branding of the film and appears on other marketing materials, for example the film posters. These are simple in their execution and reinforce the 'everyman' role of the central character. His raised fist is a gesture of defiance reflecting his fight against the system. The wall behind him in the poster is populated with quotes from reviews of the film, with the emotional 'pleasures' the audience will experience higlighted in red. View the trailer and the poster here: https://www.imdb.com/title/tt5168192/.

Quickfire 3.38

Why was the disruptive-display advertising used in the *Daily Mirror* effective for this particular film?

Tip

While there is no requirement to study the actual film as a media product, you will be expected to have explored how the trailer, as part of the film's distribution strategy, markets the film.

Quickfire 3.39

How might the on-screen graphics in the trailer help to market the film?

Quickfire 3.40

What is the importance to the industry of directors and producers such as Ken Loach?

Stretch and Challenge 3.24

Research the BBC Film website and other websites used in the marketing of the film to broaden your understanding of how this film was distributed.

Stretch and Challenge 3.25

Read Simon Hattenstone's 2016 interview: 'Ken Loach: "If You're Not Angry, What Kind of Person are You?"' in the *Guardian* online to gain a greater understanding of Ken Loach and his impact as an individual producer.

The effect of individual producers on media industries

It is important to consider the role of Ken Loach in the success of *I, Daniel Blake*. He is an established director and cinema practitioner known for his social realist films, which have had an impact upon audiences and the social systems of the time. Loach has been directing films in this genre since the 1960s and could be said to be responsible for the continued existence of this sub-genre. As a result, his status in the film industry may have helped to secure funding for the film. Although Ken Loach is a well-known and successful figure within the film industry, his films have always sought to challenge social ills and, in tackling difficult themes and issues, what he produces belongs firmly in the independent film genre in its style and subject matter. He has seemingly not been tempted to become more mainstream.

His longevity and credibility within the industry means that he can make films that may not have secured the funding if pitched by other lesser-known directors. Therefore, as an individual producer he is seen as an important force within the industry. He is also important in the marketing of the film as he is recognisable and during the launch he appeared on news and current affairs programmes and was interviewed in newspapers.

As a socialist and political activist himself, Loach's film embodies a left-wing political message and his decision to set the film in the North East, focusing on characters struggling with poverty, reinforces his political and social message. This message resonated around the country, as it was seen to represent the very real situation of many people living in the UK today. Loach is an ally of Jeremy Corbyn, Leader of the Labour Party at the time and made a promotional video documenting his policies and highlighting the hopes of his supporters.

Members of the Unite Union staged a 'We Are All Daniel Blake' protest, outside West London job centres in November 2016, against benefit sanctions and welfare cuts (Unite, 2016).

Applying Theory

Power and Media Industries: Curran and Seaton

This film, the trailer and the marketing material in its production and distribution would appear in some way to challenge Curran and Seaton's (2009) findings, which state that the majority of companies are driven by the logic of profit and power. The production model of this film would contradict this viewpoint. The film is low budget with low production values, the aim is the communication of a social message rather than pure financial gain, which came as an unpredicted bonus.

Curran and Seaton's further assertion that variety, creativity and quality are inhibited by media concentration is also challenged by the fact that this film was able to be produced in the contemporary film industry. The film does prove the theorists' claim that more socially diverse patterns of ownership create the conditions for other varied and adventurous media productions – the funding opportunities available for the film from the BBC and the BFI, and the fact that it is a UK, French and Belgium co-production, give the producers more artistic freedom to create a film that is not necessarily constrained by the need for commercial success.

Contexts: Social and Political

As with many of his other films, in *I, Daniel Blake* Ken Loach deals with social and political issues within the narrative of the film, including the welfare system, benefits, the Work Capability Assessment, poverty and homelessness. The film very clearly reflects the time in which it was made and makes obvious social and political comment, challenging government policies and clearly apportioning blame. The trailer claims the film as of moving relevance and Daniel Blake himself states how humiliating his job is having to look for non-existent jobs.

Investigating the Set Forms and Products: The Newspaper Industry

You will be aware from your Year 1 work that newspapers as a form are set products for Component 1 Sections A and B and as such are studied in relation to all aspects of the theoretical framework: Media Language, Representation, Media Industries and Audiences. This section will focus on industry and audience in relation to the A Level/ Year 2 content.

Despite the changing face of the print press and movement to digital platforms, a range of newspaper titles is still produced daily in the UK. However, changes have been made that reflect the development of the newspaper industry. The existing newspaper titles highlight different styles and the varied political and cultural perspectives. Newspapers are being forced to make, at times, dramatic changes to the way in which they are produced and distributed in order to remain economically viable. For example, in 2018 the *Guardian* re-launched as a tabloid having previously moved from a broadsheet to a Berliner in size. This involved a redesign and a reduction of the 'extras' offered as a part of the newspaper's daily content. The aim was that the move would make substantial savings and ensure the long-term future of the print newspaper.

Press Ownership 2023

The significance of patterns of ownership and control, including conglomerate ownership, vertical integration and diversification

Title	Owner	Political affiliation
Daily Telegraph *Sunday Telegraph*	Telegraph Media Group, a subsidiary of Press Holdings owned by the Barclay brothers	**Centre-right**/Conservative
The Times/Sunday Times *Sun/Sun on Sunday*	News UK: CEO Rupert Murdoch	Centre-right/Conservative Right-wing/Conservative
Guardian *Observer*	Scott Trust: Guardian Media Group	**Centre-left**/Labour

(continued)

Rapid Recall 3.19

What is the focus of study for the newspaper products in Section B of Component 1?

Quickfire 3.41

Why did the *Guardian* made these changes? What does it tell us about the industry?

Stretch and Challenge 3.26

For more on the redesign read https://www.theguardian.com/gnm-press-office/2018/jan/14/guardianand-observer-launch-new-tabloid-format-and-digital-redesign.

Key Terms

Centre-right
Describes a person, organisation or political party that has political views which are closer to capitalism and conservatism, but are not as extreme as some political viewpoints and therefore closer to the centre.

Centre-left
Describes a person, organisation or political party that has political views which are closer to socialism than to capitalism and leans to the left.

Rapid Recall 3.20

What are some of the advantages of online newspaper sites?

Tip

It is important to consider the relevant contexts when studying the set products.

Quickfire 3.42

What conclusions can you draw about the newspaper industry from this grid?

Quickfire 3.43

What does the ownership of any newspaper tell us about the industry?

Stretch and Challenge 3.27

Read the full report on 'Changing news habits and attitudes of younger audiences' here: https://reutersinstitute.politics.ox.ac.uk/digital-news-report/2022/young-audiences-news-media.

Key Term

Reuters
An international, independent news agency formed in 1850. It sells news, including written stories, photographs and video footage, to media industries. Clients pay a subscription which entitles them to use Reuter's news stories, pictures or video footage in their papers, magazines, websites or news bulletins.

Title	Owner	Political affiliation
Daily Mail/Mail on Sunday *Metro* and *i News*	DMG Media	Right-wing/Conservative Centrist/neutral
Daily Mirror/Sunday Mirror/Sunday People	Reach plc	Left-wing/Labour
Daily Express/Sunday Express *Sunday Star*	Reach plc	Right-wing/Conservative

Source: Adapted from newspaper websites

Social and Cultural Context: Newspapers and Technological Change

The impact of digitally convergent media platforms on media production, distribution and circulation, including individual producers

Newspapers and the way in which they gather and distribute news have adapted and changed in order to reflect changes in society. All national newspapers now also have an online presence, the content of which is available through apps and social media platforms. The readership of print titles continues to fall as audiences opt for the more portable, regularly updated digital platforms. This has had a direct impact upon advertising revenue, as big advertisers have moved out of print and into more lucrative social media platforms.

Another social and cultural change is the way in which audiences access news and current affairs, which generally differ according to age. Younger people who are digital natives rely for their news on digital and social media, and do not tend to develop the same loyalty to news brands as older audiences. Twitter, Instagram and TikTok have grown as platforms through which news is disseminated and there has been a cultural shift in the way that news events are discussed and debated. This is illustrated in the fact that politicians regularly air their thoughts and views on global issues through Twitter. Use of TikTok for accessing news content increased fivefold among 18–24 year olds between 2020–2022 according to a Reuters report. The report also discovered that many younger people avoid the news altogether as they do not trust the content available.

Producing content for online platforms is also advantageous for newspapers, as this is cheaper to produce and distribute than the print version and the newspapers' multi-media and interactive content attracts a broader audience, some of whom may reject the print form as it does not suit their lifestyle. In this way, social context has directly affected the newspaper industry.

How processes of production, distribution and circulation shape media products

Some critics are unhappy about the role social media has taken in the distribution of news and fear that this poses a threat to more credible forms of journalism (see, e.g., Humphrys, 2018).

Newspapers also use a range of methods to gather their news. This may include using their own journalists and accessing stories from the more traditional news sites, for example **Reuters**.

However, it is increasingly the case that newspapers also rely on the ordinary person submitting their images and stories. The ease with which people can become producers of the news has contributed to the rise in citizen journalism. Traditional journalism is characterised by the fact that it is a one-way broadcast from the news organisation to the individual reader/viewer/listener. In this case, it is the responsibility of the editor and journalists to be the gatekeepers, validating the news selected, deciding what is newsworthy and what their audience need to know. With the less traditional user-generated content, everyone can be a prosumer.

Advances in technology mean that anyone can report on an event as it happens.

Characteristics of Citizen Journalism

- Citizen journalists have well-established links to a range of social media platforms to facilitate the rapid dissemination of information.
- Due to improvements in technology, mobile phones allow the production of high-quality images and video footage.
- There is quick access to the internet.
- The stories can be subjective and emotional, particularly as citizen journalists are often witnesses of events as they happen and unfold. For example, the first images from the terrorist attack on the Ariana Grande concert in Manchester were from mobile phones.
- The stories covered by citizen journalists are usually related to breaking news.
- The stories are produced by amateurs, not professionals, but are accepted in their raw form by audiences because of their immediacy.
- However, citizen journalists can sometimes be responsible for the wide dissemination of fake news stories because there is no responsibility for validating the stories as would be the practice in a news organisation.

The rise in the instances of content provided by citizen journalists also highlights examples of **media democracy**. The power is seen to be shifting from the big news agencies to smaller groups and, indeed, individuals. This transfer of power within the newspaper industry gives an opportunity for everyone to produce news content. In some instances of citizen journalism, for example the reporting of elections, injustices have been revealed and the story has provided evidence of systemic problems that may have otherwise been covered up.

Tip

Remember that the focus of this section is industry and audience. You will not be expected to engage in textual analysis of your chosen example of the newspaper set product, instead you will be required to demonstrate your understanding of the industry and audience, using the example of the set newspaper to support your points.

Rapid Recall 3.21

What is a gatekeeper?

Key Term

Media democracy
Refers to the way in which developments in technology have empowered citizens and promoted democratic ideals. Technology has given individuals the opportunity to participate in the media and journalism by creating content that allows them to report on current affairs and express opinions.

Quickfire 3.44

What are some of the issues associated with citizen journalism?

Quickfire 3.45

Give an example of how citizen journalism might reveal injustices or provide evidence.

Stretch and Challenge 3.28

Watch the short video that can be found on the TED website, called 'How Social Media Can Make History – Clay Shirky', in which Clay Shirky discusses the rise of citizen journalists and how they are shaping news content and the role of social media in the creation and distribution of news.

Critically Exploring Theory

Curran and Seaton

Some of the areas Curran and Seaton explored include:

- the idea that media is controlled by a small number of companies primarily driven by the logic of profit and power
- the idea that media concentration generally limits or inhibits variety, creativity and quality
- the idea that more socially diverse patterns of ownership help to create the conditions for more varied and adventurous media productions.

As you will have learned in Year 1 of the course, Curran and Seaton's (2009) theory is related to the relationship between media industries and power. While it can be applied to the more traditional news media, it is less appropriate as a theoretical perspective when discussing the new ways of making and distributing news. This is particularly true when considering the rise of citizen journalism:

- with regards to citizen journalism the control lies with the individual or the group
- the aim is the discussion of an issue or the highlighting of social ills rather than making a profit or establishing a power base
- the media consumers who are now producers are creative in the way that they 'speak back' to the media establishment
- the user-generated content does allow for more adventurous productions by individuals rather than organisations
- this content can also serve to reveal injustices and to provide evidence of events as they happen, so it has an immediate impact.

Industry: The Regulation of the Press

> The regulatory framework of contemporary media in the UK
> The role of regulation in global production, distribution and circulation

It has been proven in recent years that there is a fine line between ensuring the press is regulated effectively in order to protect the public from the excesses of certain elements of the industry and maintaining a free press that is able to work to investigate social wrongs.

The Leveson Inquiry was initiated in November 2012 in response to concerns about aggressive newspaper journalism, including phone-hacking. Because of the initial investigation into such practices, the *News of the World* was closed. As a result of the findings from his inquiry, Lord Justice Leveson put forward a range of proposals for regulating the press more effectively. He felt that, among other issues, there was, at times, an unhealthy relationship between politicians and the press, which meant that undue influence may shape a newspaper and its coverage of events, people and issues.

Link

There is more information about Lord Leveson and press regulation on page 102 of the Year 1 book.

The first part of the recommendations of Leveson's Inquiry considered the ethics and standards of the British press, and in 2012 he recommended a new, more objective and rigorous form of press regulation. His findings were not welcomed by some elements of the industry which feared a loss of press freedom.

Stretch and Challenge 3.29

Find on the BBC News website an article called 'Phone-hacking Trial Explained' (2014), which explains the phone-hacking scandal in more detail.

The findings of the Leveson Inquiry resulted in the closure of the tabloid newspaper the *News of the World*. Two former editors, Andy Coulson and Rebekah Brooks (a close friend of David Cameron, Prime Minister at the time), were charged with conspiracy to intercept mobile voicemails.

In 2014 the Independent Press Standards Organisation (IPSO) was established as one option of press regulation. It was seen to be controversial as there was no legal requirement for newspapers to be part of this organisation and, indeed, some newspapers, for example the *Guardian*, that were concerned about the restrictions which may be enforced upon them by such an organisation, continued to be self-regulatory. IPSO is seen to be anti-Leveson in terms of its opposition to the accountability he wanted to be enshrined in a new Royal Charter. IPSO is fully funded by the newspaper industry and is not backed by the government or by Royal Charter.

In 2016, a second regulatory body was formed: IMPRESS. This organisation was granted a Royal Charter and is fully compliant with the terms of the Leveson Inquiry. IMPRESS is the first officially recognised press regulator. However, most newspapers have continued to be members of IPSO, as they feel this gives them more journalistic freedom. Some are still self-regulatory. Impress states that it is a champion for news that can be trusted:

> *We are here to make sure news providers can publish with integrity; and the public can engage in an ever-changing media landscape with confidence.*
> (IMPRESS, 2023)

In 2017, Theresa May's Conservative government decided not to implement Part 2 of Lord Leveson's recommendations, which had a specific focus on police and press corruption, including the relationship between politicians and the press. This was greeted with disappointment from those who had campaigned for the implementation of the second stage, including cross-party politicians and the campaign group 'Hacked Off'.

'Hacked Off' is a pressure group that was established in 2011 in response to the phone-hacking revelations. It has been vocal in its campaigning for greater press regulation and accountability, fronted by celebrities, including Hugh Grant who was a victim of phone-hacking. Read more about the 'Hacked Off' campaign here: www.hackinginquiry.org. Issues around the regulation of the press continue to be raised. In May 2023 a trial began into allegations, some of them dating back 20 years, from Prince Harry and others that their phones had been hacked by Mirror Group newspapers.

A further stage in the attempt to make the press more accountable is Section 40 of the Crime and Court Act 2013. This was written in response to the Leveson Inquiry and required newspaper organisations to meet the legal costs of the claimant in a **libel** case regardless of the outcome. It was Lord Leveson's assertion that smaller publishers and the ordinary person who may be libelled by a newspaper, unlike celebrities, did not have the funds to take newspapers to court. This stage would also have made publishers sign up to a press regulator or be fined.

However, in March 2018 the government formally closed the Leveson Inquiry and pledged to repeal Section 40.

In 2018, the Data Protection Bill went through parliament, within which was an amendment calling for a second Leveson Inquiry into allegations of data protection breaches committed by or on behalf of news organisations. This amendment was defeated and the bill went through without the amendment.

As with other content, online newspapers and digital journalistic content are more complex in terms of regulation, and protecting the journalist and the reader. In 2022 there was an amendment to the government's Online Safety Bill with the aim of adding stronger press protections in cases where social media platforms remove journalist's articles without their consent.

Key Term

Libel
The defamation of a person's character through written or printed words or images.

Stretch and Challenge 3.30

Visit the IPSO website to find out more about its role in the regulation of the press: https://www.ipso.co.uk/what-we-do/.

Hugh Grant has been a very important ambassador for the 'Hacked Off' campaign.

Stretch and Challenge 3.31

Visit the 'Hacked Off' website, https://hackinginquiry.org/, to see the progress of its campaign.

Applying Theory

Regulation: Livingstone and Lunt

Some of the areas Livingstone and Lunt explored include:

- the idea that there is an underlying struggle in recent UK regulation policy between the need to further the interests of citizens (by offering protection from harmful or offensive material) and the need to further the interests of consumers (by ensuring choice, value for money and market competition)
- the idea that the increasing power of global media corporations, together with the rise of convergent media technologies and transformations in the production, distributing and marketing of digital media, have placed traditional approaches to media regulation at risk.

As stated above, the UK press industry is under increasing pressure to adhere to new rules and guidelines regarding its ethical behaviour in the light of recent scandals and the subsequent Leveson Inquiry. There is a need to achieve a balance between protecting citizens from material that may be harmful or, indeed, more recently 'fake' and maintaining the freedom of the press to expose wrongdoing through professional, credible investigative journalism. The increasing power of some newspaper organisations, for example News Corp, combined with digital expansion has introduced more challenges regarding regulation.

Set Products: The *Daily Mirror* and *The Times*

In studying these two set products you will gain knowledge and understanding of both newspapers as evolving media products that have been chosen to highlight important elements of the newspaper industry and to illustrate audience issues. In order to develop your understanding of both newspapers at A Level/Year 2 you must consider:

- one complete print edition of each newspaper chosen by your teacher/centre
- selected pages from the website of each newspaper, including the homepage and at least one other page.

Quickfire 3.46

Why do you think these two newspapers have been chosen as set products?

Rapid Recall 3.22

What is a 'splash' in newspaper terms?

Tip

It is not a requirement to study every page of the set editions in detail. However, it is important to be able to refer to specific pages from the set editions that exemplify, for example, ideology, political and social contexts and the target audience of the newspaper.

Useful Pages to Study From the Set Newspapers

- **The front page**: this will allow you to discuss news values, ideology, mode of address and political contexts.
- **A news story covered inside the paper**: this may link to the splash on the front page and will cover the main stories in more detail.
- **The editorial**: this is where the newspaper gives its opinion on the day's news and where the political allegiance and ideology of the publication may be most explicit. The mode of address used here will also give an indication of the target audience. For example, a quality broadsheet may still use a formal mode of address in the editorial, whereas a tabloid may be more informal.
- **The letters page**: this is where readers can interact with the newspaper and the stories and features that are included. Studying the letters pages for your set products gives you an insight into the papers' readers and their repsonses.
- **The advertisements**: these will often give an indication of the demographic profile of the reader.

Set Product: The *Daily Mirror*

The significance of patterns of ownership and control, including conglomerate ownership, vertical integration and diversification

How processes of production, distribution and circulation shape media products

This set product is covered in detail in the Year 1 book. The *Daily Mirror* is a good example of how newspaper ownership may evolve and change to reflect the economic situation.

In 2018 the *Daily Mirror* embarked upon a £200 million deal to buy the *Express* and *Star* newspapers. This included the *Daily Express*, the *Sunday Express*, the *Daily Star*, the *Star on Sunday* and *OK!* magazine. The merging of the two companies meant savings for the *Daily Mirror* in a time of falling print sales. The newspaper estimated a £20 million saving through the pooling of editorial resources. Some editorial teams, for example sport, remained, whereas other less compatible ones, for example politics, remained separate. The combined strength of the titles meant greater competition for digital advertising that was at the time largely soaked up by the giants Facebook and Google.

There were obvious concerns at the time that the move by the *Daily Mirror* could impact upon the freedom of opinion at the *Express* and *Star* newspapers. However, Simon Fox, the chief executive of Trinity Mirror (now Reach plc) at the time, asserted his aim to maintain the editorial independence of the papers and that the *Mirror* was not going to go right-wing or the *Daily Express* go left-wing. Both would have their editorial independence (Sweeney, 2018).

The new combined company was renamed Reach and would become the UK's second largest newspaper group with 24% of newspaper sales. This is still less than the sales of *The Sun*. However, this raised issues regarding both the freedom of opinion at the *Express* and *Star* and concerns about whether there was sufficient plurality of views and editorial independence across the industry.

The merger was referred to the **Competition and Markets Authority (CMA)**, whose job it is to investigate wider issues of competition in the industry. Ofcom also launched an investigation. In June 2018 all concerns were cleared and the merger was allowed to go ahead. In 2023 Reach plc owns more than 130 national and regional print and online brands and has over 11 million registered users (https://www.reachplc.com/about-us).

Set Product: *The Times*

The Times is a UK national newspaper which was first published in 1785 and is part of the Times Newspaper Group, a subsidiary of News UK, a spinoff of the American multi-media conglomerate News Corp, owned by **Rupert Murdoch** and focusing specifically on newspapers. *The Times* has been described as 'credible', 'responsible', 'trusted' and 'part of the nation's heritage' (Gallagher, 2022). The company also publishes the *Sunday Times*, *The Sun*, the *Sun on Sunday* and, until it closed, the *News of the World*.

Tip

To avoid confusion and to develop understanding, you are required to study a different edition of the newspaper from that set for Section A. For Section B you need to establish an overall understanding of the newspaper and its place in the industry; however, you will not be engaging in textual analysis of the pages as is required for Section A.

Quickfire 3.47

What was unusual about the *Daily Mirror*'s bid to buy the *Express* and the *Star* newspapers?

Quickfire 3.48

Why did the *Daily Mirror* make the decision to buy the *Express* and *Star* newspapers?

Link

The *Daily Mirror* is covered for Section B of Component 1 on pages 102–106 of the Year 1 book.

Key Figures

Competition and Markets Authority (CMA)
A non-ministerial UK government department, responsible for investigating any mergers that could restrict competition within a particular market, e.g. the press. The aim is to protect consumers and offer choice.

Rupert Murdoch
An Australian-born media mogul whose empire at one time included several newspapers and shares in Fox and Sky. In 2018 his reign at Sky TV ended when his company 21st Century Fox agreed to sell its shares in Sky to US media firm Comcast after a long-running battle.

Although *The Times* adopts a more neutral position, along with *The Sun* it has a predominantly right-wing allegiance and supports the Conservative party at key times, for example general elections. The newspaper was one of the first to have an online presence, launching its website in 1996, and was also one of the first to introduce a **paywall**, offering a range of subscription opportunities for audiences.

The Front Page

Although you are not required to engage in textual analysis of the newspaper pages from your chosen edition, the front page can tell you a lot about the industry that produces the paper.

The masthead is the name of the paper and can signify the ideology of the publication. *The Times* is a long-running paper and the name suggests that it is up to date and reflects current issues of 'the time'.

The typography used for the masthead is bold and strong and has a commanding place either side of the newspaper's crest and logo. This reflects the more traditional aspect of the newspaper and its long history in the industry. The lion and the unicorn are symbolic of England and is a royal coat of arms. Unlike other newspapers, other than some changes to the font type, *The Times* has kept the masthead unchanged, reinforcing its place in press history. The royal crest has been part of the paper since it was first published in 1785 and the slogan *Dieu et Mon Droit* meaning God and My Right, was reputedly first used as a battle cry by Richard I. The combination of the modern typeface and the traditional emblem signifies different aspects of the newspaper.

The plug is an important element of *The Times* front page. It is eye-catching and in colour, suggesting that this traditional paper also covers stories related to lifestyle and popular culture, so broadening the audience appeal.

The front-page stories usually focus on political topics, suggesting the newspaper is a quality publication dealing with serious issues. Compared with the tabloids and middle-market dailies, there is much more copy on the front page and a greater number of stories dealt with in detail.

The **bylines** accompanying the main front-page story suggest the serious nature of the story and the calibre of the journalists and their specialisms. The fact that there are specific editors for political and economic stories suggests the regular content of the newspaper and the target audience.

Key Terms

Paywall
A method of restricting access to a website other than by a subscription payment. Some newspapers introduced this as a way of creating revenue to make up for losses from print newspapers and advertising.

Bylines
A line in a newspaper story naming the writer or contributor.

Rapid Recall 3.23

What is a standalone?

Quickfire 3.49

Give an example of a middle-market daily.

The Inside Pages

It is important to remember that for Section B you are using selected elements of the whole publication to consider aspects of the industry and the newspaper's readership. A newspaper such as *The Times* includes a wide variety of stories and features, all of which communicate messages about the paper, its readers and its ideology. With a quality publication such as this, the ideology may at times be more implicit and, in fact, *The Times* may be considered neutral and unbiased when reporting on some political stories. However, there are some pages where the paper's opinion is clearly communicated and these are explicitly signalled, for example, by the title 'Comment'. Here, as in the editorial, *The Times* gives its opinion on stories of the day or particular issues or events. It is often evident from the headline for this section that it is pro-government and anti-Labour, criticising Labour policies and asserting its right-leaning allegiance.

The editorial is another part of the paper where opinions can be aired and, as the name indicates, this is supposedly written by the paper's editor, there are no bylines from journalists. This page in the paper is set out slightly differently with a more traditional graphic at the top 'Times Past' and 'Future' reinforcing the longevity of the publication. It is here that the articles may demonstrate more overt political bias, for example the sub-heading in the 23 June 2023 paper, which can be seen at https://www.thetimes.co.uk/article/the-times-view-on-ending-the-nhs-strikes-healthy-alternatives-j6t68q7mx.

- **Sections**: quality, broadsheet newspapers such as *The Times* will have a 'Global' section of the paper where they will deal with news from around the world. As part of the news values of the paper, these will tend to focus on elite nations whose dealings may impact upon the UK, for example Putin and the war in Ukraine (February 2023). There is also a large 'Business' section focusing in the 7 February edition on interest rates, the recovery of the new car market and Amazon's plans for Alexa, all suggesting the interests of the readers.
- **News stories**: the main news stories on the front page will usually be followed up in more detail inside the newspaper. The construction of these stories, including the headlines, subheadings and standfirsts, may reflect the ideology of the newspaper and give an indication of the readers.

Rapid Recall 3.24

What is the difference between readership and circulation?

Audiences

> How media industries target audiences through content and the appeal of media products and through the ways in which they are marketed, distributed and circulated
>
> How media organisations reflect the different needs of mass and specialised audiences, including through targeting

You will already have considered newspaper audiences in Year 1, when you studied your set edition of the *Daily Mirror*. You will need to transfer that knowledge to the analysis of *The Times*. The readership of this paper is very different and the two examples studied together will give you a good understanding of how newspapers target, attract, reach and address their potential audience.

Key Figure

PAMco
The Publishers' Audience Measurement Company Ltd is funded by UK national publishers. It surveys 35,000 people including 5,000 whose digital reading habits are monitored by computer software.

Who Reads *The Times*?

The data in the table on the following page are collated by **PAMco**, the company that took over from the National Readership Survey (NRS). Unlike the NRS, PAMco does not only focus on print publications but also surveys the total brand reach across print, mobile phones, tablets and desktop computers. Its findings are particularly useful to advertisers, thus aiding the newspaper industry.

Quickfire 3.50

Why is the data collected by PAMco useful for advertisers?

Rapid Recall 3.25

What is a standfirst?

Stretch and Challenge 3.32

The following websites will give you more detailed information about the readership of newspapers:

- www.newsworks.org.uk
- www.pamco.co.uk.

Stretch and Challenge 3.33

Consider what conclusions you can draw about the audience for *The Times* from this table and how this could be incorporated into an examination response.

Key Terms

Rolling news
A 24-hour, continuously updated news service, broadcast on television and online.

Edition-based digital format
An online newspaper distributed in electronic form but formatted identically to the print version.

Quickfire 3.51

Why do you think the newspaper decided to create an edition-based rather than a rolling news format?

PAMCo collects data about the readership of newspapers and their online platforms.

GB Adults 15+	Entities included	
	Print	Digital
The Times	*The Times*	times.co.uk

Monthly reach					
Total	Print	Total digital	Computer	Smartphone	Tablet
15,473	2,767	13,748	1,447	12,001	1,448

Weekly reach					
Total	Print	Total digital	Computer	Smartphone	Tablet
7,991	1,942	6,412	547	5,403	834

Daily reach					
Total	Print	Total digital	Computer	Smartphone	Tablet
2,745	937	1,866	131	1,506	308

Source: PAMCo H1 2023 June 2021–December 2022 print data fused with November 2022 iris data
Notes: Print estimates are for 6 day. Base: GB adults 15+

The Digital Newspaper Audience

The interrelationship between media technologies and patterns of consumption and response

The newspaper industry has changed dramatically with regards to the way in which the product is distributed to audiences. While print production is falling, the digital access of news is growing. However, the newspaper must ensure that the digital versions on offer are suitable for the newspaper's readership.

In 2016, *The Times* and the *Sunday Times* launched a combined website and upgraded the smartphone apps. The newspaper made the decision to move from **rolling news** to an **edition-based digital format**. Research undertaken for the newspaper revealed that readers of *The Times* look at digital platforms at certain points in the day, the newspaper therefore decided to produce one main digital edition of the paper, which would be updated at 9am, midday and 5pm, correlating with the daily routines of their readers. This model was seen to suit the needs of the audience while still giving the newspaper the flexibility not available in the print version to change the content to cover a breaking story. John Witherow, the then editor of *The Times*, said:

> *The power of an edition has endured at* The Times *for more than 230 years. Our challenge is to update this concept for the digital age: to put readers first.* (Witherow, 2016)

What Can the Inner Pages of the Newspaper Tell You About the Audience?

How the front page of any newspaper attracts an audience has been considered, but the inner pages also communicate messages about who the newspaper perceives its target audience to be.

- **The letters page** in *The Times* offers an opportunity for the readers to respond to the stories and topics chosen by the newspaper as newsworthy for their readers.

Unlike the '#Madeuthink' page in the *Daily Mirror*, the 'Letters to the Editor' in *The Times* are longer, more detailed and tend to focus on serious topics.

They all address the editor as 'Sir', reflecting the formal mode of address. The lead letter on 7 February 2023 was about artificial intelligence (AI) and the future of jobs, suggesting the more serious social and cultural topics covered, while other letters focused on scientific research, the UK possible withdrawal from the European Convention on Human Rights, and slavery reparation. The language used in the letters is formal and the writers are generally in a position of knowledge and, at times, authority, for example doctors will often write in to comment on medical issues covered in the newspaper. This reflects the intellectual readership of the paper and contrasts with the more light-hearted style of the letters pages in the *Daily Mirror*. However, both these items included in the papers allow the reader to interact and feel that their point of view is important and can be aired. The readers' letters also often reflect the ideology and political allegiance of the newspaper and its readers.

> How audiences are grouped and categorised by media industries, including by age, gender and social class as well as by lifestyle and taste

- **Features**: these are usually **soft news** items relating to, for example, the arts, lifestyle or human interest stories. They are lighter in tone but still address the target audience. In *The Times*, these articles are included in a lifestyle supplement, *Times2*, which is separate from the **hard news** items. The focus of the supplement on 7 February 2023 was relaxation treatments. The articles in Times2 tend to appeal to a younger demographic evident in the topics chosen, focusing on lifestyle and the less formal language. In this edition features included online dating, binge watching and Beyoncé at the Grammys.

In this edition of *Times2* (7 February 2023) there is a feature on burning calories while doing the housework. The images used feature women, this is clearly targeting a female audience of a specific demographic, further reinforced by equating the calories used completing a domestic chore with a food, clearly suggesting a particular reader.

Key Terms

Features
Items in the newspaper that are typically longer than a hard news story. They cover topics of interest to the audience range of the newspaper and offer a contrast to the more serious items.

Soft news
Refers to items that are primarily entertaining or of personal interest to the reader, for example celebrity and lifestyle.

Hard news
'"Hard" news is typically used to refer to topics that are usually timely, important and consequential, such as politics, international affairs and business news' (digitalnewsreport.org, 2018).

Stretch and Challenge 3.34

Read 'Distinctions Between Hard and Soft News' (Reuters Institute for the Study of Journalism, 2018), which is a useful article about the distinctions between the two aspects of news.

Tip

Apply the information here to the edition of the newspaper you have studied in class.

Stretch and Challenge 3.35

Read about *The Times*' advertising campaign and related articles by registering on the *Campaign* website:
https://www.campaignlive.co.uk/article/times-pledges-cut-noise-new-tv-ad/1410754.

Stretch and Challenge 3.36

Explore *The Times* website. There is a range of different subscription offers, including a student subscription which offers a one-month free trial.

In What Other Ways Does *The Times* Target, Attract and Reach Readers?

As mentioned earlier in this section, as well as the print edition, *The Times* also has a digital presence across a range of platforms. The website for any newspaper is an important method of engaging readers, as it offers a range of additional features including:

- **Interactive opportunities**: these are elements of the website that allow the reader to become part of the newspaper's community through the use of blogs, forums, surveys and the opportunity to email the newspaper.
  - **The navigation bar**: allows for ease of movement around the website and enables readers to choose the content they want to read.
  - **Multi-media features**: allow readers to explore news stories in more detail by accessing audio and video aspects of the story.
  - **Regular updates**: *The Times* updates its edition-based format at key points during the day, ensuring that the reader is receiving the most up-to-date news stories.

In return for subscribing to the website, readers are offered additional opportunities to become part of the newspaper's community.

Accessing news online offers different opportunities and is more convenient for some audiences.

Advertising Campaigns

Another way that *The Times* has sought to engage with readers is through advertising campaigns. In 2016 *The Times* and *Sunday Times* launched a joint brand awareness campaign 'Know your times' with the additional slogan 'Cut through the noise to the stories that matter'. The campaign included a 30-second TV and cinema audio-visual advert, which included footage of big news stories including the refugee crisis, the NHS and the Donald Trump election campaign trail. At one point the advertisement focuses on the crying of one child and all other sound is muted. This relates to the fact that the newspaper always cuts to the important part of news stories, echoing the brand positioning of 'know your times'. Catherine Newman, the then marketing and sales director of *The Times* and the *Sunday Times*, said:

> *The 'Know your times' campaign aims to demonstrate how our titles ensure readers are not just informed, but well-informed, about the fast changing world we live in today.* (Gwynn, 2016)

Quickfire 3.52

What does the 'Know your times' campaign tell us about the newspaper and its readers?

Applying Theory: Newspapers

Power and Media Industries: Curran and Seaton

The key points of Curran and Seaton's (1981) theory are covered earlier in this section in relation to citizen journalism. This theoretical perspective can also be used with respect to *The Times* newspaper and its place within the press industry.

- The major newspaper titles are owned by a small number of companies whose main concern is profit and power. *The Times* itself is part of a powerful multi-media conglomerate that is both a horizontally and vertically integrated company.
- It could be said that being part of such an organisation, the additional increased restrictions on press freedom could inhibit variety, creativity and quality.
- Rupert Murdoch, as owner of the paper, is often accused of using excessive control over its content, point of view and the freedom of the journalists.
- It could also be suggested, however, that the ownership model of Murdoch, whereby a more **pluralistic pattern** is adopted, could create the conditions for more adventurous media productions.

Cultural Industries: Hesmondhalgh

Some of the areas **David Hesmondhalgh** explored include:

- the idea that cultural industry companies try to minimise risk and maximise audiences through vertical and horizontal integration, and by formatting their cultural products
- the idea that the largest companies or conglomerates now operate across a number of different cultural industries
- the idea that the radical potential of the internet has been contained to some extent by its partial incorporation into a large profit-orientated set of cultural industries.

Hesmondhalgh is an A Level/Year 2 theorist whose theories can be applied and critically explored, in relation to the newspaper set products:

- *The Times* is part of a large, powerful company that operates both vertical and horizontal integration. The company, News Corp, and its wider ownership have a broad range of titles and related media companies that help to minimise financial and commercial risks. There have been instances, for example, where a print version of *The Times* has been sold cheaper than usual as this loss can be offset by other companies owned by Murdoch.
- In contrast to Hesmondhalgh's assertion that the radical potential of the internet has been contained, News Corp has engaged in digital expansion in order to broaden the readership of its titles. Its establishment of a paywall allows it to still generate income while offering subscribers up-to-date-news and flexibility of access.
- As part of the wider conglomerate of News Corp, *The Times* has access to the benefits offered by association with other cultural industries.

Key Term

Pluralist pattern
Describes the way in which some media content is shaped by consumer demand with the idea of giving people what they want rather than the content being dictated by the editor or owner. This concept of the reader wanting to know, was used by Rupert Murdoch to explain some of the more controversial stories in the *The Sun.*

Stretch and Challenge 3.37

Look at page 106 of the Year 1 book where Gerbner's theory is applied to the *Daily Mirror*. Consider how you can apply this theory to the set product of *The Times* you have chosen to study in your centre.

Named Theorist

David Hesmondhalgh
He is Professor of Media, Music and Culture at the University of Leeds. He is the author of several books and articles on media industries and production. His book *The Cultural Industries* is an analysis of changes in television, film, music, publishing and other industries since the 1980s, and of the rise of new media and cultural industries during that time. This has been recently updated and re-issued.

Stretch and Challenge 3.38

Consider how *The Times* reflects social and cultural contexts through its selection of news stories and representation of social groups.

Contexts: Political

A study of the UK press lends itself easily to a consideration of political contexts. *The Times* is a right-leaning newspaper, which is less explicit in its political allegiance compared with other titles. However, as may be seem from the pages you have studied, the newspaper is often critical of left-wing policies and less so of those of the Conservative party.

When studying the examples of the set products in relation to what they tell us about the industry you need to consider:

- how political contexts have shaped the product
- the influence the political context has had upon the product and the processes whereby it was constructed
- how the ownership of the newspaper affects the political context
- how the political agenda of the newspaper and its ideology affect the way in which stories are covered
- how the news values of the paper reflect the political context, including how specific stories are treated and what is deemed appropriate for the newspaper's readers and what is omitted from the news agenda.

Often, the content inside the paper is influenced by political contexts, for example *The Times'* cartoons are famous for their treatment of politicians and their policies.

Link

Pages 107–114 of the Year 1 book give an introduction to advertising and cover the Year 1 specification content.

Tip

Although the primary emphasis of this specification is on contemporary media, you are also required to explore how products relate to their wider historical contexts.

Link

Key points related to all aspects of audience are covered in Chapter 1 of this book.

Investigating the Set Forms and Products: Advertising

As you will remember from the Year 1 course, Advertising, as a Component 1 Section B form, is only studied in relation to audiences, not industry.

You will already have studied the two set products, *Tide* and *Super. Human.*, in Year 1 of the course and in this book for Section A of the specification. Unlike some of the other forms, there is no additional advertising set product in Year 2 of the course; the expectation is that you will explore the existing set products in relation to the additional content, theories and theoretical perspectives required for A Level/Year 2.

In Section A you studied media language and representation in relation to the two set products. In this section you will develop your knowledge and understanding of the same two products in terms of the relevant audience issues they illustrate. You will also be aware that the two examples have been chosen as they reflect different historical, social and cultural contexts, different purposes, and target different audiences.

In studying these two very different products you will gain an understanding of how advertising has always been one of the most powerful and persuasive media forms. These adverts, produced at key times in different decades, also serve to reflect the time in which they were made and provide information about the social and cultural contexts in which they were created.

How audiences are grouped and categorised by media industries, including by age, gender and social class, as well as by lifestyle and taste

It does not matter when the advertisement was made; the aim of advertising has always been to create a brand and a brand identity that will communicate messages to potential consumers. The producer of the advertising campaign will research the target audience in detail in order to effectively reach the core consumer. The creators of advertisements and other media products divide audiences into categories to more effectively target them. They will create a profile of the audience based on:

- **Demographics**: categorising audiences by dividing them into groups based on certain aspects including, age, gender, income, occupation, marital status, etc. Although perceived as out-moded by some media organisations, this way of categorising audiences is still used by, for example, the advertising industry.
- **Psychographics**: here audiences are categorised according to their values, attitudes and lifestyles. This model considers how people think and behave, what is important to them and how this then affects how they spend their money.

Other methods used to categorise audiences relate to the time in which they were born and how the social and cultural contexts affect their lifestyle and behaviour.

Advertisers regularly devise new ways of categorising audiences in order to reflect changes in society and culture. Consumers no longer only buy a product for what it does, but also what is says about them and how it helps to establish an identity. A contemporary way of considering the audience is to divide them into **tribes**, which are constructed according to lifestyle, beliefs and brand identification. Advertising agencies are very aware of these 'tribes' and use this information to target audiences:

> *On our journey to work we will be sat in our Land-Rover and reconnect with the dream we had when buying it – the 'explorer' dream of taking it off road for an adventure and to discover new experiences. We get to work and power up our Apple iMac which subconsciously is telling us to 'Think Differently' and we become part of a rebel tribe trying to disrupt the norm. In the evening we decide to go for a run. We reconnect with our Nike trainers and their message of 'just do it'. We join the Nike tribe of heroes slaying apathy and pushing through barriers to succeed. Each of these brands says something about the people we are at the time of interacting with them.* (fifteen, 2017)

In 2018, **Rachel Pashley** published the results of a five-year-long survey, the aim of which was to re-define the ways in which women are categorised by advertisers. Eight thousand women aged from 17–70 across 19 countries were included in the survey. Pashley coined the term 'female capital' to describe the value women bring to the world, which she feels is unrecognised and untapped by advertisers.

As a result of her research, Pashley came up with four 'female tribes' that can be used to categorise the modern global woman:

- **Alpha females**: these women are driven and confident. They play a key role in society, founding companies and sitting on boards. They are defined by their careers and are ambitious women keen to make their mark.

Victoria Beckham is an example of an alpha female.

Rapid Recall 3.26

What is brand identity?

Key Term

Tribe
An advertising tribe is a group of people who together identify themselves with a particular lifestyle and set of behaviours. They will also identify with particular products and share similar views about specific brands. These tribes are important to advertisers as they can be influential and play a role in marketing the product and raising brand awareness.

Key Figure

Rachel Pashley
The Planning Partner and Founder Female Tribes at Wunderman Thompson. Her book *New Female Tribes: Shattering Female Stereotypes and Redefining Women Today*, published in 2018, explores the ways in which advertisers target women and the assumptions they make about this audience.

Rapid Recall 3.27

Which New York advertising agency first developed the idea of the psychographic audience profile based on motivational needs?

Stretch and Challenge 3.39

Rachel Pashley discusses her research and her ideas for new tribes in 'Alphas, Hedonists, Traditionalists & Altruists: Which New Female Tribe Are You?' (2018b), which can be found online.

Stretch and Challenge 3.40

Read 'The 4 Different Female Tribes You'll Find in London', from the *Evening Standard* (Law, 2018), which discusses Rachel Pashley's ideas and gives examples of the brands associated with each tribe.

- **Hedonists**: this tribe enjoy having a good time. They are more likely to postpone marriage and children in favour of exploring cultural experiences. They are digital natives and use social media as part of their daily lives and so are seen to be influencers. They are a similar group to the 'explorers' suggested in Young and Rubicam's theory. Pashley (2018b) considers hedonists to be self-focused but have pleasure and enjoyment as their goal:

  > *Within Hedonists we have the Explorer Tribe, driven by the desire to see the world, take risks and challenge themselves, much like a female Indiana Jones; think Pippa Middleton.* (Pashley, 2018b)

Pippa Middleton is an example of the 'hedonist' tribe and is a digital influencer.

- **Altruists**: this tribe are focused on others rather than just themselves. They want to make a difference and are seen promoting charity, social and health campaigns. They are often activists who have used the power of social media to spread the word about their concerns and to raise awareness of key social issues, for example the women of the #MeToo campaign. Pashley uses the term 'culture shapers' to define women in this tribe who use their creative power as writers and artists to serve their local and global communities.
- **Traditionalists**: this group equates to the 'mainstreamers' of Young and Rubicam's model. They may be older but not necessarily so. They are more concerned with family values and their family is their priority, although they may also engage in entrepreneurial schemes. Pashley calls this group 'spouse-focused' to describe women who have willingly given up careers to support those of their partners.

Altruists are activists and 'culture shapers'.

How media products target, attract, reach, address and potentially construct audiences

Knowing who the target market is and how best to appeal to them has always been an essential part of marketing strategy. What Young and Rubicam in the past and Rachel Pashley in 2018 have shown, is that audiences need to be continually re-examined and re-categorised as society adapts and changes. Advertisers have moved away from defining audiences solely in terms of demographics and now engage in research which provides them with detailed information about the attitudes, aspirations and beliefs of their audience.

Gaining an understanding of the developing ways in which audiences are surveyed and categorised will help you to discuss the contexts of the set products in more detail and with greater knowledge and understanding.

Link

Look at page 37 of the Year 1 book where you will find information on Channel 4's UK Tribes research project.

Jools Oliver gave up a career as a model to have a family and support husband Jamie in his career.

Set Product: *Tide* Print Advertisement (1950s)

Background Information

The *Tide* advertisement, seen on page 71, is an example of an historical media product from the 1950s, chosen to give an understanding of how products reflect the time in which they were produced and the audiences that they targeted.

Tide was a soap powder produced by **Procter & Gamble**, an American company that had always seen the value of advertising in order to attract audiences to its products. Its first colour print advert for *Ivory* soap appeared in *Cosmopolitan* magazine in 1886, and in 1939, five months after the introduction of television in the US, Procter & Gamble aired its first TV commercial for the same product.

From the beginning, Procter & Gamble saw the importance of appealing to its female audience for both beauty and domestic cleaning products. It sponsored radio 'soap operas', encouraging listeners to become loyal consumers of its products.

In 1946, Procter & Gamble introduced *Tide*, 'the washing miracle', with a new formula that cleaned better to meet the demands of the new, advanced domestic appliances. By 1950 it had become the leading laundry product.

In order to market the product, Procter & Gamble used the advertising agency D'Arcy Masius Benton and Bowles. The print adverts were also supported by radio and television adverts reinforcing the brand identity.

Historical, Social and Cultural Contexts: The Female Audience of the 1950s

> The way in which different audience interpretations reflect social, cultural and historical circumstances

As the advertisement for *Tide* was launched nearly 70 years ago, it is important to consider the world in which it was produced in order to be able to discuss the product in relation to relevant contexts.

- America joined in World War II in 1941. This changed the employment picture of the USA dramatically as, just as in the UK, it became a national necessity for women to work as the men left to fight in the armed forces. The positive outcome of this situation was the increase in family income, with more money available to buy food and household durables. Women became used to earning money and having a job outside of the home. This was valued at the time as it was essential to help the war effort.
- However, with the end of the war, women were encouraged, and at times forced, to return to their pre-war roles and the importance of this nurturing role and the family were actively echoed in society and across advertising at the time.

Stretch and Challenge 3.41

Information about Procter & Gamble can be found online. Search for 'P&G' (P&G, 2023).

Key Figure

Procter & Gamble
William Procter and James Gamble emigrated from England and Ireland, respectively, and set up a company making soap and candles in Cincinnati, Ohio in 1837. By 1890 they were producing 30 different types of soap. It is still a large global brand today, trading as P&G and producing many of our everyday cleaning products and toiletries including Pampers, Crest, Gillette, Ariel, Fairy and Always products. Their slogan, which echoes their aim in the 1950s, is 'Touching lives, improving life'.

Link

Information about *Tide* and its audience is also available in the Year 1 book, pages 109–111.

Quickfire 3.53

What changes did advertisers have to make to the way in which they targeted women in post-war America?

While women were actively encouraged to work during the war, once the war was over they were expected to happily return to a domestic life.

- As men attempted to assert a post-war patriarchal control, linked to concerns that they had been displaced by women in the world of work during the war, women were held personally accountable for all things domestic. According to Ad Council (2018) 'Women in War Jobs' was the most successful recruitment advertising campaign in American history, with social change as the underlying theme, requiring women to enter the workforce as a patriotic responsibility for both women and employers:

  > *Those ads made a tremendous change in the relationship between women and the workplace. Employment outside of the home became socially acceptable and even desirable.* (Ad Council, 2018)

- After the war, even if they wanted to, women found it difficult to have a career, as the workforce was generally made up of the men who had returned, placing women in direct competition with them. A battle they couldn't win in 1950s America.
- At this time there was a post-war boom and new products appeared as new technologies rapidly developed. Many of these were in the domestic sphere, for example vacuum cleaners, fridge-freezers and washing machines. This also meant that related products also appeared, for example *Tide*, which was created for the new types of washing machines. The target audience was obviously women and advertisers had to think of ways to persuade women to buy these products.
- One way was to make the role of wife and mother culturally important, creating the stereotype of the 'happy housewife', which all women were expected to aspire to.

  As **Betty Friedan** said:

  > *For fifteen years and longer, there has been a propaganda campaign, as unanimous in this democratic nation as in the most efficient of dictatorships, to give women 'prestige' as housewives.* (Friedan, 1963)

Link

Betty Friedan is discussed in relation to the Component 2 magazine covers on page 169 of the Year 1 book.

Key Figure

Betty Friedan
An American writer and activist who was a leading figure in the US feminist movement. Her 1963 book *The Feminine Mystique* discusses the stifling and narrow roles for women in contemporary America and was said to be the impetus for the second wave feminist movement.

- Women's identity was constructed by advertisers and became inextricably linked to nurturing and specifically to the cleanliness of her house and her family's clothes. A range of adverts appealed to women as homemakers, regardless of whether this is what they wanted. The adverts invariably showed women as happy in their domestic role, reinforcing the cult of home-making.

- In post-war adverts, the roles of women and men were seen to be very different. Women were rarely portrayed in the world of work and were only seen in the domestic sphere, whereas men were depicted as the breadwinners in employment settings, for example an office. There were no obvious role models of working women for post-war females to aspire to. Ironically, for many families to be able to afford the new products available, they would need two incomes.

Quickfire 3.54

How does Betty Friedan's theory from the 1960s relate to Rachel Pashley's more contemporary research?

- Advertisements also often focused on winning approval of the male and advertisers perpetuated the stereotypes by showing that the woman's domestic role could lead to a happy marriage. These post-war advertisements created an unattainable dream world and caused women to feel confused about their roles in society.

> *A woman was told by advertisers to purchase an increasingly spell-binding array of goods so as not to cheat her family. But the only way for her to do this was by going to work outside the home, thereby (according to advertising's imagery) cheating her family in another way. It is this paradox which emerges from an analysis of advertising in the post-war period.* (Freeman, 2014)

- In addition to domestic roles, women were also bombarded by adverts for beauty products featuring flawless women. In fact, the two stereotypes often came together in the adverts for domestic products, which invariably featured women who closely resembled Hollywood screen stars such as Grace Kelly and Doris Day, doing the washing and cleaning in the latest fashions. This placed additional pressure on the female audience, not only must her home and clothes be spotless, but she must be beautiful and fashionable too. Friedan (1963) thought that this produced an unmistakable message about the maternal role, which many women in the post-war period identified with.

The stereotype of the 'happy housewife' was reinforced in advertisements of the time.

Tide: How Did this Advert Attempt to Appeal to the 1950s Female Audience?

How media producers target, attract, reach, address and potentially construct audiences

It is important to consider what has been said above about the social, cultural and historical contexts in relation to the set product:

- The target audience was middle-class American women who were wives and mothers with the disposable income to afford the new washing machines on the market at the time.
- The copy in the advertisement places the responsibility of cleanliness firmly with the woman. The advertisement portrays the happy, satisfied, fulfilled woman discussed by Friedan as being misleading for the women of the time. The women in the advert are attractive, fashionable and well made up, not a typical washday look.
- The advertisement perpetuates Friedan's stereotype of the 'happy housewife' and constructs the idea of the woman who can be everything to her family.
- The product, as well as being made to appear different and exciting by the use of hyperbole, is also seen to make the woman's life easier. The lexis used includes *'miracle'*, *'world's cleanest'* and *'nothing like'* suggesting its role in facilitating household chores.

Stretch and Challenge 3.42

Freeman's academic study, 'The Distorting Image: Women and Advertising, 1900–1960', has an interesting section on the 1950s female audience for advertisements. Read it online.

Women of the 1950s had to aspire to the ideal of the perfect family.

Link

This advertisement and its audience are also covered on pages 109–110 of the Year 1 book.

Rapid Recall 3.28

What is meant by encoding and decoding in relation to advertising?

- The audience are encouraged to personally identify with the women in the advertisement, *'you women'*, and make links between their lives and their own.
- The advertisement puts pressure on women to purchase not only *Tide* but also the new time-saving, technologically advanced washing machines. The image of the old machine with suds pouring from it is seen to be outdated and *Tide* is marketed as *'What Women Want'* creating an identity for the woman.
- The inclusion of a woman from a similar demographic hanging out her washing, having used the product, encouraged women to feel part of a community of valued homemakers.

Audience Responses

How audiences interpret the media, including how and why audiences may interpret the same media in different ways

Applying Theory

Reception Theory: Stuart Hall

Hall's theory is useful in considering how the women of the time may have responded to the *Tide* advertisement and others like it which sought to construct an image of domestic perfection. Hall's theory states:

- the idea that communication is a process involving encoding by producers and decoding by audiences
- the idea that there are three hypothetical positions from which messages and meanings may be decoded:
  - the dominant-**hegemonic** position: the encoder's intended meaning (the preferred meaning) is fully understood and accepted
  - the negotiated position: the legitimacy of the encoder's message is acknowledged in general terms, although the message is adapted or negotiated to better fit the decoder's own individual experiences or context
  - the oppositional position: the encoder's message is understood, but the decoder disagrees with it, reading it in a contrary or oppositional way.

Some 1950s women may have accepted the preferred, largely dominant, patriarchal view encoded in the *Tide* advertisement. They would have then also had a literal response and been persuaded by the advertisement to buy the product in the hope that it would make their lives easier.

Other women may have had a negotiated response, accepting that this is a new product which may be useful, but also acknowledging that it would not transform their lives into the glamorous representation of domesticity constructed by the advertisement.

Oppositional responses may have come from those 1950s women who felt frustrated and unhappy by their enforced return to domesticity after the war. They may still have wanted a life outside the home and would not be convinced by the persuasive devices employed in the advertisement, which do not reflect the reality of their actual lives (see Freeman, 2014).

Key Term

Hegemonic
Something that is dominant – a dominant set of values or ideas, for example.

Quickfire 3.55

In what way could the advertising of the 1950s be said to be misleading audiences by 'avoidance'?

Link

On pages 111–112 of the Year 1 book, Gerbner's cultivation theory is applied to the *Tide* advertisement.

Stretch and Challenge 3.43

Consider how you could apply Gerbner's theory to the *Tide* product in a more detailed way, using the additional information about the 1950s female audience from this chapter.

Set Product: *Super. Human.* Audio-Visual Advertisement (2020)

The second advertising set product *Super. Human.* has been specifically chosen to offer a contrast with the *Tide* advertisement. It is a contemporary product from a different advertising sub-genre. Advertisements for specific events and those whose aim is to raise awareness of an issue or to address the under-representation of a social group have a different purpose from those selling consumable products or services. Consequently, these advertisements use a range of different techniques as persuasive devices. They are not selling the audience something tangible, but often are arresting them with images and text to catch their attention, make them listen and perhaps encourage the audience to be active in some way. *Super. Human.* as an example of marketing is relatively unique as it covers all those elements, it is marketing the Tokyo 2020 Paralympic Games, Channel 4's coverage of the event and raising awareness about attitudes to disability and the under-representation of certain social groups.

Quickfire 3.56

Why do you think using shock tactics has been successful as an advertising strategy in the past?

Super. Human.: The Facts, A Reminder

- The advertisement was made by cinematographer Bradford Young who has previously worked in film and television. It was devised and created by 4Creative, Channel 4's in-house creative agency, and was produced by global production company Serial Pictures and Somesuch. The advertisement was part of a larger marketing campaign for the 2020 Paralympics.
- The 2020 Paralympics were postponed due to the pandemic and were re-scheduled, taking place in 2021. This is addressed in the advertisement to highlight the extra pressures this placed on the athletes.
- Channel 4 had also produced the marketing campaigns for the two previous Paralympic Games, with the aim of ensuring that the event was promoted in a similar way to other sporting events. The coverage of the 2021 games were Channel 4's biggest and most ambitious campaign with over 1,300 hours of coverage on linear TV, Channel 4 and More 4.
- During the coverage the programme *The Last Leg* was broadcast every night of the Paralympics. '*The award-winning series began as part of Channel 4's London 2012 Paralympic programming to highlight the Games and tackle the tricky questions viewers wanted to ask using the hashtag #isitok.*' This programme was subsequently given a weekly slot and covers news and political events as well as focusing on issues related to the Paralympics and issues of disability. The main presenter Adam Hills describes the show as '*three guys with four legs talking about the week*' (British Comedy Guide, 2023) highlighting the disabilities of the presenters and its inclusion in the Channel 4 schedule reinforces the broadcaster's commitment to diversity in its programming.
- The Channel 4 coverage also included more disabled senior production roles than ever before and some of the coverage also specifically focused on issues related to disability, for example presenter Ade Adepitan, a former professional wheelchair basketball player, broadcast his highlights show from a converted Tokyo taxi in which he travelled around the venues giving a unique perspective. His *Today in Tokyo* was awarded Best Sport Entertainment Programme in the Broadcast Awards (Channel 4, 2023).

Rapid Recall 3.29

What is soft-sell advertising?

How do media industries target audiences through the content and appeal of media products and through the ways in which they are marketed, distributed and circulated.

The target audience for this event and for the marketing material including the advertisement, is a relatively broad demographic including: loyal viewers of Channel 4, which generally encompasses the 16–14 age range; those who recall the success of the previous two campaigns for the event and so will anticipate this event; general fans of sport; fans who will watch for coverage of specific sports; those who admire Channel 4's ethos to include more representation of diverse social groups; and those who want to see people like themselves participating in such a high-profile event. The Paralympics gave Channel 4 an opportunity to:

- challenge and change public attitudes
- attract a significant audience at a home Paralympics
- appeal to advertisers as well as audiences
- reflect its remit: innovation, young people, diversity (Channel 4, 2022).

The content of the advertisement appeals to the target audience range:

- A range of different sports are featured along with a training regime that will be recognisable to audiences familiar with the different sports. The technique of personalisation will appeal to audiences as the advertisement features actual people with human stories that will resonate with audiences. The struggles of the athletes and their training is juxtaposed with the struggles of everyday life: dealing with a young baby, missing a birthday party and wanting to be diverted from a task, in this case by playing the drums.
- The content of the advertisement forces the audience to also engage with very real aspects of the struggles the disabled athletes go through in order to achieve success. The household names will be recognisable to audiences, for example Ellie Symonds, Jordanne Whiley and Kadeena Cox and others are less well known, but the aim, according to Zaid Al-Qassab, Chief Marketing Officer for Channel 4, was to move from the 'superhumans' concept of the previous campaigns and focus on the 'human' element, so encouraging audiences who may have no experience of disability to engage with the athletes.
- The appeal for many audiences will be the way in which Channel 4 has approached the marketing of this event in the advertisement. The advertisement reinforces the channel's aim to go beyond producing a promotional advertisement and instead create a product that will challenge audiences to consider how they view disability. It combines an upbeat audio track with humour but also does not shy away from showing the grittier aspects of the training regime, some of which is uncomfortable for audiences to watch, including the popping of a blister.
- The technical and audio codes engage and hold the attention of the audience with rapid editing, use of close-ups, dramatic scenarios all designed to reflect what the Paralympics has to offer audiences. The opening scene with the combination of images, sports commentary voiceover and dramatic music hook the audience. The choice of the soundtrack from *Bugsy Malone* will be recognised by audiences and is synonymous with the need for the determination to succeed by the athletes.

Quickfire 3.57

How are the athletes in the advertisement constructed to be relatable to audiences?

Grittier images are juxtaposed with humour.

The way in which different audience interpretations reflect social, cultural and historical circumstances

- Some audiences who view the advertisement will be less familiar with the struggles of the Paralympian athletes and may find some of the images uncomfortable to watch. Socially and culturally, they may have less experience with disability and could have their preconceptions challenged by this advertisement. One way the advertisement does this is through the use of language by the inclusion of the phrase, '*To be a Paralympian there's got to be something wrong with you*', focusing on historically outdated language use.

- The construction of the advertisement and the focus on the human element of the athlete's stories may shock audiences into re-examining the ways in which certain social groups are treated in society and represented in the media.
- The construction of the advertisement reflects a social and cultural context. Recent research suggests that audiences are becoming desensitised to the negative images used in some advertising campaigns designed to raise awareness and have reached saturation level, as emotive shocking images are seen regularly in the media, not solely in particular advertising campaigns, but on the news and in newspapers. Audiences are becoming harder to shock.
- It is now the case that campaigns are increasingly using more soft-sell tactics to reach the target audience. Read what Ian Heartfield, Creative Director at advertising agency BBH, has so say about soft-sell advertising in Isaac's (2016) article 'Have Charity Shock Ads Lost their Power to Disturb?'
- In contemporary advertising, the important aim is to establish a brand that has popular appeal and an advertising campaign that is memorable, not just for being shocking (see Isaac, 2016). The *Super. Human.* advertisement achieves this through its combination of engaging personalities and interesting human stories, the focus is on the athletes as people striving to succeed.

The advert uses visual metaphors to illustrate the challenges the athletes face.

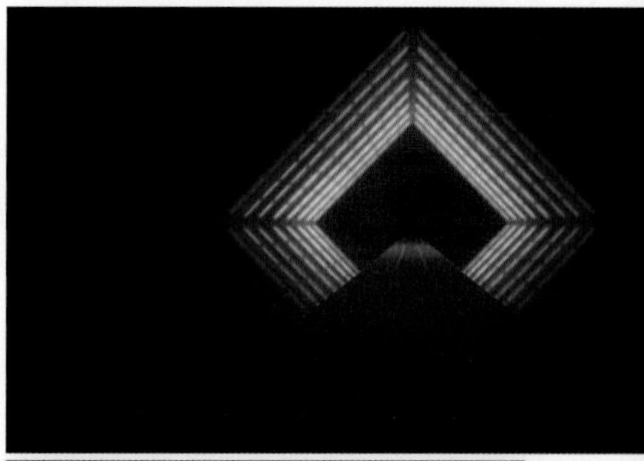

The advertisement ends positively with images of success and celebration.

Applying Theory

Stuart Hall

How audiences use media in different ways, reflecting demographic factors as well as aspects of identity and cultural capital

- Some audiences may accept the encoder's intended meaning in creating the advertisement. The upbeat soundtrack fast paced editing, use of personalisation, elements of humour and positive representations of the event and the athletes as both 'Super' and 'Human', encourages an audience to accept the ideologies and the preferred reading intended by Channel 4. The use of real people creates a preferred reading that the audience should invest in their narratives and subsequently watch the Paralympic Games.
- Some audiences may adopt a negotiated position, acknowledging the legitimacy of the encoder's position, but may feel more distanced from the sporting theme of the event. However, this audience may be more open to the positive approach of the advertisement and part of their negotiated position may involve them examining their misconceptions about disabled people in general.
- Oppositional responses may come from those who are not supporters of Channel 4 and see their coverage of the event as a means of virtue-signalling, rather than promoting its ideology of giving voice to those who are under- represented. These may be older, less liberal audiences who are not regular viewers of Channel 4. Other oppositional responses may come from those audiences who are not interested in sport of any kind and may disagree with the amount of time devoted to this event. Or they may have 'compassion fatigue', which may be caused by saturation with negative images or a questioning of the high production values of the advertisement.

Link

Look back to earlier in this section where Stuart Hall's theory in relation to the *Tide* set product is outlined.

Link

Page 113 of the Year 1 book discusses the role of the active audience and examples of possible literal responses to the advertisement.

Link

On page 114 of the Year 1 book there is information about how to apply Gerbner's theory to this set product.

Rapid Recall 3.30

What literal responses could there be to this advertisement?

Social and Cultural Contexts

- Advertising campaigns, whether for consumable products, events or charities, reflect the concerns and issues of the society that produces them. In promoting the Paralympics and creating the advertisement for the event and its coverage, Channel 4 was also seeking to address the under-representation or misrepresentation of a particular social group.
- The advertisement reflects the contemporary social context whereby broadcasters are much more aware about the need to reflect diversity in what they include on their channels. The creators of the advertisement focus on the fact that the athletes are real people – 'Human' rather than 'Super' – which makes them and their everyday struggles more relatable and accessible to the audience.
- The representation of disability in this advertisement is affected by social and cultural circumstances. Channel 4 has taken the active decision to present the athletes neither as victims nor as heroes, but just ordinary sports people facing extraordinary challenges. This constructs a more compelling narrative reflecting social issues and the appetite of the time for success stories that are accessible. Lynsey Atkin, 4Creative's executive creative director explains that the agency saw an opportunity to present the Paralympians in a way that hadn't been used before, *'by pointing a camera at the realities of their lives and, as with any elite athlete, the sacrifices they make in pursuit of greatness'* (The Drum, 2021).
- Research into the impact of the 2012 Paralympics on perceptions of disability found that:
  - Two-thirds of viewers (65%) felt the coverage of the Paralympics had a favourable impact on their perceptions towards people with disabilities.
  - More than four in five adults agreed disabled athletes were as talented as able-bodied athletes.

This rose to 91% among those who had watched Channel 4's coverage of the Paralympics.

Link

Video games are also covered on pages 115–119 of the Year 1 book.

Investigating the Set Forms and Products: Video Games

As you will have discovered during Year 1 of the course, video games is the media form that appears only in Section B of Component 1, and is therefore studied in relation to industry and audience specifically. There is no requirement for you to study video games in relation to media language and representation, and this form will not appear as an unseen product in Section A. You will be required to consider contexts in relation to this form, including social and cultural, economic and political.

Key Term

Virtual costuming
Where new costumes or skins can be bought for characters in the virtual world of the game. Gamers can be involved in making choices about how they want their characters to be represented and the games' publishers can add to their revenue from the cash used to do this.

Economic Context

Video games are surviving in a competitive market where different hardware and software manufacturers are competing for audiences. Global production, circulation and distribution are also very important to the industry. New video games are marketed aggressively in order to secure audiences.

In 2017 a new video game was launched: *Fortnite: Battle Royale*. This game received a lot of media attention as it rapidly became one of the world's most popular online games with over 40 million users each month. The creators of new games have to be innovative in the way they make money in order to achieve economic success. **Virtual costuming** proved to be a financial success in the case of *Fortnite*.

Fortnite continues to be a hugely popular and economically successful game and has gained iconic status in popular culture. Chapter 4 was launched in 2022 and has managed to remain relevant and financially viable as a franchise through, for example, collaborations and cross-overs involving Ariana Grande, Travis Scott and Marvel.

Social and Cultural Context

Video games are one of the forms that clearly reflect social and cultural changes with regards to the ways in which audiences interact with and use media products. The form, since its introduction, has also raised issues and started debates in society regarding regulation and the effect of media products upon audience behaviour. Developments in technology have allowed the games industry to offer innovative experiences to audiences that are not available on other platforms.

However, there have also been well documented problems surrounding this media form. In June 2018 the World Health Organisation (WHO) classified gaming addiction as a medical disorder. It was also announced that the first patients in the UK were to be treated on the NHS for games addiction.

Set Product Recap

The role of regulation in global production, distribution and circulation

The regulation of video games is essential, as the form has become more prolific and popular. However, this has also proved to be an increasingly difficult task both for the UK and other countries, particularly regarding technological developments within the industry.

In 2012 the UK government moved to tighten the regulation of video games. This was largely as a result of recommendations made in two key reviews of the industry: Tanya Byron's *Safer Children in a Digital World* (2008) and Reg Bailey's *Letting Children be Children* (2011). In June 2012 all games sold in the UK were registered under the PEGI system, making it illegal to sell 12-rated video games to younger children. The PEGI system also gave more information about each game's content and the reason for the age certification. This was mainly aimed at parents to guide them in what was suitable gameplay for their children.

However, due to the advances in technology since the original change in legislation, games can now be accessed more easily by children through downloads and streaming for those who can purchase games online, and further measures to protect children have been introduced over recent years.

Although in the past there have been debates about the links between video gameplay, transgressive behaviour and acts of violence, this has often been irresponsibly reported in the media and the empirical evidence for these claims is limited and frequently unsubstantiated.

The video games industry continues to put in place measures to ensure that games are played by people of the appropriate age. In addition, the Entertainment Software Rating Board (ESRB) provides information for players and parents, about the content and suitability of games. Its aim is to create a positive, safe experience for all gamers and '*to help parents make informed decisions about the video games and apps their children play*' (www.esrb.org). The information is divided into Rating Categories, Content Descriptors and Interactive Elements, offering a comprehensive guide for parents and young gamers. The ESRB work in all areas of the games industry including marketing and distribution to ensure responsible processes are in place.

***Fortnite* was an unexpected gaming success in 2017.**

Stretch and Challenge 3.44

Read about *Fortnite's* business model in 'How *Fortnite* Conquered the World', https://www.theguardian.com/games/2018/may/27/fortnite-conquered-the-world-video-game-teenagers-parents.

The rise in the popularity of video games has caused society to question the effect on young people.

Rapid Recall 3.31

What does PEGI stand for?

The PEGI system regulates who is allowed to buy video games in the UK.

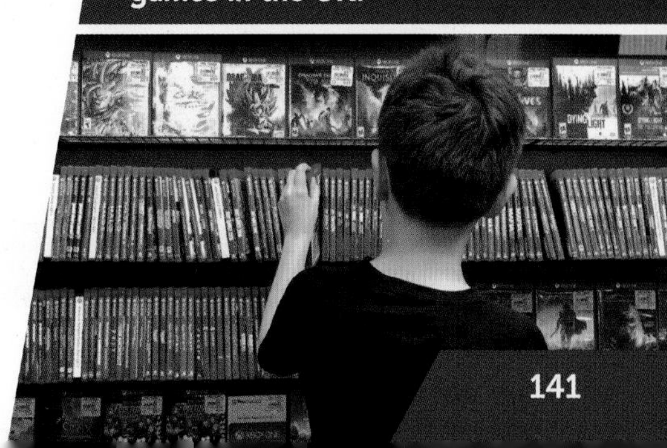

Stretch and Challenge 3.45

You can access the Online Safety Bill factsheet here: https://www.gov.uk/government/publications/online-safety-bill-supporting-documents/online-safety-bill-factsheet. This gives more details of the bill's proposals and how it may impact the video games industry.
The possible global effects of the bill is discussed in this article:
https://www.gamesindustry.biz/could-uk-online-safety-bill-change-gaming-worldwide.

Stretch and Challenge 3.46

In the USA, the trade association for the video games industry is The Entertainment Software Association. Its website and annual report offer a wealth of information about the gaming industry in the US: www.theesa.com.

Quickfire 3.58

What interesting statistics are there in these graphics about US gamers?

Regulation of video games continues to be monitored and discussed in different countries. In 2020, the UK's Department for Digital, Culture, Media and Sport asked the games industry for evidence on loot boxes which can be purchased with real money, and their links to gaming-related harm including gambling and mental health issues. The government stated:

> *Games companies and platforms should provide spending controls and transparent information to all players. Protections should support the minority of players who spend a disproportionate amount of money on loot boxes, and who may be at a greater risk of harm.* (Rt Hon Dorries, 2022)

It called for the purchase to be unavailable to children and young people unless approved by a parent or guardian.

A further development in the regulation of all online content is the UK's Online Safety Bill which is going through parliament at time of writing (February 2023). Some of the changes the bill proposes will have implications for the video games industry. Previously, it had been the responsibility of the games providers to regulate the content, with the advent of this bill new responsibilities have been set out for online user-to-user service providers that may be accessed by children.

Audiences: What is the Appeal of Video Games?

How media organisations reflect the different needs of mass and specialised audiences, including through targeting

Who Plays Video Games?

The profile of the gamer is broad, as is the genre of games they are playing. The ESA gathers data related to the US gaming audience and publishes a yearly report highlighting its findings. The graphic below is taken from the 2022 report.

Ukie (UK Interactive Entertainment) in the UK performs a similar service for the games and interactive industry.

Video gaming is no longer exclusively enjoyed by the young. As generations who regularly play video games grow older so has the average age of the gamer. In the US in 2022 36% of gamers were 18–35, 24% were under 18 and 13% were 35–44 (www.statista.com).

Source: ESA, 2022

The modern gaming audience is diverse in terms of age and gender, more so now than at any time in the industry's history. This is matched by the diverse range of game genres available to play. Gamers gain a range of different experiences from playing video games:

- One of the main attractions of playing video games is the levels of interactivity compared with other media platforms. The choices that can be made by the participant directly influence the gameplaying experience and give a sense of control and ownership not available in other media forms.
- Gameplaying is a collaborative experience often related to the creation of a narrative. This is enhanced by the persistent world experience that is unique to the form.

- This collaboration extends also to being part of an online community involving multi-players (MMORPG).

The psychological immersion involved in some gameplaying can be said to help to create a sense of identity. This may be through, for example, identification with in-game characters, living through virtual avatars and also identifying with real-life gaming communities. Read more about gaming in the virtual environment in Ecenbarger (2014).

People play video games for a diverse range of reasons, some of which are often not considered, particularly by critics of the form. These may include:

- **Competition**: very often the gamer may be playing against members of a group from an online community. If not, the player, depending on the game, may have to succeed at a range of increasingly more complex tasks and challenges to proceed to the next level.
- **Social interaction**: some platforms, for example the Xbox Series X and PlayStation 5, allow the gamer to speak directly to other gamers, who then become part of the virtual world experience. Certain games can facilitate multi-generational playing and this can be a social bonding experience. As Brian Mazique says, after playing video games with every one of his four children he's been able to uniquely bond with each one:

  Thanks to video games, I've learned more about each of my sons and daughters, and about myself as a father. (Mazique, cited in ESA, 2018)
- **Skills development**: a lot of research has been done into the positive outcomes of playing video games responsibly; this research unearthed some positive advantages of playing certain video games, particularly with regards to the development of technical and social skills. This has provided more evidence to suggest that responsible and supervised video gaming can be a positive experience (see Granic et al., 2014).
- **Enhancing creativity**: it must also be remembered that not all video games are violent, although it is examples from this genre that tend to receive the most media coverage. Other game genres can encourage the player to be creative in the way in which they interact with the avatar and the choices they make about different narratives.

The research around the real-world psychosocial benefits of gaming has contributed to the rise in what are being termed 'serious games'. These games focus on the social interaction elements and the decision-making skills inherent in some video games. These 'serious games' are now being designed for use by the military, economists and healthcare providers to educate employees and equip them for certain real-life situations. Newbury (2017) thinks that the success of serious games is partly due to there being a growing nation of gameplayers. Serious games allow gamers to learn, experience and develop skills that have not previously been easily accessible:

> *By giving audiences direct experience with new learning environments, we capitalize on the positive impact that games can have …* (Newbury, 2017)

Applying Theory

Media Effects: Bandura

The information in the previous section, relating to the more positive outcomes of playing video games, will enable to you to consider Bandura's theory (2008) from another perspective. While some may say that certain video-game genres may encourage transgressive behaviour, although there is no concrete evidence, there is also another school of thought that says the 'modelling' suggested by Bandura could be of positive behaviours. In the same way, his suggestion that audiences acquire

Rapid Recall 3.32

What is meant by persistent worlds in gaming?

Rapid Recall 3.33

What is MMORPG?

Stretch and Challenge 3.47

Read Charles Ecenbarger's (2014) paper entitled 'The Impact of Video Games on Identity Construction', about gaming in a virtual environment, online.

Quickfire 3.59

Why might the immersion in a virtual world with other online gamers be perceived negatively by those who are concerned about the gaming experience?

Some video games can encourage sociability and multi-generational collaboration.

Quickfire 3.60

Which audience theory can be applied to the way in which the audience 'uses' video games?

Link

Page 119 of the Year 1 book discusses Albert Bandura's effects theory.

attitudes and emotional responses through such modelling could be the positive effects of collaboration and decision making and empathy with online characters. This may have a positive effect on the player in the real as well as the virtual world. For example, a man playing through a virtual female avatar may broaden his emotional experience, which may help in real-life situations.

Tip

Remember that at A Level the expectation is that you will use a range of complex theories appropriately to develop your analysis of the set products.

Rapid Recall 3.34

What is meant by transgressive behaviour?

Set Product: *Assassin's Creed* Franchise

Set Product Recap: *Assassin's Creed* franchise

You may already have studied this product in Year 1 of the course; this product carries through into Year 2 of the course, there are no additional video games to be studied. You are required to have knowledge and understanding of the *Assassin's Creed* franchise in terms of the relevant video games industry and audience issues it illustrates. It is not expected that you will study all of the games in the franchise. One game must be studied in detail. This could be *Assassin's Creed III: Liberation*, or in your centre you may study more recent releases within the franchise. In order to develop an awareness of industry and audience issues, you should consider at least one extract from the chosen game.

How processes of production, distribution and circulation shape media products

- The *Assassin's Creed* franchise was developed by Ubisoft, a French global computer game publisher, which is one of the largest independent game publishers:

  > *Ubisoft is a creator of worlds, committed to enriching players' lives with original and memorable gaming experiences.* (Ubisoft, n.d.)

- In terms of production the games in the franchise are part of a multinational development, which is typical of game production in larger studios such as Ubisoft.
- Video games production techniques have evolved and become increasingly innovative as the industry has become more competitive and the demand for games has increased. Advances in technology have shaped video games by the inclusion of more complex gameplay, highly developed graphics and advanced CGI.
- The marketing of each game in the *Assassin's Creed* franchise also includes a trailer and subsequently gameplay videos to appeal to the audience. During the early stages of a new game's introduction, the gameplayer is usually also able to download additional content in the shape of props, loot and additional memory, offering different immersive experiences.

The impact of digitally convergent media platforms on media production, distribution and circulation, including individual producers

- Digital convergence is important to Ubisoft as an individual producer in a competitive market, it also benefits fans as like-minded communities and individual producers of game content, for example through gameplay videos
- For example, in January 2014, *Assassin's Creed III: Liberation* was re-released as a high-definition re-work. It was no longer confined to only the PlayStation format but also was made available on Xbox 360, PS3 and PC. While the game was impressive for its **open world play** on a portable platform, with the re-release the opportunities for more complex gameplay were developed. The game's cinematics were remastered and the HD elements made the game more impressive to play. The re-released game also has **backward compatibility**, allowing gamers to play this on older games consoles.

Key Terms

Open world play
Refers to the type of game where the player is given freedom to explore a virtual world and can make choices that determine the next moves. This gives the player a feeling of control in contrast to linear game play.

Backward compatibility
The property of the system that allows interoperability with an older system. It allows gamers to play video games that were developed for previous versions of the console.

Link

There is information about this set product on pages 117–119 of the Year 1 book.

- In addition, the convergence between social media platforms promotes gamer engagement and identification with the games across the fan community. Walkthroughs and gameplay videos are created by fans to introduce new gamers to the franchise, thus ensuring the appeal to a new audience. This benefits Ubisoft, as fans promote elements of the game across different platforms thus broadening reach.
- Convergence has developed further across the most recent games in the franchise. This is significant in terms of promotion and circulation, and facilitates the development and re-release of games incorporating more complex elements. For example, *Assassin's Creed Odyssey* offered a more immersive experience for players than previous games and *Assassin's Creed Infinity* was released in 2022 as a fully live service game, inspired by the success of games like *Fortnite*. This enabled the franchise to expand and develop new experiences for the gamer.

Audiences

How audiences interact with the media and can be actively involved in media production

Video games differ from other media products in that they offer interactive, multiplayer experiences for the gamer. Part of their appeal is that they are role-playing games and encourage participants to work together on a particular mission, so interacting with other players within a gaming community. Interaction involves becoming immersed in the persistent game world and making decisions as a character within the game. Fan forums, walkthroughs and gameplaying videos with instructive voiceovers allow gamers to produce their own content and distribute it online.

Interactive opportunities in the *Assassin's Creed* franchise:

- Interactivity in the games is through an avatar, immersing the gamer in the world of the game through identification with a character; interestingly, in *Assassin's Creed 111: Liberation*, the avatar is female, thus encouraging a different target audience of female gamers. The female gamers' interaction with Aveline may offer an opportunity for identification not available in other video games. In *Assassin's Creed Odyssey* players are offered a choice between playing as a male or female character, Alexios or Kassandra, allowing for different interpretations of the narrative.
- The games' technology is used to create a realistic, life-like world, giving an immersive, interactive experience for the audience. Escaping into a historically accurate virtual world enhances the interactive experience as well as providing both escapism and knowledge and understanding of the time period.
- Some of the games in the franchise include interactive elements such as gamers collecting supplies and tokens to enhance the gameplaying experience. Content can be pre-ordered, for example in *Assassin's Creed 111: Liberation* the 'Mysteries of Bayon' pack, including props and upgraded ammunition. There is a range of different trailers offering tastes of the interactive game experience.

The role and significance of specialised audiences, including niche and fan, to the media

- Interactivity is facilitated through online fan communities and the games in the *Assassin's Creed* franchise have a strong fanbase of **core gamers** and **casual gamers**. Games producers often listen to the criticism and praise of the fans, which can have a direct impact on how the game is developed.
- Walkthrough videos created by fans highlight aspects of the game and encourage interactivity in the gaming community as well as within the game itself. They are an important element of the game's marketing and distribution.

Key Terms

Core gamers
Players with a wide range of gaming interests, who actively engage with different types of games but do not have the intensity of a hardcore gamer.

Casual gamers
Gamers who play more spontaneously and may only play a few games a year. They tend to choose games that are less challenging and lacking in complexity.

Fans are vital to the success of video games.

Key Term

Cosplay
A shortened version of the term costume play, this is a performance art in whereby fans dress up and assume the roles of characters from video games, television and film, usually at organised events for fan communities.

Cosplay events are an important element of the fan community.

Stretch and Challenge 3.48

Consider how Charles Ecenbarger's (2014) research into video games and identity construction can be used to support elements of Jenkins' theory.

Stretch and Challenge 3.49

Consider how you could use Livingstone and Lunt's theories to discuss the issues that arise over the regulation for the games industry, particularly in the light of technological developments and convergence of platforms.

- The Ubisoft website encourages engagement with fans and fan created websites reinforce a sense of community for the specialised gaming audience from diverse social and cultural backgrounds, providing a platform for sharing ideas, comments and gaming experiences. The *Assassin's Creed* website includes discussion forums, fan-created content including AC Wiki, a digital *Assassin's Creed* encyclopaedia created by the fan community and a feature on fans who participate in **cosplay**. Interviews with these fans reinforces the strength and importance of the fan community to the promotion and development of the franchise. One fan thought that *Assassin's Creed* ticked all of their interest boxes, exploring history with great characters, detailed outfits and storylines: *'It was a way for me to explore worlds which I'd only ever read about in history books or daydreamed about during school'* (Psycadillo, 2022).

Applying Theory

Fandom: Jenkins

Some of the areas Jenkins explored include:

- the idea that fans are active participants in the construction and circulation of textual meanings
- the idea that fans construct their social and cultural identities through borrowing and inflecting mass culture images, and are part of a participatory culture that has a vital social dimension.

As has been discussed earlier in this chapter, online fan communities and the importance of fan culture are significant to the success of the gaming industry. Video games offer social, collaborative experiences as part of gameplay and fan communities.

Interaction in video games allows fans to construct their identities through the shared online gaming experience and the role-playing environment.

The developments in video games technology have expanded the ways in which fans can interact with games producers and the fan community, creating a participatory culture.

The *Assassin's Creed* franchise has a well-developed, vocal fanbase of core gamers who have been instrumental in the development of the game and the wider franchise.

Cultural Industries: Hesmondhalgh

Some of the areas Hesmondhalgh explored include:

- the idea that cultural industry companies try to minimise risk and maximise audiences through vertical and horizontal integration, and by formatting their cultural products
- the idea that the largest companies or conglomerates now operate across a number of different cultural industries
- the idea that the radical potential of the internet has been contained to some extent by its incorporation into large, profit-orientated sets of cultural industries.

The video games industry is designed to make a profit, it operates in a competitive market.

One of the ways it minimises risk is through genre-formatting, this is evident in the *Assassin's Creed* franchise. The promotion strategies used in the marketing of a new game focus on audience recognition of the game and the brand as part of the established franchise. Audiences therefore know what to expect.

The video games industry is dominated by large multi-national conglomerates, but companies like Ubisoft are now in competition with tech companies including Facebook, Google and Amazon, who have recently become major players in the games industry backed by huge financial reserves.

Component 1: Media Products, Industries and Audiences: Assessment

4

OVERVIEW

How will I be assessed?

Written examination: 2 hours 15 minutes

35% of the qualification

90 marks

A Level Component 1 assesses media language, representation, media industries, audiences and media contexts. You will also be assessed on your use of relevant theories and theoretical approaches, and your correct use of subject-specific terminology.

Section A: Analysing Media Language and Representation

45 marks

This section of the examination paper assesses your ability to analyse media language and representation in relation to two of the media forms studied for this section. These are: advertising, marketing, music video or newspapers. There will be two questions:

- One question will assess media language (15 marks). This question requires the analysis of an unseen audio-visual or print resource. This will be taken from one of the media forms studied for this section.
- One question will assess representation (30 marks). This question will require you to compare one of the set products you have studied with an unseen audio-visual or print product taken from one of the forms studied for this section. In the examination you may be required to compare products in the same or different forms. You may also be required to refer to relevant media contexts. This is an **extended response question**.
- Across Section A as a whole, there will always be one unseen audio-visual resource and one unseen print-based resource; Question 1 will relate to an audio-visual resource and Question 2 will relate to a print-based resource.

Understanding the demands of the different sections of the examination papers will help to focus your revision.

Tip

It is important that you are aware of what is required in each section of the examination. This should help to guide your revision and the organisation of your notes.

Key Term

Extended response question A question with a higher mark tariff, which is more demanding. It requires the ability to construct and develop a sustained line of reasoning that is coherent, relevant, substantiated and logically structured.

Tip

Time to view and study the unseen resources is built into the time given for the examination. Make sure you use this time productively.

Tip

Engaging with a range of different examples from the set forms outside of those studied in class will help to prepare you for the demands of the examination.

Tip

At A Level it is important that you understand the set theories and theoretical perspectives in some detail and are able to discuss their relevance in relation to the set forms and products.

Tip

It would be impossible to know all the aspects of the key theorists, as many of them are prolific writers on a range of subjects related to the media. To help you there is a summary of the key ideas of each of the set theorists at the end of this book.

Tip

It will help to read articles and extracts from books related to the set theories and theoretical perspectives in order to extend your knowledge and understanding.

Tip

The mark allocations between questions and part-questions will vary across different examination series.

Key Term

Stepped question
Refers to when an examination is split into different sub-parts with the mark tariffs usually increasing as the question parts become more difficult. In Component 1 Section B there are some questions that test your knowledge and are lower in tariff than those that require you to discuss and explain.

At A Level you will be expected to apply and critically explore relevant theories. Not all the theories to be assessed are applicable to every form. The grid below will help to show which theories are required for Section A.

	Theory/theoretical perspective	Component 1 forms
Media Language	Semiotics, including Roland Barthes	Advertising and marketing Music video Newspapers
	Structuralism, including Claude Lévi-Strauss	Advertising and marketing Music video Newspapers
Representation	Theories of representation, including Stuart Hall	Advertising and marketing Music video Newspapers
	Theories of identity, including David Gauntlett	Advertising and marketing Music video
	Feminist theory, including Liesbet van Zoonen and bell hooks	Advertising and marketing Music video
	Theories around ethnicity and postcolonial theory, including Paul Gilroy	Advertising and marketing Music video

Section B: Understanding Media Industries and Audiences

45 marks

This section will assess knowledge and understanding of media industries, audiences and media contexts in relation to any of the forms studied for Section B. These are: advertising, film, newspapers, radio and video games. There will be two questions:

- Question 3 will be a **stepped question** assessing knowledge and understanding of media industries in relation to at least one form studied.
- Question 4 will be a stepped question assessing knowledge and understanding of audiences. It will assess a different form from that assessed in Question 3 and may assess more than one form.

The grid on the following page will help to show which theories are required for Section B.

Link

Examples of examination questions can be found in Chapter 9 of this book.

	Theory/theoretical perspective	Component 1 forms
Media Industries	Power and media industries, including James Curran and Jean Seaton	Film Newspapers Radio Video games
	Regulation, including Sonia Livingstone and Peter Lunt	Film Newspapers Radio Video games
	Cultural industries, including David Hesmondhalgh	Film Newspapers Video games
Audiences	Media effects, including Albert Bandura	Video games
	Cultivation theory, including George Gerbner	Advertising Newspapers
	Reception theory, including Stuart Hall	Advertising Newspapers Radio Video games
	Fandom, including Henry Jenkins	Radio Video games
	'End of audience' theories, including Clay Shirky	Newspapers Radio Video games

Tip

It is also acceptable that you refer to other theories you may have been taught during your course, as long as they are relevant to the question.

Tip

The theories required for Year 2 of the A Level course are more challenging and demand a higher level of understanding. It is important that you spend time in your independent study exploring the key aspects of these more complex theoretical perspectives.

Tip

The products you studied at Year 1/AS will also be assessed in Year 2 of the A Level course. It is important that you regularly revise products you have covered earlier in the course.

Tip

It is very important that in an examination response you do not merely download the theories that you have learned but that you read the question carefully and select the most appropriate.

The grid below will help to remind you of where and how the products will be assessed for Component 1, the areas of the theoretical framework that must be covered and the relevant contexts.

Media forms	Set products	Section A		Section B		Suggested contexts
		Media Language	Reps	Ind.	Aud.	
Advertising and marketing	*Tide* print advertisement	✓	✓		✓	Historical Social and cultural
	Super. Human. Tokyo 2020 Paralympic Games audio-visual advertisement (2020)	✓	✓		✓	Social and cultural Economic
	Kiss of the Vampire (1963) film poster	✓	✓			Historical Social and cultural

(continued)

Media forms	Set products	Section A		Section B		Suggested contexts
Music video	One option from Group 1 and one option from Group 2 must be studied **Group 1** *Formation*, Beyoncé (2016) or *Turntables*, Janelle Monáe (2020) or *Underdog*, Alicia Keys (2020) **Group 2** *Riptide*, Vance Joy (2013) or *Seventeen Going Under*, Sam Fender (2021) or *Little Bit of Love*, Tom Grennan (2021)	✓	✓			Social and cultural
Newspapers	*Daily Mirror* 1 February 2022 front page and article on 'Partygate'	✓	✓			Social and cultural Economic political
	Daily Mirror Complete edition; online and social media content			✓	✓	Social and cultural Economic Political
	The Times 1 February 2022 front page	✓	✓			Social and cultural Economic Political
	The Times Complete edition; online and social media content			✓	✓	Social and cultural Economic Political
Film	*Black Panther* (2018) Cross-media study			✓		Economic Political Social and cultural
	I, Daniel Blake (2016) Cross-media study			✓		Economic Political
Radio	*Woman's Hour* or *Have You Heard George's Podcast?*			✓	✓	Social and cultural Economic Political
Video games	*Assassin's Creed III: Liberation* (2012) Set product and related online and social media content			✓	✓	Social and cultural Economic

Component 2: Media Forms and Products in Depth

5

Section A: Television in the Global Age

The Specification

If you are following the linear Eduqas specification, television is one of the media forms that you are required to study in depth. At A Level, you are required to study two set television products, including one that has been produced for a non-English-speaking audience.

This section builds on the material covered in Chapter 5 of the Year 1 book, where some of the key approaches and theories that can be used to study television products were introduced. As well as providing a framework for analysing the non-English-language products, in this section we will introduce the more advanced critical theories that you are required to apply to the set television products at A Level.

Link

An introduction to the study of television as a media form can be found in the Year 1 book, pages 123–158.

WJEC

If you are following the modular WJEC specification, you will study television as part of the A2 module 'Media in the Global Age'. For this unit, you will study three television crime dramas – the Welsh crime drama *Hinterland*, one European crime drama produced outside the UK, and one UK crime drama produced in the 1990s. There are four European crime dramas to choose from (*The Bridge*, *The Killing*, *The Disappearance* and *Arne Dahl*) and four UK crime dramas from the 1990s (*Prime Suspect*, *Inspector Morse*, *Touching Evil* and *Cracker*).

Before reading this section of the book, which includes a discussion of Nordic noir and its influence on contemporary crime dramas such as *Hinterland*, we would recommend that you look at the section on television in the Year 1 book as it provides a useful overview of key issues and debates regarding the study of television as a media form and also offers an introduction to the codes, conventions and historical development of the crime drama genre.

Tip

The set products shown here are correct at the time of writing. However, it is important to note that these may change from time to time. Before choosing which option to study, you should check the Eduqas website to see if there have been any changes to the set products.

Television Options

For Section A of Component 2, you are required to study two television products, including one that has been produced for a non-English-speaking audience. There are three options to choose from.

OPTION 1: Crime Drama

Set Product 1: *Peaky Blinders* (UK, 2013), Series 1, Episode 1

- *Peaky Blinders* is a British crime drama that was created by Steven Knight and which stars Cillian Murphy. It was produced for the BBC by Caryn Mandabach Productions and Tiger Aspect Productions. It was first broadcast on BBC Two on 12 September 2013.

Set Product 2: *The Bridge* (Denmark/Sweden, 2015), Season 3, Episode 1

- *The Bridge* (*Bron/Broen*) is an example of Nordic noir – a Scandinavian sub-genre of crime drama. It is co-produced by Filmlance International and Nimbus Film. The opening episode of the third season was first shown on Sweden's SVT1 and Denmark's DR1 on 27 September 2015. Its first UK screening was on BBC Four at 9pm on 21 November 2015.

OPTION 2: Science-Fiction and the Supernatural Thriller

Set Product 1: *Black Mirror* (UK/US, 2016), Series 3, Episode 4: 'San Junipero'

- *Black Mirror* is a British science-fiction **anthology series**, created by Charlie Brooker. The fourth episode of Series 3, 'San Junipero', which stars Mackenzie Davis and Gugu Mbatha-Raw, was produced by House of Tomorrow for Netflix. It was released on Netflix on 21 October 2016.

Key Term

Anthology series
A series that is comprised of entirely separate, self-contained stories. The individual episodes may be connected by a common, over-arching theme but they generally feature different characters.

Set Product 2: *The Returned* (France, 2012), Season 1, Episode 1

- *The Returned* (*Les Revenants*) is a French supernatural thriller. Produced by Haut et Court, it was originally shown on the French television network Canal+ on 26 November 2012. In the UK, it was first broadcast on Channel 4 at 9pm on 9 June 2013.

OPTION 3: The Spy Thriller

Set Product 1: *Killing Eve* (UK, 2018), Series 1, Episode 1

- *Killing Eve* is a British spy thriller, starring Jodie Comer and Sandra Oh. It was produced for BBC America and BBC Three by Sid Gentle Films. It was first broadcast on BBC America on 8 April 2018 and on BBC Three on 15 September 2018.

Set Product 2: *Tehran* (Israel, 2020), Season 1, Episode 1

- *Tehran* is an Israeli spy thriller created by Moshe Zonder, Dana Eden and Maor Kohn. Produced by Donna and Shula Productions in association with Paper Plane Productions, it was originally broadcast on Kan 11 in Israel on 22 June 2020 before its international streaming release on Apple TV+ in September 2020.

Using the Theoretical Framework

In exploring your set television products, you will need to consider all four areas of the theoretical framework:

- **Media Language**: how television products communicate meanings through their forms, codes, conventions and techniques.
- **Representation**: how television products portray issues, individuals and social groups.
- **Media Industries**: how ownership, production, distribution and regulation affect television products.
- **Audiences**: how television products target, attract, reach and address audiences, and how audiences interpret and respond to television products.

MEDIA LANGUAGE

Genre

Genre is one of the key aspects of media language that you need to explore when studying your set television products.

The dynamic and historically relative nature of genres such as crime drama, science-fiction and the spy thriller was discussed in the Year 1 book along with Steve Neale's theory of genre.

This section builds on some of these ideas as it addresses:

- the socially relative nature of genre conventions
- genre hybridity
- the way in which genre conventions can be challenged or subverted
- how Neale's theory of genre might be evaluated
- the specific generic contexts of *The Bridge*, *The Returned* and *Tehran*.

Link

Pages 126–139 of the Year 1 book introduce key critical approaches for studying television genres and outline the defining conventions of crime drama, science-fiction and the spy thriller.

Link

Steve Neale's theory of genre is outlined on page 127 of the Year 1 book.

Comparing the Set Television Products

While the two television products you study will belong to the same genre or two genres that are closely related, they will have been produced within different national or cultural contexts:

- Option 1 features a British crime drama (*Peaky Blinders*) and a Scandinavian crime drama (*The Bridge*).
- Option 2 features a British science-fiction series (*Black Mirror*) and a French supernatural thriller (*The Returned*).
- Option 3 features a British spy thriller (*Killing Eve*) and an Israeli spy thriller (*Tehran*).

The set products therefore provide useful opportunities for comparison. Taking a comparative approach to the two television products will enable you to:

1. Develop a greater understanding of the genre(s) they belong to and the patterns of repetition and difference that exist within those genres.
2. Explore how social and cultural contexts shape and influence the way in which genre conventions are used.

OPTION 1: Nordic Noir and *The Bridge*

The non-English-language product in Option 1 is *The Bridge*. This is an example of Nordic noir – a sub-genre of crime drama comprising films, television programmes and other works of fiction that are set or produced in Scandinavian countries and that feature dark, unsettling themes and a bleak or melancholy **aesthetic**.

Notable examples of Nordic noir include Danish crime drama *The Killing*, as well as the Swedish series *Wallander* and *Beck*.

According to Glen Creeber (2015), the defining conventions of Nordic noir include:

- *multi-layered storylines*
- *a slow and melancholic pace*
- *a dimly lit aesthetic*
- *an interest in uncovering the dark underbelly of contemporary life.*

Key Term

Aesthetic
The look, style or feel of a media product.

Rapid Recall 5.1

What is a sub-genre?

Key Terms

Film noir
A mode of filmmaking that emerged in the USA in the 1940s and which features a distinctive visual style, characterised by low-key or chiaroscuro lighting, claustrophobic framing and unsettling camera angles.

Low-key lighting
A technique that leaves significant areas of the shot in shadow. In low-key lighting set-ups, the fill light (a secondary light source that is typically used to eliminate areas of shadow) is removed or reduced.

Chiaroscuro lighting
Chiaroscuro is an Italian term used in the visual arts to describe a dramatic contrast between darkness and light. In film and television products, this effect is produced through particular lighting techniques.

Many of these conventions are derived from **film noir** – a mode of filmmaking that emerged in the USA in the 1940s. Films in the noir tradition tended to offer a bleak or pessimistic view of society. The darker tone of these films was reflected in their visual style. **Low-key lighting** or **chiaroscuro lighting** would often be used, leaving large parts of the shot in shadow. This added to the mood of uncertainty and paranoia.

Expressive use was also made of framing and mise-en-scène to convey a sense of anxiety, alienation and claustrophobia. In his overview of film noir, Andrew Spicer points to '*a pervasive use of claustrophobic framing devices including doorways, windows, stairways, and metal bed frames that seem to invade the space of the characters, trapping them*' (2010). Venetian blinds – a common visual motif in film noir – were often used to similar effect, creating the impression of characters being trapped behind bars. This pervasive use of claustrophobic framing devices is particularly noticeable in the set episode of *The Bridge*.

From Film Noir to Nordic Noir

Nordic noir programmes such as *The Killing* and *The Bridge* borrow heavily from film noir. They too explore dark, unsettling themes and use similar visual codes, as the shot below illustrates.

However, while Nordic noir draws heavily on the American tradition of film noir, its aesthetic is distinctively Scandinavian. As Marit Waade and Pia Majbritt Jensen (2013) point out:

> *Nordic Noir uses recognisably Nordic phenomena, settings, light, climate and seasonal conditions as well as language(s), characters and themes.*

This illustrates the idea that genre conventions are socially and culturally relative. For example, while *Peaky Blinders* offers a distinctively British take on the quintessentially American gangster genre, *The Bridge* brings a Scandinavian sensibility to the American noir tradition.

Low-key or chiaroscuro lighting and an expressive use of mise-en-scène are common conventions of Nordic noir shows such as *The Killing*.

Key Term

Desaturation
A process through which colours are made to appear more muted. In film and television programmes, this is typically achieved through colour grading, as more white, black or grey is added to the image.

Stretch and Challenge 5.1

Develop your understanding of Nordic noir by reading Anne Marit Waade and Pia Majbritt Jensen's (2013) article 'Nordic Noir Production Values: *The Killing* and *The Bridge*', which can be found online.

The Significance of Setting in Nordic Noir

As well as conveying a strong sense of place, the Scandinavian landscapes that feature in Nordic noir also have a significant aesthetic and narrative function. For example, programmes such as *The Killing* and *The Bridge* often use the desolate beauty of the Nordic landscape to convey a sense of isolation or alienation. The cold Scandinavian climate and the wintery quality of the light add to the melancholy mood, while post-production techniques such as colour grading are used to create a **desaturated** look, accentuating this effect.

This promotional image for the first season of *The Bridge* illustrates the way in which Nordic noir uses setting and mise-en-scène expressively to convey mood and atmosphere.

From Nordic Noir to Celtic Noir

The success of Nordic noir has also given rise to **Celtic noir**. Set in Celtic-speaking regions of the United Kingdom rather than Nordic countries, Celtic noir, like its Scandinavian cousin, is characterised by dark themes and a prevailing sense of melancholy.

Examples of Celtic noir include:

- Welsh series *Y Gwyll* (*Hinterland*) and *Craith* (*Hidden*), which were shown on the Welsh-language channel S4C as well as BBC Four and BBC One Wales.
- Scottish-Gaelic series *Bannon* (*The Ties that Bind*), which was shown on the Scottish Gaelic-language station, BBC Alba.
- Irish-Gaelic series *Corp + Anam* (*Body and Soul*), which was shown on the Irish public service channel TG4.

Like Nordic noir, Celtic noir has a strong sense of place. For example, Ed Thomas, the co-creator of *Hinterland/Y Gwyll* has described the show as '*a love letter to a disappearing Wales*', suggesting that the makers of the programme were '*using the genre, a cop show, to tell stories about Wales*' (Mathias, 2014).

Key Term

Celtic noir
A sub-genre similar in style, mood and aesthetic to Nordic noir, but which is set in Celtic- or Gaelic-speaking regions of Wales, Scotland and Ireland.

OPTION 2: Supernatural Thrillers and *The Returned*

The non-English-language product in Option 2 is the French supernatural thriller *The Returned*. Like science-fiction programmes, supernatural thrillers usually focus on the extraordinary or otherworldly. However, while science-fiction's exploration of 'other worlds' is grounded in science, the narratives of supernatural thrillers involve events that defy rational explanation.

For example, the science-fiction anthology series *Black Mirror* has a strong basis in scientific reality; its exploration of the impact of artificial intelligence, social media and new technologies on everyday life reflects recent scientific advances. In contrast, the central premise of *The Returned*, which involves characters returning from the dead, defies scientific reason.

Key Term

The uncanny
A sensation commonly produced in the supernatural genre, whereby the familiar is made to feel strange or unfamiliar. In Freudian theory, the uncanny is often associated with the return of something that has been repressed.

Key Figure

Sigmund Freud
An Austrian theorist who is widely credited with founding psychoanalysis. His work has had a profound influence in many different fields, including literature, film and media studies.

Stretch and Challenge 5.2

What examples of the uncanny can you find in the set episode of *The Returned*? How are ordinary landscapes and settings made to seem unsettling or strange, for instance?

Key Term

Zombie drama
A sub-genre of horror and the supernatural that focuses on the 'undead'.

Stretch and Challenge 5.3

Develop your understanding of *The Returned* by reading Louisa Mellor's interview with the producer and director of the show, 'The Returned: Fabrice Gobert and Caroline Benjo interview' (4 June 2013), which can be found on the *Den of Geek* website.

A useful concept for exploring the way in which supernatural thrillers project a sense of unease is **Sigmund Freud**'s idea of **the uncanny**. Freud used this term to describe the sensation that is produced when something that is familiar comes to seem strange or frightening. For him, the uncanny belongs '*to all that arouses dread and creeping horror*' (Freud, 1919). He used the German terms '*heimlich*' (homely) and '*unheimlich*' (unhomely) to describe this relationship between the familiar and the strange.

More specifically, Freud's theory suggests that:

- the sense of anxiety associated with the uncanny can '*come from something repressed which recurs*' or returns (Freud, 1919)
- the uncanny is often experienced with regard to '*death and dead bodies, to the return of the dead, and to spirits and ghosts*' (Freud, 1919).

Not only does a sense of the uncanny play a central role in the narrative of *The Returned*, it can also be seen to inform the programme's aesthetic or visual style (see, e.g., the image shown here). The show's director, Fabrice Gobert, cites the work of American photographer Gregory Crewdson (Mellor, 2013) as a particular influence on the look of the series, noting that Crewdson has a unique way of playing with frame and lighting in order to make ordinary urban landscapes seem strange.

The Zombie Sub-genre

The Returned could also be classified as a **zombie drama** – a particular sub-genre of horror that includes American shows such as *The Walking Dead* and *iZombie*. However, in terms of theme, tone and style, *The Returned* is closer to the British zombie show *In the Flesh* than these American series. As the producer of *The Returned*, Caroline Benjo, points out, '*even though [...] zombies are quintessentially North American*', Dominic Mitchell, the writer and creator of *In the Flesh*:

> *twists the genre and makes it very British with a strong artistic and personal angle.*
> (Mellor, 2013)

Again, this shows that genre conventions are socially and culturally relative. For example, while French, British and North American zombie dramas may all draw on the same basic repertoire of elements, the way in which those elements are used is likely to differ according to the cultural context in which the show is produced. Therefore, in the same way that *The Bridge* offers a Scandinavian take on noir, *The Returned* provides a French twist on a 'quintessentially North American' genre (the zombie drama).

OPTION 3: The Spy Thriller and *Tehran*

While spy thrillers have achieved significant transnational appeal, crossing international borders much like the assassins and intelligence operatives that populate their narratives, they often address concerns that are specific to the national and cultural contexts in which they are produced. For example, many post-war British spy thrillers, such as the Bond movies based on the works of Ian Fleming and the film and television adaptations of John Le Carré's spy novels, can be seen to offer a commentary on Britain's changing place in the world following the decline of the British empire.

Spy thrillers produced in other countries also provide a vehicle for exploring issues relating to national history, geopolitics and cultural identity. Significantly, the German spy thrillers *Deutschland '83* and *Kleo* both look back to a watershed moment in German history – the period leading up to and immediately following the fall of the Berlin Wall, an event that paved the way for German reunification, marking the end of the Cold War.

Geopolitics is also at the heart of many Israeli spy thrillers produced over the past two decades. A significant number of these shows address the ongoing Israeli–Palestininan conflict. Notable examples of this include *Fauda*, which follows the work of an Israeli special forces unit working undercover to track down terrorists operating in the Palestinian West Bank territory, and the critically acclaimed Israeli thriller *Prisoners of War* (*Hatufim*), which provided the basis for the popular American spy thriller *Homeland*, produced by Showtime.

Rather than Israeli–Palestinian relations, *Tehran* is framed by Israel's long-standing conflict with Iran. The central narrative of the show, which sees a Mossad agent sent on an undercover mission to disable an Iranian nuclear reactor, reflects particular cultural anxieties about Iran's nuclear capabilities and has notable parallels with recent real-world events. For example, in 2021, shortly after the series was aired, a nuclear facility in Natanz in Iran was the subject of a cyber-attack widely believed to have been carried out by Israeli agents from Mossad. Resonances such as these could be seen to enhance the show's cultural verisimilitude, giving it greater topicality or socio-political relevance.

Stretch and Challenge 5.4

Develop your understanding of *Tehran* and the Israeli spy thriller by reading Yael Friedman and Maryam Ghorbankarimi's article 'The Politics of the Political Thrillers: De-othering Iran in *Tehran* (Kan, 2021–)', available online at https://www.tandfonline.com/doi/full/10.1080/25785273.2022.2107685.

***Tehran* focuses on the undercover mission of a Mossad agent, Tamar Rabinyam, who is sent by the Israeli intelligence agency to disable a nuclear reactor in Iran.**

Genre Hybridity

As discussed in the Year 1 book, one of the key elements in Steve Neale's theory of genre is the idea that genres change, develop and vary as they borrow from and overlap with one another. This shows that genre conventions are dynamic and can be used in a hybrid way.

HBO's *Westworld*, which is based on the Michael Crichton film of the same name, is a good example of this, as it combines the codes and conventions of science-fiction with those of the western.

Similarly, Disney's *WandaVision*, the first television series in the Marvel Cinematic Universe, combines the conventions of the fantasy or superhero genre with those of the television sitcom.

Key Term

Genre hybridity
The result of combining conventions from different genres. Genre hybridity may be produced by combining the conventions of a western with those of a crime drama, for example.

Genre hybridity is something that you will need to explore when analysing your set television products. For instance:

- If you are studying Option 1, consider how *Peaky Blinders* produces genre hybridity by combining the gangster genre with elements of the western and the period drama.
- If you are studying Option 2, consider how the 'San Junipero' episode of *Black Mirror* produces genre hybridity by combining science-fiction with elements of romance and the coming-of-age drama.
- If you are studying Option 3, consider how *Killing Eve* produces genre hybridity by combining the spy thriller with elements of comedy.

Challenging or Subverting Genre Conventions

As well as exploring how genre conventions can be used in a hybrid way, you also need to consider how they can be challenged or subverted. Steve Neale's description of genres as '*instances of repetition and difference*' (1980) is particularly relevant here. This suggests that while genres offer audiences a pleasing sense of familiarity, there is also pleasure in having our expectations challenged. Neale argues that audiences would soon lose interest in a genre if it simply relied on repetition alone. Challenging or subverting conventions is therefore necessary for a genre to survive.

Peaky Blinders, *Black Mirror* and *Killing Eve* can all be seen to challenge or subvert genre conventions in certain ways. For example:

- *Peaky Blinders* could be seen to subvert the conventionally American nature of the gangster and western genres through its Birmingham setting. By focusing on the reality of working-class life in the interwar period rather than offering a nostalgic and idealised representation of an imaginary national past, it could also be seen to subvert the conventions of the period drama.
- The 'San Junipero' episode of *Black Mirror* could be seen to subvert the conventions of the science-fiction genre by focusing primarily on themes of love and romance rather than science and technology. The utopian nature of the episode could also be seen as relatively unconventional for a genre that more commonly focuses on dystopian worlds and narratives.
- *Killing Eve* could be seen to subvert the conventions of the spy thriller by featuring female characters in the two leading roles, thereby challenging the traditionally male-dominated nature of the genre. By introducing moments of comedy and **bathos**, it could also be seen to subvert the dramatic mode of address and sense of importance that are conventional features of the spy thriller.

Evaluating Steve Neale's Theory of Genre

THEORY: Steve Neale's Theory of Genre

- the idea that genres may be dominated by repetition, but are also marked by difference, variation, and change
- the idea that genres change, develop and vary as they borrow from and overlap with one another
- the idea that genres exist within specific economic, institutional and industrial contexts

In the Component 2 exam, you may be required to evaluate Steve Neale's theory of genre. This means assessing its validity, relevance or usefulness. Therefore, something that you may want to investigate is Neale's suggestion that genres are marked by difference and variation as well as repetition, and that they change, develop and vary over time.

For example, the extent to which genres such as crime drama, science-fiction and the spy thriller do, in fact, change, develop and vary is open to debate; it might be argued that the fundamental conventions that underpin these genres remain relatively consistent and do not actually change that much over time.

Similarly, the degree of difference and variation within these genres can also be questioned. One way of testing this would be to consider how much the two television products you have studied differ from other products in the same genre.

- If you are studying Option 1, consider how much *Peaky Blinders* differs from other crime dramas such as *Boardwalk Empire* or *The Sopranos*, or how different *The Bridge* is from *The Killing*.
- If you are studying Option 2, consider how much *Black Mirror* differs from other science-fiction shows such as *Westworld* or *Philip K. Dick's Electric Dreams*, or how different *The Returned* is from other zombie horror shows such as The *Walking Dead*, *The Last of Us* or *In the Flesh*.
- If you are studying Option 3, consider how much *Killing Eve* and *Tehran* differ from each other and from other spy thrillers such as *Homeland*, *The Americans*, *Kleo* or *Slow Horses*.

Key Term

Bathos
The effect that is produced when there is an abrupt switch from something that is serious, grand or important to something that is trivial, commonplace or ludicrous. A sense of anticlimax. This technique is often used for comic effect.

Link

Steve Neale's theory of genre is discussed on page 127 of the Year 1 book while the main codes and conventions of the crime, science-fiction and spy thriller genres are discussed on pages 127–139.

Stretch and Challenge 5.5

What evidence can you find in your set television products to support Neale's claim that genres change, develop and vary over time? Is there any evidence to suggest that genres do *not* change, develop and vary?

Tip

Remember that evaluating a theory does not mean that you necessarily have to disagree with it. It simply means that you need to critically appraise it.

Key Terms

Intertextuality
The process by which one text makes reference to another.

Eclecticism
A practice that involves combining or drawing on a wide range of sources or styles. Eclecticism is concerned with plurality and diversity as opposed to singularity and similarity. Postmodern products are often highly eclectic, as they reference a diverse array of cultural forms and styles.

Irony
A knowingness or acute self-awareness. This is a common characteristic of postmodern media products.

Tip

You are only required to explore the use of intertextuality in *Peaky Blinders*, *Black Mirror* or *Killing Eve*. You do not have to consider how intertextuality is used in the non-English language product you are studying.

Stretch and Challenge 5.6

Consider the different ways in which intertextuality is used in *Peaky Blinders*, *Black Mirror* or *Killing Eve* (depending on which of the three television options you have chosen to study). What different purposes and functions do the intertextual references in your chosen product perform?

Key Figure

Fredric Jameson
A Marxist critic who has written extensively on postmodern culture. His theory of postmodernism is outlined in the essay 'Postmodernism and Consumer Society' (1988).

Postmodernism

Postmodernism is one of the critical perspectives that you are required to use in the television unit of Component 2.

- If you are studying Option 1, you will need to explore postmodernism in relation to *Peaky Blinders*.
- If you are studying Option 2, you will need to explore postmodernism in relation to *Black Mirror*.
- If you are studying Option 3, you will need to explore postmodernism in relation to *Killing Eve*.

The term 'postmodern' can refer to a number of different things. It can be used to describe a particular *era* or historical moment (an era that began in the mid-twentieth century, following the age of modernism). It can be used to describe a particular body of critical theory (postmodern theory), and it can also be used to describe a particular type of *culture* – postmodern film or literature, for example, or postmodern architecture.

Postmodern culture is commonly identified with the following characteristics or features:

- reflexivity
- **intertextuality**
- hybridity and **eclecticism**
- bricolage
- parody or pastiche
- hyperreality
- **irony** or knowingness.

This does not mean that a postmodern product will necessarily feature *all* these characteristics. Nor does it mean that these features are *only* to be found in postmodern products.

For example, most television products use some form of intertextuality; this is an important aspect of media language and a fundamental way in which media products of all kinds are understood. However, what is often distinctive about the use of intertexuality in postmodern television products is that the intertextual references serve to remind the viewer that the programme they are watching is itself a textual construct, as the allusions to other texts become part of a knowing and playful exchange between programme-maker and audience.

Postmodern Culture as an 'Imaginary Museum'

Many critics see postmodern culture as a response to a crisis of originality. For example, in his landmark essay, 'Postmodernism and Consumer Society', **Fredric Jameson** (1998) claims:

> *In a world in which stylistic innovation is no longer possible, all that is left is to imitate dead styles, to speak through the masks and with the voices of the styles in the imaginary museum.*

What Jameson is suggesting is that media producers in the postmodern era find themselves turning back to the past, as they have little choice but to copy styles and products that already exist. This is because all creative possibilities seem to have been used-up or exhausted; everything seems to have been said or done before.

The Jack Rabbit Slim's scene in Quentin Tarantino's *Pulp Fiction* provides a perfect illustration of Jameson's idea of postmodern culture as an 'imaginary museum', as the décor, costumes, characters and dance routines that feature in this scene are all borrowed from earlier eras. John Travolta's character, Vincent Vega, even describes the diner as being 'like a wax museum with a pulse'.

Jameson therefore sees **pastiche** and nostalgia as the dominant **tropes** of postmodern culture. A particular example of this that he discusses is the film *Back to the Future* (right). Like the 'San Junipero' episode of *Black Mirror, Back to the Future* explores the idea of time travel, as the main protagonist, Marty McFly, finds himself transported back in time to 1955. The key point that Jameson makes about the film's representation of 1950s America is that it is derived entirely from representations found in other popular texts.

What is significant for Jameson, then, as John Storey (2015) points out, is that films such as *Back to the Future*

> *do not [try to] represent the 'real' past, but [...] make do with certain cultural myths and stereotypes about the past, [offering] films about other films, representations of other representations (what Baudrillard calls simulations).*

Postmodern Parody

However, while Jameson claims that postmodern texts simply reproduce dominant cultural myths in a superficial and nostalgic fashion, not all theorists share this view. For example, **Linda Hutcheon** sees parody as just as vital an element of postmodern culture as pastiche.

Although parody and pastiche are both forms of imitation, a parody has some form of satirical purpose as it simultaneously mocks the thing that it imitates. Parody is therefore an important critical tool as it can be used to challenge dominant discourses, ideologies and representations.

Parody can also be thought of as a stage in the evolutionary cycle of a genre. As theorists such as Christian Metz and **Thomas Schatz** have pointed out, genres typically move from an initial experimental stage to a classical stage as they mature. They then reach a stage when the conventions of the genre start to feel overfamiliar or clichéd. It is here that genres become subject to parody. The way in which popular television genres such as crime drama, science-fiction and the spy thriller evolve over time can be seen to reflect this movement towards parody.

Key Figures

Linda Hutcheon
An academic and theorist whose work on postmodern culture has proved particularly influential. Notable publications include the books *A Theory of Parody* (1985), *A Poetics of Postmodernism* (1988) and *The Politics of Postmodernism* (1989).

Thomas Schatz
A prominent film theorist whose work focuses primarily on Hollywood cinema. His theory of genre is outlined in the book *Hollywood Genres: Formulas, Filmmaking, and the Studio System* (1981).

However, this does not mean that *all* television products within a given genre become parodies after a certain point. Many continue to use the established conventions of the genre in a straightforward manner, without any broader satirical purpose.

Key Terms

Pastiche
A form of imitation. Unlike parody, which mocks or satirises the object of imitation, pastiche is a neutral form of mimicry as it simply reproduces that which it copies or imitates.

Trope
A significant recurring device, motif or theme.

Quickfire 5.1

Why do you think that Fredric Jameson describes postmodern culture as an 'imaginary museum'? What does this tell us about media production in a postmodern age?

Stretch and Challenge 5.7

Consider whether the set product you are studying includes elements of parody or pastiche. How might *Peaky Blinders* be seen as a pastiche of old westerns or gangster movies, for example? In what ways could the 'San Junipero' episode of *Black Mirror* be seen as a pastiche of 80s teen movies such as *Pretty in Pink* or *The Breakfast Club*? How does *Killing Eve* parody the conventions of the spy thriller?

Named Theorists

Jean Baudrillard
A French cultural theorist and leading figure in the development of postmodern theory. His theory of postmodernism explores the idea that the distinction between reality and simulation has broken down in contemporary culture. This theory is outlined in the book *Simulacra* and *Simulation*, which was first published in 1981.

Key Terms

Implosion
A process in which things collapse in on themselves (as opposed to explosion which involves an outward dispersal of energy). In postmodern theory, the term is commonly used to describe the way in which the boundaries separating the 'real' world from the world of the media have collapsed in on one another.

Deepfake
A video that has been digitally manipulated using a form of artificial intelligence called deep learning in order to produce a fake image of a person or event. This often involves replacing the face or voice of one person with that of someone else. Due to the sophisticated nature of these artificial intelligence systems, deepfake videos can appear highly convincing.

Examples of television parodies include:

- Charlie Brooker's *A Touch of Cloth*, which parodies popular crime dramas such as *A Touch of Frost* and *Inspector Morse*.
- The Finnish series *NoPoFo*, co-produced by Ilkkas' Creative Studio and BBC Studios Nordics, which parodies Nordic noir shows such as *The Bridge* and *The Killing*.
- Seth MacFarlane's *The Orville*, which parodies sci-fi shows such as *Star Trek*. *Star Trek* is also parodied in the 'USS Callister' episode of *Black Mirror*, which featured in the show's fourth season.
- FX's animated series, *Archer*, which parodies spy thrillers such as the James Bond movies.

Baudrillard's Theory of Postmodernism

The key postmodern thinker whose work you need to be familiar with is French cultural theorist **Jean Baudrillard**.

KEY THEORY: Jean Baudrillard's Theory of Postmodernism

- the idea that in postmodern culture the boundaries between the 'real' world and the world of the media have collapsed and that it is no longer possible to distinguish between reality and simulation
- the idea that in a postmodern age of simulacra we are immersed in a world of images that no longer refer to anything 'real'
- the idea that media images have come to seem more 'real' than the reality they supposedly represent (hyperreality)

At the heart of Baudrillard's theory is the idea that we now live in a postmodern age that is dominated by images and simulations. In this postmodern era, it is difficult to tell the real from the fake, as the distinction between the real world and the world of the media is no longer clear – these two worlds have **imploded** or collapsed into one another. Baudrillard talks, for example, about the way in which television seeps out and dissolves into real life while real life merges into television; he refers to this as the '*dissolution of TV in life [and the] dissolution of life in TV*' (Baudrillard, 1994).

Baudrillard also argues that, in a hyperreal world, images and simulations can come to seem more real than reality itself. Rather than *representing* reality, these images and simulations *take the place of* reality so that the fake becomes the real.

The cultural phenomenon of **deepfakes** is a perfect illustration of these ideas, as the sophisticated nature of artificial intelligence today makes it far easier to produce convincing fake images of people or events. This was explored in BBC One's political thriller series, *The Capture*. For example, one of the scenes in the second series showed a deepfake video of a politician being interviewed on a news programme. ITV has also created deepfake images of celebrities such as Kim Kardashian, Idris Elba, Nicki Minaj and Greta Thunberg in its comedy impressions show, *Deep Fake Neighbours Wars*, using artificial technology to depict the celebrities as suburban neighbours in everyday scenarios.

Science-fiction also provides a rich terrain for exploring Baudrillard's ideas. For example, the idea that it is no longer possible to distinguish between reality and simulation is a key theme in science-fiction products from *Black Mirror* and *Westworld* to the *Blade Runner* films, where androids are often indistinguishable from their human counterparts (in *Blade Runner*, the androids or 'replicants' are said to be 'more human than human'), and the 'real' world is often displaced by the virtual world. In this way, science-fiction products can be seen to illustrate Baudrillard's notions of hyperreality and the **simulacrum**, as copies or **simulations** come to seem more 'real' than reality itself.

Significantly, in an essay about science-fiction in the hyperreal era, Baudrillard suggested that:

> *In its artificial resurrection of 'historical' worlds, [science-fiction] can only try to reconstruct [...] the perimeters of a prior world, the events, the people, the ideologies of the past, emptied of meaning.*

The replicants in *Blade Runner 2049* can be seen to exemplify Baudrillard's notion of the hyperreal and the simulacrum.

If you are studying the 'San Junipero' episode of *Black Mirror*, this is something that you may find it useful to consider. Is San Junipero's 'artificial resurrection' of the historical world of the 1980s 'emptied of meaning' in the way that Baudrillard suggests? Does it offer any *real* understanding of the 1980s or does it simply reconstruct films and popular culture that depict that era rather than the era itself? You should also consider how Baudrillard's concept of hyperreality and the simulacrum could be applied to the world of San Junipero.

Similarly, if you are studying *Peaky Blinders*, you may want to consider whether the historical period it tries to reconstruct is emptied of meaning. Does its heightened aesthetic and **anachronistic** soundtrack suggest that the programme privileges style over substance, for instance? Does the mixing of fictional characters and real historical figures such as Winston Churchill suggest that the boundaries between reality and simulation have imploded or collapsed in the way that Baudrillard suggests? You might also consider the fact that the programme inspired particular fashion trends, with many people imitating the hairstyle adopted by the Peaky Blinders. Does this illustrate Baudrillard's point about the dissolution of TV in life, or the idea of the simulacrum (a copy of a copy)?

The suggestion that postmodern culture privileges style over meaning is something that you might also want to consider if you are studying *Killing Eve*. The opening episode also provides an opportunity to explore Baudrillard's suggestion that, in the postmodern world, images have come to seem more real than the reality they supposedly represent. Consider the references to CCTV and photographs in the opening episode, for instance. Do these references suggest that images now play a key role in determining reality, for instance (much like the 'pics or it didn't happen' phrase which became the mantra of the social media age), or do images still simply document reality?

Key Terms

Simulacrum
A term used by postmodern theorist Jean Baudrillard to describe a copy without an original (a copy of a copy) or a copy that has taken the place of the original.

Simulation
An imitation of something; a fake.

Anachronism
Something that is placed in the wrong time period, for example a reference to a book or a song in a period drama that had not yet been written at the time the period drama is set.

Evaluating Baudrillard's Theory of Postmodernism

Baudrillard's theory of postmodernism has provoked much critical debate. For example, his suggestion that we are now immersed in a world of images that no longer refer to anything real has been disputed by many critics.

A particular focal point for these debates was an essay provocatively titled 'The Gulf War Did Not Take Place' (1991), in which Baudrillard argued that the Gulf War was a virtual war rather than a real war as it was experienced primarily as a series of images, whether by people watching it play out in real time on TV screens around the world, or those undertaking bombing missions who saw their targets presented as digitised images on computer monitors.

However, Baudrillard's conceptualisation of the Gulf War as a 'virtual' war was denounced by many commentators, who saw this as a dangerous denial of the real human consequences of such conflicts.

As Kim Toffoletti (2011) pointed out:

> *[The Gulf War] involved real people and real events, and to suggest that it didn't happen because lots of the footage shown on television looked like a computer game is absurd.*

In evaluating Baudrillard's theory, you may find it useful to consider where you stand in relation to this debate:

- How far do you agree with the idea that in today's postmodern culture we experience reality primarily in the form of mediated images?
- Have the boundaries between the real world and the world of the media really collapsed in the way that Baudrillard suggests?
- Are we no longer capable of distinguishing between reality and simulation (between television and real life)?

Postmodernism, Reflexivity and the Collapse of Absolute Truth

Another highly influential thinker whose work has had a significant impact on postmodern theory is **Jean-François Lyotard**. He argued that the **grand narratives** or metanarratives that have traditionally been used to make sense of the world around us should be regarded with suspicion, as the postmodern world is far too complex for any single narrative, theory or perspective to fully account for or explain. According to Lyotard, there is no such thing as **absolute truth**; what we have instead are multiple 'truths' and different versions of reality.

One of the ways in which postmodern texts challenge the idea of absolute truth is by reminding us of the processes through which they are produced instead of trying to maintain the illusion that what they are presenting is real. This is known as **reflexivity**.

A notable example of this is Oliver Assayas's 2022 television series, *Irma Vep*, which is about an American film star who is hired to play the leading role in a television remake of the French silent film serial *Les Vampires*. The series blurs the lines between the real and the fake, and provides a reflexive commentary on the processes through which films and television programmes are produced. The fact that Oliver Assayas's television series is itself a remake of his own 1996 film of the same name, which in turn was based on the film serial *Les Vampires*, adds a further layer of reflexivity to the show and provides a useful illustration of Baudrillard's notion of the simulacrum as it is effectively a copy of a copy.

Key Figure

Jean-François Lyotard
A French theorist who defines postmodernism in terms of a scepticism towards grand narratives. Lyotard's postmodern theory is outlined in the book *The Postmodern Condition: A Report on Knowledge* (1984).

Key Term

Grand narrative
A term used for '*any theory claiming to provide universal explanations and to be universally valid*' (Sim, 2011).

Absolute truth
A truth that is not subject to interpretation and cannot be questioned. Postmodernists challenge the idea of absolute truth as they suggest that all truths are relative and vary according to perspective.

Reflexivity
Defined by Tim Woods (2009) as the '*self-conscious incorporation of the processes of production, construction or composition*'. A reflexive media product will therefore reveal rather than conceal the ways in which it has been constructed. Also described as self-reflexivity or self-referentiality.

The Sky/HBO drama *Landscapers*, which is based on real events involving a husband and wife who are accused of a double murder, is another good example of reflexivity, as the show repeatedly draws attention to its status as a textual construct. For instance, at the beginning of the first episode, a voice from off-screen (presumed to be that of the director) is heard calling for 'Action' and then 'Rain'. On this command, fake rain suddenly begins to fall as characters burst into life and start walking across the shot. A caption stating 'this is a true story' then appears onscreen. However, the word 'true' fades out, so the caption effectively changes from 'this is a true story' to 'this is a story'. The effect of these reflexive strategies is to immediately raise questions about the relationship between truth and fiction, while making the viewer aware that what they are watching is a narrative construct rather than a definitive account of real events.

This pattern is repeated throughout the series. For example, in a later episode, the space in which a police interview scene takes place is suddenly revealed to be a studio set built on a soundstage. As the actors (still in role) move from one set to another, various production crew members, including a camera operator, are clearly visible within the shot. Again, this has the effect of rupturing the realistic illusion on which most television dramas depend.

The programme also challenges the idea of absolute truth by offering multiple versions of the same event. We see contradictory accounts of events on the night of the murders, for instance. As the series itself provides no single, definitive version of events, it suggests that truth is relative rather than absolute. The radical eclecticism of the show's visual style, which switches from colour to black and white and borrows from a wide range of genres, presenting the murder in the style of a horror movie in one scene before reimagining it as a scene from a western in another, further highlights the indeterminacy of the postmodern world.

Structuralism

Structuralism is another theoretical perspective that you will need to apply to your set television products. This has had a profound influence not only in Media Studies but also in other academic disciplines such as linguistics, literature and anthropology.

As a critical approach, structuralism encompasses a broad range of theories. Tzvetan Todorov's theory of narratology is a structuralist theory, for example, as is Roland Barthes' theory of semiotics. What these theories have in common is an interest in the underlying systems and structures through which meaning is produced. For example, a structuralist analysis of a television product will typically involve an examination of the deeper patterns of meaning that operate both within the text and across the broader culture to which it belongs.

Lévi-Strauss's Theory of Structuralism

KEY THEORY: Claude Levi-Strauss's Theory of Structuralism

- the idea that texts can best be understood through an examination of their underlying structure
- the idea that meaning is dependent upon (and produced through) pairs of oppositions
- the idea that the way in which these binary oppositions are resolved can have particular ideological significance

Named Theorist

Claude Lévi-Strauss
A structuralist theorist who worked primarily in the field of cultural anthropology. Lévi-Strauss is best known for his theory of binary oppositions – the idea that meaning is produced through, and dependent on, pairs of opposing ideas, concepts or values.

Claude Lévi-Strauss's structuralist theory is based on the idea that meaning is dependent upon and produced through binary oppositions. In other words, an idea or value only has meaning in relation to its binary opposite (for instance, without the concept of 'good', 'bad' has no meaning). It is the dynamic interplay between these opposing ideas or values that gives television products their narrative momentum.

A useful starting point when applying Lévi-Strauss's theory to your set television products is to identify the binary oppositions that structure the narratives. Here are some examples of binary oppositions that can be seen to operate in the set products for each television option.

OPTION 1: Crime drama

Peaky Blinders	Crime – Law and order Loyalty – Betrayal The working class – The ruling class Communism – Capitalism
The Bridge	Sweden – Denmark Saga – Hanne The nuclear family – Non-nuclear families Political correctness – Political incorrectness

OPTION 2: Science-fiction and supernatural thrillers

Black Mirror	Reality – Simulation Heaven – Hell Life – Death Kelly – Yorkie
The Returned	The living – The dead Past – Present Acceptance – Denial Inside – Outside

OPTION 3: The spy thriller

Killing Eve	Eve – Villanelle Hunter – Hunted The mundane/everyday – The thrilling/extraordinary Obeying the rules – Breaking the rules
Tehran	Israel – Iran Liberalism – Conservativism Freedom – Constraint Safety – Danger

Key Figure

John Fiske
An academic and theorist whose work focuses on media, communication and popular culture. His books *Reading Television* (1978) and *Television Culture* (1987) have proved particularly influential in the field of television studies.

When studying your television products, you need to do more than just identify the binary oppositions they set up; you also need to explore their function and ideological significance. Think about how we are positioned in relation to these binary oppositions:

- Which characters are we encouraged to identify or side with?
- What ideas or values do the set products support or promote?
- How are the binary oppositions resolved? In other words, is one side of the binary opposition privileged over the other? Does one set of ideas or values overcome another?

Another important element in Claude Lévi-Strauss's theory is the concept of myth. **John Fiske** in *Television Culture* (1987) explains that for Lévi-Strauss myth is:

an anxiety-reducing mechanism that deals with unresolvable contradictions in a culture and provides imaginative ways of living with them. These contradictions are usually expressed in terms of binary oppositions.

Therefore, in order to deal with these unresolvable contradictions, a myth may create a hero or heroine who is able to mediate between opposing ideas or values, embodying characteristics from both categories (Fiske, 1987).

According to Fiske, an example of this would be the heroes of crime shows who exhibit characteristics drawn not only from the value system of society but also from the value system of the criminals.

- If you are studying *Peaky Blinders*, consider how the gangster, as a mythical figure, could be seen to deal with the unresolvable contradictions in a culture that promotes success and material wealth yet denies the working classes a legitimate means of achieving this.
- If you are studying *Black Mirror*, consider how Yorkie and Kelly mediate between two different worlds – the virtual world and the physical world – as well as between past and present, and life and death.
- Similarly, if you are studying *Tehran*, consider how Tamar could be seen to mediate between two different worlds as she moves between Israel and Iran.

Evaluating Lévi-Strauss's Structuralist Theory

In order to evaluate Lévi-Strauss's structuralist theory, you need to think about its strengths and weaknesses. For many critics, structuralism marked a significant step forward from earlier approaches to textual analysis. This is because, instead of focusing on the intentions of the author or producer of a text, it shifted attention onto the texts themselves. By providing a set of tools through which the underlying structure of a text could be analysed and understood, structuralism was said to offer a more scientific and reliable way of investigating how meanings are produced.

However, one of the main criticisms of structuralism is that it does not give enough attention to the role of audiences or readers in determining meaning. The emergence of post-structuralism can be seen as an attempt to address this weakness, as it places much greater emphasis on the way in which audiences interact with texts.

One theorist who moved away from structuralism to adopt a more post-structuralist position later in his career was Roland Barthes. His essay 'The Death of the Author' (1967), which argued that textual meaning is not determined by the producers of texts but is created in the act of reading, illustrates this cultural shift.

Evaluating Todorov's Theory of Narratology

KEY THEORY: Tzvetan Todorov's Theory of Narratology

- the idea that all narratives share a basic structure that involves a movement from one state of equilibrium to another
- the idea that these two states of equilibrium are separated by a period of imbalance or disequilibrium
- the idea that the way in which narratives are resolved can have particular ideological significance

Link

Tzvetan Todorov's theory of narratology is discussed on pages 141–142 of the Year 1 book.

As well as evaluating Lévi-Strauss's structuralist theory, you should also be prepared to evaluate Todorov's theory of narratology. Consider, for example, whether all television products share a basic narrative structure that involves a movement from one state of equilibrium to another, as Todorov suggests. Is Todorov's theory too rigid or too formulaic to account for the range of different narrative structures that television products today adopt?

Named Theorist

Stuart Hall
A highly influential cultural theorist whose work covered a range of topics from reception theory to representations of race and ethnicity. His theory of representation is outlined in *Representation: Cultural Representations and Signifying Practices* (2001).

Link

The key elements of Hall's theory are summarised on pages 142–143 of the Year 1 book.

Key Terms

Discourse
A particular way of talking and thinking about a topic; a system of representation. For example, when looking at the representation of gender or ethnicity in a media product, it may be useful to think about the discourses that are used – the ways in which gender or ethnicity are talked about, and the ideas and values that these systems of representation convey.

Ideology
A set of attitudes, values and beliefs; a way of looking at the world.

Realism
A mode of representation that conceals the processes of construction, creating the illusion that the product offers a window onto the real world.

Verisimilitude
Having the appearance of truth ('verity' means truth, while 'similitude' means having a similarity or resemblance to something).

Quickfire 5.2

What term describes the technique that postmodern media products use to draw attention to the processes through which they have been constructed?

REPRESENTATION

As well as media language, another key area of the theoretical framework that you will need to consider when studying your set television products is representation.

Of course, media representations do not function independently of audiences, industry or media language; these different areas of the theoretical framework interrelate in a variety of ways. For example, it is through media language that representations are constructed – this is one of the key points that **Stuart Hall** makes in his theory of representation.

Therefore, as well as analysing the codes, conventions and techniques that are used to construct the representations in your set television products, you will also need to think about:

- how audiences interpret and respond to those representations
- the impact of industry contexts on the choices media producers make about how to represent issues, individuals and social groups.

Discourse and Ideology

In addition to this, you will need to consider the way in which representations invoke discourses and ideologies. **Discourse** is defined by Stuart Hall (2001) as a system of representation that governs the way in which a topic can be talked about meaningfully. Discourses therefore shape and influence not only how we talk about particular topics but also how and what we think about them; they carry ideas and values. For example, patriarchal discourse is a way of talking and thinking about gender that promotes male dominance. In contrast, feminist discourse seeks to challenge sexist ideas and values.

As this suggests, representations have a significant ideological function; they position us to look at issues, events, individuals and social groups in certain ways. As Glen Creeber (2006) points out:

> *Whatever approach to* **ideology** *you take, it will usually involve similar issues of representation. Ideological criticism consistently reminds us that rather than innocently reflecting the world, television re-presents reality.*

Realism and Verisimilitude

While some postmodern programmes draw attention to the processes through which they have been constructed, rupturing the illusion that what they are showing is real, most television products disguise or conceal their ideological function, hiding the fact that their representations have been constructed from a certain perspective.

One of the ways in which television products conceal their ideological function is through **realism**. This is to do with how accurate or true-to-life the representations in a programme appear to be, and how an illusion of reality can be manufactured through the deployment of certain codes, conventions and techniques.

There are, however, different ways of gauging the realism of television products. For instance, we are likely to judge a documentary in a different way from a crime drama, a spy thriller or a science-fiction show. This is because, as Steve Neale (1990) points out: '*Regimes of* **verisimilitude** *vary from genre to genre*'. Neale therefore draws a distinction between cultural verisimilitude and generic verisimilitude:

- **Cultural verisimilitude** is established through references to the social and cultural world that exists outside of the text. References to real figures or actual historical events can help to establish a sense of cultural verisimilitude for instance. Similarly, the inclusion of authentic forensic techniques in a police procedural can make it seem more true-to-life.
- **Generic verisimilitude** is to do with the internal rules of the genre rather than the social world outside the text. For example, when someone launches into a song-and-dance number in a musical, we accept it, not because we think it would be likely to happen in everyday life, but because it fits our expectations of the genre. Similarly, when we are watching a science-fiction show, a spy thriller or a crime drama, we expect certain things to happen. Provided these expectations are met, we are usually willing to suspend our disbelief.
- **Surface realism** is another feature of many television products. This is where aspects of mise-en-scéne, such as costumes, sets and props, are used to convey an impression of authenticity or historical accuracy. Period dramas rely heavily on surface realism to maintain their credibility.

Key Terms

Cultural verisimilitude
A form of realism that is established when a media product corresponds with what we know about the social and cultural world that exists outside the text.

Generic verisimilitude
The degree to which a media product conforms to the rules of its genre, facilitating a willingness to suspend disbelief on the part of the audience.

Surface realism
A particular form of realism in which aspects of mise-en-scéne such as costumes and props are used to convey an impression of authenticity. This technique is widely used in period dramas.

Representations of Gender

The Year 1 book established a basic critical framework for analysing the representation of gender in television products. In particular, it addressed issues regarding:

- the under-representation of women both on-screen and in key off-screen roles within the television industry
- the significance of the roles and contexts in which men and women are shown
- the construction of gender stereotypes.

At A Level, you should be prepared to use feminist theories, including those of Liesbet van Zoonen and bell hooks, to analyse the representations that your set television products offer. You will also need to explore Judith Butler's theory of gender performativity.

The Influence of Feminism on the Television Industry

While feminism has had a significant impact on the academic study of the media, its influence can also be seen in the work of many writers and directors currently working in the television industry. For example, Jane Campion's *Top of the Lake* is a feminist crime drama that explores the way in which the subordination, oppression and abuse of women is normalised within patriarchal culture.

Similar themes regarding patriarchal oppression and the subjugation of women are explored in the science-fiction serial *The Handmaid's Tale*. Based on the Margaret Atwood novel of the same name, the programme depicts a dystopian future in which women have been forced into sexual servitude by the state.

Therefore, while patriarchal representations of gender still circulate widely within the media, what shows such as these demonstrate is that television can also be a vehicle for the expression of feminist values, ideas and viewpoints.

bell hooks' Feminist Theory

KEY THEORY: bell hooks' Feminist Theory

- the idea that feminism is a struggle to end sexist/patriarchal oppression and the ideology of domination
- the idea that feminism is a political commitment rather than a lifestyle choice
- the idea that race and class as well as sex determine the extent to which individuals are exploited, discriminated against, or oppressed

bell hooks is one of the main feminist theorists whose ideas you are required to explore. A crucial part of her theory is the idea that feminist struggle is directed against an ideological system rather than against men per se. In this way, she debunks the myth that feminism is 'anti-men', arguing instead that feminism is a struggle to end patriarchal oppression and the ideologies that facilitate the domination of one sex over another (hooks, 1984). This is a useful starting point for thinking about how feminist theory can be used to analyse television products.

For example, if feminism is a struggle to end sexist oppression and the ideology of domination, a key question that we need to ask is: What form(s) does this sexist/patriarchal oppression take?

- Is it evident in the representational codes used to portray men and women on television?
- Can it be seen in the division of gender roles?
- Is it apparent in the objectification of women?

As already suggested, not all television products reinforce patriarchal ideology. It is important, therefore, not to confuse representations that *express* patriarchal ideology with those that *challenge* it by highlighting or exposing where and how it operates.

Another important point bell hooks makes is that social factors such as race and class work alongside sexism to determine the extent of oppression, discrimination and exploitation that an individual may be subjected to (hooks, 1984). Arguing that women do not all share a common social status, she points out that a woman from a white, middle-class background will not necessarily have the same experience of oppression as a black, working-class woman. This critical perspective, which explores the way in which various social structures overlap with one another to produce different experiences of inequality, is commonly described as **intersectional feminism**.

This sense of intersectionality is a key feature of Michaela Coel's critically acclaimed BBC drama series *I May Destroy You*, as the programme provides an incisive exploration of the way in which social attitudes regarding race, class, gender and sexuality inform institutional responses to sexual violence and shape cultural understandings of consent, leading to some voices being heard while others are ignored.

The Portrayal of Violence Against Women on Television

According to bell hooks' theory, violence is also a manifestation of '*the ideology of domination that permeates Western culture on various levels*'. As she points out:

> *Television screens are [...] flooded daily with tales of male violence, especially male violence against women. It is glamorized, made entertaining and sexually titillating.* (hooks, 1984)

Named Theorist

bell hooks
A renowned feminist theorist and cultural critic who wrote extensively on racial and sexual politics in film, music and popular culture. Her work on feminist theory includes the books *Feminist Theory: From Margin to Center* (1984) and *Feminism is for Everybody* (2000). She presented her name all in lower-case letters to suggest that her work is more important than she is as an individual.

Key Term

Intersectional feminism
A particular body of feminist thinking which recognises that women's identities and experiences of oppression differ. More specifically, intersectional feminism explores the way in which different forms of discrimination, such as sexism, racism, classism and homophobia, overlap or intersect with one another, impacting on different women in different ways, according to their race, class and sexuality as well as their gender.

Tip

As well as thinking about *how* men and women are represented in your set television products, you also need to consider the ideological significance of these representations. To what extent can they be seen to support or challenge patriarchal ideology, for instance?

Stretch and Challenge 5.8

How is violence against women represented in your set television products? Is it normalised, trivialised or fetishised, for example? Are representations of female victims reductive or stereotypical?

This issue has been widely discussed in recent years, with growing criticism of the levels of violence against women shown on television. For example, crime dramas such as *True Detective* and *The Fall* have been accused of a voyeuristic fascination with violence against women, as the bodies of female victims are frequently represented as simply part of the crime scene – objects offered up for the scrutiny of investigators within the diegetic world of the programme as well as the extradiegetic audience. This accusation has also been levelled against fantasy series such as *Game of Thrones*.

However, some television programmes have started to challenge the dominant tropes of television violence. Discussing the way in which her show, *Happy Valley*, approached this issue, screenwriter Sally Wainwright pointed out that it was the main character who was shown to be a victim of violence rather than '*just a naked, dead female who we don't know*' (Williams, 2016). The programme also sought to offer a '*realistic response to what violence is really like*' by showing the aftermath of the violent attack and the lengthy recovery period of the main character who remained in hospital for several weeks.

van Zoonen's Feminist Theory

KEY THEORY: Liesbet van Zoonen's Feminist Theory

- the idea that gender is constructed through discourse, and that its meaning varies according to cultural and historical context
- the idea that the display of women's bodies as objects to be looked at is a core element of Western patriarchal culture
- the idea that in mainstream culture the visual and narrative codes that are used to construct the male body as spectacle differ from those used to objectify the female body

Another feminist theorist whose ideas you will need to consider when analysing your set television products is Liesbet van Zoonen. Her work builds on that of several other feminist theorists, most notably **Laura Mulvey**.

For example, van Zoonen argues that the display of women's bodies as objects to be looked at is a core element of Western patriarchal culture. Like Mulvey, she discusses the way in which women in mainstream media products function as objects of visual pleasure both for male characters within the text and for the viewing audience. In this way, women are relegated to a passive role as objects of a **male gaze** (they are the ones being looked *at*), whereas men are seen to occupy an active role as they are the ones *doing* the looking. Furthermore, it is the actions of male characters that typically '*drive the narrative forward*' (van Zoonen, 1994).

However, where van Zoonen starts to diverge from Mulvey is in exploring the idea of a female gaze, as she discusses the various ways in which the male body is displayed within popular culture. Crucially, though, she suggests that the visual and narrative codes that construct the male body as spectacle differ from those used to objectify the female body, as the male body appears to resist straightforward visual eroticisation (van Zoonen, 1994). This is because it is more commonly represented as an object of romantic rather than sexual interest. Furthermore, as displays of the male body are often accompanied by the suggestion of action, van Zoonen argues that there is not the same degree of passivity associated with displays of the male body as there is with displays of the female body.

Key Figure

Laura Mulvey
A feminist theorist whose work on sexual politics and the gaze has had a significant influence on film and media studies. Her male gaze theory was outlined in the essay 'Visual Pleasure and Narrative Cinema', which was first published in 1975.

Key Term

Male gaze
A term used by Laura Mulvey to describe the way in which the media position us to view women's bodies as objects of visual pleasure, adopting a heterosexual male perspective, regardless of our own gender or sexual orientation.

Stretch and Challenge 5.9

Consider whether van Zoonen's ideas can be applied to your set television products.
Are women constructed as objects of visual pleasure, for example? Is it men who drive the narrative forward?

The Construction of Gender Through Discourse

Another key aspect of van Zoonen's theory is the idea that gender is constructed through discourse as notions of masculinity and femininity are not determined by biology, they are produced through systems of representation.

For instance, she suggests that the dominant discourse of gender within the media identifies women with the world of family and domestic life and men with the world of politics and work, conveying the idea '*that femininity is about care, nurturance and compassion, and that masculinity is about efficiency, rationality and individuality*' (van Zoonen and Sreberny, 2000).

However, van Zoonen also points out that the meaning of gender varies according to cultural and historical context. In other words, understandings of what it means to be male or female are not fixed or constant. Western norms of femininity may be quite different from those in non-Western cultures, for example. Similarly, the hegemonic models of masculinity that we see in the media today may be quite different from those of the 1950s or 1960s.

Supporting her claim that the meaning of gender changes over time, van Zoonen (1994) cites the American cop show *Miami Vice*, in which one of the male heroes shows stereotypical feminine qualities such as sensitivity, a caring nature and physical attractiveness, along with the more conventionally masculine qualities associated with the archetypal tough-guy cop. For van Zoonen, this demonstrates the idea that '*more and more popular culture is beginning to explore the contradictions of gender*'.

Your set products provide a number of opportunities to examine these aspects of van Zoonen's theory.

- In Option 1, you could explore the extent to which the representation of female characters such as Polly Gray, Ada Shelby and Grace Burgess in *Peaky Blinders* reinforce or challenge the dominant discourses of gender that have traditionally circulated in mainstream media. You may also want to consider whether the representation of Saga Norén in *The Bridge* reflects the growing interest in the '*contradictions of gender*' that van Zoonen associates with contemporary popular culture.
- Similarly, in Option 2, you could consider the extent to which the representations in the 'San Junipero' episode of *Black Mirror* support van Zoonen's claims. To what extent do male characters such as Wes and Greg exhibit 'traditional female qualities' for instance? How far do these representations, along with the representation of Kelly and Yorkie, reflect a historical shift in the meaning of gender? You could also compare these representations with those of Jérôme, Claire and Léna in *The Returned*.
- In Option 3, you might want to consider whether characters such as Eve and Villanelle in *Killing Eve* exhibit the 'contradictions of gender' that van Zoonen refers to, and whether they challenge the dominant discourses of gender that have traditionally identified women with the world of family and domestic life, and men with the world of politics and work. You could also consider whether *Tehran's* representation of sexual politics, and the contrasting value systems of Israel and Iran, support van Zoonen's claim that the meaning of gender varies according to cultural context.

Butler's Theory of Gender Performativity

Another critical approach that you will need to consider when analysing your set television products is **Judith Butler**'s theory of gender **performativity**.

Quickfire 5.3

van Zoonen suggests that the representations of gender that circulate in the media today are more contradictory and more varied than those of the past. Which other named theorist makes a similar argument?

Named Theorist

Judith Butler
An American academic and cultural theorist. Their work on gender performativity has had a significant influence in many different fields. Two of their most notable publications, in which they outline their theory of gender performativity, are *Gender Trouble: Feminism and the Subversion of Identity* (1990) and *Bodies That Matter: On the Discursive Limits of 'Sex'* (1993). Butler's preferred pronouns are they/them.

Key Term

Performativity
The idea that identity is constructed through a series of performative acts.

KEY THEORY: Judith Butler's Theory of Gender Performativity

- the idea that identity is performatively constructed by the very 'expressions' that are said to be its results (it is manufactured through a set of acts)
- the idea that there is no gender identity behind the expressions of gender
- the idea that performativity is not a singular act, but a repetition and a ritual

The central premise of Butler's theory is the idea that gender is constructed through a series of performative acts. Crucially, these acts are not the expression of an underlying or pre-existing gender identity; they are the means by which gender identities are produced. In other words, people do not act in the way that they do because of an innate gender that they already possess; their gender is a product of the way that they act. This is what Butler means by performativity.

It could be argued that shows such as *RuPaul's Drag Race All Stars* draw attention to the performative acts through which gender is constructed.

According to Butler, we do not freely choose how we perform our identities; our performances are regulated by social and cultural norms that tell us how we should act. Therefore, if gender is a performance, it is one that is scripted by our social context to a significant extent.

However, there are opportunities to subvert the social script we are given. For example, Butler (1990) argues that cultural practices such as cross-dressing and drag cause 'gender trouble' by drawing attention to the performative construction of gender, mocking or parodying the notion of a 'true' gender identity.

Evaluating Butler's Theory of Gender Performativity

You are only required to explore Butler's theory of gender performativity in relation to one of the set television products you are studying:

- If you are studying Option 1, you need to use Butler's theory to explore the representations in *The Bridge*.
- If you are studying Option 2, you need to use Butler's theory to explore the representations in *Black Mirror*.
- If you are studying Option 3, you need to use Butler's theory to explore the representations in *Killing Eve*.

Each of these set products offers interesting opportunities to test and explore Butler's theory. For example, in *The Bridge*, the murder of Helle Anker, a prominent LGBT activist and founder of Denmark's first gender-neutral pre-school, provides the catalyst for an investigation of contemporary gender politics, as Anker's claim that '*gender is not biological but rather a social construction*' is debated at the diegetic level of the text. The extent to which Saga causes what Butler refers to as 'gender trouble' through her subversion of particular gender norms is also worth considering.

This is something that can be explored in relation to Villanelle's character in *Killing Eve* too. For example, one way of causing 'gender trouble' is by challenging what Butler describes as 'the heterosexual matrix' – a form of binaristic thinking which suggests that one's sex determines one's gender, which in turn determines one's sexuality, producing heteronormativity or 'compulsory heterosexuality'. Villanelle might therefore be seen as a transgressive figure who causes 'gender trouble' through her refusal to adhere to gender norms and the compulsory heterosexuality that the heterosexual matrix demands. It is also worth exploring whether Villanelle's gender performativity further reveals what Butler refers to as the '*imitative nature of gender itself*'. Consider her interactions with Konstantin, for example, particularly

Tip

While cultural practices such as cross-dressing and drag are perhaps more obvious examples of gender performativity, it is important to note that *all* gender identities are performatively constructed according to Butler's theory.

Stretch and Challenge 5.10

Butler argues that gender '*must be understood as the mundane way in which bodily gestures, movements, and styles of various kinds constitute the illusion of an abiding, gendered self*' (1990). Consider how this idea could be applied to the set product you are studying.

Tip

As well as exploring representations of gender and ethnicity, you may also find it useful to analyse the representation of issues in at least one of your set products.

If you are studying Option 1, you may find it useful to explore the representation of LGBT rights and sexual politics in *The Bridge*.

If you are studying Option 2, you may find it useful to explore the representation of issues such as euthanasia and same-sex marriage in *Black Mirror*.

If you are studying Option 3, you may find it useful to explore the representation of international relations between Israel and Iran in a nuclear age.

when she mockingly imitates the way in which he speaks to her. More than simply demonstrating her own talent for mimicry, think about whether this also reveals the way in which Konstantin's masculinity is performatively constructed through the way that he speaks and acts.

Butler's suggestion that gendered identities are performatively produced through a set of acts or rituals can also be used to explore the representations of gender in the 'San Junipero' episode of *Black Mirror*. Think about the way in which Harvey's masculinity is performatively constructed through the way that he sits, moves and talks, for instance. It is also worth considering the makeover scene in which Yorkie tries on a series of different 80s outfits, effectively rehearsing or trying out a number of different selves. However, in order to establish the extent to which this ultimately supports or challenges Butler's theory of gender performativity, it is important to consider whether this performance actually produces Yorkie's gender identity or whether she is still presumed to have a core identity (an authentic self) that exists outside of performance.

Representations of Race and Ethnicity

As well as looking at representations of gender, you will also need to explore how race and ethnicity are represented in your set television products. You may find a comparative approach particularly useful here. Are there any differences between the two products in terms of ethnic diversity, for example?

In comparing the representations of race and ethnicity in your set products, consider the significance of the following factors:

- The cultural contexts in which the two products were made. How far do they reflect the ethnic composition of the countries in which they were filmed or produced?
- The institutional contexts of the two products. For example, public service broadcasters such as the BBC and Channel 4 are required to represent the cultural diversity of the UK as part of their remit. This can have an impact on representations of race and ethnicity.

Ethnocentrism is another important issue to think about. For example, Stuart Hall discusses the way in which racial stereotypes marginalise those who are perceived to be different by constructing them as 'other'. This establishes a particular set of power relations, as it presupposes the inferiority of those who are different, while the values of the dominant group are treated as a universal norm.

Therefore, when exploring some of these issues, you may find it useful to consider the following questions:

- Are black, Asian or minority ethnic groups constructed as 'other' in either of your set products?
- Is there any evidence of racial stereotyping?
- To what extent do the set products reinforce or challenge racial hierarchies and racialised discourse?

INDUSTRY

In the Year 1 book, we introduced some of the main issues that you will need to consider as you study the television industry. These include:

- Patterns of ownership and the difference between publicly and privately owned companies.
- The different ways in which television companies are funded.
- The role of public service broadcasting in the television industry.

Link

See pages 148–155 of the Year 1 book for an introduction to the television industry.

- How the television industry is regulated.
- The way in which television products are marketed.

Building on these ideas, this section looks at the global context in which television production, distribution and regulation takes place and provides an overview of David Hesmondhalgh's theory of cultural industries and Livingstone and Lunt's theory of media regulation.

Rapid Recall 5.2

List four ways in which television channels might be funded.

Television as a Global Industry

Globalisation has had a significant impact on the television industry. This is reflected in:

- the international context in which television programmes are produced (international co-productions have become increasingly prevalent in recent years)
- the way that television programmes and formats are distributed around the world (for instance, BBC Studios, the commercial arm of the BBC, sells BBC programmes and formats to different international territories. It also operates a number of channels in countries outside the UK; a notable example of this is BBC America, which it co-owns with AMC Networks)
- streaming platforms such as Netflix, Apple TV+ and Disney+ (e.g. Apple TV+ is available in over 100 countries worldwide, while Netflix is available in every country except for China, Crimea, North Korea, Russia and Syria)
- the international popularity of genres such as Nordic noir (the third season of *The Bridge* was shown in over 150 countries).

The Rise of Non-English-Language Programming on British Television

While American programmes have been a significant part of the British television landscape since the early days of broadcasting, non-English-language programmes have become increasingly prominent in recent years. The rise of global streaming platforms such as Netflix, which has a production base in several international territories and distributes content from countries around the world, has been instrumental in this regard. The popularity of South Korean shows such as *Squid Game* and *All of Us Are Dead*, as well as Spanish television dramas such as *Money Heist* and *Elite*, and the French crime drama *Lupin*, demonstrate the growing cultural appetite for non-English programming.

The BBC and Channel 4 have also been at the forefront of this trend. For example, European crime dramas such as *The Killing*, *The Bridge* and *Modus* have become a key part of BBC Four's brand identity, with the channel positioning itself as the British home of Nordic noir.

Many of Channel 4's non-English-language shows are offered through the 'Walter Presents' strand of its online video-on-demand service. In order to push viewers towards its online platform, Channel 4 will often show the opening episode of a new foreign-language series on its main channel before making the rest of the series available via the video-on-demand service.

Sky has also invested heavily in non-English programming in recent years, co-producing the big budget, German period noir series *Babylon Berlin* and the critically acclaimed Italian crime drama *Gomorrah*.

The Rise of International Co-Productions

The way in which television programmes are funded and produced also reflects the increasingly global nature of the television industry, as international co-productions have become more common. For example:

- *The Bridge* was co-produced by Swedish independent production company Filmlance International and Danish company Nimbus Film. The series also received financial support from several European public service broadcasters, including Sweden's SVT, Denmark's DR, Germany's ZDF and Norway's NRK.
- *Tehran* was commissioned by the Israeli public service broadcaster Kan and the American streaming platform Apple TV+. It also received funding from Cineflix Rights, the UK's largest independent TV content distributor.

Co-productions are attractive to broadcasters as the costs of production can be shared between the different parties involved. Without this collaborative approach to production, many projects would not have the funding to get off the ground.

International co-productions can also result in higher production values as programme-makers have bigger budgets to work with. For example, the BBC has worked with a variety of international partners in recent years, producing several big budget, quality drama series. *McMafia* was co-produced with American network AMC, for instance, while *Troy: Fall of a City* was co-produced with Netflix, and Hugo Blick's western *The English* was co-produced with Amazon Studios.

Explaining why the BBC has entered into these types of international partnership, Piers Wenger, the Controller of BBC Drama Commissioning, points out in an interview:

> *We can put more money on screen, whilst also keeping editorial control. [...] With our current BBC drama partners, [...] we can make drama that might not otherwise get made.* (Gill, 2017)

The Economic Context of Television Production

As you study the television industry, you will need to develop an understanding of the economic contexts in which television production and distribution take place. Looking at how television products are funded is an important part of this. There are, for example, many regional agencies that provide funding and support for companies working in the audio-visual sector.

For instance, the third season of *The Bridge* received funding from:

- the Copenhagen Film Fund (a Danish organisation that provides funding and support for film and television projects in the Capital Region of the country)
- the Ystad-Österlen Filmfond (a Swedish organisation that provides funding and support for film and television projects in the Ystad-Österlen region)
- Film i Skåne (a Swedish organisation that provides funding and support for film and television projects in the Skåne region of the country).

Similarly, *The Returned* received funding from:

- the Rhône-Alpes Regional Fund (a French organisation that provides funding and support for film and television projects in the Rhône-Alpes region)
- Centre National de la Cinématographie (a national organisation that provides support and funding for the French film and television industry).

The decision by the producers of *Tehran* to film the scenes set in Tehran on location in Athens also enabled them to access regional funding from EKOME – the National Centre of Audiovisual Media and Communication (an organisation that supports the Greek audio-visual industry by offering cash rebate and tax relief schemes to productions filmed in Greece).

The European Commission's 'Creative Europe' Programme

The European Commission (EC) also provides grants to support the production and distribution of European television products. This is done through the MEDIA sub-programme, which is part of the EC's 'Creative Europe' programme.

Among the television productions to benefit from this funding are:

- *Hinterland*: having received an initial development grant of €45,000, the programme-makers, Fiction Factory, received a further grant of €500,000 for the first season in 2013. Another grant of €500,000 was awarded for the third season in 2015.
- *The Bridge*: Filmlance International received a grant of €1 million for the third season of the show in 2014. It had previously been awarded €400,000 for the first season in 2010.
- *The Returned*: Haut et Court was awarded grants totalling €450,000 for the first season of the show in 2012, and €1 million for the second season in 2014.

The Influence of Economic Factors on Television Production

The way in which a programme is funded can influence its production in various ways. For example, to qualify for funding, production companies usually have to meet certain criteria. These may include:

- a requirement to film in a particular region or location
- a requirement to employ crew members from a particular nation
- a requirement to work collaboratively with other international companies.

In some cases, programmes may also have to demonstrate potential for wider international distribution. For example, Creative Europe's MEDIA sub-programme is designed to support European television programmes '*with the potential to circulate within the European Union and beyond*' (2017b).

While programme-makers may have to consider whether their programme will work in other international territories, this does not necessarily mean that they have to sacrifice their cultural specificity.

For example, when asked by an interviewer whether she thought non-French audiences would have trouble finding a way into *The Returned*, one of the show's producers, Caroline Benjo, rejected this idea, suggesting that the story was universal enough to work for other cultures:

> *If your themes are universal enough, you don't have to be afraid to be local.* (Mellor, 2013)

Ed Thomas, co-creator of the Welsh Celtic noir show, *Y Gwyll/Hinterland* made a similar point in an interview, saying that he didn't think that audiences were necessarily scared or deterred by programmes that have culturally specific content:

> *As long as the stories and the characters and the world of the story is attractive enough, then it will have a universal appeal.* (Mathias, 2014)

Quickfire 5.4

How might the need to appeal to international audiences impact on the decisions that programme-makers make?

Named Theorist

David Hesmondhalgh
An academic whose work focuses primarily on media policy and the creative industries.

Key Terms

Cultural Industries
Defined by David Hesmondhalgh (2013) as industries that '*deal primarily with the industrial production and circulation of texts*'.

Formatting
A term used by theorists such as David Hesmondhalgh and Bill Ryan to describe the way in which cultural industry companies use market research to deal with '*the uncertainties of the cultural marketplace*' (Ryan, 1992). Formatting a product may involve the use of genre or stars to deliver an audience, for instance.

Rapid Recall 5.3

What is vertical integration?

Tip

Further aspects of David Hesmondhalgh's theory of cultural industries will be discussed later in this chapter. For example, in the section on Online Media we will examine Hesmondhalgh's suggestion that the radical potential of the internet has been contained to some extent by its incorporation within the cultural industries.

Hesmondhalgh's Theory of Cultural Industries

KEY THEORY: David Hesmondhalgh's Theory of Cultural Industries

- the idea that cultural industry companies try to minimise risk and maximise audiences through vertical and horizontal integration, and by formatting their cultural products (e.g. through the use of stars, genres and serials)
- the idea that the largest companies or conglomerates now operate across a number of different cultural industries
- the idea that the radical potential of the internet has been contained to some extent by its partial incorporation into a large, profit-orientated set of cultural industries

An important theory you will need to consider when exploring the industry contexts of your set television products is **David Hesmondhalgh**'s theory of **cultural industries**.

Hesmondhalgh suggests that companies in the cultural industries tend to be risk-averse and use a number of strategies to make as much profit as possible.

Horizontal Integration

According to Hesmondhalgh's theory, one of the strategies that cultural industry companies use to minimise risk and maximise audiences is horizontal integration. This is where one company buys or merges with another that is involved in the same sector, thereby reducing competition.

The acquisition of Télévision Par Satellite (TPS) by Vivendi's Canal+ Group in 2006 is a good example of this. In the mid-1990s, TPS emerged as a competitor in the French pay television market that Canal+ had previously dominated. Therefore, buying out its main rival enabled Canal+ to re-establish its control over this sector of the television market.

Vertical Integration

Another way in which cultural industry companies minimise risk is through vertical integration. The BBC, Netflix and Canal+ are all examples of vertically integrated companies as they have the means to both produce and distribute content. Some of the BBC's programmes are produced by BBC Studios, for instance. This is the commercial arm of the BBC, which is also responsible for distributing BBC brands, formats and programmes around the world.

Internationalisation

Cultural industry companies also minimise risk through internationalisation. This involves buying or partnering with other companies abroad, enabling better access to international markets. As previously discussed, international co-productions enable television companies to spread costs and financial risk.

Formatting

According to Hesmondhalgh's theory, another key strategy that cultural industry companies use to minimise risk and maximise audiences is **formatting**. Hesmondhalgh suggests that the cultural industries carry a higher level of risk than other industries because the way in which audiences use and respond to cultural products is difficult to predict. Formatting helps to address this issue, as cultural industry companies use market research to ensure there is an audience for their products.

The **star system** is one means of formatting that Hesmondhalgh discusses. This is based on the premise that media products featuring well-known writers, directors or performers can be pre-sold, as fans of those stars will be drawn to any new projects their names are attached to.

While some stars are known primarily in their native countries, others may have broader global appeal. Global stars can be particularly useful in terms of selling television products in different international markets.

Another way to maximise audiences is by including stars who collectively or individually have **cross-demographic appeal**. This enables programme-makers to simultaneously target different audiences.

Genre is another way in which cultural industry companies format their products. As Hesmondhalgh points out, '*genres suggest to audiences the kinds of satisfaction and reward they might attain by experiencing the product*' (Hesmondhalgh, 2013). Again, this is very useful in terms of targeting and attracting audiences.

Serials are also a common means of formatting products. A specific example of this that Hesmondhalgh cites is the use of prequels and sequels in Hollywood cinema. These products have a ready-established audience, making them easier to sell.

Stretch and Challenge 5.12

Look at the marketing materials used to promote the set television products you are studying (posters, trailers, etc.). What evidence can you find of formatting? How prominently do stars feature in the marketing materials? How is the genre of the set product established and how is this used to create audience appeal?

Television Formats and International Remakes

Another way in which companies in the television industry reduce their financial risk is by selling copyrighted formats. For example, the **format** for *The Returned* (*Les Revenants*) was sold to A&E Studios which remade the show for the American market in 2015.

The Bridge has also been adapted for different international markets. A UK/French version called *The Tunnel*, produced by Kudos for Sky Atlantic and Canal+, ran for three series from 2013 to 2017. An American version, set on the US/Mexican border, was produced for the FX network, while a Russian version, set on the border of Russia and Estonia, was produced for the Russian NTV network.

Diversification

Another important element of Hesmondhalgh's theory is the idea that the largest companies and conglomerates operate across a range of cultural industries.

For example, many privately owned television companies are part of larger conglomerates that are involved in different industries:

- Sky is a **subsidiary** of the American multinational conglomerate Comcast, which has significant business interests in telecommunications, film production and theme parks, as well as the television industry.
- Canal+ is a subsidiary of the French multinational conglomerate Vivendi SA, which has significant business interests in the film industry, the music industry and magazine publishing as well as video games and the television industry.

Stretch and Challenge 5.11

Research the main stars of your set television products. Try to find out how well-known they are and whether their fame is limited to their own native countries or whether they have broader global appeal.

Quickfire 5.5

In what way could genre hybridity be seen as a way of maximising audiences?

Key Terms

Cross-demographic appeal
The capacity of a media product to simultaneously appeal to more than one audience.

Format
A term used in the television industry to refer to the concept of a programme. David Hesmondhalgh (2013) pointed out that this is frequently developed in an initial market, then sold as a copyrighted idea to overseas markets.

Subsidiary
A company that is owned by a larger company. The company that owns the subsidiary is often referred to as the parent company or the holding company.

Rapid Recall 5.4

What is a conglomerate?

Link

For an explanation of the differences between publicly and privately owned media organisations see page 148 of the Year 1 book

Key Term

Diversification
The process through which a company expands its operations into new or different areas of business.

Stretch and Challenge 5.13

Try to find out more about the companies, organisations or conglomerates that commissioned your set products or that own the companies that commissioned or produced them.

While the BBC and Channel 4 are publicly rather than privately owned organisations, they also show evidence of **diversification**. The BBC operates in radio, publishing and film as well as television, while Channel 4 has its own feature film division, Film4.

Netflix has also diversified in recent years, moving beyond film and television into the gaming industry, acquiring several existing development studios as well as launching a number of new ones in different international territories.

Evaluating Hesmondhalgh's Theory of Cultural Industries

In evaluating Hesmondhalgh's theory of cultural industries you may find it useful to think about the following questions:

- Is the television industry as risk averse as Hesmondhalgh suggests?
- Is maximising audiences of equal importance to all television companies?
- Do some television companies cater for more niche audiences?
- Is there less pressure on public service broadcasters to maximise audiences? Are these types of broadcaster more able to take risks?

Regulation

Another important aspect of the television industry that you will need to explore is regulation. Having discussed the role of Ofcom in regulating the UK television industry in the Year 1 book, we will now consider how Livingstone and Lunt's theory of regulation can be applied to the television industry as well as exploring the impact of regulation on global television production, distribution and circulation.

Livingstone and Lunt's Theory of Regulation

KEY THEORY: Sonia Livingstone and Peter Lunt's Theory of Regulation

- the idea that there is an underlying struggle in recent UK regulation policy between the need to further the interests of citizens (by offering protection from harmful or offensive material) and the need to further the interests of consumers (by ensuring choice, value for money and market competition)
- the idea that the increasing power of global media corporations, together with the rise of convergent media technologies and transformations in the production, distribution and marketing of digital media, have placed traditional approaches to media regulation at risk

Tip

In order to explore and evaluate Livingstone and Lunt's theory, you will need to look at your set television products as part of a broader media landscape rather than just analysing them in isolation.

A key aspect of **Livingstone and Lunt**'s theory of regulation is the idea that there is an underlying struggle in recent UK regulation policy between the need to further the interests of citizens on the one hand, and the need to further the interests of consumers on the other.

For example, if we look at the main regulatory duties that Ofcom is required to perform, we can see that some of these duties appear to address the needs of citizens while others seem to address the needs of consumers.

Ofcom attempts to further the interests of citizens by:

- protecting viewers from offensive or harmful material
- protecting people from unfair treatment and ensuring that their privacy is not invaded.

At the same time, it attempts to further the interests of consumers by:

- ensuring that television services are provided by a range of different organisations (maintaining market competition and value for money)
- ensuring that a wide range of high-quality programmes are provided, which appeal to a range of tastes and interests (maintaining choice).

However, Livingstone and Lunt argue that the interests of citizens and those of consumers cannot easily be reconciled. They suggest that there is an increasing tendency in recent UK regulation policy to place the interests of consumers above those of citizens.

For example, the Communications Act of 2003 saw a significant shift towards **deregulation** as it liberalised media ownership rules in order to attract more investment in British media markets. This was meant to make it easier for companies to compete in the global marketplace. However, the relaxation of rules regarding ownership placed more power in the hands of major companies and removed some of the protection that regulation offers to citizens.

> **Key Term**
>
> **Deregulation**
> A process that involves the loosening of regulatory constraints that are seen as hurdles to economic growth. This is generally associated with marketisation or privatisation. For example, Watson and Hill (2015) suggest that deregulation typically involves a shift '*from public to commercial, largely corporate, control*'.

Regulation in a Global Age

Another important aspect of Livingstone and Lunt's theory is the idea that traditional approaches to media regulation have been put at risk by globalisation and the rise of convergent media technologies.

For example, the different ways in which audiences can access television content in a digital age present new challenges for regulators. The rise of streaming and video-on-demand services, coupled with the fact that viewers can now watch television on phones, PCs, laptops and other portable devices, makes regulation far less straightforward than it was in the traditional broadcast era.

The global market in which television companies now operate also presents certain challenges in terms of regulating the flow of television content. As Livingstone and Lunt (2011) point out:

> *the increasing power of global media corporations operating across national borders [...] makes it increasingly difficult for governments to implement media and communications policies based on shared national values.*

However, while this may be the case, there are still significant variations in terms of how television is regulated around the world. For example, individual nations tend to have their own regulatory codes, as attitudes towards sex, nudity, violence and bad language vary widely according to social and cultural context. This means that a television product that is produced in one country will sometimes have to be edited in order to be shown in another.

Rules Regarding Advertising on Television

Regulations regarding how much television advertising a broadcaster can carry also vary from nation to nation.

In the UK, Ofcom stipulates that:

- Non-public service channels such as Sky Atlantic can show no more than an average of 12 minutes of television advertising per hour.
- Public service channels such as Channel 4, ITV and Channel 5 can show no more than an average of eight minutes of television advertising per hour during primetime, with an average of seven minutes per hour across the entire broadcasting day, while BBC channels do not carry any advertising at all as they are funded by the licence fee.

In contrast, the Federal Communications Commission (FCC), which regulates US television, does not impose any limit on the amount of advertising that American channels can carry. This means that UK shows often have to be edited for US broadcast in order to accommodate more commercial breaks.

Significantly, Ofcom launched a consultation in July 2022, looking at whether the current restrictions on the amount of advertising public service broadcasters in the UK are permitted to show should be loosened to bring the PSBs in line with non-PSBs. This could be seen to support Livingstone and Lunt's claim that there is an increasing tendency in UK regulation policy to place consumer interests over those of citizens as commercial interests and the need to generate revenue are privileged over the need to protect the quality of the viewing experience.

Again, this can be seen as part of a pattern of growing deregulation, as the rules preventing product placement in programmes produced for UK audiences were lifted in 2011.

AUDIENCES

Link

Read about Stuart Hall's reception theory in the Year 1 book, page 264.

In the Year 1 book, we looked at the way in which television companies target and attract audiences through the content and appeal of their products and through marketing. We also discussed how audiences interpret television products, using Stuart Hall's reception theory to explore the idea that audiences may respond to the same television product in different ways.

In this section, we will explore how the different ways in which audiences use television products reflect demographic factors as well as cultural capital and other aspects of identity. We will also look at Henry Jenkins' theory of fandom.

Audience Readings and Responses

By now, you should be familiar with the idea that media products can be read by audiences in a variety of ways. What you will also need to think about when you are exploring your set television products is the way in which audience interpretations reflect social, cultural and historical circumstances.

- If you are studying Option 1, consider how cultural and historical circumstances might influence audience interpretations of *Peaky Blinders*. Think about the way in which audience readings of characters such as Tommy Shelby and Danny Whizz-Bang might be shaped by current understandings of conditions such as post-traumatic stress disorder, looking at the programme's depiction of the aftermath of the Great War through a contemporary lens.
- If you are studying Option 2, consider how social, cultural and historical circumstances might influence audience interpretations of *The Returned*. Think about the way in which audience readings might be shaped by recent debates about migration in French society. Claire Mouflard, for example, has read the programme as an allegory of '*the treatment of migrant Others in contemporary French society*' (2016).
- If you are studying Option 3, consider how social, cultural and historical circumstances might influence the way in which audiences interpret *Tehran*. Think about the different ways in which the programme might be received in Israel and Iran in light of ongoing political hostilities between the two countries and debates regarding Iran's nuclear programme.

The Significance of Demographic Factors and Other Aspects of Identity

Demographic factors such as gender, age, nationality or social class can also influence the way in which audiences use television products. For example, Danish audiences and Swedish audiences may each find that *The Bridge* reaffirms particular long-standing stereotypes they hold of one another. In this way, the programme could be used to consolidate a sense of national identity based on the cultural differences that are seen to exist between the two countries.

According to Hans Rosenfeldt, the Swedish co-creator of the series, '*Danes look at Swedish people like we're all a little like Saga Norén, by-the-book, politically correct [and] always in full control of ourselves.*'

Other aspects of identity such as religion and ethnicity can also affect the way in which audiences read and respond to television products. This could have a significant influence on audience responses to the representation of religious conservatism in *Tehran*, for instance.

Sexual orientation can influence how audiences use television products too. Many lesbian, gay and bisexual viewers have discussed how the positive representation of a same-sex relationship in the 'San Junipero' episode of *Black Mirror* provided a sense of affirmation or validation, while LGBT audiences responded positively to the relationship that develops between Eve and Villanelle over the first three series of *Killing Eve*.

Cultural Capital

Another factor that influences the way in which audiences use television products is **cultural capital**. Cultural capital is a form of knowledge that gives those who possess it power or social status. The French sociologist **Pierre Bourdieu** originally used the term to describe the way in which knowledge about various aspects of high culture could be seen to confer particular social advantages.

More recently, the term has been broadened to include subcultural knowledge as well as knowledge about popular culture. John Fiske, for example, has discussed the way in which popular cultural capital operates within fan communities. Those fans who are seen to possess cultural capital are more likely to win the respect of their peers, whereas those whose knowledge is deemed to be superficial or lacking may find themselves disregarded or marginalised. This is often seen in the discussions that take place in online fan forums.

Cultural capital can affect how audiences read and respond to television products in a variety of ways. For example, as a Media Studies student, you may find that you view a television programme differently compared with someone who lacks the specialist knowledge of codes, conventions and techniques that you have gained over the course of your studies.

The pleasures that a television product offers its audience may also depend on the cultural capital of the viewer. Viewers who are unfamiliar with 1980s popular culture will not fully appreciate the intertextual allusions to movies such as *Pretty in Pink* or *Ferris Bueller's Day Off* that feature in the 'San Junipero' episode of *Black Mirror*. The pleasure of identifying intertextual references such as these requires a certain level of cultural capital.

Similarly, those with a more detailed knowledge and understanding of Israel–Iran relations may respond to *Tehran* differently compared with those who are unfamiliar with the political history of the two countries.

Key Term

Cultural capital
A form of cultural knowledge that endows those who possess it with power or social status. The ability to speak knowledgeably about media products, to identify intertextual references, or to distinguish between the 'good' and the 'bad' are all forms of cultural capital.

Key Figure

Pierre Bourdieu
A French sociologist whose work on cultural taste has had a significant influence in a range of different fields, including Media Studies. In one of his most influential works, *Distinction* (1986), Bourdieu discusses the way in which cultural capital reproduces and reinforces social hierarchies.

Quickfire 5.6

How might a fan of a television programme demonstrate their cultural capital? What kind of things might they be expected to know?

Fandom

Jenkins' Theory of Fandom

A key theory you will need to use when exploring the relationship between audiences and television products is **Henry Jenkins**' theory of fandom.

KEY THEORY: Henry Jenkins' Theory of Fandom

- the idea that fans are active participants in the construction and circulation of textual meanings
- the idea that fans appropriate texts and read them in ways that are not fully authorised by the media producers ('textual poaching')
- the idea that fans construct their social and cultural identities through borrowing and inflecting mass culture images, and are part of a participatory culture that has a vital social dimension

Jenkins uses the term 'textual poaching' to describe the way in which texts can be appropriated by fans and adapted to suit their own purposes. According to Jenkins, '**appropriation** *involves both accepting certain core premises in the original work and reworking others to accommodate our own interests*' (Jenkins, 2013).

Textual Poaching and the Subversion of Dominant Messages and Meanings

In some cases, textual poaching may be used to challenge or subvert the **heteronormative** premise of the original work. For example, a piece of **fanfiction** may take two characters of the same sex from a television programme and place them in a romantic or sexual relationship that was not depicted in the original work. This genre of fanfiction is commonly referred to as **slash fiction**. The HBO series, *Euphoria*, explores this idea through the character of Kat, as in one of the episodes we see examples of the fanfiction that she writes, depicting Harry Styles and Louis Tomlinson from One Direction in an explicitly sexual relationship.

Slash fiction will typically tease out a homoerotic subtext that is either latent or implicit within the original work, or it will introduce a sexual dimension to a relationship between two characters of the same sex that is entirely absent from the source text. For example, the homoerotic subtext of Villanelle and Eve's relationship that develops over the first season of *Killing Eve* inspired numerous works of slash fiction depicting the relationship between the two female characters in more explicitly sexual or romantic terms. *Peaky Blinders* has also given rise to numerous works of fanfiction, some of which subvert the operation of heteronormativity in the original text by imagining a sexual relationship between Thomas Shelby and Alfie Solomons, a character who was introduced in the second series of the show (see also the example of fanart on the next page).

Textual poaching does not necessarily have to involve the subversion of heteronormativity in the original work, though; there are other ways in which fans can appropriate and rework the premises in the source text to suit their own interests. For example, many fans of *Killing Eve* who were dissatisfied with the final episode of the show wrote their own endings instead. Similarly, many works of fanfiction inspired by the 'San Junipero' episode of *Black Mirror* created alternative endings for the characters or extended the story in new directions.

Named Theorist

Henry Jenkins
Henry Jenkins is an academic and theorist whose work focuses primarily on fandom, media convergence and participatory culture.
His theory of fandom is outlined in the book *Textual Poachers: Television Fans and Participatory Culture*, which was first published in 1992. An updated twentieth anniversary edition was published in 2013.

Key Terms

Appropriation
A process that involves taking or claiming something for one's own use. Fans may appropriate images, characters or ideas from popular television programmes, for example, using them as the basis for their own artwork or fanfiction.

Heteronormativity
A set of assumptions or presuppositions that treat heterosexuality as normal and natural.

Fanfiction
Stories or works of fiction that are based on existing films, television programmes or literary works, and which are produced by fans rather than the original creators of those products. Sometimes referred to as fanfic.

Slash fiction
A genre of fanfiction that depicts two fictional characters or famous people of the same sex in a romantic or sexual relationship with one another. Slash fiction focusing on female characters is often called femslash.

Tip

You only need to apply Jenkins' theory of fandom to one of your set television products (either *Peaky Blinders, Black Mirror* or *Killing Eve*, depending on the option you are studying). You are not required to apply this theory to the non-English-language product you are studying.

These examples show how fans appropriate texts and read them in ways that are not fully authorised by the original producers – a key element of Jenkins' theory.

Fandom as an Example of Participatory Culture

Jenkins sees fandom as part of the broader phenomenon of participatory culture. The idea that fans are active participants in the production and circulation of textual meanings challenges the notion that audiences are simply passive consumers of media content.

For Jenkins, the type of meaning-making that fans engage in has a vital social dimension. This has been facilitated to a significant extent by the growth of digital technologies as fans are able to interact with one another in a variety of ways. For example, the rise of social networking platforms such as **Tumblr** has made it easier for fans to share and exchange **gifs**, **memes** and other user-generated content online.

Jenkins has pointed out that media industries have had to make wider use of participatory strategies in order to attract and build relations with fans. A notable example of this was the competition that the BBC ran to mark the launch of the fifth series of *Peaky Blinders*, following its move from BBC Two to BBC One, as fans were invited to submit their own art inspired by the show. After receiving over 1,000 entries, the work of the 16 competition winners was then used in the marketing campaign promoting the series. Chris Hooper, Head of Marketing for BBC One and iPlayer, said that the aim of the marketing campaign was to harness the power of *Peaky Blinders*' existing fandom in order to bring new viewers 'into the fold'.

Social media plays a particularly important role in maintaining relations with fans in the television industry today as Twitter, Facebook, Instagram and TikTok are widely used to facilitate audience interaction. Hashtags have become a notable feature of marketing materials such as trailers and posters. They have also become increasingly prominent in the programmes themselves as audiences are encouraged to participate in online discussions about the programmes while they watch.

The responses posted by audiences on social media provide broadcasters with valuable information about who is watching their programmes and how they are being received. Companies such as Nielsen and Canvs analyse these responses before providing television networks with demographic data and behavioural insights into the audience. For example, Canvs uses semantic analysis technology to track and categorise emotional reactions to television products as revealed through posts on Twitter.

Evaluating Henry Jenkins' Theory of Fandom

Remember that you should be prepared not only to apply Jenkins' theory of fandom but also to evaluate it. Therefore, you may want to consider whether, in emphasising the social and participatory aspects of fandom, Jenkins' theory overlooks or downplays the significance of other types of fan response.

- Are fans necessarily part of broader communities or social networks, for instance? What about individual fans who engage with television products without the mediation of these broader networks?
- Do all fans read texts in ways that are not fully authorised by their producers? How typical is this of the way in which fans engage with television products?
- Does Jenkins overstate the participatory nature of fandom? To what extent do fans actually play an active role in the construction and circulation of textual meanings?

Key Terms

Tumblr
A blogging or social networking site that enables users to share music, art, photos, videos and various other types of content.

Gif
An image format that is commonly used for simple animations and low-resolution videos.

Meme
An image, phrase, idea or video disseminated by internet users – a screenshot from a television programme which has an amusing quote or phrase added to it before it is posted online, for example.

Stretch and Challenge 5.14

Explore some of the fanart or fanfiction that has been produced in response to your set television product. Examples of fanfiction based on *Peaky Blinders*, the 'San Junipero' episode of *Black Mirror*, and *Killing Eve* can be found on Fanfiction.net and archiveofourown.org.

Evaluating Stuart Hall's Reception Theory

Another audience theory that you should be prepared to evaluate is Stuart Hall's reception theory. The key principles of this theory were introduced in the Year 1 book.

KEY THEORY: Stuart Hall's Reception Theory

- the idea that communication is a process involving encoding by producers and decoding by audiences
- the idea that there are three hypothetical positions from which messages and meanings may be decoded:
  i. the dominant-hegemonic position: the encoder's intended meaning (the preferred reading) is fully understood and accepted
  ii. the negotiated position: the legitimacy of the encoder's message is acknowledged in general terms, although the message is adapted or negotiated to better fit the decoder's own individual experiences or context
  iii. the oppositional position: the encoder's message is understood, but the decoder disagrees with it, reading it in a contrary or oppositional way

In evaluating Hall's reception theory, you may find it useful to think about how well it works for different types of television product. For example, some critics have suggested that, while it offers a useful framework for exploring audience responses to factual genres such as television news, it is less relevant for genres such as crime drama, science-fiction or the spy thriller. Some would argue that a preferred reading is much harder to locate in these genres, as they are more concerned with offering audience pleasures than with encoding ideological messages.

Another criticism that has been made of Hall's theory is that it tends to ignore the contexts in which audience reception takes place, focusing instead on the way in which individual audience members decode and interpret texts.

Link

For more on fans playing an active role in the construction and circulation of textual meanings, see pages 232–233 of this book

Summary

Having read this section on television, you should now be familiar with:

- the way television products such as *Peaky Blinders*, *Black Mirror* and *Killing Eve* use genre conventions in a hybrid way
- the way the conventions of popular television genres such as crime drama, science-fiction and the spy thriller can be challenged or subverted
- the idea that the genre conventions of television products are socially and culturally relative as they reflect the social and cultural contexts in which they are produced
- the main characteristics and conventions of postmodern television products, including intertextuality, reflexivity, parody and pastiche
- the way representations in television products invoke discourses and ideologies
- the way representations of gender in television products may support or challenge patriarchal ideology
- the way cultural and institutional factors can be seen to influence representations of race and ethnicity in television products
- the global nature of the television industry
- the significance of international co-productions in the television industry today
- the different sources of funding in the television industry and the impact of funding on production and distribution

- the role of regulation in the global production and distribution of television products
- the impact of cultural capital, demographic factors and other aspects of social identity on the way in which audiences use and interpret television products
- the various ways in which fans use and interact with television products.

Essential Theories for Television

When discussing your set television products, you should be able to use and evaluate the following theories:

Theories of Media Language

- **Genre theory**, including Neale: for example, the idea that genres such as crime drama, supernatural horror and the spy thriller are characterised by patterns of repetition and difference, and are shaped by the institutional, industrial and economic contexts in which they are produced.
- **Narratology**, including Todorov: for example, the idea that television narratives share a basic structure involving movement from one state of equilibrium to another.
- **Structuralism**, including Lévi-Strauss: for example, the idea that television products convey their meanings through patterns of oppositions.
- **Postmodernism**, including Baudrillard: for example, the idea that in the postmodern age the boundaries between the 'real' world and the world of television have imploded or collapsed.

Theories of Representation

- **Theories of representation**, including Hall: for example, the idea that representations are constructed through aspects of media language and that stereotypical representations reflect power inequalities.
- **Feminist theories**, including bell hooks and van Zoonen: for example, the idea that feminism can be used to critique or challenge the operation of patriarchal ideology in television products, and that television representations of gender are constructed through discourses that are culturally and historically specific.
- **Theories of gender performativity**, including Butler: for example, the idea that gender is performatively constructed in television products through the repetition of acts and rituals.

Industry Theories

- **Regulation**, including Livingstone and Lunt: for example, the idea that globalisation and the rise of digital media have made regulation of the television industry increasingly difficult.
- **Cultural industries**, including Hesmondhalgh: for example, the idea that companies operating in the television industry minimise risk and maximise audiences through horizontal and vertical integration, internationalisation and the formatting of television products.

Audience Theories

- **Reception theory**, including Hall: for example, the idea that viewers may adopt different positions in relation to the television products they watch, interpreting them in different ways.
- **Fandom**, including Jenkins: for example, the idea that fans appropriate television products and read them in ways that are not fully authorised by their producers, as can be seen with examples of fanart and fanfiction.

Section B: Magazines – Mainstream and Alternative Media

The Specification

Link

An introduction to the study of magazines as a media form is available on pages 158–179 of the Year 1 book.

If you are following the linear Eduqas specification, magazines are the second of the media forms you are required to study in depth. At A Level, you are required to study two set magazine products. One of these will be a historical magazine produced in the 1960s and the other a contemporary magazine produced outside the commercial mainstream.

In the Year 1 book, some of the main theoretical approaches that can be used to study magazines were set out along with a critical framework for analysing the historical magazine products. This section builds on that material, introducing the contemporary magazines as well as some of the more advanced critical theories and concepts that you are required to study at A Level.

Tip

The set products shown here are correct at the time of writing. However, as has previously been mentioned, these may change from time to time. Therefore, before choosing which option to study, you should check the Eduqas website to see if there have been any changes to the set products.

WJEC

If you are following the modular WJEC specification, you will study magazines as part of the A2 module 'Media in the Global Age'. For this unit, you will study one historical magazine product from the 1960s (either *Vogue*, *Woman* or *Woman's Realm*), one contemporary mainstream magazine (either *Cosmopolitan*, *Hello*, *Men's Health* or *Vogue*) and one contemporary non-mainstream magazine (either *Adbusters*, *Attitude*, *Huck* or *Pride*). Both contemporary magazines will be studied in their online form.

Before reading this section of the book, it is recommended that you look at the section on magazines in the Year 1 book, as it provides an introduction to the study of magazines as a media form and sets out a framework for analysing the historical magazine products. The final section of this chapter should also prove useful, as it includes a discussion of online magazines and magazine websites, including *Attitude*.

Magazine Options

For Section B of Component 2, you are required to study two magazine products. There are three options to choose from.

OPTION 1: *Woman* and *Adbusters*

Set Product 1: *Woman* (1937–), set edition: 23–29 August 1964

- *Woman* is a weekly women's magazine. It was originally published by Odhams Press before the International Publishing Corporation (IPC) assumed ownership of the magazine in 1963. IPC was renamed Time Inc. UK in 2014, which then became TI Media in 2018. The magazine is currently published by Future plc, who acquired TI Media in 2020.

Key Term

Bimonthly
A magazine that is published every two months.

Set Product 2: *Adbusters* (1989–), set edition: May/June 2016, Vol. 23 No. 3

- *Adbusters* is a **bimonthly** activist magazine. It is published by Adbusters Media Foundation, a Canadian organisation based in Vancouver.

OPTION 2: *Woman's Realm* and *Huck*

Set Product 1: *Woman's Realm* (1958–2001), set edition: 7–13 February 1965

- *Woman's Realm* was a weekly women's magazine. Launched in 1958, it was originally published by Odhams Press before the International Publishing Corporation (IPC) took over its ownership in 1963. Publication of the magazine ended in 2001 when it was merged with *Woman's Weekly*.

Set Product 2: *Huck* (2006–), set edition: February/March 2016, Issue 54

- *Huck* is an alternative culture magazine that focuses on youth culture, subcultural lifestyles and countercultural movements. Originally a bimonthly, *Huck* was relaunched as a **biannual** in 2021 following a redesign. It is published by TCO London.

OPTION 3: *Vogue* and *The Big Issue*

Set Product 1: *Vogue* (1916–), set edition: July 1965

- *Vogue* is a monthly women's fashion magazine. The original American magazine was launched by Arthur Turnure in 1892. Since 1909, it has been published by Condé Nast. The British edition of *Vogue* was launched in 1916.

Set Product 2: *The Big Issue* (1991–), set edition: 17–23 October 2016, No. 1227

- *The Big Issue* is a weekly current affairs and entertainment magazine. Its primary purpose is to provide those who are homeless or experiencing poverty with the opportunity to earn an income as **street vendors**. The magazine is published by The Big Issue Group.

Key Terms

Biannual
A magazine that is published twice a year.

Street vendors
Those who sell goods or services to members of the public from the street. For example, magazines such as *The Big Issue*, which are commonly referred to as street newspapers, are purchased from street vendors rather than from newsagents or supermarkets.

Using the Theoretical Framework

In exploring your set magazine products, you will need to consider all four areas of the theoretical framework:

- **Media language**: how magazines communicate meanings through their forms, codes, conventions and techniques.
- **Representation**: how magazines portray issues, individuals and social groups.
- **Industry**: how processes of production, distribution and circulation affect magazine products.
- **Audiences**: how magazines target, reach, address and potentially construct audiences, and how audiences interpret and respond to magazine products.

MEDIA LANGUAGE

As you analyse your magazines, it is important to think about how the contexts in which they were produced inform their use of media language, as well as the representations they offer. In particular, you will need to explore the significance of:

- **Social and cultural contexts**: the way in which the magazines embody or express particular social and cultural values, attitudes or beliefs; the ideological significance of the codes, conventions and techniques they use.
- **Historical contexts**: how the magazines relate to the times in which they were produced.
- **Economic contexts**: how the magazines are funded and whether their purpose is primarily commercial or not-for-profit; whether the magazines are produced by a major publishing house or an independent publisher and how this might be seen to influence their house style.

Rapid Recall 5.5

What is meant by the house style of a magazine?

Key Terms

Headshot
A photograph of a person's face or their head and shoulders. Headshots are conventionally used in portrait photography and often feature on magazine covers.

Candid photograph
A photograph that appears natural or spontaneous rather than posed. The subject is often unaware that their picture is being taken.

Quickfire 5.7

Marjorie Ferguson (1978) points out that on most traditional women's magazines covers, the female face is decontextualised as there is a 'general absence of background or situational cues'. Why do you think this is the case? What is the purpose and effect of this decontextualised presentation of the female face?

Key Terms

Semantic field
A set of inter-related words that refer to the same general area or topic. The language in a specialist rock magazine such as *Kerrang!* is likely to draw on the semantic field of rock music, for example.

Magazine design
Jenny McKay suggests that: '*At its simplest, magazine design is the way in which words and images and physical elements such as paper and binding work together*' (McKay, 2000). Magazine design plays a crucial role in establishing the brand identity of a magazine as well as creating audience appeal.

Grid
A tool used in the newspaper and magazine industry to organise or format page layouts. The grid typically dictates the size of the margins, the number and width of the columns, the placement of images on the page and the use of white space, hence providing a sense of order and structure.

Analysing the Front Covers

In order to develop your understanding of the differences between your two set magazines, you may find it useful to start with a comparison of their front covers, thinking in particular about some of the following:

- **Photographic codes and conventions**: if the cover features a photographic image, what kind of shot has been used? Is it a **headshot** or a long shot, for instance? Has the subject been photographed in their usual environment or has the photograph been taken in a studio? How might the presence or absence of contextual cues such as social or cultural setting affect the way in which the image is read? To what extent has the photograph been staged or posed? Is it a **candid photograph**, for instance?
- **Visual codes**: what does the subject's clothing signify or connote? How do the subject's gestural codes or facial expression help to establish a particular mode of address? What mood does the cover model or image project? If graphics or illustrations have been used, what do they connote and how do they contribute to the meaning of the text?
- **The masthead**: what does the magazine's title signify? Does it convey a sense of the content, genre or intended audience of the magazine? What are the connotations of the typography used? Is the font style traditional or modern? Formal or informal? How does the masthead convey a sense of the magazine's brand identity?
- **Lexis**: what are the connotations of the language used? What ideological significance might the lexical choices be seen to have? What **semantic fields** do the magazines draw on?

Viewpoints and Ideologies

As you analyse the use of media language in your set magazines, you will need to explore how this incorporates viewpoints and ideologies. **Magazine design** plays an important role in this regard. As Andrew Howard (2001) points out:

> *Design is not an abstract theoretical discipline – it produces tangible artifacts, expresses social priorities and carries cultural values.*

The design of a magazine reveals a great deal about its brand values or editorial philosophy. It can signify the magazine's relationship to the mainstream and may be used to support or challenge dominant ideologies. Some magazines employ a highly commercial aesthetic, for instance, while others are more subversive in their use of media language. As you analyse your set magazines, consider the following questions:

- Is the layout of the magazine conventional or unconventional?
- How is white space used?
- Does the magazine use a traditional **grid** layout?
- Is there a uniform layout or style running through the different articles and features in the magazine or is it more eclectic?

Magazines such as *Huck* often use design elements to signify their opposition to the commercial mainstream.

These questions should then lead you to consider broader questions regarding the ideological significance of the magazine's design:

- How might the codes, conventions and techniques that the magazine uses be seen to reinforce or challenge dominant ideologies?
- What does the magazine's design suggest about its relationship to mainstream culture?
- How commercial is the magazine's aesthetic?
- In what ways can the magazine be seen to support Andrew Howard's claim that design *'expresses social priorities and carries cultural values'*?

Genre

Another important aspect of media language that you will need to look at is genre. This includes:

- the idea that genre conventions are socially and historically relative. In other words, they are not fixed or static but change and vary according to social and historical context. For example, the conventions of the women's magazine genre, which were discussed in the Year 1 book, have evolved over time to reflect changing historical circumstances and social attitudes
- the idea that genre conventions are dynamic and can be used in a hybrid way. This sense of dynamism and genre hybridity is a notable feature of each of the contemporary magazines discussed below.

Link

The idea that genre conventions are socially and historically relative, and the way in which women's magazines adapted to the new post-war context in the 1950s and 1960s, moving from a 'make-do-and-mend' ethos to one of 'shop and spend', is discussed on page 166 in the Year 1 book.

Tip

The idea that genre conventions can be used in a hybrid way is only likely to be relevant to the contemporary magazine you are studying as this is not a significant feature of any of the three historical magazine products.

OPTION 1: *Adbusters*

Adbusters belongs to the **activist magazine** genre. Activist magazines seek to bring about social or political change through **direct action**. This sense of social or political purpose is their main defining feature.

Consciousness-raising is a common aim of activist magazines, as they conventionally include essays or articles designed to raise awareness of particular issues, campaigns or causes. While activist magazines sometimes profile the activist work of individuals or collectives, they also encourage readers to become activists themselves. For example, *Adbusters* played an instrumental role in mobilising protestors during the Occupy Wall Street movement in 2011.

Key Terms

Activist magazine
A magazine that seeks to bring about social or political change through direct action.

Direct action
A means of achieving change that advocates action over discussion. This can take many forms, from protesting, demonstrating and going on marches, to boycotting goods or companies.

Consciousness-raising
A form of activism that aims to heighten public awareness of an issue.

Key Term

Culture jamming
Defined by Naomi Klein (2000) as '*the practice of parodying adverts and hijacking billboards in order to drastically alter their messages*'. Subvertising (a portmanteau word combining 'subvert' and 'advertising') is another term commonly used to describe this cultural practice.

Culture Jamming

An important issue to consider if you are studying *Adbusters* is *how* the magazine seeks to bring about social or political change. In relation to this, *Adbusters*' co-founder, Kalle Lasn, has said:

> *What we're trying to do is pioneer a new form of social activism using all the power of the mass media to sell ideas rather than products.* (Motavalli, 1996)

***Adbusters*' covers often signify the magazine's subversive politics.**

The main form that *Adbusters*' social activism takes is **culture jamming**. This involves subverting or sabotaging mass media messages, particularly those associated with advertising and consumer culture.

As **Mark Dery** (1993) points out:

> *Culture jammers often make use of what might be called 'guerrilla' semiotics – analytical techniques not unlike those employed by scholars to decipher the signs and symbols that constitute a culture's secret language, what [cultural] theorist Roland Barthes called 'systems of signification.' [...] As used by culture jammers, [semiotics] is an essential tool in the all-important undertaking of making sense of the world, its networks of power, the encoded messages that flicker ceaselessly along its communication channels.*

As *Adbusters* parodies the conventions of consumer lifestyle magazines through the spoof advertisements or 'culture jams' it incorporates, it can be seen to exhibit a certain degree of genre hybridity, albeit with subversive intent. This is something that you will need to consider as you study the set edition of the magazine.

Key Figure

Mark Dery
An American academic and cultural critic who has written extensively on cyberculture. Several of his articles were published in *Adbusters* in the early 1990s. His 1993 essay on culture jamming, 'Culture Jamming: Hacking, Slashing, and Sniping in the Empire of Signs' is available online at: http://markdery.com/?page_id=154.

OPTION 2: *Huck*

Genre hybridity is also a notable feature of *Huck*. This is evident in the eclectic nature of the magazine's content, which ranges from articles on music and skateboarding to essays on gender politics and global conflicts. *Huck* therefore combines the interest in **subcultural** lifestyles that is conventionally found in youth magazines with the political reportage of a current affairs magazine.

Key Term

Subculture
A smaller cultural group that differs in some way from the larger, dominant culture under which it exists.

Although it covers a diverse range of topics, *Huck* is said to be '*rooted in the rebellious heritage of surf and skate*' (Village, 2016). This is a sub-genre of youth magazines that is primarily concerned with documenting subcultural lifestyles.

While these magazines may include interviews with, or **profiles** of, well-known skaters or surfers, **photo essays** tend to be a key feature of the 'skate and surf' sub-genre. For example, Craig Stecyk's articles for *Skateboarder* magazine in the 1970s played an important role in documenting the skate scene that was emerging in Southern California at the time. As Kevin Duffel (2012) pointed out in an article for the April/May 2012 issue of *Huck*:

> *His* **gonzo journalistic** *style [...] pushed skateboarding away from its all-American, beachfront roots into a counterculture that embraced rebellion and danger.*

The work of photographers such as Craig Stecyk has had a significant influence on the aesthetic of more recent youth culture magazines such as *What Youth*. The photographic codes that are conventionally used in these magazines help to convey a sense of the vibrancy and authenticity of the subcultures they document as well as signifying their opposition to mainstream culture.

Radical Culture

Huck is perhaps best defined as an alternative culture magazine, as the diverse range of essays and articles that it features share a common interest in people, practices and movements that operate outside of or in opposition to the cultural mainstream.

The mission statement that appears on *Huck*'s website foregrounds this idea, highlighting the magazine's interest in radical culture. Andrea Hurland, *Huck*'s editor-in-chief, offers a useful definition of this concept, suggesting that radical culture encompasses '*anything or anyone that challenges the dominant discourse*' (Ziniophile, 2014).

The title of the magazine also invokes the idea of youthful rebellion. While 'huck' is a term sometimes used in skateboarding or snowboarding, it also refers to Huckleberry Finn, the young protagonist of Mark Twain's 19th-century American novel who rejects the norms and values of 'civilised society' and resists the attempts of his elders to 'civilise' him.

Quickfire 5.8

What is the semiotic term for signs that have more than one meaning? For example, in skateboarding 'Huck' means to leave the ground when performing a stunt; however, it could also refer to the name of the main character in *The Adventures of Huckleberry Finn*.

Key Terms

Profile
A term used in the newspaper and magazine industry for a short biographical sketch of an individual or organisation.

Photo essay
A set of photographs that present an argument or narrative about a topic or theme.

Gonzo journalism
A highly personal or subjective style of journalism in which the reporter or photographer is fully immersed in the world that they document rather than maintaining a sense of objectivity or critical distance. One of the figures most commonly associated with gonzo journalism is Hunter S. Thompson. His articles on 1960s counterculture, many published in *Rolling Stone* magazine, played a pioneering role in its development.

Tip

The key conventions of current affairs magazines are outlined on page 194.

Stretch and Challenge 5.15

Analysing other *Huck* front covers will also help you develop your understanding of the magazine's brand values. A gallery of back issues can be found on the *Huck* website.

Stretch and Challenge 5.16

Read the 'Statement of Intent' on page 10 of the set edition of *Huck* magazine. How does the intertextual reference to *Catcher in the Rye* and its main protagonist, Holden Caulfield, convey a sense of the magazine's brand values?

OPTION 3: *The Big Issue*

The Big Issue is a current affairs and entertainment magazine. While current affairs magazines focus on issues and events of social or political interest, entertainment magazines are primarily concerned with aspects of popular culture such as film, television and popular music. They conventionally include:

- profiles of music artists, actors, directors and other figures involved in the entertainment industry
- celebrity interviews
- reviews and previews of films, television programmes, festivals, concerts and albums.

Current affairs magazines can take a number of different forms. Some feature investigative journalism and political reportage, some feature more **polemical** pieces, while others are more satirical in their tone or mode of address.

There are also significant ideological differences within the genre. Some current affairs magazines try to remain politically neutral while others are more partisan. The *Spectator* is a right-wing current affairs magazine, for instance, while *New Statesman* is on the left of the political spectrum.

Alongside larger, long-established titles such as *The Economist* and *Time*, the past few years have also seen the emergence of a growing number of independent current affairs magazines. A notable example of this is American **quarterly** *Jacobin*, which, according to its website, is '*a leading voice of the American left, offering socialist perspectives on politics, economics, and culture*' (Jacobin, 2018).

Genre Hybridity in *The Big Issue*

The Big Issue's use of genre hybridity is a widely discussed issue, as its attempt to combine the conventions of a current affairs magazine with those of an entertainment magazine has not always been met with universal approval. For example, some critics have suggested that the prominence given to celebrity and entertainment in the magazine detracts from its messages about inequality and social injustice, undermining its social purpose.

From the publishers' perspective, the inclusion of more populist, mainstream content is important as, by broadening the audience, they are able to generate more revenue for the street vendors who sell the magazine. John Bird, one of the founders of *The Big Issue*, has highlighted the need to attract a wider readership, stating:

> *we're here to sell as many papers as possible in order to give work to the homeless. We're not a homeless paper: we're a paper sold by homeless people.* (Guha, 2012)

One way in which *The Big Issue* attempts to reconcile its social principles with the quest for more mainstream appeal is by using celebrity and entertainment as a vehicle for social commentary.

Key Terms

Polemical
Opinionated, controversial, argumentative or strongly critical. Polemical magazine articles are commonly found in activist magazines and current affairs magazines.

Quarterly
A magazine that is published four times a year.

Stretch and Challenge 5.17

Look at some current affairs magazines, such as *Private Eye*, *New Statesman* and *The Economist*, or visit their websites. What similarities can you identify with *The Big Issue*?

Stretch and Challenge 5.18

What evidence of genre hybridity can you find in the set edition of *The Big Issue*?

Quickfire 5.9

In what ways does the cover featuring Rose Ayling-Ellis illustrate the way in which *The Big Issue* uses celebrity as a vehicle for social commentary?

Lévi-Strauss's Theory of Structuralism

In terms of media language, the two main theories you will need to apply to the magazine products you are studying are Roland Barthes' theory of semiotics and Claude Lévi-Strauss's structuralist theory. In the Year 1 book, we discussed how Barthes' theory of semiotics can be used to analyse the processes of signification through which magazines produce their meanings. We will now explore how Lévi-Strauss's structuralist theory can be applied to the set magazine products.

KEY THEORY: Claude Lévi-Strauss's Theory of Structuralism

- the idea that texts can best be understood through an examination of their underlying structure
- the idea that meaning is dependent upon (and produced through) pairs of oppositions
- the idea that the way in which these binary oppositions are resolved can have particular ideological significance

As previously discussed, Lévi-Strauss's structuralist theory is based on the idea that meaning is dependent upon and produced through a system of binary oppositions. These binary oppositions often have ideological significance. For example, the way in which men and women are represented in binary opposition to one another may construct or reinforce particular understandings of masculinity and femininity.

The idea that 'The Working Wife is a Bad Wife', which Marjorie Ferguson (1983) found to be a recurring theme in traditional women's magazines of the 1950s and 1960s, also highlights the ideological significance of binary oppositions. To suggest that the 'stay-at-home' wife is a *good* wife is, by definition, to imply that the working wife is a *bad* wife. The construction of these ideas as binary opposites therefore reinforces patriarchal ideology.

Stretch and Challenge 5.19

Analyse how the set edition of your historical women's magazine constructs binary oppositions between men and women. Consider the representation of gender roles, for example.

Rapid Recall 5.6

In semiotic theory, what do the terms 'paradigm' and 'syntagm' refer to?

Link

The way in which semiotic theory can be used to analyse magazines is outlined in the Year 1 book, pages 162–163.

Link

A summary of the key aspects of Lévi-Strauss' structuralist theory is provided on pages 165–167.

Myth

Lévi-Strauss's suggestion that the purpose of myth is to '*provide a logical model capable of overcoming a contradiction*' (1958) is also particularly useful when it comes to analysing the ideological function of women's magazines.

As discussed in the Year 1 book, contradictory messages regarding the role of women were a common feature of popular culture during the 1960s. While the traditional 'happy housewife' stereotype of the 1950s continued to circulate throughout this decade, the sexual revolution of the 'swinging 60s' also saw the emergence of more progressive representations promoting ideas of female liberation and independence.

The representations that featured in women's magazines in the 1960s could be seen to offer magical solutions to these ideological contradictions, as they helped negotiate these different versions of femininity.

The beauty myth that circulates in women's magazines can also be seen as a way of resolving certain ideological contradictions. For example, while natural beauty is highly valued in women's magazines, these texts consistently promote the idea that beauty is something that has to be constantly worked at. As Joanne Hollows (2000) points out, fashion and beauty pages *'present looking "natural" as something which must be achieved'* by following a series of intensive beauty routines and rituals and by applying a range of cosmetic products.

This further illustrates the way in which women's magazines could be seen to '*provide a logical model capable of overcoming a contradiction*' (Lévi-Strauss, 1958).

Binary Oppositions in the Contemporary Magazines

As well as exploring Lévi-Strauss's structuralist theory in relation to your historical magazine product, you will also need to consider how it can be applied to the contemporary magazine product you are studying.

For example, the culture jams that feature in *Adbusters* often use binary oppositions to draw attention to the social inequalities that corporate capitalism creates. As Naomi Klein (2000) points out:

> *One of the most popular ways for artists and activists to highlight inequalities of free-market globalisation is by juxtaposing First World icons [such as Mickey Mouse, the Marlboro Man or Ronald McDonald] with Third World scenes.*

As a magazine that champions and celebrates '*people and movements that paddle against the flow*' (*Huck*, cited in Roberts, 2018), *Huck*'s ethos is also defined in binary opposition to mainstream culture. This is critical not only in terms of how the magazine positions and markets itself but also in terms of the angle it takes in stories and articles.

Similarly, *The Big Issue*'s tagline '*a hand up not a handout*', which appears on the cover and on the contents page as part of the magazine's manifesto, sets up a series of binary oppositions, most notably between charity and social enterprise, begging and working, and dependency and independence. This is fundamental to the magazine's ethos and the work that it does in transforming the lives of the street vendors who sell the magazine and changing public perceptions of homelessness.

Key Figure

Naomi Klein
A theorist and cultural commentator whose work focuses primarily on consumer culture. One of her most well-known works is the book *No Logo* (2000).

Evaluating Lévi-Strauss's Theory of Structuralism

Remember that in the Component 2 exam you may be required to evaluate the theories that you have studied. In evaluating Lévi-Strauss's structuralist theory, you may find it useful to consider whether this binaristic approach to textual analysis is too simplistic to fully account for the way in which meanings are produced. Are there any examples in your set magazine where binaristic understandings of culture or gender are challenged or start to break down, for instance?

REPRESENTATION

In the Year 1 book, we discussed some of the main issues regarding the representation of gender, race and ethnicity in magazines and outlined the key aspects of David Gauntlett's theory of identity. We will now build on these ideas as we consider how Gauntlett's theory might be evaluated as well as exploring how feminist theory and other relevant critical concepts and approaches can be used to analyse the representations in the set products.

Link

A framework for exploring issues regarding the representations in the historical magazine products is set out on pages 166–171 of the Year 1 book.

Evaluating Gauntlett's Theory of Identity

KEY THEORY: David Gauntlett's Theory of Identity

- the idea that the media provide us with 'tools' or resources that we use to construct our identities
- the idea that whilst in the past the media tended to convey singular, straightforward messages about ideal types of male and female identities, the media today offer us a more diverse range of stars, icons and characters from whom we may pick and mix different ideas

Link

David Gauntlett's theory of identity is outlined on page 167 of the Year 1 book.

One of the issues that you will need to consider as you study your set magazines is the effect of social, cultural and historical context on the representations they offer.

David Gauntlett's theory of identity is particularly relevant in this regard. As discussed in the Year 1 book, a key element of this theory is the idea that '*in contrast with the past [...] we no longer get singular, straightforward messages about ideal types of male and female identities*' (2008).

Gauntlett therefore suggests that, since the 1960s, the mass media has '*become more liberal [in terms of sex and gender issues], and considerably more challenging to traditional standards*'. He also argues that the media not only *reflects* changing social and cultural attitudes, it is involved in '*actively disseminating modern values*'.

An extract from the set edition of *The Big Issue*, featuring the artist Grayson Perry.

Key Term

Culture lag
The idea that changes in media representations may lag behind changes in the wider society within which those representations are produced.

Tip

It is important to bear in mind that any differences between the two set magazines in terms of the representations they offer may not be solely due to the different historical contexts in which they were produced.

Evaluating Gauntlett's Theory

These are some of the ideas that you will need to evaluate as you analyse the representations in your set magazines. Consider, for example, the extent to which the set products support Gauntlett's claim that representations of gender today are more fluid, complex and varied than they were in the 1960s.

- Do the representations in the contemporary magazine appear more liberal than those in the historical magazine, for instance?
- How traditional are the representations in the historical magazine? Are they 'singular and straightforward' as Gauntlett's theory would seem to suggest?

Gauntlett's suggestion that the media does not just reflect social and cultural attitudes but actively disseminates modern values is also worth exploring. For instance, some theorists argue that changes in media representations generally lag behind changes in society. This is referred to as a **culture lag**. For example, although over half of all working-age women were in some form of paid employment during the 1950s and 1960s, it took far longer for this social change to filter down into women's magazines.

van Zoonen's Feminist Theory

KEY THEORY: Liesbet van Zoonen's Feminist Theory

- the idea that gender is constructed through discourse, and that its meaning varies according to cultural and historical context
- the idea that the display of women's bodies as objects to be looked at is a core element of Western patriarchal culture
- the idea that in mainstream culture the visual and narrative codes that are used to construct the male body as spectacle differ from those used to objectify the female body

Key Term

Essentialism
The belief that gender and other aspects of identity are innate, natural or biologically determined rather than socially constructed. The idea that social groups such as men and women are inherently different because they are born with certain traits, for example.

Liesbet van Zoonen is one of the named theorists whose ideas you will need to consider when exploring the representations of gender in your set magazine products. As discussed in the previous section, a key aspect of her theory is the idea that gender is constructed through discourse, and that its meaning varies according to cultural and historical context.

van Zoonen (1994) therefore rejects the idea that gender is more or less stable as this **essentialist** view of gender is unable to account for the *'daily lives and experiences of [those] whose identities belie the thought of an easily identifiable distinction between women and men'*.

When applying van Zoonen's theory to your set magazine products, it is worth considering some of these issues:

- What ideas do the magazines convey about what it means to be a man or a woman? How do they construct particular notions of masculinity or femininity?
- What do you notice about the discourses the magazines use? To what extent do they serve to empower or contain women, for instance? Do the magazines challenge or support dominant discourses of masculinity?

- In what ways can the representations of gender in the two magazines be seen as historically and culturally specific? How far do the representations in the two magazines differ? How do they relate to the dominant discourses of the times in which they were produced?

Audience Responses and Feminist Analysis

van Zoonen suggests that one of the main tasks for feminist media research *'is to unravel both the dominant and alternative meanings of gender encoded in media texts'* (van Zoonen, 1994). However, while critical approaches such as semiotics and content analysis are certainly useful in this regard, van Zoonen argues that a weakness of these types of analysis is that they do not fully explain the popularity and meaning that widely consumed genres hold for their audiences.

Warning against **textual determinism** and the assumption that women's genres simply and straightforwardly oppress their female audiences, she suggests that feminist analysis of the media must also explore the pleasures that these products offer. In other words, rather than focusing on the ideologies embedded within the texts themselves, it is important to consider how these texts are actually used by female audiences.

van Zoonen (1994) therefore proposes that feminist analyses address the following questions:

- Why are cultural forms such as women's magazines so popular among women?
- Does a magazine's popularity imply acceptance of the main ideology that is embedded within it?
- How are magazines consumed and what role do they play in the daily lives of their readers?
- What do magazines mean to the women who read and enjoy them?
- Can the popularity of the women's magazine genre be reconciled with feminist concerns?
- What is the relation between feminist politics and audience pleasure?

These questions provide a useful framework for exploring audience responses to the representations in women's magazines such as *Woman*, *Woman's Realm* and *Vogue*. This is particularly important, as one of the issues you will need to consider when analysing the set magazines is how audiences interpret and respond to the representations they offer.

Key Terms

Textual determinism
The idea that the meaning of a text is inherent within and determined by the text itself. Structuralist approaches such as semiotic analysis are often criticised for their textual determinism, as they are said to neglect the role of the audience in determining textual meaning.

Stretch and Challenge 5.20

In what ways could the representations of gender in your set magazines be seen to support and illustrate van Zoonen's suggestion that gender is constructed through discourse?

bell hooks' Feminist Theory

KEY THEORY: bell hooks' Feminist Theory

- the idea that feminism is a struggle to end sexist/patriarchal oppression and the ideology of domination
- the idea that feminism is a political commitment rather than a lifestyle choice
- the idea that race and class as well as sex determine the extent to which individuals are exploited, discriminated against or oppressed

In addition to Gauntlett's and van Zoonen's theories, you will also need to look at bell hooks' theory as you explore the representations of gender in the set magazines. As discussed in the previous section, a key element of this theory is the idea that feminism is the struggle to end sexist/patriarchal oppression and the ideology of domination. Not only does this ideology affect the way in which men see women, it also shapes and influences the way in which women see themselves and each other; as bell hooks points out, women have been socialised into believing sexist thinking and values in the same way that men have (hooks, 2000).

The idea that a woman's worth is determined by the way she looks is a common example of this sexist thinking. For instance, bell hooks (2000) argues that, before women's liberation, women were socialised to believe that their value depended primarily on their appearance and whether they were perceived to be good looking, especially by men.

The emphasis conventionally placed on the value or importance of female beauty in women's magazines would seem to support this argument. In this way, women's magazines can be seen to function as agents of socialisation.

Rapid Recall 5.7

What does the term socialisation mean?

However, it is important to note that bell hooks does not reject the value of beauty altogether; it is specifically sexist understandings of beauty that she claims feminism should strive to eliminate. Arguing that the tendency to simply dismiss female longings for beauty has undermined feminist politics, she calls for healthy visions of beauty that facilitate body positivity and enhance rather than damage feelings of self-worth.

A particular focal point of bell hooks' feminist critique is the projection of an unhealthy body image as a cultural ideal. This issue has received growing attention in recent years as fashion and lifestyle magazines have been widely criticised for using unhealthily thin models and promoting the idea that thin is beautiful.

Stretch and Challenge 5.21

What evidence can you find to suggest that female readers of the historical magazine you are studying were socialised to believe that their value rests solely on their appearance?

Tip

It is important to be aware that cultural ideals of female beauty can vary from era to era. However, since the 1960s it has generally been the ultra-thin body that has been idealised in women's magazines and the fashion industry.

While some publishers have begun to respond to these concerns by including 'plus-size' models in their magazines, these representations tend to be tokenistic, as the majority of models still conform to the ultra-thin ideal. The very term 'plus-size' would also seem to suggest that thinness is still regarded as the norm in the fashion industry.

Another common response to these criticisms is to include articles drawing attention to the dangers of unrealistic and unhealthy ideals of female beauty, making this a subject of discussion. However, as ultra-thin models continue to feature in these magazines, the messages conveyed about female beauty are often contradictory. As bell hooks (2000) points out:

> *Today's fashion magazines may carry an article about the dangers of anorexia while bombarding its readers with images of emaciated young bodies representing the height of beauty and desirability.*

Ashley Graham (a so-called 'plus-size model') has featured on the front cover of many women's lifestyle magazines in recent years.

In their rush to address these issues, many magazines simply replace one form of **body shaming** with another, as pictures of celebrities who are perceived to be dangerously underweight are held up to further scrutiny. Rather than seeing the celebrities as victims of a culture that encourages women to aspire to an unhealthy body image, they often suggest that the problem lies with the individual celebrity herself. The role that the magazines themselves play in constructing unhealthy cultural ideals of female beauty is therefore ignored. As **Janice Winship** (1987) has argued, this tendency to imply that social and cultural problems can be solved at the level of the individual is a particularly common feature of women's magazines.

Key Term

Body shaming
The practice of criticising, humiliating or ridiculing someone on the basis of their body size or shape.

Key Figure

Janice Winship
An academic whose research focuses on media and film studies. Her book, *Inside Women's Magazines*, which was first published in 1987, explores the historical development of the women's magazine genre.

Representations of Race and Ethnicity

As well as looking at representations of gender in your set magazines, you should also explore how race and ethnicity are represented. Again, one of the issues you will need to consider is the impact of social, cultural and historical contexts on the representations in the two set products. How far do your set magazines suggest that representations of race and ethnicity have changed over time?

You will also need to think about whether particular racial or ethnic groups are under-represented or misrepresented in either of your magazines and across the magazine industry more broadly.

The Under-Representation of Black, Asian and Minority Ethnic Groups in the Magazine Industry

As discussed in the Year 1 book, black, Asian and minority ethnic groups have generally been under-represented in the UK magazine industry. In order to understand why this has been the case, it is important to think about the wider institutional contexts in which the magazines are produced. For example, the lack of ethnic diversity among those working in the magazine industry is often cited as one of the main reasons why black, Asian and minority ethnic groups tend to be under-represented within the magazines themselves.

Significantly, Edward Enninful, who became the first black editor-in-chief of British *Vogue* in 2017, has discussed the need to make the magazine more inclusive and more ethnically diverse. The first issue produced under his editorship, which featured the British-Ghanaian model Adwoa Aboah on the cover, set out his vision for a new *Vogue* – one designed to celebrate the true diversity of British culture.

Editor-in-Chief of British Vogue, Edward Enninful, and the model Jourdan Dunn attending the International Woolmark Prize in 2022.

Stretch and Challenge 5.22

You may find it useful to compare the front cover of the set edition of *Vogue* with the cover of the December 2017 edition featuring Adwoa Aboah. This can be found at https://www.vogue.co.uk/article/december-vogue-2017.

Key Terms

Othering
The process of treating someone or something not only as fundamentally different from one's own group but also as inferior or subordinate on the basis of those perceived differences.

Islamophobia
The irrational fear or hatred of Islam and Muslims.

Ethnocentrism, Otherness and Racial Stereotyping

Ethnocentrism and **othering** are particularly useful concepts for exploring representations of race and ethnicity. Importantly, these concepts are not only to do with notions of difference; they are also about power. For example, those who are classified as 'other' are treated as inferior because of their differences from the dominant group. For **Edward Said**, othering therefore involves '*emphasising the perceived weaknesses of marginalized groups as a way of stressing the alleged strength of those in positions of power*' (Said, 1978).

Key Figure

Edward Said
An academic and leading postcolonial theorist. One of his most influential works, *Orientalism*, which was published in 1978, provided a powerful critique of the way in which Asia and the Middle East has been represented as the inferior 'other' in Western culture.

Stereotyping is also an important concept here. As Stuart Hall points out, stereotyping tends to occur where there are inequalities of power, as subordinate or excluded groups are constructed as 'other' through ethnocentrism.

In mainstream Western media, it has often been non-white groups who have been constructed as the racial other, thereby reinforcing white hegemony or dominance. In *Learning the Media* (1987), Alvarado, Gutch and Wollen identify four main forms that stereotypical representations of the racial other have tended to take:

- the exotic
- the dangerous
- the humorous
- the pitied.

This provides a useful model for exploring the representations of race and ethnicity in the set magazines. Is there any evidence of these particular stereotypes in either of the magazines you are studying?

Link

A more detailed outline of the four main racial stereotypes identified by Alvarado et al. is available on pages 34–35.

Positive and Negative Stereotypes

When analysing the representations in the set magazines, you will need to consider how and why stereotypes can be used both negatively and positively.

In the Year 1 book, we discussed what Stuart Hall refers to as the burden of representation – the idea that when certain social groups are under-represented in the media, the few representations of them that we do see end up carrying more cultural weight as they have to stand in for an entire group. This means that stereotyping is more likely to occur. For example, it is widely argued that the limited representation of Muslims in mainstream Western media has led to the construction of **Islamophobic** stereotypes.

In order to address the misrepresentation of particular racial or ethnic groups, there are a number of strategies that can be used. For example, Stuart Hall (2013) has suggested that one strategy for addressing this issue '*is the attempt to substitute a range of "positive" images of black people, black life and black culture for the "negative" imagery which continues to dominate popular representation*'.

An image of Kuwaiti drag artist Arabia Felix, from the set edition of Huck.

Stretch and Challenge 5.23

To what extent can the representations in your set magazines be seen to support the racial stereotypes identified by Alvarado, Gutch and Wollen (1987)? See the image from *Huck* on the left for example.

Therefore, when analysing your set magazines, you should consider not only whether they could be seen to reinforce any negative racial or ethnic stereotypes but also whether they can be seen to construct more positive stereotypes.

Joel Hodgson in the set edition of *The Big Issue*, now works for a top City law firm, having previously been a *Big Issue* vendor.

Representations of National Identity

Another area of representation that you may find it useful to explore is the representation of national identity. In particular, you should consider the extent to which your set magazines challenge or reinforce dominant cultural understandings of nationality. Do they reinforce or challenge particular national myths or stereotypes, for example?

Benedict Anderson's definition of nations as imagined communities is particularly relevant here. Anderson (2006) suggests that nations are *imagined* because even members of '*the smallest nation will never know most of their fellow-members, meet them, or even hear of them, yet in the mind of each lives the image of their communion*'. In other words, it is common for individual members of a nation to imagine that they have something in common with other members of that nation (such as shared attitudes, values and beliefs or other national characteristics) even though they will never meet them. This idea is useful because it highlights the way in which notions of nationhood are constructed.

Key Figure

Benedict Anderson
A political historian whose work focused primarily on nationalism. His conceptualisation of the nation as an imagined community was outlined in *Imagined Communities: Reflections on the Origin and Spread of Nationalism*, which was first published in 1983.

Representations of Issues

The representation of issues is another topic that you may find interesting to explore. This is primarily relevant to the contemporary magazine you are studying. Here are some suggestions regarding issues you could potentially look at:

- **OPTION 1**: *Adbusters*. Consider how the magazine represents consumerism, capitalism and environmental issues. How does it challenge dominant ideologies?
- **OPTION 2**: *Huck*. Consider how the magazine represents social, cultural and political issues affecting today's youth. How does it challenge the stereotypical misrepresentation of youth, for example?
- **OPTION 3**: *The Big Issue*. Consider how the magazine represents the issue of homelessness. How can it be seen to respond to the under-representation and misrepresentation of homeless people?

In analysing the representation of issues, it is important to consider how the magazines invoke discourses and ideologies and how they position their readers to view these issues in particular ways. Think about the language that is used. How could the lexical choices be seen to have ideological significance? How might they encourage the reader to make a preferred reading of the issues that are being addressed? If there is a photograph or image accompanying the article, consider how this might be seen to have ideological significance. What meanings does it convey?

INDUSTRY

As well as conducting a textual analysis of your set magazine products, you will need to explore the industry contexts in which they have been produced. In the Year 1 book, we looked at the industry contexts of the historical magazines, focusing in particular on patterns of ownership and control in the magazine industry and the influence of economic factors on magazine products.

In this section, we will consider the impact of recent technological change on the magazine industry, looking more specifically at the industry contexts in which the contemporary magazines were produced. We will also explore Hesmondhalgh's theory of cultural industries and discuss how Curran and Seaton's theory of power and media industries might be evaluated.

Link

For more on patterns of ownership see pages 172–173 of the Year 1 book.

Quickfire 5.10

What does the term dominant discourse mean?

Key Terms

Homogeneous
Being composed of elements that are all the same or broadly similar. The opposite of this is heterogeneous, which means being composed of diverse or varied elements.

Co-opt
To adopt or appropriate something for one's own uses. In Media Studies, the term is often used to describe the way in which aspects of alternative culture are exploited and incorporated by mainstream media to make a profit.

Mainstream and Alternative Magazines

When looking at the industry contexts of the set magazines, it is important to consider the ways in which alternative media differ from mainstream media. A useful model for exploring some of these differences is provided by Bailey, Cammaerts and Carpentier (2007). They suggest that mainstream media generally tend to be:

- large scale and geared towards large, **homogeneous** audience segments
- state-owned organisations or commercial companies
- vertically or hierarchically structured professional organisations
- carriers of mainstream representations and dominant discourses.

In contrast, alternative media tend to be:

- small scale and oriented towards certain communities such as disadvantaged or marginalised groups
- independent of the state and market
- horizontally or non-hierarchically structured, allowing greater audience access and participation
- carriers of non-dominant – possibly counter-hegemonic – representations and discourses.

It is, however, important to be aware that mainstream and alternative are historically relative concepts. As Bailey et al. (2007) point out, what is considered alternative at one point in time may be regarded as mainstream at another. For example, cultural forms, traditions or genres that originate outside of the dominant culture may subsequently be appropriated or **co-opted** by the mainstream.

Stretch and Challenge 5.24

Look at the characteristics that Bailey et al. (2007) associate with mainstream media and those they associate with alternative media. Which of these can be applied to the historical magazine you are studying and which can be applied to your contemporary magazine?

The Economic Context of Magazines

Although independent publishers are not generally driven by the same '*logic of profit and power*' (Curran and Seaton, 2003) as the larger publishing houses, they still need to generate revenue in order to survive. As Megan Le Masurier (2012) points out:

> *Independent magazines may not be made purely or primarily for commercial gain, but they are deliberately made for sale.*

While most magazines generate revenue through advertising as well as their cover price, the fact that **independent magazines** are not made *purely* or *primarily* for commercial gain means that they are often more selective than mainstream magazines in terms of the advertising they choose to carry. For many independent publishers, maintaining the integrity and identity of the magazine is more important than maximising profit. In order to do this, they have to ensure that the advertisements they carry fully cohere with the magazine's brand values and editorial philosophy.

Within more commercial mainstream companies, these priorities are often reversed, as magazine content is sometimes tailored to suit the needs and interests of advertisers. For example, when a nylon company called British Nylon Spinners paid £7,000 for a double-page spread in *Woman* in 1956, the magazine's publishers agreed not to include any articles '*which prominently featured natural fibres in the same issue*' (Winship, 1987). As this demonstrates, the need to attract, retain and appease advertisers can influence the decisions that editors make about what to include in a magazine and how that content should be presented.

Key Term

Independent magazine
A magazine that is produced outside the control or ownership of the major publishing houses.

Tip

The classified advertisements that *The Big Issue* carries vary according to region. While Eduqas has suggested three particular advertisements to analyse from the set edition of the magazine, if your copy of the 17–23 October edition does not carry those particular advertisements you should analyse three alternative ones. As it is only the advertising that varies according to region, you will need to look at the specific articles and features listed on the Eduqas website, regardless of which regional edition you have studied.

Stretch and Challenge 5.25

If you are studying *The Big Issue* or *Huck*, look carefully at the advertisements the magazine carries. How do the advertisements fit with the brand values and editorial philosophy of the magazine? If you are studying *Adbusters*, think about why the magazine chooses not to carry advertising.

Industry Context: OPTION 1: *Adbusters*

Significantly, some independent magazines choose not to carry any advertising at all. For example, *Adbusters* claims to be

> *one of a handful of magazines in the world that receives zero funding from advertising (print or online), corporate sponsorship or government/foundation grants.* (Adbusters, 2017)

According to the magazine's Canadian publishers, Adbusters Media Foundation, this is what enables them to maintain their editorial independence and remain 'fiercely independent'.

As a not-for-profit organisation, Adbusters Media Foundation reinvests the revenue it generates in the magazine itself and in the causes it supports. While most of its revenue is generated through magazine sales and subscriptions, it also sells a range of merchandise, including protest art and t-shirts bearing anti-consumerist slogans, through a 'Culture Shop' on its website.

This aspect of *Adbusters*' business model has proved to be particularly controversial. Although the products it sells are designed to challenge the hegemony of major multinational corporations such as Nike, some critics have suggested that the magazine has become complicit in the very consumerist practices it purports to attack. For example, a particular criticism that has been levelled against *Adbusters* is that it has become involved in the business of commodifying political protest.

Quickfire 5.11

In what ways can *Huck's* partnership with Levi's be seen to exploit potential synergies between the two brands?

Key Terms

Content marketing
Defined by the Content Marketing Association (2018b) as *'the discipline of creating quality branded content across media channels and platforms to deliver engaging relationships, consumer value and measurable success for brands'*.

Publisher-agency
A media company that combines the functions of a magazine publisher with those of a content marketing agency. TCO is an example of this business model.

Industry Context: OPTION 2: *Huck*

Huck is published by TCO London. TCO describes itself as *'a new breed of media company'* (TCO, 2018a) as it is a **content marketing** agency as well as a magazine publisher. This means that as well as publishing *Huck* and its sister titles, the independent film magazine *Little White Lies* and the specialist food and culture magazine *Sandwich*, it produces premium content for brands such as Google, Microsoft, Levi's, Nike, Netflix and Amazon. This is a key part of its business model.

The rise of **publisher-agencies** such as TCO can be seen as a response to the increasing financial challenges faced by print magazines in a digital world. Significantly, *Huck's* co-owner, Vince Medeiros (2016), has described content marketing as *'a publisher's saviour in a converged media landscape'*.

However, as Medeiros acknowledges, the publisher-agency model does pose certain risks. In particular, there are concerns regarding the extent to which editorial independence may be compromised as the boundaries between journalism and marketing become increasingly blurred.

An example of a content marketing campaign that TCO produced for Levi's. The campaign comprised a premium print magazine, *Levi's Skate: Independence*, and a quarterly newspaper, *Lines Through the City* (above), both of which were distributed through Levi's stores, as well as online content including a series of Instagram videos.

Industry Context: OPTION 3: *The Big Issue*

The Big Issue's business model is primarily designed to support those who are homeless or experiencing poverty by enabling them to become street vendors or micro-entrepreneurs, earning an income from the magazine copies they sell. *The Big Issue* also generates revenue by selling advertising space and offering commercial partnerships with other brands. However, over the past decade, the business has diversified, moving beyond magazine publishing into a number of different areas.

Alongside the magazine, there is also an independently funded charity, The Big Issue Foundation, which provides support and guidance to vendors in areas such as training, education, health and housing. The Big Issue Group also has a social investment arm, Big Issue Invest, which helps to finance sustainable social enterprises and charities, and a social trading platform, The Big Issue Shop, which aims to promote *'social consumerism'* or *'shopping with a social echo'* (The Big Issue Shop, 2018). This is where the purchases that consumers make have a positive social impact. Purchasing eco-friendly products or buying products from organisations that use the profits to support social enterprises or charitable causes are both examples of social consumerism.

The Impact of Recent Technological Change on the Magazine Industry

One of the issues that you will need to consider as you study your contemporary magazine is the relationship between recent technological change and magazine production, distribution and circulation. You will also need to explore the impact of digitally convergent platforms on the magazine industry.

In terms of production, one of the most important changes in the magazine industry in the past 40 years has been the rise of **desktop publishing (DTP)**. Computer technology and design programs have made it far easier for individuals and smaller, independent companies to publish magazines without the support of major publishing houses. For this reason, desktop publishing is often said to have democratised the magazine industry.

Recent technological change has also had a significant impact on magazine distribution. Traditionally, distribution involves:

- persuading retailers to stock the magazines that the distributor handles
- ensuring that the magazines are delivered in the right quantity and at the right time to the most appropriate retail outlets
- marketing the magazines that the distributor is responsible for (by placing promotional displays at the point-of-sale, for instance)
- importing and exporting physical copies of magazines.

However, the growth of digital distribution has led to some significant cultural changes in the magazine industry. In particular, this has made it much easier for magazine publishers to reach specialised audiences on both a national and global scale. Megan Le Masurier (2012) points out that online marketing and distribution have allowed independents to develop a 'global niche' of readers, whose interests connect 'horizontally across national borders' and are not limited by location.

Adbusters and *Huck* are good examples of this, as online marketing and distribution have helped them to develop a global network of readers with shared values or interests.

Digital platforms have also proved particularly useful for *The Big Issue*, enabling it to reach audiences who would not otherwise be able to access the magazine, either because they live in remote locations or because there are no vendors in their local area.

The rise of digital news-stands, such as Zinio, which is a multi-platform distribution service for digital magazines, further demonstrates the impact of recent technologies on the magazine industry, as thousands of titles, including *The Big Issue* and *Huck*, are made available for distribution through these services.

Digital Convergence in the Magazine Industry

As digital **convergence** enables publishers to disseminate content across multiple platforms, this has led an increasing number of magazines to adopt a **digital-first** strategy. *Huck* is a good example of this cultural trend. As the magazine's editor-in-chief, Andrea Kurland, explains:

> *[What] we do online becomes our field notes – we can test things out, and if something seems to resonate it becomes a great entry point for features in the printed magazine.* (Berg, 2016)

Key Term

Desktop publishing (DTP)
The use of computers and software programs to design, create and publish books, newspapers or magazines.

Rapid Recall 5.8

What term is used to describe the process whereby a company acquires the means to both produce and distribute products?

Quickfire 5.12

What are some of the advantages of digital distribution for magazine publishers?

Key Terms

Convergence
A process through which different media forms merge or overlap with one another. Defined by Henry Jenkins (2006) as a '*move from medium-specific content toward content that flows across multiple media channels, toward the increased interdependence of communication systems [and] toward multiple ways of accessing media content*'.

Digital-first
A policy in which media content is first created in digital form and then adapted for other mediums. For example, in the case of a digital-first magazine, content is generally published online before it appears in print.

> **Key Terms**
>
> **Transmedia storytelling**
> Defined by Henry Jenkins (2007) as *'a process where integral elements of a [story or narrative] get dispersed systematically across multiple delivery channels for the purpose of creating a unified and coordinated entertainment experience'*.

It is commonly argued that in the new digital age publishers can no longer rely on print alone. *Huck*'s former deputy editor, Cian Traynor summed this new ethos up when he said that publishers need to think in terms of **transmedia storytelling**:

> *Is there an article [...] that would work as a short film? [Could an] illustration be turned into an animated GIF for Instagram? Could a great interview be expanded into a podcast series?* (McDermott, 2018)

The increasing importance of transmedia storytelling in the magazine industry is reflected in the way that videos are posted to accompany or supplement articles either on the magazine's website or through social media platforms such as YouTube. For example, a video to accompany the 'Teenage Utopia' feature in the set edition of *Huck* was made available through the magazine's website and YouTube channel.

To coincide with the special 25th anniversary edition of the magazine, which included a feature on former *Big Issue* vendors such as Marvina Newton, *The Big Issue* posted a video called 'Marvina Newton's Story – *The Big Issue* at 25' on its YouTube channel.

MOVING ON

Some Big Issue vendors stay with us for a long time – as long as they need us. Others use the magazine as a stepping stone to move on to new starts. Here are some of our great success stories.

STAN BURRIDGE
Healthcare Champion for Homeless People

Stan is an expert on homelessness through his own experience: he slept on the streets of London and sold The Big Issue outside the old BBC headquarters in west London during the late 1990s. "Selling The Big Issue, I learnt I had an ability to get people talking, not only talking but listening as well," he says. "I got to hear about other people's lives, marriages, divorces – it led me to where I am today."

Now in his early 50s, Stan is a project leader at Pathway, a charity that works within the NHS to get homeless people and other marginalised groups better healthcare. "I get a real sense of pride when one of the people we help gets a job or when they make a massive step forward in other areas of their lives," Stan says. "It's the same feeling that The Big Issue has when one of their flock smashes through the glass ceiling and begins to fly. The Big Issue opened the door to me and countless others."

MARVINA NEWTON
Youth Charity Boss

Marvina Newton, 30, began sleeping rough on the streets of east London when she was still a teenager. She decided to sell The Big Issue to earn an income, before finding a job as a waitress and beginning to build her career. Marvina now lives in Leeds and is a part-time biomedical technician. She has taken a career break to focus on her charity Angel of Youths, helping disadvantaged children.

Marvina's aim was to stop other teenagers ending up in the predicament she found herself in over a decade ago. "Whether they're white, black or whatever, I can see a little bit of me in them," she says. "No one's going to save you but you. You're the superhero in the story – that's what I got from The Big Issue. The only person I had was myself. I could have chosen to be a victim but I chose to sell as many Big Issue magazines as I could."

Evaluating Hesmondhalgh's Theory of Cultural Industries

KEY THEORY: David Hesmondhalgh's Theory of Cultural Industries

- the idea that cultural industry companies try to minimise risk and maximise audiences through vertical and horizontal integration, and by formatting their cultural products (e.g. through the use of stars, genres and serials)
- the idea that the largest companies or conglomerates now operate across a number of different cultural industries
- the idea that the radical potential of the internet has been contained to some extent by its partial incorporation into a large, profit-orientated set of cultural industries

One of the theories that you will need to consider when studying your set magazines is David Hesmondhalgh's theory of cultural industries. As with all the theories that you study in Component 2, you should be prepared not only to *apply* this theory to your set products but also to *evaluate* it.

As discussed in the television section of this chapter, a key element of Hesmondhalgh's theory is the idea that cultural industry companies use various strategies in order to minimise risk and maximise audiences. Therefore, a useful starting point for evaluating this theory is to consider whether the companies responsible for producing your set magazine products do, in fact, seek to minimise risk and maximise audiences in the ways that Hesmondhalgh suggests.

For example, you may want to explore whether smaller, independent publishers such as Adbusters Media Foundation, TCO London or the Big Issue Group, are as concerned with minimising risk and maximising audiences as major publishers such as IPC or Condé Nast. Is there any evidence to suggest that they have formatted their magazines to appeal to the broadest possible audience? Do they feature stars or celebrities, for instance? Have either of the companies who published your set magazines used horizontal integration to reduce competition and expand audience reach? Are either of them vertically integrated?

Think about Hesmondhalgh's claim that the largest companies or conglomerates operate across a number of different cultural industries too. What other industries, besides magazine publishing, have IPC and Advance Publications (the owners of Condé Nast) been involved in, for example?

Evaluating Curran and Seaton's Theory of Power and Media Industries

As well as Hesmondhalgh's theory of cultural industries you will also need to explore Curran and Seaton's theory of power and media industries.

KEY THEORY: James Curran and Jean Seaton's Theory of Power and Media Industries

- the idea that the media is controlled by a small number of companies primarily driven by the logic of profit and power
- the idea that media concentration generally limits or inhibits variety, creativity and quality
- the idea that more socially diverse patterns of ownership help to create the conditions for more varied and adventurous media productions.

In order to evaluate Curran and Seaton's theory, it is important to consider their arguments regarding:

- the extent of media concentration
- the effects of media concentration
- the impact of socially diverse patterns of ownership on media production.

The Extent of Media Concentration

Whether the magazine industry today is controlled by a small number of companies, as Curran and Seaton suggest, is a matter of some debate. While the acquisitions and mergers that took place in the magazine industry during the 1950s and 1960s enabled companies such as IPC to establish a dominant position within the market, power today is not as concentrated as it once was.

Link

Information about IPC and Condé Nast and their use of vertical and horizontal integration as well as diversification can be found on pages 173 and 174 of the Year 1 book.

Tip

Hesmondhalgh's suggestion that the radical potential of the internet has been contained to some extent by its incorporation within a large, profit-orientated set of cultural industries is only relevant to the contemporary magazine you are studying; the internet had not yet been developed at the time the historical magazine was published. When evaluating this claim, you may want to consider whether or not *Adbusters*, *Huck* or *The Big Issue* has, in fact, exploited the radical potential of the internet. Have they used it to agitate for social change, for instance, or to challenge or disrupt mainstream culture?

Link

An outline of Curran and Seaton's theory of power and media industries is shown on pages 172–173 of the Year 1 book.

Rapid Recall 5.9

What is an oligopoly?

Stretch and Challenge 5.26

In order to find out how concentrated power is in the magazine industry today, try to find out which publishers have the largest market share. Is the market dominated by a few major publishers or is power more widely dispersed?

This is partly due to changes that occurred during the 1980s, when several large European publishers entered the UK market, challenging the dominance of companies such as IPC and Condé Nast. Desktop publishing has also made the magazine industry more competitive than it once was. However, while there may be many more publishers operating today, some would argue that there is still a relatively small oligopoly of major companies who account for most of the market.

The Effects of Media Concentration

Another important aspect of Curran and Seaton's theory is the idea that media concentration limits or inhibits variety, creativity and quality, as companies are less likely to innovate and more likely to cut costs if competition in the markets in which they operate is reduced. For example, Howard Cox and Simon Moffatt (2008) claim that IPC's monopoly over the women's weekly magazine market in the 1960s and 1970s generated an air of complacency while '*the very size of IPC lent itself to over-centralisation and bureaucratisation, which tended to stifle entrepreneurship and creativity*'.

However, Curran and Seaton's (2003) suggestion that variety, creativity and quality are the victims of media concentration is open to question, as it could be argued that media concentration gives larger companies the necessary economic capital to produce higher-quality products. For instance, companies such as IPC and Condé Nast were able to invest in high-quality colour printing during the 1950s and 1960s because of their financial power.

Socially Diverse Patterns of Ownership

Curran and Seaton also claim that socially diverse patterns of ownership help to create the conditions for more varied and adventurous media productions. This suggests that innovation is more likely to be found in independently owned magazines, as larger media companies tend to be more risk averse.

In order to evaluate this aspect of Curran and Seaton's theory, you may find it useful to consider whether the contemporary magazine you have studied, which was produced outside the commercial mainstream, is more varied and adventurous than the historical magazine you have looked at, which was published under conglomerate ownership. However, you will need to bear in mind the significance of the historical contexts in which the magazines were produced. A magazine that appears relatively safe and commonplace by today's standards may not have been seen in the same way at the time it was produced.

AUDIENCES

Link

The main ways in which audiences are grouped and categorised by the magazine industry and the key aspects of Gerbner's cultivation theory and Hall's reception theory are introduced on pages 175–178 of the Year 1 book.

The final area of the theoretical framework that you will need to consider when studying your set magazine products is audiences. In particular, you will need to explore:

- how magazine publishers categorise, target, attract, reach, address and potentially construct audiences
- how magazine publishers reflect the different needs of mass and specialised audiences, and how specialised audiences can be reached through different technologies and platforms
- the different ways in which audiences use and interpret magazines and how this reflects aspects of identity as well as social, cultural and historical circumstances.

You also need to be able to apply and evaluate Gerbner's cultivation theory and Hall's reception theory in relation to your set magazine products.

Audience Targeting

While some magazines target a mass audience, others are aimed at more specialised, niche audiences. Since the mid-20th century, the general trend within the magazine industry has been away from mass-market publications and towards more specialised titles aimed at specific audience segments.

The circulation figures shown in the grid below provide a general indication of the audience reach for each of the set products. However, when analysing these circulation figures, it is important to bear in mind that *Adbusters* and *Huck* both target global audiences, whereas the other magazines are made specifically for the UK market (although there are different international editions of *Vogue* and *The Big Issue*, the circulation figures here relate specifically to the British editions of these magazines). Historical context is also a significant issue, as traditional print magazines have seen a steady decline over the past 50 years. For example, while *Woman*'s circulation in 1965 was close to three million, today it is under 100,000.

OPTION 1	***Woman*** Circulation in 1965: 2,960,000	***Adbusters*** Circulation in 2017: 120,000
OPTION 2	***Woman's Realm*** Circulation in 1965: 1,300,000	***Huck*** Circulation in 2017: 60,000
OPTION 3	***Vogue*** Circulation in 1965: 139,000	***The Big Issue*** Circulation in 2017: 83,073

The Content and Appeal of Magazine Products

In exploring how magazine publishers target their audiences, you will need to consider the content and appeal of your set products.

Magazines that feature more mainstream content are likely to have broader appeal than those that feature alternative, non-mainstream content. For example, *Adbusters* and *Huck*, which focus primarily on radical culture, have more niche appeal than traditional women's weeklies such as *Woman* and *Woman's Realm*, which are far more mainstream in terms of the topics they cover.

Woman and *Woman's Realm* are both defined as general interest women's magazines, whereas *Vogue* is a high-end women's fashion magazine and therefore has a more specialised focus.

The Big Issue also differs from *Adbusters* and *Huck* as it caters for both mass and specialised audiences. While the ethics and purpose of the magazine would appeal primarily to **reformers**, it also uses entertainment, celebrity and popular culture to target a more mainstream audience.

Quickfire 5.13

Why do you think the general trend in the magazine industry since the mid-20th century has been away from mass-market publications towards more specialised titles aimed at specific segments of the audience?

Tip

When exploring how your set magazines reflect the different needs of mass and specialised audiences, you should consider their content or subject matter, their mode of address and their brand values.

Key Term

Reformers
One of the psychographic groups in the 4Cs system of consumer classification developed by advertising agency Young and Rubicam. Reformers tend to be tolerant, socially aware and anti-materialistic. Their core need is for enlightenment.

Tip

In analysing the content and appeal of your set magazines, you should also consider how audiences are targeted through any advertisements they carry.

Marketing and Distribution

As well as considering how magazine publishers target audiences through the content and appeal of their products, you also need to explore how audiences are targeted through marketing and distribution. Some of the points made in the previous 'Industry' section of this chapter can also be applied here. For example, the role of digital technologies and platforms in reaching specialised audiences is particularly relevant in terms of audience targeting.

The internet and social media have become increasingly important in magazine marketing in recent years. Platforms such as Twitter and Facebook are commonly used to alert readers when a new issue of a magazine is about to be published. These social media posts often include links that direct readers to the magazine's website, where the readers can preview articles or access additional content. The use of hashtags also encourages user participation and facilitates viral marketing, as key messages are passed from user to user through social networks.

This form of online engagement is particularly useful for publishers and marketing companies, as it enables them to develop a clearer understanding of a magazine's readership. As *Huck's* former deputy editor, Cian Traynor, has pointed out, this means that they can target audiences more effectively.

The internet and social media can also be used to target different demographics. For example, Ben Sullivan, *The Big Issue*'s digital editor, has talked about the need to reach a younger audience who have '*grown up aware that* The Big Issue*'s on the street but because they're digital-only, mobile-only, [...] perhaps might not buy the magazine*' (Clarke, 2018). Making content available online is an important way of reaching this demographic.

As well as using social media, magazine producers may also use other channels and platforms to market their products.

For example, in order to promote the 25th Anniversary edition of *The Big Issue*, the magazine's co-founder, John Bird, appeared on *The One Show*, which is shown at peak-time on BBC One, and BBC Radio 4's late-night show *Westminster Hour*.

When analysing a marketing campaign, it is important to consider why particular platforms, channels or programmes have been chosen. Who are the producers of the campaign trying to reach? Is the marketing message aimed at a similar demographic to the magazine's existing audience or is it attempting to broaden the audience by targeting a different demographic?

One of the ways in which *Huck* has been marketed is by exploiting synergies with other brands. The content that TCO produced for Levi's made prominent use of the *Huck* logo, for instance, broadening awareness of the *Huck* brand within Levi's key youth demographic.

A potential cross-over between *Huck* and its sister title, *Little White Lies*, was also developed when, in 2009, the artist Geoff McFetridge was commissioned to produce a piece of cover artwork that would run across the two magazines. In order to collect the complete artwork, readers had to buy the relevant editions of both *Huck* and *Little White Lies*.

In the case of Adbusters Media Foundation, buying advertising space can prove challenging due to its explicitly anti-consumerist ideology. For example, several North American television networks have refused to carry its 'anti-advertisements' or 'uncommercials' as they are seen to be inimical to the networks' commercial interests. However, these refusals to air the advertisements can also generate useful publicity, encouraging readers to seek out the videos online through the magazine's website or its YouTube channel.

Gerbner's Cultivation Theory

KEY THEORY: George Gerbner's Cultivation Theory

- the idea that exposure to repeated patterns of representation over long periods of time can shape and influence the way in which people perceive the world around them (i.e. cultivating particular views and opinions)
- the idea that cultivation reinforces mainstream values (dominant ideologies)

Link

Details of Gerbner's cultivation theory can be found on page 177 of the Year 1 book.

More than simply *targeting* audiences, magazines can also be seen to *construct* their audiences in various ways. For example, Gerbner's cultivation theory suggests that regular exposure to repeated patterns of representation over long periods of time can shape and influence the way in which people perceive the world around them. This idea is particularly applicable to women's magazines, as they could be seen to cultivate certain understandings of gender, thereby shaping the identities of their readers.

Adbusters, *Huck* and *The Big Issue* could also be said to construct their audiences in various ways:

- *Adbusters* could be said to construct and cultivate its audience as it aims to turn readers into political activists. Its instrumental role in mobilising support for the Occupy Wall Street movement is a good example of this. The anti-capitalist ideology that underpins the representations in the magazine could also be seen to shape and influence the way in which the audience sees the world around them.
- Similarly, *The Big Issue* could be seen to shape and influence audience understandings of social inequality. By challenging the dominant discourses that surround homelessness and poverty, the magazine aims to change public perceptions, shaping the values, attitudes and beliefs of its readers.
- *Huck* could also be seen to construct an audience by fostering a sense of subcultural belonging and identity in its readers. Significantly, **Sarah Thornton** (1995) argues that '*Niche media like the music press construct subcultures as much as they document them.*' Therefore, through its coverage of different subcultural scenes and countercultural movements, *Huck* shapes audience understandings of what those scenes and movements mean and represent.

Key Figure

Sarah Thornton
A writer and theorist whose work on popular music and subcultural identity has had a significant influence in the field of subcultural studies. One of her most well-known works is the book *Club Cultures: Music, Media and Subcultural Capital* (1995).

Evaluating Gerbner's Cultivation Theory

One of the issues to think about when evaluating Gerbner's cultivation theory is the suggestion that cultivation reinforces mainstream values. You may want to explore whether this is always necessarily the case. To what extent could magazines that operate outside the commercial mainstream, such as *Adbusters*, *Huck* and *The Big Issue*, be seen to cultivate *alternative* values, attitudes and beliefs, for instance? Could long-term exposure to the repeated patterns of representation in these magazines *challenge* rather than reinforce mainstream values and dominant ideologies?

How Audiences Use and Interpret Magazine Products

Link

Details of Stuart Hall's reception theory and how it can be applied to magazines can be found on pages 177–178 of the Year 1 book.

You will also need to explore how audiences use and interpret your set magazines. The audience theories that we introduced in the Year 1 book are particularly relevant here. For example, Hall's reception theory outlines the different ways in which audiences may read or decode media products, while Blumler and Katz's uses and gratifications theory looks at how media products can be used by audiences to satisfy different needs.

Further to this, you will need to consider:

- **The way in which audience interpretations of your set magazines may reflect social, cultural and historical circumstances**. For example, audiences at the time when the historical magazines were published are likely to have viewed them differently compared with audiences today. This is because social and cultural norms, values, attitudes and beliefs change over time.
- **The influence of demographic factors, identity and cultural capital on the way in which magazines are used**. Demographic factors such as gender, age or social class are likely to have a significant effect in terms of how readers use a magazine. Whether they see it as a form of escapism, whether they identify with or relate to the representations that it features, or whether they aspire to become more like the people who feature in the magazine will be determined to some extent by these demographic factors as well as other aspects of identity such as the reader's values, attitudes and beliefs. Cultural or subcultural capital can be another influential factor; how much the reader already knows about the subcultural and countercultural movements magazines such as *Adbusters* and *Huck* document is likely to determine how they use the magazine.

In the 'My Pitch' section of the set edition of *The Big Issue*, Donato Barbieri discusses his experiences of homelessness and what becoming a *Big Issue* vendor has meant to him.

How Audiences Interact with Magazines

Another issue that is worth considering when analysing your set magazines is how readers engage and interact with these products. To what extent do the magazines solicit and facilitate audience interaction and participation? This is likely to vary from publication to publication. *Adbusters* often invites readers to submit their own photographs or artwork, for example, while *The Big Issue* provides a space for vendors to tell their own stories in the 'My Pitch' section.

You may also find it useful to see whether your set magazine has a letters page or a problem page where readers' voices are heard. For the contemporary magazine products, you could also look at the magazines' websites and social media accounts, thinking about how they facilitate audience interaction.

Summary

Having read this section on magazines, you should now be familiar with:

- the genres that your set magazines draw on
- the way in which magazine design and other aspects of media language incorporate viewpoints and ideologies
- the influence of social, cultural and historical context on magazine representations of gender, race and ethnicity
- the way in which magazine representations of gender, race and ethnicity invoke discourses and ideologies
- the factors that can lead to the under-representation or misrepresentation of particular social groups in magazines

- the use of positive and negative racial or ethnic stereotypes in magazines and the processes through which particular racial or ethnic groups come to be represented as 'other'
- the differences between mainstream and alternative magazines
- the industry contexts of the set magazines, including how they are funded
- the impact of recent technological change on the magazine industry, including the rise of digital convergence and the impact of digital distribution
- how magazine producers target their audiences through the content and appeal of their products and through marketing and distribution
- how magazine producers can be seen to construct their audiences
- how audience interpretations of magazines may reflect social, cultural and historical circumstances
- how demographic factors and other aspects of identity may influence the way in which audiences use magazines
- how audiences may interact with magazines in various ways.

Essential Theories for Magazines

When discussing your set magazine products, you should be able to use and evaluate the following theories.

Theories of Media Language

- **Semiotic theory**, including Barthes: for example, the way in which magazines convey messages and meanings through signification.
- **Structuralism**, including Lévi-Strauss: for example, the way in which magazines convey meanings through patterns of oppositions.

Theories of Representation

- **Theories of identity**, including Gauntlett: for example, the idea that, in the past, magazines offered singular, straightforward messages about ideal types of male and female identities.
- **Feminist theories**, including bell hooks and van Zoonen: for example, the idea that feminism can be used to critique or challenge the operation of patriarchal ideology in magazine products.

Industry Theories

- **Cultural industries, including Hesmondhalgh**: for example, the idea that companies operating in the magazine industry use vertical and horizontal integration and format their products by including stars and celebrities in order to minimise risk and maximise audiences.
- **Power and media industries**, including Curran and Seaton: for example, the idea that historically the magazine industry has been controlled by a small number of companies driven by profit, and that concentration of ownership in the magazine industry has led to a loss of variety and creativity.

Audience Theories

- **Cultivation theory**, including Gerbner: for example, the idea that repeated exposure to similar patterns of representation in magazines cultivates particular attitudes and beliefs in their readers.
- **Reception theory**, including Hall: for example, the idea that readers may adopt different positions in relation to the magazines they read.

Section C: Media in the Online Age

The Specification

If you are following the linear Eduqas specification, online media is the third of the media forms that you are required to study in depth. For this topic, you will study the work of one blogger or vlogger, as well as an online magazine or magazine website that targets, or is produced by, a minority audience.

In Chapter 5 of the Year 1 book, some of the key approaches that can be used to study online media products were introduced, with a particular focus on blogs and vlogs. This book looks more specifically at online magazines and magazine websites, as well as exploring some of the more advanced critical theories and concepts that you are required to apply to the set online products at A Level.

Link

Some of the key approaches that can be used to study online media products were introduced on pages 180–185 of the Year 1 book.

WJEC

If you are following the modular WJEC specification, you are required to study an online newspaper and a news website for the 'News in the Online Age' topic that forms part of the AS module 'Investigating the Media'. You will also study an online magazine that has been produced outside the commercial mainstream for a niche or specialist audience as part of the A2 module 'Media in the Global Age'. The material in this chapter about online magazines and magazine websites will be of particular relevance in this regard.

Online Media Options

As part of your investigation into online media in Component 2, you are required to study **one** product from **Group 1** and **one** product from **Group 2**:

GROUP 1	GROUP 2
Zoe Sugg https://www.youtube.com/channel/UCrUbqTCagwsaP2Fmr0p1TsA https://zoella.co.uk/ or **JJ Olatunji/KSI** www.youtube.com/user/KSIOlajidebtHD	The ***gal-dem*** website https://gal-dem.com/ or The ***Attitude*** website https://www.attitude.co.uk/

Note

At the time of writing *gal-dem* was the approved set product. Please make sure you double check the WJEC/Eduqas website or Illuminate (https://bit.ly/3r1d7at) for the most up-to-date information on which set products you should be studying.

JJ Olatunji/KSI

- JJ Olatunji, better known as KSI, is a successful YouTuber, music artist and entrepreneur who has built a significant following from his gaming and entertainment vlogs.

Zoe Sugg

- Zoe Sugg is a successful British blogger, YouTuber and entrepreneur. As well as her YouTube channel, where she posts videos about her day-to-day life, she has also previously operated a beauty and lifestyle blog under her 'Zoella' brand.

Tip

It is important to note that it is specifically the *Attitude* or *gal-dem* ***website*** that you are required to study, not the print magazine. Remember that Section C is concerned with *online* rather than print media.

gal-dem

- *gal-dem* was an independent print and online magazine that shared the perspectives of people of colour of marginalised genders. Produced by GAL-DEM LIMITED, it shut down in March 2023.

Attitude

- *Attitude* is a gay lifestyle magazine and website. The brand was launched in 1994 and was bought by Stream Publishing Limited in 2016.

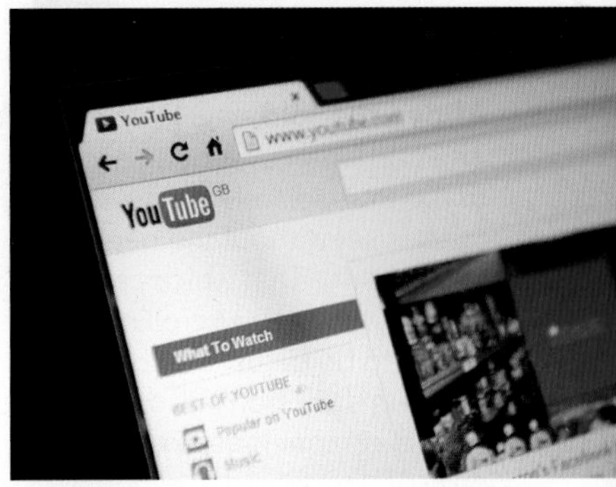

What to Study

When studying your set online products, you will need to explore:

- The codes and conventions of the homepage, including aspects of layout and design.
- Examples of posts, such as specific blogs, vlogs or articles from the online products.
- Examples of interactivity, including links to, and use of, social and participatory media.

Using the Theoretical Framework

In exploring your set online products, you will need to consider all four areas of the theoretical framework, looking at:

- **Media language**: how vlogs, blogs, online magazines and magazine websites convey meanings through their forms, codes, conventions and techniques.
- **Representation**: the way individuals, social groups, issues and (where relevant) events are represented in blogs, vlogs, online magazines and magazine websites.
- **Industry**: the impact of recent technological change on media production, distribution, circulation and regulation, and the significance of economic factors to online media products.
- **Audiences**: how the producers of blogs, vlogs, online magazines and magazine websites target, attract, reach, address and potentially construct audiences, and how audiences interact with and respond to online media products.

MEDIA LANGUAGE

The main codes and conventions associated with different types of vlog and blog were outlined in the Year 1 book. Before exploring how theories of structuralism and postmodernism can be applied to online media, this section introduces some of the key conventions of websites and online magazines, establishing a critical vocabulary that you can use when analysing your set online products.

Multimodality and Hypermodality

When analysing different media forms, it is important to think about the modes of communication they use – for instance, whether they use images, sound, speech or writing. Websites are **multimodal** as they use a combination of modes to convey their meanings. While this is true of many other media forms, what makes websites different is their use of **hyperlinks**.

As Jay Lemke points out, this means that there is a wider range of connections than those traditionally found in print products: '*It is not simply that we juxtapose image, text, and sound; we design multiple interconnections among them*' (Lemke, 2002). Lemke uses the term **hypermodality** to describe this extra level of interconnectedness that online products typically possess.

Key Terms

Multimodality
Defined by Theo van Leeuwen (2005) as '*the combination of different semiotic modes – for example, language and music – in a communicative artefact or event*'. For example, websites are multimodal as they combine images, text and sound.

Hyperlink
A word, phrase or image in an electronic document or webpage that the user can click on to navigate to a different part of the document or a different page.

Hypermodality
A term used to describe the way in which the linkages in online media products such as webpages '*go beyond the default conventions of traditional multimodal genres*' (Lemke, 2002). For example, while there may be links between images and text in a film poster or print advertisement, a webpage also provides links to other pages or documents, introducing another layer of connectivity.

Key Term

Above the fold
The portion of a webpage that is immediately visible to the user without the need for scrolling. That which can only be viewed via scrolling is said to be below the fold. The terms are borrowed from the newspaper industry, as newspapers would traditionally be folded in half before being put on display on newsstands. Therefore, passers-by would only be able to see material that appeared above the fold.

Layout and Design

In terms of the layout and design of webpages, a distinction is often drawn between content that appears **above the fold** and that which appears below the fold. Content above the fold is immediately visible to the user without the need for scrolling, while content that is below the fold only becomes visible when the user scrolls down the page. A basic principle of web design is that the most important information should appear in the upper part of the page and be visible without the need for scrolling. This establishes a clear sense of visual hierarchy.

Although this seems relatively straightforward, where the fold appears is likely to vary depending on the size, shape and resolution of the screen on which the webpage is viewed. For example, a mobile phone screen differs significantly from a desktop monitor. Therefore, some designers now talk about a secondary fold, which is where the fold appears on devices that present content in portrait format. A common way of dealing with these presentational issues is through responsive web design as this enables content to be displayed appropriately on different devices.

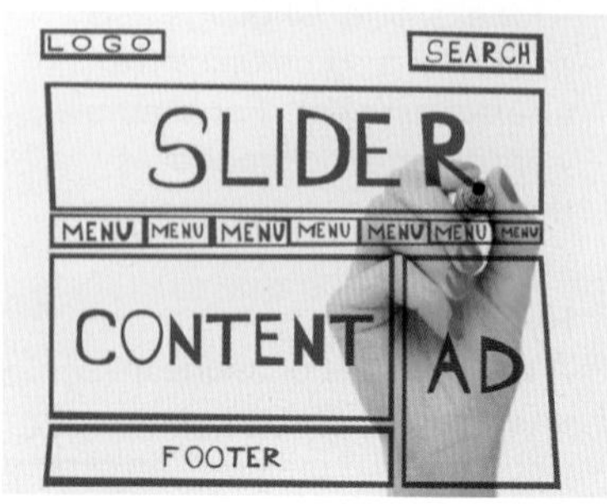

Website Codes and Conventions: The Homepage

As the homepage is typically the first page that a visitor will see, it is one of the most important parts of a website.

The conventions most commonly found on the homepage include:

- A **logo**: this is an important part of the website's visual branding as it helps to create continuities of iconography between the different pages of the website and the different platforms across which the brand operates. The logo is conventionally positioned in the upper left corner or top centre of the homepage.
- **Main navigation**: this usually takes the form of a menu bar or navigation bar and provides links to the main sections of the website.
- A **carousel** or **slider**: this enables multiple pieces of content to be presented sequentially in the form of a slideshow. The slides generally advance automatically, although arrows and/or buttons are usually included, enabling the user to navigate between slides themselves.
- A **footer**: this is the information that appears at the bottom of the homepage. Contact details will generally be provided here. Information about the website may also be included in an 'About Us' section. A copyright notice is generally included in the footer as well.
- A **search box**: this enables users to look for particular topics or articles. It generally appears towards the top of the homepage.
- **Social media icons**: these provide links to Facebook, Twitter, TikTok and Instagram pages as well as the relevant YouTube channel.
- **Banner ads**: these are advertisements that are embedded in the webpage and link directly to the advertiser's website. They can be animated or static.

Evaluating Barthes' Theory of Semiotics

KEY THEORY: Roland Barthes' Theory of Semiotics

- the idea that texts communicate their meanings through a process of signification
- the idea that signs can function at the level of denotation, which involves the 'literal' or common-sense meaning of the sign, and at the level of connotation, which involves the meanings associated with or suggested by the sign
- the idea that constructed meanings can come to seem self-evident, achieving the status of myth through a process of naturalisation

A basic critical framework for analysing blogs and vlogs using semiotic theory was outlined in the Year 1 book. The same principles can also be applied to websites and online magazines. For example, when analysing the layout and design of a webpage, semiotics can help you understand the connotations of the various signs that are used and the way in which paradigmatic choices regarding images, colour, typography and lexis convey particular meanings. Semiotics can also be used to explore the way in which these paradigmatic elements work together syntagmatically to establish a sense of brand identity.

At A Level, as well as being able to apply relevant critical theories, you also need to be able to evaluate them. This means that you will need to consider the relative strengths and weaknesses of semiotic theory as a critical approach.

For instance, when applying semiotic theory to webpages, there is often a tendency to focus on the static elements of the text while ignoring the dynamic and interactive elements that distinguish online products from other media forms. This could be seen as a potential weakness or limitation of semiotic theory.

Another criticism that is widely levelled against semiotics, as well as the broader body of structuralist thinking to which it belongs, is that this kind of critical approach tends to ignore the social contexts in which communication takes place, treating texts in isolation from those who produce them as well as those who use them.

For instance, Robert Hodge and Gunther Kress argue that the emphasis placed on structures and codes in mainstream semiotics means that the social uses and functions of semiotic systems tend to be overlooked:

> *[Mainstream semiotic theory] stresses system and product rather than speakers and writers or other participants in semiotic activity as connected and interacting in a variety of ways in concrete social contexts.* (Hodge and Kress, 1988)

In order to address some of these limitations in traditional semiotic approaches, Hodge and Kress (1988) advocate what they refer to as **social semiotics** – *'a critical theory of sign-making which sees all acts of communication as social'* (cited in Burn and Parker, 2003). In this way, they draw on the work of semiotic theorists such as Roland Barthes while exploring the significance of the social contexts in which media production and communication take place.

Key Term

Social semiotics
A critical approach that addresses the perceived limitations of mainstream semiotics by acknowledging and exploring the social contexts in which meaning-making takes place.

Lévi-Strauss's Theory of Structuralism

KEY THEORY: Claude Lévi-Strauss's Theory of Structuralism

- the idea that texts can best be understood through an examination of their underlying structure
- the idea that meaning is dependent upon (and produced through) pairs of oppositions
- the idea that the way in which these binary oppositions are resolved can have particular ideological significance

In addition to Roland Barthes' theory of semiotics, you will also need to consider how Lévi-Strauss's structuralist theory can be used to explore the way in which meanings are produced in your online products. Consider, for example, the extent to which they rely on binary oppositions. These may be between competing sets of ideas or values (such as bigotry and tolerance, freedom and oppression, belonging and alienation, success and failure, good and bad, before and after), or between opposing individuals, groups or cultures.

The article above, which features on the *gal-dem* website, explores a series of binary oppositions, most notably between black pride and anti-blackness, representation and marginalisation, and power and powerlessness.

Binary oppositions often play an important role in the construction of cultural or subcultural identity as they set up borders and boundaries between different social groups. Therefore, as the online magazine or magazine website you are studying has been produced for a minority audience, you may find it useful to explore the extent to which it operates in binary opposition to the majority culture.

Another useful concept that can be applied both to online magazines and to blogs and vlogs is Lévi-Strauss's notion of myth. For instance, his suggestion that the purpose of myth is to *'provide a logical model capable of overcoming a contradiction'* (Lévi-Strauss, 1958) could be used to explore the way in which YouTubers such as JJ Olatunji/KSI and Zoe Sugg maintain the illusion of personal, face-to-face communication while addressing a mass audience. It could also be used to explore how the binary opposition between the public and personal domain is negotiated in these blogs and vlogs.

The Way Media Language Incorporates Viewpoints and Ideologies

As well as considering how meanings in your set online products are conveyed through binary oppositions, you will also need to explore how their use of media language incorporates viewpoints and ideologies. Of course, these two aspects of the theoretical framework are by no means mutually exclusive. As already suggested, one of the ways in which media products incorporate viewpoints and ideologies is *through* the binary oppositions they set up. For example, when encoding messages and meanings in terms of binary opposites, media producers will often favour or value one side over another.

The discourses that are used in online products can also be seen to express viewpoints and ideologies. For instance, the discourses of self-improvement that conventionally circulate within fashion, beauty and lifestyle blogs generally promote a particular set of ideas about gender and identity. Similarly, the discourses of consumerism that circulate in certain types of blog, vlog and online magazine have a significant ideological function as they promote a particular set of ideas, values and beliefs.

Tip

Remember that you may be required to *evaluate* Levi-Strauss's theory of structuralism, rather than simply applying it to your set online products. Some tips for evaluating this theory can be found in the Television section of this chapter, on page 167.

In considering how media language incorporates viewpoints and ideologies, you will need to think about how and why particular codes and conventions have been used.

Look at the use of visual and technical codes, for instance. How could they be seen as ideologically significant? What messages and values do they convey?

It is also important to consider the way in which elements of media language are *combined* to convey certain meanings. Think about the relationship between image and text or image and narration, for example.

Tip

When exploring how media language incorporates viewpoints and ideologies, it is important to remember that this is not to do with the *content* of the media product; it is about how that content is presented through particular codes, conventions and techniques.

Baudrillard's Theory of Postmodernism

One of the theories that you will need to explore when analysing your set online products is Jean Baudrillard's theory of postmodernism.

KEY THEORY: Jean Baudrillard's Theory of Postmodernism

- the idea that in postmodern culture the boundaries between the 'real' world and the world of the media have collapsed and that it is no longer possible to distinguish between reality and simulation
- the idea that in a postmodern age of simulacra we are immersed in a world of images that no longer refer to anything 'real'
- the idea that media images have come to seem more 'real' than the reality they supposedly represent (hyperreality)

As discussed in the television section of this chapter, a key aspect of this theory is the idea that the boundaries between the real world and the world of the media have collapsed or imploded so that it is no longer possible to distinguish between reality and simulation.

The rise of social media and online forms such as vlogs and blogs could be seen as symptomatic of this cultural shift, as the lines separating real, everyday life from the world of the media have become increasingly blurred. In a digital age where we now live much of our lives online, it might reasonably be argued that the real, everyday world *is* the world of the media.

Baudrillard therefore argues that in the postmodern world, instead of referring to anything real, we simply get signs referring to other signs – texts referring to other texts. Again, the very nature of the web could be seen to illustrate this idea, as we are presented with a seemingly endless network of links and connections, continually referring us to other sites, documents, images and pages.

A visitor to the Madame Tussauds museum in London taking photos of the Zoe Sugg and Alfie Deyes waxworks.

Online Media and the Loss of Meaning

Significantly, many of the criticisms that Baudrillard makes of postmodern culture have also been levelled against online media, and vlogs and blogs more specifically. For example, in an essay called 'Figures of the Transpolitical' (1999), Baudrillard talks about the 'obscenity' of over-representation, arguing that things that are unimportant and which were once kept secret are now represented 'beyond all necessity'.

This idea could be considered in relation to online media:

- How might vlogs, blogs and social media be seen to represent things that would once have been kept secret? Consider how they blur the boundaries between private and public, for example.

Stretch and Challenge 5.27

As reflexivity is a characteristic that is often associated with postmodern products, you may find it useful to consider the degree to which the vlogs you are studying draw attention to their own processes of construction. Does the vlogger make any reference to the filming or editing process for example?

Key Term

Phatic internet technologies
According to Wang, Tucker and Haines (2012), these are *'special forms of communications technologies devoted to personal and social needs and goals'*.

Key Figure

Marshall McLuhan
An academic and media theorist whose work has had a profound influence on studies of the internet and online media. His concept of 'the global village', which explores the way in which electronic media establish communication networks, making the world seem like a smaller place, has proved particularly useful in this regard.

Key Figure

Neil Postman
A media theorist and cultural critic whose work focused particularly, although not exclusively, on television, popular culture and the cultural influence of technology. Two of his best-known works are *Amusing Ourselves to Death: Public Discourse in the Age of Show Business*, which was published in 1985, and *Technopoly: The Surrender of Culture to Technology*, which was published in 1993.

- Can we see in these new media forms what Baudrillard describes as *'the representation of nothing at all'*? Do they simply represent the trivial and the mundane, for instance? Are they symptomatic of the superficiality or lack of depth that Baudrillard associates with postmodern culture?

Baudrillard's (1994) claim that the world we live in has more information with less meaning is also worth considering here. Think about the way in which information proliferates online. Has the digital age led to information overload?

The Medium is the Message

You might also consider how significant this lack of substance or meaning actually is. As Wang, Tucker and Haines (2012) point out, Facebook, Twitter and YouTube are examples of **phatic internet technologies**. This means that their primary purpose is to *'establish, develop and maintain personal and social relationships'*. Therefore, in phatic communication, *'it does not matter that the message sent and received may be meaningless or even empty'* because it is the act of communication that is important rather than the content of communication (Wang et al., 2012). This is equivalent to the use of greetings such as 'Hi' or 'Hello' in everyday conversations. The purpose of such greetings is not to convey information but to establish contact and facilitate social interaction. This is what is meant by phatic communication. Wang et al. are therefore suggesting that what is actually said on social media platforms is often not as important as the act of communication itself.

Marshall McLuhan's famous phrase *'the medium is the message'*, which Baudrillard cites in *Simulacra and Simulation* (1994), could be seen to make a similar point. Baudrillard (1990) himself talks about the phatic function of communication, although in much more critical terms, when he says:

> *Contact for contact's sake becomes the empty form with which language seduces itself when it no longer has anything to say.*

Hyperreality and Digital Media

Baudrillard's notion of the hyperreal can also be applied to digital media. This is where simulations displace reality and come to seem *'more real than the real'* (1994).

Evidence for this can be seen in the way that people attending concerts simultaneously record and watch the performance on their smartphones, almost as if the image on the screen is more real than the band or artist in front of them.

Discussing the way in which technology shapes and determines our interactions with the world around us, **Neil Postman** (1993) wrote:

> *[To someone] with a pencil, everything looks like a list. To [someone] with a camera, everything looks like an image. To [someone] with a computer, everything looks like data.*

In the Web 2.0 era, we might add that, to someone with a camera and an internet connection, everything looks like a vlog.

REPRESENTATION

Another important area of the theoretical framework you will need to consider when analysing your set online products is representation. In terms of the vlogs or blogs you are studying, you will need to look at self-representation as well as the representation of relevant aspects of social identity such as gender. These topics were discussed in the Year 1 book.

With regard to the online magazine or magazine website you are studying, you will also need to consider how and why particular social groups may be under-represented or misrepresented, as well as exploring how representations invoke discourses and ideologies and position audiences. In addition to this, you will need to explore the effect of social and cultural context on the representations in *both* your set products while also considering how audience responses to representations reflect social, cultural and historical circumstances.

As well as Hall's theory of representation and Gauntlett's theory of identity, you will need to explore Butler's theory of performativity and theories around ethnicity, including Gilroy's postcolonial theory.

The Under-Representation of LGBT People in the Media

As already stated, one of the issues you will need to explore in relation to the online magazine or magazine website you are studying is how and why particular social groups may be under-represented. This is often to do with power relations, as the under-representation of minority groups can be seen to both reflect and reinforce social inequalities.

For example, the under-representation of **LGBT** people in mainstream media can be seen to maintain social hierarchies by marginalising those who do not comply with heterosexual norms. Larry Gross (1991) has argued that, historically, gay people have been largely invisible in the media:

> *[They have been] ignored or denied –* **symbolically annihilated** *[and] when they do appear, they do so in order to play a supportive role for the natural order and are thus narrowly and negatively stereotyped.*

Since Gross' article was originally published in the early 1990s, LGBTQ representations have started to become more prominent within the media. These representations matter because, as Sander de Ridder et al. (2011) point out:

> *The right to be visible, acknowledged, and in this way legitimated, is indispensable for social change. Therefore, media representations of gay and lesbian identities in popular culture are crucial.*

This provides a useful context for thinking about the representations that appear on the *Attitude* and *gal-dem* websites. Consider, for example, the following questions:

- To what extent can these representations be seen as a response to the historical under-representation of LGBTQ people in mainstream media?
- What significance might these representations hold for marginalised and minority groups who use these websites?
- What references do these websites make to representations of LGBTQ people in *mainstream* media products and what is the function of these references? Can they be seen to promote and encourage further representations in mainstream media, for example?

Tip

The under-representation and misrepresentation of social groups only needs to be explored in relation to *gal-dem* or *Attitude*. You do not need to explore this aspect of the theoretical framework in relation to JJ Olatunji/KSI or Zoe Sugg.

Key Term

LGBT
An acronym that stands for lesbian, gay, bisexual and transgender. Other variations include LGBTQ and LGBTQ+. The Q in these variations stands for 'questioning' or 'queer', while the addition of the '+' is intended to make the category more inclusive by encompassing other related groups such as those who identify as pansexual or asexual.

Symbolic annihilation
The idea that the under-representation of particular social groups works to maintain social inequalities by denying those groups any meaningful presence, thereby rendering them silent or invisible.

The Under-Representation of Black, Asian and Minority Ethnic Groups in the Media

It is also important to think about issues regarding visibility and representation when exploring media representations of race and ethnicity.

Significantly, it is outside of the mainstream where representations of minority groups are more commonly found. For example, a growing number of independent online magazines specifically targeting black, Asian and minority ethnic audiences have emerged in recent years. Notable examples of this include *Mille World*, which is aimed at a global audience of young Arab readers, the UK Asian lifestyle magazine *DesiMag* and *melanmag*, which is a digital magazine for women of colour.

In many ways, these products can be seen as a direct response to the under-representation of black, Asian and minority ethnic groups in the mainstream media. This is something that is explicitly referenced in the 'About Us' section of the *gal-dem* website, where it notes that:

> *The current journalistic landscape is 94% white and 55% male and* gal-dem *is actively trying to redress this imbalance in media more broadly through both our editorial and commercial work. [...] We believe that taking control of the way we are portrayed in media is essential. [...] We empower and support the creative work of our communities through disrupting tired stereotypes and showcasing their thoughts and work as a vital part of discussions in a whitewashed media environment.* (gal-dem, 2022)

Similarly, Natasha Syed, one of the founders of *DesiMag* and *British Muslim Magazine*, pointed out in a 2017 interview that young British Muslims are '*becoming publishers and [...] website owners because they're completely sick of reading media that just doesn't represent them*' (Mahmood, 2017).

Rapid Recall 5.10

Which of the named theorists uses the term 'burden of representation' to describe the extra cultural weight that representations of under-represented groups often have to bear? If you can't remember, look at page 147 of the Year 1 book.

Quickfire 5.14

In what way could institutional factors be seen as a reason for the under-representation or misrepresentation of particular social groups?

Gay Stereotypes and the Misrepresentation of LGBTQ People in Mainstream Media

As well as thinking about how particular social groups are *under*-represented in the media, you also need to explore how and why they may be *mis*represented. As discussed in the Year 1 book, the under-representation of minority groups can often lead to misrepresentation in the form of stereotyping, as the few representations of those groups that *do* find their way into the media end up representing or standing in for whole communities.

For example, when LGBTQ people appear in mainstream media, they are often represented in narrow and stereotypical terms. Gay men are frequently represented as camp, effeminate, theatrical or flamboyant. Representations such as this, while representative of *some* gay men, do not reflect the diversity of gay male identities.

It could also be argued that these stereotypes shore up hegemonic understandings of masculinity by constructing gay men as 'other'. Masculinity is often equated with heterosexuality in mainstream media, perpetuating the myth that in order to be masculine one has to be heterosexual. Therefore, stereotypical representations that present effeminacy as an intrinsic part of gay male identity could be seen to reinforce this idea. Effeminacy, theatricality and flamboyance often function as visible markers of difference; they mark and construct gay men as other in relation to heteronormative models of masculinity.

These are issues that can usefully be explored when analysing the *Attitude* website. Whether the representations that are shown there challenge or reinforce dominant stereotypes of gay male identity is something you may wish to consider.

Racial Stereotypes and the Misrepresentation of Minority Ethnic Groups in Mainstream Media

The misrepresentation of black, Asian and minority ethnic groups in the media is also a long-standing issue. Stuart Hall, whose theory of representation was outlined in the Year 1 book, has written extensively on this topic, highlighting the ways in which minority ethnic groups are represented as 'other'. As we have already seen, a key aspect of his theory is the idea that '*stereotyping tends to occur where there are gross inequalities of power*' (Hall, 2013).

For example, in their study of Muslim representations in the British press, Sian et al. (2012) found that:

> *The portrayal of Muslims has been largely negative and stereotypical, informed often by a virulent, racialised Islamophobic discourse.*

The '*recurring use of words such as "fanatic", "terrorist", "fundamentalist", "radical" and "extremist"*' (Sian et al., 2012) systematically constructs Muslims as 'other', representing them as a threat to Western norms and values.

While these stereotypes are more commonly seen in media representations of Muslim *men*, there are also certain stereotypes of Muslim women that tend to circulate in Western culture. For example, Muslim women are often stereotypically represented as passive, submissive or oppressed in the mainstream media.

One of the issues to consider when studying the *gal-dem* or *Attitude* website is whether it might be seen to challenge some of these stereotypes. Do they substitute negative representations with more positive images of black, Asian or minority ethnic groups, for instance?

Tip

Western media tend to present Asians and Muslims as synonymous despite the fact that not all Asian people are Muslim. For example, many are Hindu or Sikh. There are also many different branches and traditions within Islam (the religion that Muslims follow). This is often overlooked in mainstream media, as Muslims tend to be represented in narrow and stereotypical terms. The term Asian itself can also be problematic as it tends to homogenise a vast array of different cultures. More specific terms such as South Asian and Southeast Asian are sometimes preferred for this reason.

Gilroy's Theory of Ethnicity/Postcolonial Theory

A key theorist whose work addresses some of these issues is **Paul Gilroy**.

KEY THEORY: Paul Gilroy's Theory of Ethnicity/Postcolonial Theory

- the idea that colonial discourses continue to inform contemporary attitudes to race and ethnicity in the postcolonial era
- the idea that civilisationism constructs racial hierarchies and sets up binary oppositions based on notions of otherness

Colonial discourses are particular ways of thinking and talking about race, ethnicity and culture that privilege white people or Western norms and values over non-white people and the norms and values of other groups or cultures. Historically, these discourses were often used as a justification for colonial conquest as they emphasised the supposed cultural superiority of the **colonisers** over the colonised.

Named Theorist

Paul Gilroy
Paul Gilroy is an academic who has published widely in the field of postcolonial studies. Some of his most notable publications include *There Ain't No Black in the Union Jack: The Cultural Politics of Race and Nation* (1987), *The Black Atlantic* (1993) and *After Empire: Melancholia or Convivial Culture?* (2004).

Key Term

Colonisers
People who settle in and assume control over another country. Those whose countries are occupied and taken over are the colonised.

Gilroy argues that, even though the age of colonial rule is now largely over, these ideas about white, Western superiority are still evident in the discourses that circulate in contemporary culture. One of the examples he discusses is a speech given by then British Prime Minister, Tony Blair, in October 2001. Describing the armed forces as the front line in our struggle for freedom and justice, Blair talked about the need not to '*let fanatics and extremists determine our fate*' and refers to '*a belief that we will create a better world*' (Gilroy, 2004).

Gilroy describes the speech as '*an update on older themes*' as he claims that its key features '*echo arguments in support of the legitimacy of European colonial [conquest]*' (2004). He also sees this as an example of civilisationism – the tendency to present geopolitical conflicts as a battle between civilisations. According to Gilroy's theory, civilisationism constructs racial hierarchies as it sets up binary oppositions based on notions of otherness.

Identity and Diaspora

Another key concept that Gilroy uses is the idea of **diaspora**. This term is used to describe a group of people who share a common ethnicity but are widely dispersed outside their ancestral homeland. Gilroy (1997) argues that it is generally through '*forced dispersal and reluctant scattering*' that diasporas are formed. For example, war, famine, enslavement and political repression are all factors that may force people from their homeland.

Gilroy is particularly interested in the cultural exchanges that arise in and through diasporas and the different experiences that diasporas encompass. Someone who is British-Asian is likely to have a different set of experiences compared with someone who is Asian-American, for example. For Gilroy, therefore, identity is '*as much about difference as about shared belonging*' (1997).

There are various ways in which Gilroy's theory can be used to explore the representations of race and ethnicity that feature in the online magazine or magazine website you are studying. As a starting point, you may find it useful to consider the attitudes, values and beliefs that these representations convey, thinking more specifically about the following questions:

- Do the representations in the set product reproduce or challenge colonial discourses of race and ethnicity in any way?
- Is there any evidence of civilisationism? Are different cultures set in binary opposition to one another, for instance? Do the representations set up a clash of civilisations or construct racial hierarchies?
- To what extent do the representations on the website construct a sense of diasporic identity?

Key Term

Diaspora
Defined by Chris Barker (2008) as '*a dispersed network of ethnically and culturally related peoples*'. For example, the Asian or South Asian diaspora refers to people of Asian descent who live outside of their ancestral homeland in different parts of the world. British Asians are therefore said to be part of the Asian diaspora, along with other people of Asian descent such as Asian-Americans. A significant factor in the formation of the Asian diaspora was the Partition of India in 1947, which saw millions of people displaced.

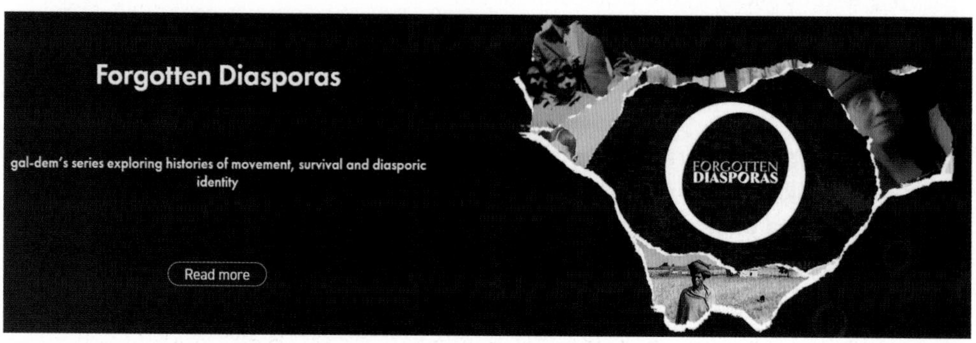

The Effect of Social and Cultural Context on Representations

When analysing your set online products, you will also need to consider the effect of social and cultural contexts on the representations they offer. Some of the issues we have already discussed, particularly regarding the under-representation and misrepresentation of minority groups, are again relevant here, as this is part of the cultural context in which products such as the *gal-dem* and *Attitude* websites are produced. In many ways, the representations in these products can be seen as a response to the narrow and stereotypical images that appear in mainstream media.

When considering the effect of social and cultural contexts on representations, it is important to remember that attitudes, values and beliefs regarding gender, sexuality and ethnicity vary widely across different cultures. For example, same-sex relationships are still illegal in some countries around the world. Not only can this affect *how* LGBT people are represented, in many cases it determines whether they are represented at all.

How Audiences Respond to and Interpret Representations in Online Products

When studying your set online products, you will need to explore the way in which audiences might respond to and interpret the representations that they contain.

You will also need to consider how audience responses to the representations in the set products reflect social, cultural and historical circumstances. Think about the different ways in which these representations might be interpreted or read.

- Would audiences in the past be likely to read these representations differently compared with audiences today, for instance?
- What about audiences in different parts of the world? How might those living under regimes with more repressive attitudes towards same-sex relationships read and respond to the representations on the *Attitude* website, for instance?
- Consider how the social and cultural circumstances of diasporic communities living in the UK might affect the way in which they read and respond to the representations on the *gal-dem* website.

Evaluating Gauntlett's Theory of Identity

As discussed in the Year 1 book, a particularly useful theory for thinking about the way in which audiences might respond to the representations in online products is Gauntlett's theory of identity.

KEY THEORY: David Gauntlett's Theory of Identity

- the idea that the media provide us with 'tools' or resources that we use to construct our identities
- the idea that whilst in the past the media tended to convey singular, straightforward messages about ideal types of male and female identities, the media today offer us a more diverse range of stars, icons and characters from whom we may pick and mix different ideas

Gauntlett's suggestion that the media provide us with 'tools' or resources that we can use to construct our identities is not only relevant to the blogs and vlogs of content creators such as JJ Olatunji and Zoe Sugg, it can also help to explain an important function that the representations which feature on the *Attitude* and *gal-dem* websites perform for their users.

Rapid Recall 5.11

What is an oppositional reading?

Tip

It is also important to remember that social and cultural values may change over time. For instance, homosexuality was not decriminalised in the UK until 1967. This means that representations of gay and lesbian identities today are likely to differ significantly from those produced 50 or 60 years ago.

Tip

When analysing JJ Olatunji or Zoe Sugg, you may find it useful to consider how the representations they offer reflect the dominant norms and values of the society in which they are produced. Think about the emphasis that is placed on image and appearance in Western culture, for example, or the dominance of consumerist and materialist ideology. How far can these values be seen to inform the representations in your set online products?

Link

A brief outline of the way in which Gauntlett's theory of identity might be applied to vlogs and blogs is provided on pages 184–185 of the Year 1 book.

The new emphasis on men's emotions that Gauntlett refers to can be seen in articles on men's mental health that feature on the *Attitude* website.

Tip

Remember that Gauntlett is talking about broad patterns of representation across a significant period of time. Therefore, when evaluating his theory, it is important not to invest too much significance in individual products. For example, if one particular product does not fit neatly within the model that Gauntlett proposes, this in itself does not necessarily disprove or discredit his whole thesis.

Tip

Although this topic only needs to be explored in relation to the *Attitude* or *gal-dem* website, you may find it useful to think about the way in which the representations that feature on JJ Olatunji's and Zoe Sugg's blogs and vlogs invoke discourses and ideologies and position audiences as well.

Tip

Remember that it is *through* media language that representations are constructed. Stuart Hall (2013) makes this clear when he says that '*representation is the production of meaning through language*'.

Another key element of Gauntlett's theory is the idea that the media today offer a more diverse range of representations than was the case in the past, when messages about ideal types of male and female identities tended to be more singular and straightforward. For example, Gauntlett (2008) argues that, since the 1990s, representations of, '*confident, successful and assertive women*' have come to seem entirely normal, displacing the traditional image of women as submissive housewives.

He also suggests that the stereotypical masculine ideals of '*toughness, stubborn self-reliance and emotional silence have been shaken by a new emphasis on men's emotions, need for advice and the problems of masculinity*'.

When evaluating Gauntlett's theory, you should consider the extent to which his ideas are borne out or supported by each of your set products. For example:

- How far can your set online products be seen to project 'images of confident, successful and assertive women' in the way that Gauntlett suggests?
- To what extent has the stereotypical representation of women as housewives been displaced by other, more progressive representations? Are there any traces of more traditional gender stereotypes in either of your set online products?
- To what extent is there 'a new emphasis on men's emotions, need for advice and the problems of masculinity' in your set online products?

These questions should provide a useful basis for evaluating Gauntlett's theory.

Discourses, Ideologies and Audience Positioning

When you are analysing the *gal-dem* or *Attitude* website, you will also need to think about how representations invoke discourses and ideologies. As previously discussed, representations have a significant ideological function as they position us to view issues, events, individuals and social groups in certain ways. Therefore, when analysing the representations in the online magazine or magazine website you are studying, it is important to think about the attitudes, values and beliefs they convey.

Consider, for example, the ideological significance of the representational codes that are used. Think about the images that have been selected. Why have these images been chosen rather than others? How do they help to construct a particular impression of the issue, event, individual or social group that is being represented? How are visual and technical codes used to convey messages and meanings?

You should also analyse the use of language. Think about the ideological significance of the lexical choices that the encoder has made. How do they frame your view of people, issues or events? Look at the headlines or captions that have been used. How do they provide anchorage for the images that feature in these products? What is the preferred reading that you are encouraged to make? What discourses can you identify in these representations?

It is also important to consider the kind of response that the representations are intended to elicit. Are you positioned to pity, admire or empathise with particular individuals, groups or causes, for example? Do the representations have an emotive function? If so, how is this constructed?

Butler's Theory of Gender Performativity

Another theory that you will need to explore in relation to JJ Olatunji/KSI or Zoe Sugg's online representations is Judith Butler's theory of gender performativity.

KEY THEORY: Judith Butler's Theory of Gender Performativity

- the idea that identity is performatively constructed by the very 'expressions' that are said to be its results (it is manufactured through a set of acts)
- the idea that there is no gender identity behind the expressions of gender
- the idea that performativity is not a singular act, but a repetition and a ritual

Crucially, for Butler, performativity is not about expressing an identity that we already possess; it is the idea that our identities come into existence only as a *result* of these performative acts.

Vlogs and blogs provide an interesting focal point for these ideas. For example, Butler's suggestion that performativity often has to do with the repetition of oppressive gender norms could usefully be explored in relation to the series of beauty rituals that conventionally feature in fashion, beauty and lifestyle blogs and vlogs as well as the series of acts or rituals through which masculinity is performatively constructed in the videos of male YouTube stars such as JJ Olatunji/KSI.

However, as discussed earlier in this chapter, while Butler highlights the way in which we are encouraged to perform our identities in accordance with dominant gender norms, there are also opportunities to subvert or deviate from this social script, causing what they refer to as 'gender trouble'. Again, this is something that you may want to consider when exploring the representations that feature in the blogs or vlogs of your chosen YouTuber. For instance, do they consciously draw attention to the performative construction of gender by mocking or parodying '*the notion of a true gender identity*' thereby causing '*gender trouble*' (Butler, 1990)? Collaboration videos posted on the channels of Zoe Sugg's brother, Joe Sugg, and her partner, Alfie Deyes, in which she does their make-up in order to make them look like women, could be seen as particular examples of this.

INDUSTRY

When looking at the industry contexts in which your set online products are produced, there are certain issues that you need to explore. As well as considering the impact of digitally convergent platforms on media production, distribution and circulation, you will need to think about the significance of economic factors to online media products and their producers, looking at the ways in which blogs, vlogs and magazine websites can be monetised.

It is also important to be aware of the economic challenges that smaller, independent companies such as the publishers of *gal-dem* face. These challenges ultimately led to *gal-dem*'s closure in March 2023. Announcing the decision to close the business in a letter posted on its website, it highlighted the financial and structural difficulties of '*keeping a small, independent media company that is reliant on partnerships afloat [particularly in the context of] a global pandemic, brand budget reductions and [an] economic downturn*' (*gal-dem*, 2023). The challenges of making an independent magazine sustainable were also acknowledged by Rhona Ezuma, the founder and editor-in-chief of *Thiiird magazine*, in an interview with Pierre De Villiers for *FIPP*, where she discussed the barriers regarding funding and distribution that independent

Tip

You are not specifically required to explore Butler's theory of gender performativity in relation to the representations on the *Attitude* or *gal-dem* websites, although you may find it useful to do so.

Tip

Remember that as well as applying Butler's theory of gender performativity, you also need to be able to evaluate it. Chapter 7 of David Gauntlett's *Media, Gender and Identity* (2008) provides a useful summary of some of the main criticisms of Butler's work.

Stretch and Challenge 5.28

Butler has talked about the way in which their theory of gender performativity is often misinterpreted. In an interview with Liz Kotz (1992), they pointed out that a common misreading is to suggest that someone can simply get up in the morning, look in their wardrobe and decide what gender they want to be that day: '*I can take out a piece of clothing and change my gender, stylize it, and then that evening I can change it again and be something radically other.*' Why would this be a misreading of Butler's theory?

Link

For an outline of these key industry issues, see page 227 of the Year 1 book.

Tip

The impact of digitally convergent platforms on the magazine industry was discussed in the magazines section of this chapter. This material is also particularly relevant to the *gal-dem* and *Attitude* websites.

publishers face: '*It's something we are always working against [... That's why people who buy] an issue, [attend] an event, [or buy] merch [are] doing more than just purchasing a product of ours – they're supporting what we do and stand for*' (De Villiers, 2023).

In addition to thinking about the economic contexts in which your online media products are produced, you will also need to consider the impact of 'new' digital technologies on media regulation as well as exploring David Hesmondhalgh's theory of cultural industries and Livingstone and Lunt's theory of regulation.

Hesmondhalgh's Theory of Cultural Industries

KEY THEORY: David Hesmondhalgh's Theory of Cultural Industries

- the idea that cultural industry companies try to minimise risk and maximise audiences through vertical and horizontal integration, and by formatting their cultural products (e.g. through the use of stars, genres and serials)
- the idea that the largest companies or conglomerates now operate across a number of different cultural industries
- the idea that the radical potential of the internet has been contained to some extent by its partial incorporation into a large, profit-orientated set of cultural industries

Democratisation or Commercialisation?

Hesmondhalgh's (2013) suggestion that the potential of the internet has been '*contained by its partial incorporation into a large, profit-orientated set of cultural industries*' is a matter of much debate.

While many theorists and commentators suggest that the internet has challenged or undermined the power of cultural industry companies to a significant extent, resulting in a democratisation of the media, Hesmondhalgh takes a slightly different view. While acknowledging the radical potential that the internet offers for social change, he suggests that its progressive uses risk being '*submerged by commercialism*' (Hesmondhalgh, 2013).

Hesmondhalgh sees the prominence of online advertising as symptomatic of this growing commercialisation, claiming that advertising intrudes on most aspects of internet communication to the point that it is sometimes difficult to distinguish between advertisements and web content.

Rather than operating independently of business and commerce, Hesmondhalgh argues that the internet has been incorporated within the cultural industries. The growing power of tech companies such as Meta Platforms, which owns Facebook, Instagram and WhatsApp, and Alphabet Inc., the conglomerate that owns Google and YouTube, could be seen to illustrate this idea.

Hesmondhalgh's suggestion that businesses in the cultural industries try to use horizontal and vertical integration to maximise profit and minimise risk is also relevant in this regard. As the Digital, Culture, Media and Sport (DCMS) Committee noted in an interim parliamentary report published in July 2018: '*a series of mergers and acquisitions means that a handful of tech companies own the major platforms*'.

Tip

In exploring the significance of economic factors for the producers of *gal-dem* and *Attitude*, you will need to consider how they monetise their online content through sponsorships and brand partnerships, and by selling advertising space on their websites. The relative costs of producing their print magazines compared with their online content is also worth considering.

Quickfire 5.15

In what ways could it be argued that the internet has led to a democratisation of the media?

Rapid Recall 5.12

Name two strategies that cultural industry companies use to minimise their financial risk.

Stretch and Challenge 5.29

Look at the homepage of the online magazine or magazine website you are studying. How far does it appear to support Hesmondhalgh's claims about the encroachment of advertising online?

Power and Surveillance in the Digital Age

Hesmondhalgh (2013) argues that while new forms of Web 2.0 technology have been interpreted by **digital optimists** as empowering ordinary people, the fact that these technologies are typically used to capture and sell information about users raises important questions about surveillance and power. Using Facebook to illustrate this idea, he discusses the way in which it generates revenue by gathering information about its users' cultural tastes and habits that it sells on to third parties.

Hesmondhalgh therefore suggests that digital technologies have consolidated the power of cultural industry companies, providing them with a more effective way of gathering data on audiences, which can then be sold to advertisers.

Evaluating Hesmondhalgh's Theory of Cultural Industries

In order to evaluate Hesmondhalgh's theory, you will need to test and explore some of these ideas in relation to your set online products and in relation to online media more generally. What evidence can you find to support or challenge the arguments that Hesmondhalgh makes? Are your set online products primarily designed to make a profit for their producers? What other interests and purposes might they serve?

Regulation

When looking at the industry that surrounds online media, one of the issues you will need to consider is the impact of digital technologies on regulation. As Hesmondhalgh (2013) notes, the development of these technologies raises important questions about power and surveillance. Several events in recent years have brought these questions firmly into the spotlight. A notable example was the Cambridge Analytica scandal in 2018, which revealed that a data analysis firm had harvested the personal data of millions of Facebook users to carry out a political **microtargeting** campaign.

As well as the issue of **data harvesting**, concerns have also been raised about the impact of the internet and social media on young people's health and wellbeing. This has resulted in calls for:

- more robust age verification systems
- firmer action against cyber-bullying and online abuse
- screen-time limits.

While tech companies and platforms such as Apple, Google, TikTok, Facebook and Instagram have started to respond to some of these concerns, introducing 'time well spent features' designed to help users cut back on screen time, and setting age limits for their platforms, a number of countries, including the UK, have begun to establish new legal frameworks to regulate online media.

Platforms or Publishers?

One of the difficulties of regulating the internet and social media is establishing who should be held responsible for material that is posted online. A key issue here is whether tech companies such as Facebook and YouTube should be regarded as platforms or publishers. In other words, do they simply provide a neutral service that enables others to communicate and share information, or do they have editorial control over the content that is posted on their sites?

Key Term

Digital optimists
Those who believe that the internet and digital technologies have a positive impact on culture and society. David Hesmondhalgh defines digital optimism as *'the view that digitalisation and the Internet have democratised cultural production and consumption'* (Hesmondhalgh, 2013). He cites Clay Shirky and Henry Jenkins as two notable proponents of digital optimism.

Stretch and Challenge 5.30

Read how Hesmondhalgh uses Facebook to further illutrate his ideas on power and surveillance in *The Cultural Industries* (2013).

Key Terms

Microtargeting
A marketing strategy in which personal data are used to identify the particular interests of an individual or small group, enabling them to be targeted more effectively. This is sometimes referred to as psychographic microtargeting.

Data harvesting
The process of extracting large amounts of data from a website to use for other purposes.

Stretch and Challenge 5.31

Compare Hesmondhalgh's view of the internet with those of Clay Shirky and Henry Jenkins. Which of these arguments do you find most convincing?

Stretch and Challenge 5.32

Conduct some research into the Cambridge Analytica data scandal. What issues has this case raised?

Livingstone and Lunt's Theory of Regulation

KEY THEORY: Sonia Livingstone and Peter Lunt's Theory of Regulation

- the idea that there is an underlying struggle in recent UK regulation policy between the need to further the interests of citizens (by offering protection from harmful or offensive material) and the need to further the interests of consumers (by ensuring choice, value for money and market competition)
- the idea that the increasing power of global media corporations, together with the rise of convergent media technologies and transformations in the production, distribution and marketing of digital media, have placed traditional approaches to media regulation at risk

Livingstone and Lunt's theory of regulation can be used to explore a number of these issues. As was discussed in the television section of this chapter, an important aspect of their theory is the idea that traditional approaches to media regulation have been put at risk by globalisation and the rise of convergent media technologies.

Significantly, many of these issues were highlighted in a government committee report on disinformation and 'fake news', published in July 2018. For example, the report noted that there was '*no regulatory body that oversees social media platforms and written content, including printed news content, online, as a whole*'. While acknowledging that '*the globalised nature of social media creates challenges for regulators*', the report concluded that the UK's existing legal framework was '*no longer fit for purpose*'.

In order to address some of these problems, the UK Government's Online Safety Bill, which started its passage through Parliament in 2023, put Ofcom in charge of regulating online media. The Bill made Ofcom responsible for checking that online platforms were taking sufficient measures to protect internet users, and gave it power to issue significant fines against companies and platforms that failed to do so, regardless of whether or not they were based in the UK.

These are ideas you will need to explore in greater depth in relation to your set online products. For example, you will need to consider how globalisation and the rise of convergent media technologies have placed traditional approaches to media regulation at risk. What challenges do these cultural and technological developments present?

Another important aspect of Livingstone and Lunt's theory is the idea that there is an underlying struggle in recent UK regulation between protecting the interests of citizens and furthering those of consumers. For example, while the general trend towards deregulation in UK policy can be seen to further the interests of consumers by making it easier for companies to compete, there are concerns this has given too much power to corporations, placing the interests of citizens more and more at risk.

Hesmondhalgh (2013) summed this struggle up when he asked if allowing companies to capture information about us is a worthwhile price for the conveniences and pleasures that search engines and social networking sites offer.

This provides a useful context for examining recent legislation such as the General Data Protection Regulation (GDPR), which was introduced in May 2018, and the Online Safety Bill. In what ways could these pieces of legislation be seen as an attempt to redress the balance between the respective interests of citizens and consumers?

Stretch and Challenge 5.33

Consider how recent debates about privacy, data collection and disinformation/'fake news' could be seen to highlight the struggle between furthering the interests of consumers and furthering those of citizens.

Stretch and Challenge 5.34

Conduct some research into the GDPR. What regulatory requirements has it introduced? How has it tried to establish greater control and transparency regarding the way people's data are collected, processed, stored and used? What impact is this likely to have on your set online products?

AUDIENCES

An introduction to some of the key issues concerning online audiences, including how they can be targeted and the ways in which they are able to interact with online media forms, was provided in the Year 1 book. This section builds on these ideas by exploring how specialised audiences can be reached through different media technologies and platforms. It also looks at the way in which online products address the needs of mass and specialised audiences, including niche audiences and fans, and considers how Jenkins' theory of fandom and Shirky's 'end of audience' theory can be applied and evaluated in relation to online products.

How Specialised Audiences Can Be Reached through Different Media Technologies and Platforms

In today's digital age, new media technologies play an increasingly important role in reaching specialised audiences. Online platforms provide a particularly valuable space for those social groups that have traditionally been alienated or marginalised by mainstream media, enabling them to assume control over their own representations and write their own narratives.

As Myria Georgiou (2013) points out:

> *in the digital media world, diversification of platforms creates opportunities for different voices within minorities to find expression.*

How Online Products Address the Needs of Mass and Specialised Audiences

One of the issues you will need to consider when analysing your two set products is how they address the different needs of their respective audiences. With regards to the *gal-dem* or *Attitude* website, you might want to explore how they address the need of specialised audiences for greater visibility. The way in which they foster a sense of community, belonging or cultural identity is another idea you might find useful to explore.

In contrast to *gal-dem* and *Attitude*, which are produced for specialised audiences, JJ Olatunji/KSI and Zoe Sugg target a broader mass audience. However, while their YouTube channels attract millions of subscribers, a particular source of appeal is the sense of personal connection they are able to establish with their fans. This is partly achieved through parasocial interaction.

In exploring how JJ Olatunji/KSI or Zoe Sugg address the needs of their fans, consider the following questions:

- What kinds of function do these products perform for their fans, and what kinds of role do the content creators adopt in relation to them? Do they assume the role of a friend or mentor, for example? If so, how is this relationship constructed?
- What kind of mode of address do the content creators use? How might the content of their blogs and vlogs be seen to address the needs of their fans? Do they offer advice, guidance, support or instruction, for example?
- How do the content creators interact with their fans? Do they respond to fans' messages, tweets and suggestions for videos? How might the Q&As they host on their channels be seen to address the needs of fans?

Tip

When thinking about the way in which the producers of *gal-dem* and *Attitude* target and attract audiences, you may want to consider the following:

- The significance of *gal-dem's* takeover of the *Guardian* Weekend supplement in August 2018 (e.g. using the platform of a national newspaper to reach a broader audience of readers who are likely to share similar liberal/left-wing values).
- The significance of *Attitude*'s annual awards events, the 'Attitude Awards' and the 'Attitude PRIDE Awards' (e.g. in terms of generating publicity and building awareness of the *Attitude* brand).
- The way in which *Attitude* has used its online platforms to host the *Attitude Pride at Home* digital festival since 2020.

Tip

The question of how specialised audiences can be reached through different media technologies and platforms only needs to be considered in relation to the *gal-dem* and *Attitude* websites. It is not necessary to consider this in relation to JJ Olatunji/KSI or Zoe Sugg, who reach a wider, more mainstream audience.

Quickfire 5.16

In what ways could online magazines and websites be seen as a more effective way of reaching specialised audiences than print media?

Rapid Recall 5.13

What is parasocial interaction?

How Audiences Use Online Products

As well as considering how your set online products address the needs of their audiences, you will also need to explore how audiences use these products. The focus here is on what audiences or users do with the products rather than what the products and their producers do to target, reach, attract, address or appeal to their audiences.

Quickfire 5.17

Which of the named theorists suggests that audiences use the representations they find in media products as resources that they can draw on as they construct their identities?

Although it is not one of the specified theories you are required to study at A Level, Blumler and Katz's uses and gratifications theory provides a useful model for exploring the different ways in which online products might be used by their audiences. Rather than seeing the audience as a passive, undifferentiated mass that is controlled and manipulated by the media, this theory suggests that audiences actively seek out and use media products in order to satisfy four main needs:

- the need for information (surveillance needs)
- the need for diversion, escapism or entertainment
- the need for personal identity
- the need for social interaction and integration.

When you are analysing your set online products, consider how audiences might use them to satisfy these particular needs:

- What can they learn or find out from these products?
- In what ways might the products be used for entertainment? How might they provide a sense of diversion from the user's own day-to-day life?
- How might audiences use these products to help construct, affirm, validate or consolidate their sense of identity? Think about the ways in which black African audiences might use articles on the *gal-dem* website such as 'The Flavours of Home: How food can be used as a social glue for African diaspora communities', for instance, or the ways in which LGBTQ audiences might use articles on the *Attitude* website such as 'LGBTQ Stars Who Came Out in 2022'. Look too at the comments that users have posted in response to vlogs on JJ Olatunji/KSI's YouTube channel, such as 'I Was Feeling A Bit Down' or posts on Zoe Sugg's YouTube channel such as 'Anxiety Update & Christmas Work Party'. What do they tell us about the ways in which audiences use these products?
- In what ways might someone use these products for social interaction and integration? Consider how they might offer users a sense of community and belonging. Think also about the interactive opportunities that online media offer.

How Demographics and Other Aspects of Identity Affect the Way in which Audiences Use Online Products

Stretch and Challenge 5.35

How might younger audiences use online products such as JJ Olatunji/KSI and Zoe Sugg's vlogs differently compared with older audiences?

You also need to consider how the different ways in which audiences use online products reflect demographic factors as well as cultural capital and other aspects of identity.

Gender, age, ethnicity, nationality and social class can all affect the way in which audiences use online products. For instance, whether someone uses a feature on high fashion just for diversion or as a resource for constructing their own image is likely to depend, to some extent at least, on their socio-economic status.

Similarly, the way in which audiences use YouTube videos will vary according to age. Those who are of a similar age to JJ Olatunji/KSI or Zoe Sugg may be more likely to identify with the life experiences they share online. For instance, the pregnancy and baby content that features on Zoe Sugg's YouTube channel may be of particular interest to those who are going through similar experiences themselves.

Jenkins' Theory of Fandom

KEY THEORY: Henry Jenkins' Theory of Fandom

- the idea that fans are active participants in the construction and circulation of textual meanings
- the idea that fans appropriate texts and read them in ways that are not fully authorised by the media producers (**textual poaching**)
- the idea that fans construct their social and cultural identities through borrowing and inflecting mass culture images, and are part of a participatory culture that has a vital social dimension

One of the theories that you are required to explore specifically in relation to JJ Olatunji/KSI or Zoe Sugg is Henry Jenkins' theory of fandom.

A useful starting point for exploring this theory is to look at the comments that fans have posted on the channels, blogs and social media sites of the content creator you are studying.

- To what extent can the conversations taking place across these sites be seen to support Jenkins' claim that fans are part of a participatory culture that has a vital social dimension?
- What kinds of interaction appear to be taking place on these sites? Is there any evidence of fans interacting with one another or are they only interacting with the blog or vlog? Is there a sense of fan community?

You may also find it useful to look at examples of fanart or fanfiction, considering how these fan-produced works might illustrate the idea of textual poaching.

Shirky's 'End of Audience' Theory

KEY THEORY: Clay Shirky's 'End of Audience' Theory

- the idea that the internet and digital technologies have had a profound effect on the relations between media and individuals
- the idea that the conceptualisation of audience members as passive consumers of mass media content is no longer tenable in the age of the internet, as media consumers have now become producers who 'speak back to' the media in various ways, as well as creating and sharing content with one another

Another theory that you will need to explore in relation to your set online products is **Clay Shirky**'s 'end of audience' theory. Like Jenkins' theory of fandom, this also suggests that media users are actively involved in the construction and circulation of textual meanings.

As Shirky points out, the growth of the internet and digital technologies in the Web 2.0 era has made it much easier for users to create and share content with one another. Again, fanart and fanfiction are good examples of this, as are the GIFs and memes that circulate widely across the internet and social media.

Tip

Although you are only required to apply Jenkins' theory of fandom to JJ Olatunji/KSI or Zoe Sugg, you will need to explore Shirky's 'end of audience' theory in relation to both of your set products.

Rapid Recall 5.14

What are the key characteristics of the Web 2.0 era? How does internet use in the Web 2.0 era differ from earlier uses?

Tip

You only need to study Jenkins' theory of fandom in relation to JJ Olatunji/KSI or Zoe Sugg; you are not required to study this in relation to the *Attitude* or *gal-dem* website.

Key Term

Textual poaching
A term used by Henry Jenkins to describe the way fans may appropriate a text and read it in a way that was not originally intended by its producer.
In this way, media texts are reinterpreted and given new meanings.

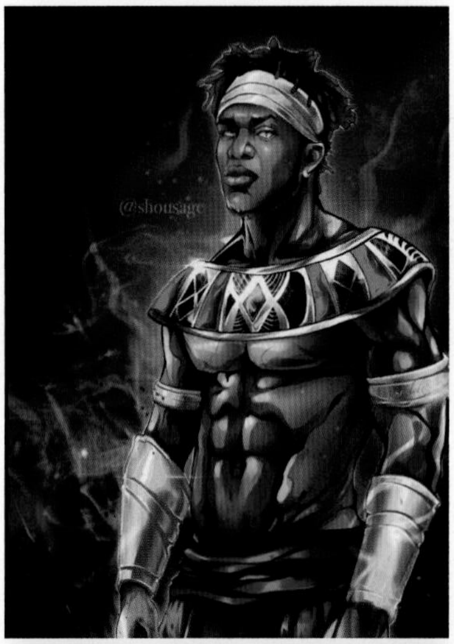

An example of fanart that reimagines KSI as the fictional character Beerus, the God of Destruction, that features in the Japanese *Dragon Ball* franchise Courtesy of Shoury Sinha.

Named Theorist

Clay Shirky
An academic and theorist whose work focuses on the effects of the internet on society. This is the principal subject of his books, *Here Comes Everybody: The Power of Organising Without Organisations* (2008) and *Cognitive Surplus: Creativity and Generosity in a Connected Age* (2010).

For instance, when *The Sun* ran a salacious article about a relatively innocuous image that Zoe Sugg had posted on Snapchat (the headline of the article was 'YouTube Star Zoella Ditches Wholesome Image with Bedtime Snapchat ... of Her in Her Knickers'), fans and supporters, including Alfie Deyes, responded with a series of memes using the hashtag #WeStandWithZoe.

Similarly, when, in 2014, the *Independent* ran an article that was critical of Zoe Sugg (which can be seen at https://www.independent.co.uk/voices/comment/sure-teenage-girls-need-role-models-but-not-of-the-zoella-kind-9809136.html), many of her fans used social media and their own blogs to challenge the arguments outlined in the article, speaking back to the media in the way that Shirky describes.

Stretch and Challenge 5.36

In evaluating Jenkins' theory of fandom, you might want to consider whether his emphasis on participatory culture and the social dimension of fandom serves to obscure other forms of fan engagement.

Evaluating Jenkins' Theory of Fandom and Shirky's 'End of Audience' Theory

As well as applying Jenkins' theory of fandom and Shirky's 'end of audience' theory, you will also need to evaluate them. While there is no doubt that the internet and digital media technologies have made it much easier for media users to create and disseminate content themselves, the extent to which users *actually* participate in this form of cultural activity is open to some debate. As Nico Carpentier (2011) points out:

> *The presupposition of a hyperactive and hyperproductive audience [...] is not always substantiated by actual audience practices.*

Tip

Remember that another audience theory you will need to apply and evaluate in relation to your set online products is Gerbner's cultivation theory. The way in which this theory can be used to explore online products was discussed on page 194 of the Year 1 book. When evaluating Gerbner's theory, you may want to consider whether media products might have a more direct and immediate effect than Gerbner suggests. In other words, is it only exposure to repeated patterns of representation over long periods of time that can shape and influence an audience's attitudes, values and beliefs? Could a single article published on the *Attitude* or *gal-dem* website feasibly change the way in which an audience member sees the world around them, for instance?

In order to evaluate the claims that Jenkins and Shirky make about participatory culture, it may be instructive to look at how many people comment on the videos that content creators such as JJ Olatunji/KSI or Zoe Sugg post. Comparing this with the number of times those videos have been viewed or the number of subscribers these YouTube channels have, may give you a general idea of the levels of interaction and participation among users of these products.

Similarly, in terms of the *Attitude* and *gal-dem* websites, you will need to see whether there is any evidence to suggest that users *are* actually speaking back to the media in the way that Shirky suggests. To what extent do these websites exploit the opportunities to interact and participate that online media offer? Is there a facility for users to comment on the stories and articles that appear on these sites, for example?

The social media accounts that these websites link to are also worth exploring. Again, a key issue to consider is how these social media accounts are being used. Are they used primarily for the transmission of information from producers to audiences, or are these sites a space for dialogue, conversation and audience interaction?

From Consumers to Producers?

Another question concerns the extent to which posting a comment on a YouTuber's blog, vlog or social media site constitutes creative activity on the part of the user. Is it reasonable to claim that simply by doing so the media user becomes a media producer, as Shirky's theory appears to suggest? Theorists such as David Hesmondhalgh and David Buckingham are rather more sceptical about these claims. As mentioned in the Year 1 book, Buckingham (2012) argues that:

> *There's a big difference between posting an occasional comment on an online forum or a social networking profile, and filming, editing and posting a video.*

In evaluating Shirky's 'end of audience' theory, you may find it useful to consider the claims he makes about the *traditional* relationship between the mass media and consumers *before* the age of the internet and the way in which the internet is said to have changed these relations, culminating in what he characterises as 'the end of audience'. These ideas were set out in an essay called 'RIP the Consumer, 1990–1999', which was published on Shirky's website in 2000. In the essay, Shirky suggested that the mass media in the pre-internet era was characterised by a 'noisy advertiser/silent consumer relationship'. In other words, while the media were able to 'speak' to audiences and sell them products, the audience had no means to respond or 'speak back' to the media. According to Shirky (2000), the internet has radically changed this dynamic:

> *In the age of the Internet, no one is a passive consumer anymore. [...] In a world where an email address constitutes a media channel, we are all producers now.*

This provides a particularly useful basis for exploring and evaluating Shirky's theory. Consider, for instance, the claims that Shirky makes here:

- Is it *really* the case that, before the internet, consumers had no way to respond to the things they would see, read or hear in the media? Were all audiences before the age of the internet necessarily passive?
- Does the internet *really* herald the disappearance of the consumer altogether? Could it be argued instead that online media is being used to '*package consumers and sell their attention to advertisers*' in just the same way as more traditional media forms?
- Has the internet *really* destroyed the noisy advertiser/silent consumer relationship, or could it be argued that advertisers remain a noisy presence on the internet?
- Do *all* users now speak back to the media as Shirky suggests? Are we really *all* producers now?

Summary

Having read this section on online media, you should now be familiar with:

- the way in which online products can be seen to exhibit multimodality and hypermodality
- the codes and conventions of webpages, including their layout and design
- the way in which online products incorporate viewpoints and ideologies through their use of media language
- issues regarding the under-representation and misrepresentation of minority groups in the media
- the effect of social and cultural context on the representations that online products offer
- the way in which the representations in online products invoke discourses and ideologies and position audiences
- the way in which online platforms and digital technologies can be used to reach specialised audiences
- the way in which online products address the needs of mass and specialised audiences
- the factors that influence how audiences use online products.

Essential Theories for Online Media

When discussing your set online products, you should be able to use and evaluate the following theories:

Theories of Media Language

- **Semiotic theory**, including Barthes: for example, the idea that blogs, vlogs and websites convey their meanings through a process of signification.
- **Structuralism**, including Lévi-Strauss: for example, the idea that binary oppositions play a fundamental role in the production of meaning in online products.
- **Postmodernism**, including Baudrillard: for example, the idea that, in the online age, the boundaries separating the real world and the world of the media have imploded or collapsed.

Theories of Media Representation

- **Theories of identity**, including Gauntlett: for example, the idea that online media products provide users with an array of resources with which to construct their identities.
- **Theories of representation**, including Hall: for example, the idea that online representations are constructed through media language.
- **Theories of gender performativity**, including Butler: for example, the idea that gender is performatively constructed in blogs and vlogs through a ritualised set of acts.
- **Theories around ethnicity and postcolonial theory**, including Gilroy: for example, the idea that online products can create a sense of diasporic identity, and can challenge or reinforce colonial discourse.

Industry Theories

- **Cultural industries**, including Hesmondhalgh: for example, the idea that the internet has become part of the cultural industries and is increasingly used to make profit.
- **Regulation**, including Livingstone and Lunt: for example, the idea that globalisation and digital convergence present particular challenges for regulators in the online age.

Audience Theories

- **Cultivation theory**, including Gerbner: for example, the idea that, with repeated use over time, online products may come to shape and influence the way in which users see the world around them.
- **Fandom**, including Jenkins: for example, the idea that fans of content creators are part of a participatory culture that has a vital social dimension.
- **'End of audience' theories**, including Shirky: for example the idea that in the digital age we have all become producers, as online media and digital technologies enable us to 'speak back' to the media in various ways.

Component 2: Media Forms and Products in Depth: Assessment

6

How Will I Be Assessed?

The Component 2 examination assesses your knowledge and understanding of media language, representation, media industries, audiences and media contexts in relation to the three media forms that you have studied in depth: television, magazines and online media.

The examination is 2 hours 30 minutes long. It counts for 35% of the qualification.

The paper consists of three sections, each worth 30 marks:

- Section A is on Television
- Section B is on Magazines
- Section C is on Online media.

In each section, you will answer **one two-part question** or **one extended response question** based on the set products you have studied for that particular media form.

Each part of a two-part question will be based on one set product. Extended response questions will be based on both of the set products for that media form.

In **Section A**, there will be:

- one question on *Peaky Blinders* and *The Bridge*
- one question on *Black Mirror* and *The Returned*
- one question on *Killing Eve* and *Tehran*.

In **Section B**, there will be:

- one question on *Woman* and *Adbusters*
- one question on *Woman's Realm* and *Huck*
- one question on *Vogue* and *The Big Issue*.

In **Section C**, there will be:

- one question on **either** Zoe Sugg or JJ Olatunji/KSI **and** the *gal-dem* website **or** the *Attitude* website.

You will have to answer one question from each section.

Key Points to Remember

- The questions may be on any area of the theoretical framework.
- Some questions may ask you to explain, apply or discuss a particular theory or theoretical approach.
- One question will ask you to **evaluate** a particular theory or theoretical approach.

The grid on the following page shows which theories you need to have studied for each of the three media forms.

Tip

Further tips about how to prepare for the Component 2 examination can be found in Chapter 9.

Tip

Remember that the set products for each media form may change periodically during the life of the specification. Check the Eduqas website to make sure that you have the most up-to-date information about the set products.

Tip

The grid on the following page shows the key theories that you must be able to use when studying each media form. This does not mean that you have to limit yourself to just these theories. For example, although you are not specifically required to use Butler's theory of gender performativity to analyse the representations in your set magazine products, you may find it useful to do so. Nor do you have to use every theory you have studied in each question; you should only use a theory where it is relevant and appropriate to do so.

Tip

A short summary of the key ideas of each of the named theorists you are required to study is included at the end of this book.

Required theories for each media form in Component 2

	Television	Magazines	Online media
Semiotics, including Barthes		✓	✓
Narratology, including Todorov	✓		
Genre theory, including Neale	✓		
Structuralism, including Lévi-Strauss	✓	✓	✓
Postmodernism, including Baudrillard*	✓		✓
Theories of representation, including Hall	✓		✓
Theories of identity, including Gauntlett		✓	✓
Feminist theories, including van Zoonen and bell hooks	✓	✓	
Theories of gender performativity, including Butler**	✓		✓
Theories around ethnicity and postcolonial theory, including Gilroy***			✓
Power and media industries, including Curran and Seaton		✓	
Regulation, including Livingstone and Lunt	✓		✓
Cultural industries, including Hesmondhalgh	✓	✓	✓
Cultivation theory, including Gerbner		✓	✓
Reception theory, including Hall	✓	✓	
Fandom, including Jenkins****	✓		✓
'End of audience' theories, including Shirky			✓

* In Section A, postmodernism only needs to be studied in relation to *Peaky Blinders*, *Black Mirror* or *Killing Eve* depending on your chosen option.

** In Section A, theories of gender performativity only need to be studied in relation to *The Bridge*, *Black Mirror* or *Killing Eve*. In Section C, they only need to be studied in relation to Zoe Sugg or JJ Olatunji/KSI.

*** In Section C, theories around ethnicity and postcolonial theory only need to be studied in relation to the *gal-dem* or *Attitude* website.

**** In Section C, fandom only needs to be studied in relation to Zoe Sugg or JJ Olatunji/KSI.

Component 3: Cross-Media Production

7

OVERVIEW

Overview of A Level/Year 2

The aim of this component is to:

- synthesise your knowledge and understanding of the media theoretical framework gained over the course through the application of your knowledge and understanding to a practical production
- allow you to demonstrate the knowledge and understanding of media language, representation, media industries and audience learned across the course, through practical application
- enable you to demonstrate your knowledge and understanding of the digitally convergent nature of the media
- enable you to use your knowledge and understanding of the media theoretical framework to create an individual production for an intended audience.

Tip

Your teachers will manage the delivery and execution of the production work. They will set you deadlines which must be adhered to.

This component allows you to demonstrate your knowledge and understanding of the media theoretical framework in a practical way.

The Non-Exam Assessment

Component 3 is the non-exam assessment of the linear A Level course and will usually be completed during Year 2 of the course.

It is 30% of the overall qualification and is worth 60 marks.

It is internally assessed by the teachers in your centre and externally moderated by WJEC to ensure that all centres are working at the same standard. To check this, a sample of work from your centre will uploaded digitally and viewed by an external moderator.

WJEC will release the briefs each year on 1 March in the year prior to assessment. They will be published on the WJEC Eduqas website. The briefs will be detailed and have some prescriptive elements, but they will also offer options and allow you to follow your own interests and build upon work you have done during the course. Some aspects of the set production briefs will change every year. In particular, the intended audience and the industry context will differ each time. It is important that you develop a response to the specific requirements of the brief by addressing the key elements appropriate to the specific intended audience and industry context. It is also very important to consider how you will address the cross-media element of this component.

Quickfire 7.1

How might the industry context change for the music marketing brief?

The Production Briefs

You are required to create an individual cross-media production in two forms for an intended audience, applying knowledge and understanding of the theoretical framework.

The following forms will always be set:

- **Television**: a cross-media production that will include a sequence from a new television programme and related print or online products.
- **Advertising and marketing: music**: a cross-media production that will include an original music video for a new or local/unsigned artist or band and related print or online products.

Tip

It is very important that you follow the cross-media brief closely and complete all the tasks set. Part of the assessment is related to your ability to meet the requirements of the brief.

Tip

The following website design sites are useful:

- Wix
- Weebly
- WordPress.

Key Term

Statement of Aims and Intentions
An assessed element of Component 3. It must be completed before you embark upon your production. It facilitates your planning, ensuring you have considered how to address the main elements of the theoretical framework.

- **Advertising and marketing: film**: a cross-media production that will include a print marketing campaign for a new film and related audio-visual or online products.

Film production work must not include a complete short film, film sequence or film trailer.

- **Magazines**: a cross-media production that will include a new print magazine and related audio-visual or online products.

For website production it is acceptable to use web design software or templates, but you must be responsible for all the design of the website and all the related content, for example images, copy and audio-visual material, all of which must be original. You will be required to acknowledge any software or templates, and how they have been used, on the cover sheet you will submit with your work..

What Do I Need to Submit for A Level Component 3?

You need to complete the following:

- a **Statement of Aims and Intentions**
- a cross-media production in two forms
- a completed cover sheet containing relevant information related to the execution of your production work. This is available from the WJEC/Eduqas website.

Key Points to Remember

You can use other people to help you in your production work, but they must operate under your direction.

- Your production must be individual. You can use other unassessed people, for example other students, in your work, but you must be in overall control. They must be directed by you and all aspects of the work must be your own. You will be required to state on the cover sheet details of any unassessed contributors you have used.
- All of the elements of your production work must be original, for example the images in magazines and the film footage you use. You must take this into account when you choose your brief and plan your production. The use of existing brands or products is not permitted. One exception is the music for the music marketing option. It is not expected that the music is original but the chosen track must not already have a music video associated with it. Any music you use in other products, for example a soundtrack, must be copyright free and be acknowledged on your cover sheet.
- You are permitted to use existing generic logos such as those for production companies, age certification logos and barcodes.
- Your cross-media production is required to demonstrate the knowledge and understanding of the theoretical framework you have gained during the course. This can be demonstrated in a range of ways including your use of media language, how you decide to construct particular representations, how the intended audience will be targeted and how you intend to conform to the industry context set out in the brief.
- Your teacher is required to monitor your progress and authenticate your work at key stages. They will set you deadlines that you must meet. They will record feedback on the cover sheet.
- On the cover sheet you are also required to give brief details of the software packages you used and how they were used in your production.

Link

Other ideas for research are outlined in the Year 1 book on page 202. However, you must remember that the focus at Year 1/AS is a single media product.

Research and Planning

It is important that before you embark upon the actual production pieces you engage in a range of research and planning tasks related to your chosen brief. Although this is not assessed directly, it will develop your understanding of the theoretical framework and be evident in the finished production. Your teacher will also be required to review your progress at regular intervals and this will be recorded on the cover sheet.

In order to create a professional media product, you will need to explore the type of products you want to create in detail. There is a range of different research tasks you can engage in related to the theoretical framework including:

- **Analysis of similar products** to the ones you want to produce, considering how media language is used. It is important that your analysis identifies the key codes and conventions of your chosen form, including, for example, how the characters and narrative are introduced and developed in a specific product. You will also need to consider how layout, design, and technical and visual codes are used to create meanings.
- You will also need to **explore how particular representations are constructed**, for example, individuals and social groups, considering how the choice and combination of elements of media language influences meaning and conveys viewpoints and ideologies.
- **Industry context**: you need to consider how this impacts upon what is produced and how you can reflect this in your own production. You will need to consider the specific media organisation, the production processes, how the products are marketed and distributed, scheduling, and placement and regulatory issues, in relation to products similar to the ones you want to create.
- **Digital convergence**: as you are creating a cross-platform media production you will need to broaden your understanding of how media industries work across different digital platforms and how these can be used to promote and distribute products. You also need to be aware of how products establish a brand identify across different platforms to make their products recognisable to a range of audiences and therefore easier to market.
- **Audience research**: you may need to engage in primary and secondary audience research and to consider the methods used by media industries to target, appeal to and position their audience. It may also be useful to explore how audiences interact with and respond to media products similar to the ones you want to create.

Tip

Your teacher will be able to guide you in your research and planning tasks, but once you start your production only very generic observations can be made. It is therefore very important that when you meet with your teacher for your reviews you have your research and planning evident and are prepared to talk through your ideas in detail.

Link

Page 203 of the Year 1 book gives some tips for conducting focus group research.

Quickfire 7.2

What is meant by primary and secondary research?

Tip

Presenting your ideas to your teacher and peer group as a pitch helps you to focus on the validity of your production and allows others to offer constructive help and advice.

Planning

Planning allows you to ensure you are able to apply your knowledge and understanding of the theoretical framework to your chosen cross-media production. The research you have done will be invaluable in helping you to plan your production, as it will have developed your understanding of your chosen form and genre. Planning tasks may include:

- **A pitch or treatment** for your cross-media production. This must consider the convergence of the products in the two forms, for example audio-visual and print, and how you will demonstrate that they are inter-related but also distinct and particular to their form. For example, an online magazine and a print magazine will have clear elements that link them, including house style and branding, but yet will have distinctive elements related to their platform.
- **A project plan**: this is a way to organise the time allocated to complete the production project and may include a timeline, a list of resources and equipment, and availability of individuals involved in the production.
- **Planning documents** appropriate to the forms and products you have opted to create. These may include:
  - a step outline
  - a shot list
  - a storyboard
  - a script
  - draft designs
  - recce photographs
  - mock-ups of layout and designs.

A storyboard is an important planning document for audio-visual productions. This one shows scenes from a rap music video.

Researching Specific Forms and Products: Television

Example brief:

A cross-media production for a new television programme in a factual or fictional genre (or sub-genre/hybrid) of your choice.

Create an audio-visual sequence from a new television programme and associated print or online materials to promote the programme.

Your cross-media production should be created for a mainstream broadcaster (such as BBC One or ITV) and target a mainstream audience of 16–34 year olds who have an interest in the genre/topic of the television programme.

Task	Details	The production must include as a minimum:
Audio-visual AND	**An original pre-title and title sequence** Length: 2.30–3 mins	• Original title and logo for the programme • Two or more filming locations • At least three different characters or contributors representing at least two social groups • Exposition of narrative/topic or issue, including conflict and equilibrium • Wide range of camera shots, angles and movement, to establish locations, narrative/topic or issue/and representations • Diegetic sound (including dialogue and/or narration as appropriate) and non-diegetic sound (including soundtrack) • Editing of footage, dialogue and soundtrack. Continuity editing in the pre-title sequence; montage of footage for the title sequence • Graphics/titles to include the title of the programme, episode title, names of key personnel
Either: Option (a) online	**A new, functioning website, to include working homepage and one linked page to promote your new television programme to its target audience** Length: two pages, including 30–45 seconds of embedded audio or audio-visual material related to the topic	**Homepage:** • Original title and logo for the programme (same as above) • Menu bar • Main image plus at least two other images (all original) that establish the locations, characters/social groups and narrative/topic of the programme • A written synopsis that introduces the narrative or topic/issue of the programme (approximately 200 words in total) • An original audio or video 'blog' (30–45 seconds) by the director, detailing either the research undertaken for the programme or a production diary **Working link to one further page from the website:** • Either an 'Episodes' page or 'Further information' page on a topic/issue (factual programme) or 'Characters' page (fictional programme)

OR Option (b) print	**A front cover and double-page spread feature article for a new mainstream TV listings magazine to promote your programme to its target audience** Length: three pages	**Front cover:** • Original title and masthead for the magazine; strapline • Cover price and barcode • Main cover image relating to the new programme plus at least 1 smaller/minor image (both original) • Main cover line relating to the new programme plus at least 3 further cover lines **Double-page spread:** • Feature article (approximately 300 words) promoting the new television programme (including its topic/narrative and characters/representations). The article should include an interview with either the director or an actor/presenter • Headline and standfirst, sub-headings, columns • One main image and at least two smaller/minor images (all original and different from the images on the cover) • Pull quotes and/or sidebar

Responding to the Brief

When you have chosen which brief you want to follow you will have some decisions to make:

- if you want to produce a factual or fictional television programme
- the genre, sub-genre or hybrid elements of your programme
- the theme/subject/topic of your programme
- which broadcaster would show your programme.

Your choice of sub-genre will influence your filming style.

Analysing Similar Products

As the A Level Component 3 production is cross-media, it is important that once you have decided which second option to choose, you explore how similar products are inter-related and how they work together to promote the television programme. It is also important that you make clear links between the different forms you are producing, while showing their distinctive conventions.

Audio-Visual Products

Choose products that are similar to the ones you want to create and focus on how they incorporate aspects of media language, construct representations, demonstrate industry elements and target their audience.

One of the decisions you will need to make is between a television programme in the fictional or factual sub-genre. Your decision may be influenced by which products you have enjoyed studying in the other components of the specification. In this section the focus will be on factual programmes, which includes the following sub-genres:

- news
- current affairs
- investigative
- reality
- docudramas, including true crime
- wildlife.

Tip

The specific detail of the production brief will change each year, for example the industry element and the target audience. The print task may detail a different type of publication. It is very important that you check you are following the correct brief for your year of assessment.

Tip

You must give close consideration to the cross-media elements of the brief and think about how you will demonstrate this in your own production.

Tip

You will need to adhere closely to the requirements of the brief as this will form the basis of your assessment for this component.

Tip

Use the skills, knowledge and understanding that you have gained in other areas of the course to help you with Component 3. For example, you have studied television genres in Component 2.

Link

On pages 213–217 of the Year 1 book there is an analysis of *Luther*, an example of a fictional television programme.

Reality television programmes are a very popular sub-genre, which employ a set of recognisable codes and conventions and cover a range of topics.

The Traitors (BBC One, 2022) is a new, very popular reality television programme hosted by Claudia Winkleman and set in the Scottish Highlands. It involves contestants from the general public. Some reality programmes, like this one, are hybrids and include elements of other genres, for example competition and game shows where contestants have to complete tasks and are eliminated, while the winners receive a cash prize.

Educating Yorkshire is a reality/documentary television programme commissioned by Channel 4, is now available on All 4. *Educating Yorkshire* was the second series in the franchise after the success of *Educating Essex* in 2011 and since then there have been three more in the series. In 2018 the series returned to the school featured in the most recent *Educating …* series, Harrop Fold in Greater Manchester.

The programme opened with the same sequence each week, which is stylistically similar to the other programmes in the franchise, giving an overall brand identity. In the title sequence the school, key students who will appear in specific episodes and the teachers are introduced, establishing the programme's sub-genre.

Media Language

- The codes and conventions of the sub-genre are introduced, including shots of the real location of the school to establish realism.
- There is also the audio code of the ringing of the school bell at the beginning and a voiceover, a common convention of documentaries, with the purpose of guiding the audience through the narrative, offering explanations and missing background information. The title sequence also employs sound bites where short, catchy phrases are taken from other parts of the programme and are edited over images, where they can create humour if they are contrapuntal.
- Realism is also constructed through the use of technical codes including handheld cameras, **fly-on-the-wall style filming**, poor lighting where subjects are not always seen clearly and indistinct sound. This suggests that the footage was shot as it happened and as if we had been there ourselves, further reinforcing the sense of reality.

Key Terms

Reality television
A sub-genre of television that is largely unscripted and focuses on the lives of ordinary people. The intention of the programmes in this genre is to present everyday life or, alternatively, 'real-life' situations created by the producers. The programmes tend to be entertaining rather than informative.

Fly-on-the-wall filming
Refers to a style of documentary filming whereby the cameras are unobtrusive, and the subjects are observed in everyday situations unaware that they are being filmed. The technique is used to portray realistic representations of people and institutions. The production team filmed for a year in the schools featured in the *Educating* ... series.

Stretch and Challenge 7.1

Discover further historical background to the fly-on-the-wall filming style by reading '"Fly on the Wall" TV', on the BFI website (Sieder, 2014).

- These sub-genres are also termed observational documentaries as they have sequences where the viewer is observing a subject. This allows the audience to believe that they are eye witnesses and are more likely to engage with the programme and believe what they see. These observational sequences are also often used as evidence highlighted in the voiceover or sound bites.
- The programme creates a separate narrative in each episode and in this sense this sub-genre blurs the lines between fact and fiction as the audience is persuaded to believe that they are seeing the story as it happens, when in fact the programme is often highly constructed in a similar way to a television drama.
- During the filming of the programme the directors will have carefully selected footage and particular students and teachers who will appeal to an audience. All of the elements seen by the audience are part of actuality, but particular sequences have been edited together to make more interesting television. The title sequence includes some of these selected shots and also focuses on 'larger than life' characters whose individual stories will feature in the series; close-ups are often used to introduce these 'characters'. Bailey and Ryan were two such 'characters'. Bailey's eyebrows (1.48) and Ryan's dream to be a politician (18.30–20.16) were widely covered in the media. Both achieved notoriety beyond the programme and helped to generate audience interest.
- The programme also uses interviews, a typical documentary convention. In this programme the interviewer is hidden from view and we only hear the questions. The interviews are used to develop characters and the narrative. Sometimes the programme manipulates time and space, a narrative device, as the interview has been conducted at a later date, for example after the examination results. The style of interviews is formulaic across all programmes in the series. A medium or close-up shot is used and the subject talks directly to the camera as if they are addressing the audience. Mr Mitchell the headteacher is interviewed with the iconography of the whiteboard behind him emphasising the topic and the credibility of the subject.
- The music builds to a crescendo towards the end of the title sequence and, immediately after, the voiceover introduces the narrative focus for that particular episode. For Episode 2 it is a fight in the school and the subsequent repercussions. An equilibrium is initially established as we observe Mr Mitchell doing a crossword with a sound bite where he talks about raising standards in the school. The narrative then ironically develops as the fight is investigated. The unobtrusive cameras enhance audience involvement in the narrative, in one shot we observe the student phoning her mum to tell her about the fight.
- At one point the student, Georgia (3.26–9.13), is whispering and instead of enhancing the sound, subtitles are shown on the screen to make the audience believe they are witnessing the scene as it happened.
- Georgia's friends are interviewed about what they think about her and the incident. These interviews enhance the narrative and break-up the observational filming, they also allow characters to be developed. This style of filming the students in pairs or individually is used throughout the series and becomes a distinctive convention.

Tip

Consider how you could use documentary filming techniques in your production if you choose the non-fiction option. Consider how your filming style will reflect your chosen sub-genre.

Tip

Consider how you can use iconography to communicate messages to an audience.

Tip

Documentaries are factual but still have a clear narrative structure. Consider how you will construct a clear narrative in the extract you create.

Representation

This is closely related to the **exposition** of the reality documentary, in this case: *'A warm and humorous exploration of what it's like to grow up or work in a secondary school in the heart of a diverse northern community'* (All 4, 2018). The main areas of representation covered in the programme are issues relating to education and young people. Each episode focuses on specific teenagers and their stories, and their representation seems to reflect reality, but is constructed in order to create entertaining television. The representations of young people are negative at times, focusing on those students who seem without hope or are difficult, but also celebrates successes, for example Musharaf, who, with the help of his English teacher, manages to overcome his stammer. The representations are constructed through the actual edited footage and the interviews with the young people, their families and teachers. The positive representation of teenager Musharaf touched audiences.

Media Industries

- *Educating Yorkshire* was commissioned by Channel 4 and produced by Twofour Group, an independent family of companies that produces and distributes programmes for a range of channels including Channel 4, BBC and ITV. Channel 4 is a publicly owned and commercially funded UK public service broadcaster, with a statutory remit to deliver high-quality, innovative, alternative content that challenges the status quo.
- Channel 4 was set up with a unique model as a 'publisher-broadcaster', meaning that the channel does not have any in-house production, but instead commissions content from production companies, for example Twofour, throughout the UK.
- Channel 4 is a self-sufficient business that reinvests all profits back into programmes, at zero cost to the taxpayer. *'A "Robin Hood" model of cross-funding means programmes that make money pay for others that are key to delivering our remit but that are loss-making e.g. News and Current Affairs'* (Channel 4, 2018). The channel operates this cross-funding model whereby typical loss-making genres are funded by more commercially viable programmes.
- *Educating Yorkshire* was marketed through trailers and posters building on the recognition of the brand from the earlier series, *Educating Essex*.
- The 2023 remit of Channel 4 is to represent unheard voices, challenge with purpose and reinvent entertainment. It has always set itself out to be different from the other broadcasting companies in its ethos and programming.

Audiences

Educating Yorkshire is distributed by Channel 4. The audience have certain expectations of the output of the channel. Channel 4's statutory public service remit includes:

- *To champion unheard voices*
- *To innovate and take bold creative risks*
- *To inspire change in the way we lead our lives*
- *To stand up for diversity across the UK*

(Channel 4, 2023)

- *Educating Yorkshire* was number 1 in the top 10 Channel 4 programmes in September 2013 with four million viewers (BARB, 2018).

Key Term

Exposition
With regard to the documentary form, this refers to the elements of the narrative that are revealed to the audience, allowing them to more fully understand characters. It also serves to mediate a message for the audience, persuading them of a particular viewpoint.

Tip

In your planning you must take into account how you intend to represent social groups in your production.

Tip

Your chosen brief will usually give you some industry information that you must adhere to, for example the broadcaster. For this example brief the production was for a mainstream broadcaster. It is therefore important that part of the research explores the output and ethos of this type of channel. This should then be reflected in the style of programme created.

Stretch and Challenge 7.2

To find out more about the industry context you can read the annual report, for example Channel 4's most recent report can be found here: https://annualreport.channel4.com.
Consider how you can reflect this industry context in what you produce.

- The programme inherited an audience due to the successful first series *Educating Essex* and the subsequent press coverage, this audience therefore had certain expectations of the programme.
- The teachers and pupils in this programme proved very popular with the audience. Ryan appeared on *The One Show* and Musharaf later went on to be a contestant on *Celebrity First Dates* accompanied by his English teacher Mr Burton. Musharaf Asghar is now 24, and a journalist and keynote speaker raising awareness about stammering and encouraging resilience in young people who feel vulnerable.
- Specific pupils and teachers that would appeal to the audience were used across all the marketing material to encourage the audience to feel involved in the life of the school and the journey of the students. The concept of 'the journey' is used regularly in documentary narratives.
- Audiences responded regularly to the programme via social media, expressing their opinions and interacting with each other, this is also an important marketing device to maintain the popularity of the programme.
- The programme's legacy continues to provide entertainment for audiences. In 2022 the British Youth Music Theatre staged a theatrical version of the successful documentary in Halifax.

Tip

Consider how you can demonstrate understanding of the theorists and theoretical perspectives you have studied during the course in your production. For example, how relevant are Henry Jenkins' theories related to fandom to your research products and the products you choose to create?

Cross-Media Products

At A Level you will need to demonstrate your ability to produce two products and to illustrate cross-media links. In order to do this it is important to explore how your research products appeared on different platforms and what were seen to be the important links made to establish the brand.

The website for *Educating Yorkshire* featured the key characters from the programme that will have become familiar to the audience. This website existed long after the programme had finished, encouraging new viewers. The 'One Year On' trailer was for an additional programme that built on the success of the original series.

All episodes are now available on the Channel 4 website.

The main image that was on the homepage established one of the key 'characters', the headteacher, in a recognisable setting related to the topic and sub-genre: in front of the school lockers. His visual codes, including expression, gesture and clothing, communicate clues to his character and role within the documentary. His image is also shown at the top of the Channel 4 *Educating Yorkshire* page.

There was an 'Episodes' page, which included written text and images. This allowed the narrative of each episode to be explained and included enigmas. The images featured the pupils who have been the focus of the series and were constructed for the purpose of the website. The direct mode of address of the subjects established a relationship with the audience.

The 'Further Information' page reflected the public service ethos of the channel, offering support and information related to the topics covered in the programme. This is a common convention of the documentary genre.

The 'Clips and Extras' page had 45 seconds of original footage in different forms including the 'One Year On' trailer, the Christmas message and a catch-up about where the subjects of the documentary had progressed after leaving school.

Tip

One of the aspects of the brief that will change each year will be the website pages you are required to produce. Make sure that you look at these closely and engage in relevant secondary research to prepare you to create your own pages.

A further option in the television brief is to create the front cover and double-page spread of a mainstream listings magazine like *The Radio Times*. It is appropriate to research other magazines that may feature television programmes on their front covers and inner pages. Consider how the front cover for *The Big Issue* for January 2023 promotes the new series of *Happy Valley*. What cross-overs are there between the television programme and the print product?

Planning for the Television Brief

Once you have completed your research into cross-media products similar to the ones you want to produce, you need to use your findings to influence your decisions regarding the planning tasks you must undertake. These could include the following.

A Pitch or a Treatment

This allows you to set out your ideas and ensure that you are adhering to the requirements of the brief and that you have taken into consideration:

- the cross-media elements of the brief
- how you will use your research into similar products
- media language, including establishing the codes and conventions of your chosen sub-genre
- the construction of representations of social groups
- industry aspects, including reflecting the ethos of the chosen channel and the production, distribution and marketing of your product
- how to target, appeal to and attract your audience.

A Recce

Visit the different locations you may want to use in your television extract and your second production piece and take photographs. Your research will help you to select locations that reflect your chosen sub-genre. You will need to take into account other considerations, for example the time of day, lighting and access. The images you collect will help to construct your storyboard.

Tip

Your recce photographs can be used for your storyboard but with careful planning they could also feature in your print productions.

A Storyboard

This is an essential planning device used by the creators of film and television products. It allows you to plan in advance the range of shots you want to include and the development of the narrative. Consider what you have learned through your research about the codes and conventions of the sub-genre you want to produce and ensure that you use them in your planning.

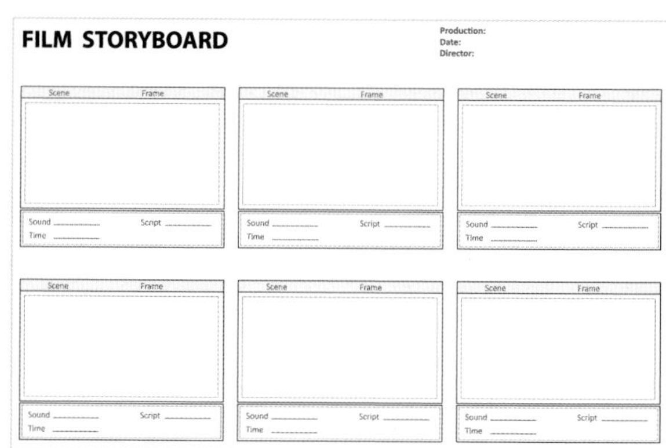

Quickfire 7.3

How can your website reflect elements of your television programme extract?

Consider the elements of media language that you can use in your production, for example the narrative techniques that are employed in the sub-genre. Documentaries and other non-fictional products often involve a journey, they also use voiceovers to give additional information to the audience and, unlike fictional products, the subjects often use a direct mode of address. You may want to introduce a presenter – another typical convention of this genre.

Consider how you are going to construct representations. For the sample brief you are required to include characters from at least two social groups. How will you use elements of media language, for example visual and technical codes, to introduce and develop your characters? In non-fiction products it is often the case that you will also be dealing with an issue or event; a storyboard will help to plan how you 'show' this to your audience.

The following elements should be included in your storyboard:

- **Shot length**: use your research as a guide, as this is frequently overestimated by students.
- **Visuals**: in the storyboard cell you need to draw or place a photograph of the shot you want to use. The standard of your drawing is unimportant, but you must ensure that the shot description and your drawing/photograph correspond.
- **Technical codes**: remember that the brief may require you to employ a wide range of shots, angles and movement, and that you use different editing techniques including **continuity editing**.
- **Audio**: this may include dialogue and diegetic and non-diegetic sound. Remember, the sound used must be copyright free.
- **Commentary**: it is often useful to include a commentary box in your storyboard to explain some of your decisions or any aspects that are not clear. This will also help in discussions with your teacher.
- **Transitions**: consider how your shots will move from one to another and how this will affect the pace of your extract.
- Make sure that your planning takes into account the requirements of the brief. For example, the sample brief requires that you include two or more filming locations, at least three different characters, a wide range of technical codes and diegetic and non-diegetic sound.

Remember to build in plenty of time to edit your footage.

A Script

A script is another planning option and should be influenced by your research and reflect the conventions of the sub-genre. Not all the elements of your extract may need to be scripted; it may seem more realistic in a documentary, for example, if your characters improvise a conversation guided by you regarding what you want them to say. Other characters, for example your presenter or voiceover, may need a more formal script.

Your storyboard can be hand-drawn, or you can use some of your recce photographs. A template is useful to record all the elements.

Tip

The storyboard you create will be useful in the discussions with your teacher, as it shows your ideas for your audio-visual production.

Tip

Creating a storyboard should not just be a print exercise. It is important that you visualise the sequence you want to create before you commit your ideas to paper. It is also helpful to talk through the construction of your extract with someone, explaining the technical and audio codes you want to include.

Key Term

Continuity editing
Editing that combines a series of shots into a sequence in order to effectively convey the narrative.

Link

More information about storyboarding can be found on pages 219–220 of the Year 1 book.

Link

'Tips for Writing a Script' can be found on page 220 of the Year 1 book, along with an example.

Stretch and Challenge 7.3

Research examples of scripts related to your chosen sub-genre. These are often related to the channel and will have a house style. Examples of different scripts can be found online at the TV Calling 'Script Library' (n.d.).

Link

'Tips for Success' for producing a television sequence can also be found on page 223 of the Year 1 book.

Tip

Your teacher will inform you of how long you have to complete the Component 3 brief. This should not be longer than 16 weeks. You must then plan your time accordingly remembering to build in time for editing and sorting out anything that may go wrong.

Stretch and Challenge 7.4

Consider how this student has applied her understanding of Hall's theoretical perspective in her production work.

Mock-Ups

For your website and print options for the television brief you will need to spend time considering layout and design. Elements, for example font style and colour scheme, should link to your chosen sub-genre and the other product you are creating. As you are producing more than one page for your website or magazine you must consider how they will be linked, and you need to establish a house style that will be consistent across your product. Use your research to guide you on the format of these products.

You will need to produce a draft of each of the pages you want to create, ensuring that you have incorporated all the requirements of your chosen brief.

Produce any other planning tasks you require for this project to help you manage your time and resources, for example a timeline, equipment list, permissions, and health and safety considerations.

When you have completed all your research and planning, and before you start your production, you need to complete your Statement of Aims and Intentions. This aspect of the production is covered in more detail in Chapter 8 of this book.

Producing a Cross-Media Television Production: Tips

- Plan in advance the equipment you will need, when you will need it and for how long. Ensure that you know how to use it and that it is compatible with, for example, the editing software you intend to use.
- Think carefully about audio, it is often overlooked by students, but poor sound can be very detrimental to the overall quality of your piece. In your recce you should have taken note of any sound issues that may affect your filming sequence.
- Use your planning tasks to help in your organisation, for example your shooting schedule and storyboard. Make sure your actors and crew are sure about when you need them and for how long, then stick to your schedule.
- Consider continuity when you are filming to avoid confusion in your narrative.

Television Brief: Examples of Student Work

When you have researched and planned the two elements of your television brief you are ready to start your cross-media production as you will now have a clear idea of how to make your two products inter-related, yet different. You will also be more informed regarding how to reflect the theoretical framework in your own production. The clips on this page and the top of the next page, from a documentary television programme created by a sixth-form student, illustrate some of the key points to bear in mind when creating a media product in this form. Consider how this student has interpreted some of the elements of the sample brief and has been influenced by research into the *Educating ...* programmes.

The application of knowledge and understanding of the media theoretical framework is clear through the inclusion of the conventions of the reality documentary genre. The sequence opens with speeded up shots of the school corridors rapidly establishing the setting and sub-genre. This is accompanied by the audio of strident pop music. There is also the audio code of the voiceover introducing the theme of the documentary: the misrepresentation of teenagers. The iconography of the school uniform reinforces the sub-genre.

On-screen graphics, a convention of the documentary genre, serve to introduce elements of the narrative and link the sections of the extract.

Similar to *Educating Yorkshire*, close-ups are used to interview the characters and the construction of the representations of young people, talking about how they are generally perceived, challenges typical representations as they discuss what they think of each other.

Extracts from the television documentary, when adults were asked what words they would use to describe teenagers, courtesy of Rachel Wells of Heaton Manor School.

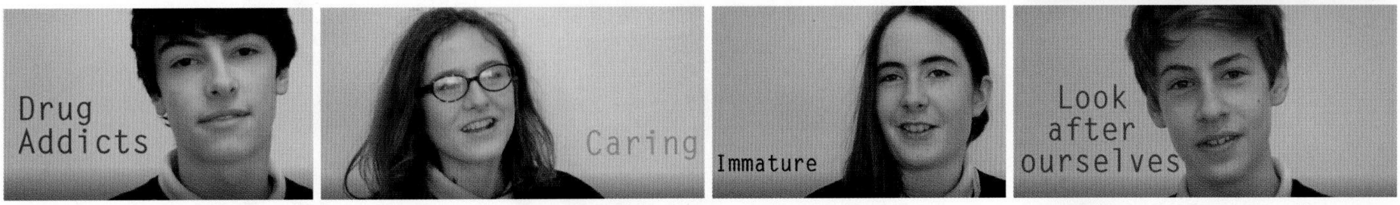

The student used visuals including on-screen graphics to illustrate the differing representations of young people and how they view themselves. This also establishes a style for the documentary, which reflects the target audience of 16–34 year olds. This is consistent throughout the sequence and these shots are intercut with shots of the school. Close-ups create a relationship between the pupil, the off-screen interviewer and the audience. An expectation is created that the audience will experience a day in the life of the students that will be positive rather than negative.

The student also employs a minimalist style for the on-screen information, linking to the younger target audience. Relevant industry information is included, comprising the programme title and names of key personnel as required by the brief.

Quickfire 7.4

What else would need to be included in this television extract to fulfil the requirements of the brief?

Tip

Try not to be over ambitious when creating your audio-visual extract. Consider the settings and people that are around you and how you could use them in your production.

Cross-Media Elements

An option in this sample brief is to create a functioning website promoting the new television programme and including a working homepage and one other linked page. **While the student work featured here is not for the same programme as the audio-visual extract, this website for a television drama does include some of the requirements of the sample brief and is therefore useful for illustration.**

There is a clear sense of house style and links are well established between the different pages of the website. The industry aspect is addressed with the inclusion of the Channel 4 logo and industry information is also included at the bottom of each page.

Original images are used throughout the website and there is a clear awareness of the codes and conventions of the chosen sub-genre demonstrated through the use of media language, including iconography and lexis.

The homepage includes an original video interviewing one of the key characters, giving background information and introducing elements of the narrative.

The written synopsis introduces the narrative and areas of representation that will be explored in the drama, including gender and mental health issues, while also establishing the crime drama sub-genre. This has allowed the student to effectively demonstrate understanding of aspects of the theoretical framework.

Stills from the *Deception* website courtesy of Sophie Johnston from Varndean College.

The 'Episodes' page includes original images and iconography related to the sub-genre and demonstrates an evident appeal to the Channel 4 demographic.

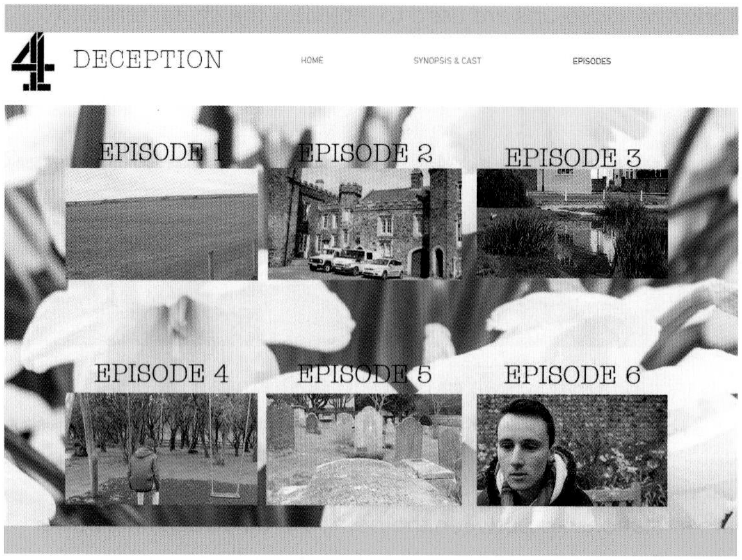

Cross-Media Products

The second option for the sample Television brief is to create a front cover and double-page spread feature article for a new mainstream listings magazine to promote the television programme to its target audience. The front cover on the next page is a student production that reflects some of the requirements of the brief and shows knowledge and understanding of the media theoretical framework.

- The cover conforms to the codes and conventions of the magazine form and to the sample brief; there is an original title and masthead with the name reflecting the sub-genre and linking to the television audio-visual brief. The main cover image relates to the new programme *Blind Dates* with obvious reference to existing programmes *Love Island* and *First Dates*. It is part of the promotion of the programme, which adheres to the demands of the brief.
- There is adherence to a house style with the use of the three-colour scheme which also adds a level of sophistication to the product, indicating the target audience as fans of the genre and of the required demographic.
- The main cover line relates to the new programme and there are at least three further cover lines. The genre-specific language used on the front cover relates to the reality sub-genre and the 16–34 year old target audience.
- The double-page spread is focused on a feature article promoting the new television programme, as required by the brief, and includes an interview with the winner of the new programme *Blind Dates*. The student has constructed a double-page spread that matches the house style for the magazine.
- The conventional codes of a double-page spread article are demonstrated and the student has considered how to use visual codes to construct a representation of masculinity that links to the sub-genre of the television programme. The pull quote reinforces the desired representation.

Tip

The pages of the magazine that you produce must link together and be obviously from the same publication. They must also have cross-media links with the primary media product you have created.

Tip

When you are constructing your production pieces, consider how you are going to reflect your knowledge and understanding of representation. You need to decide whether you want to conform to, or challenge, the typical stereotypes of your chosen sub-genre.

- The target audience of 16–34 year olds are addressed through the choice of character and the mode of address employed in the article.
- There is clear evidence that the student has applied their knowledge and understanding of the theoretical framework in their construction of these pages.

Magazine pages courtesy of Scott Maxwell from Keswick School.

Researching Specific Forms and Products: Magazines

A cross-media production for a new lifestyle magazine in a genre (or sub-genre) of your choice. Create a front cover, contents page and double-page spread article for a new magazine and associated audio/audio-visual or online material to promote the same magazine.

Your cross-media production should be created for a mainstream publisher (such as Hearst or Time Inc. UK) and target an audience of **25–44 year old affluent 'aspirers'**.

Task	Details	The production must include as a minimum:
Print AND	**An original magazine cover, contents page and double-page spread article** Length: four pages	**Front cover plus double-page spread article, four pages including at least eight original images in total** **Front cover:** • Original title and masthead for the magazine • Strapline • Cover price and barcode • Main cover image plus at least three smaller/minor images (all original) • At least five cover lines **Contents page:** • Full list of contents for the whole magazine • At least three images related to different articles (all original and different from the images used on the cover and double-page spread) **Double-page spread:** • Headline and standfirst, subheadings, columns • One main image and at least two smaller/minor images (all original and different from the images on the cover and contents page) • Representations of at least one specific social group • Feature article (approximately 400 words) relating to one of the cover lines on the front cover • Pull quotes and/or sidebar

Either: Option (a) online	**A new, functioning website to include a working homepage and one other linked page to promote your new lifestyle magazine to its target audience** Length: 2 pages, including 30–45 seconds of embedded audio or audio-visual material related to the topic	**Homepage:** • Original title and masthead for the magazine (as above) • Menu bar • Main image plus at least two other images (all original) that relate to the chosen genre of magazine **Working link to one further page from the website:** • One feature relevant to the genre of magazine (this must be different from the main feature article in the print double-page spread) • These pages must include: ◦ written text appropriate to the content of the magazine (approximately 200 words in total) ◦ 30–45 seconds of original audio or audio-visual material related to the topic embedded into one of the pages (e.g. interview with someone featured in the magazine or audio/video footage relating to the topic of one of the articles)
OR: Option (b) audio/ audio-visual	**A sequence from a new mainstream radio or television culture programme to promote the launch of your magazine to its target audience** Length: 2–2.30 mins	• Introduction/overview of the item by the presenter • Interview with the editor of the magazine detailing the concept for the magazine and production process • Filming or recording in a studio and at least one other location, e.g. at the publishers or another location relevant to the content of the magazine • Diegetic sound (including dialogue and narration) and non-diegetic sound (including soundtrack) • Editing of sound (including narration, dialogue, music) and visual images as appropriate • Review by a critic or audience responses to the magazine (audio only) • Range of camera shots, angles and movement (audio-visual only)

Tip

Remember all the elements of your magazine must be original. You cannot use the name of an existing magazine or include found images in your production.

Tip

This magazine brief includes a lot of detail, which is the minimum you should include. You should also ensure that you adhere to all the requirements of the brief.

Tip

The specific detail of the production brief will change each year, for example the industry element and the target audience. The audio-visual task may detail a different sub-genre of programme. It is very important that you check you are following the correct brief for your year of assessment.

Responding to the Brief

When you have chosen which brief you want to produce you will have some decisions to make:

- the magazine sub-genre
- which second option to choose
- how you will incorporate cross-media elements into your production
- which existing products to research
- the facilities and equipment you will need to realise your ideas. Are they achievable?

Analysing Similar Products

Once you have made your decision about the sub-genre of magazine you want to create, you will need to analyse existing magazines, magazine websites and audio/audio-visual products that are similar. With regard to the briefs, you must take particular note of the industry element, for example the suggested publisher and the target audience. In the sample brief you are required to produce a new **lifestyle magazine** created by a **mainstream publisher** and targeting a 25–44 year old audience. It is therefore important that the existing examples you explore fulfil these requirements.

Researching Print Products: *Elle* Magazine

Elle is a mainstream lifestyle magazine published by Hearst:

> *This important luxury fashion brand sits at the cross-section of style, beauty and culture with added new 2023 elements: value systems and identity.* (Hearst, 2023)

As a research product, *Elle* magazine links effectively to the sample brief in terms of its style, industry elements and target demographic. Look at a front cover of *Elle* magazine and consider the following aspects of the theoretical framework:

Media Language

- The *Elle* front covers usually feature a female model/celebrity recognisable to the target demographic, for example Emma Corrin (March 2023), Emily Ratajkowski (December 2022) and Emma Raducanu (August 2022). This is a convention of an upmarket lifestyle magazine, although *Vogue* magazine has broken with convention featuring men on its cover, including Harry Styles and Timothée Chalamet.
- *Elle* magazine employs visual codes to attract the audience. The house style incorporates a minimalist colour scheme, suggesting it is a more sophisticated magazine aimed at a slightly older and more discerning target reader.
- The layout and design are formal and conventional for an upmarket lifestyle magazine. The font styles are bold and consistent with the overall aesthetic of the magazine, and the typography of the magazine's title ensures it is easily recognisable to audiences. The choice of *Elle* as a title signifies sophistication associated with being female and French.
- Technical codes are employed to construct the main images: the models/celebrities are often photographed from a low angle to make them seem more powerful. Direct mode of address and positive codes of expression engage the audience, welcoming them into the community of *Elle* magazine.
- The cover lines communicate the discourse of the magazine and add to the construction of the representation of the female cover lead. For example, 'Finding Her Voice' (Emma Corrin), 'On Babies, Body Politics and Bitch Eras' (Emily Ratajkowski) and 'Serving Greatness' (Emma Radacanu). The magazine frequently employs lexis related to power and achievement, reinforcing the positive representation of women. The magazine's producers also use the cover lines to suggest that *Elle* can shape the life and future of the reader, presenting itself as a style guide.
- Some of the cover lines also suggest that the magazine is ethical and responsible, and concerned about global issues as well as fashion and beauty. For example, '*Don't Be Scared: The Truth About Eco Anxiety*' (April 2022).

Key Terms

Lifestyle magazine
A genre of magazine that relates to how people live their lives and what interests them. These are usually popular men's and women's magazines.

Mainstream publisher
A publisher that publishes popular magazines that have a wide, rather than niche, appeal and have high circulation figures. These magazines are termed 'mainstream' as they are generally conventional in style and content and reflect the attitudes and interests of the majority of people.

Rapid Recall 7.1

What is meant by the discourse of a magazine?

Tip

Consider how you could replicate some of the codes and conventions of this mainstream magazine in your production.

Stretch and Challenge 7.5

Consider how you can apply your knowledge and understanding of semiotics to the analysis of the magazine pages you have looked at as part of your research.

Tip

Consider how you can use cover lines to contribute to the construction of representations in your magazine front cover.

Representation

- The representations in *Elle* magazine are constructed through the choices the media producer makes regarding the front cover and how they convey the values and attitudes of the magazine.
- This selection communicates messages about the magazine's ideology and at times the choices suggest that they are not afraid to push the boundaries and offer more diverse representations, challenging the more conventional style of lifestyle magazines. In September 2018 the editor of *Elle* magazine chose to feature Slick Woods on the front cover, a woman of colour who was also pregnant. View the magazine cover here: https://fashionista.com/2018/08/fashion-magazine-september-issues-covers-2018.
- In this edition, the visual codes of gesture, expression and costume constructed a representation of a confident woman in control of her life, suggesting this is what the audience will gain from purchasing the publication.
- The focus of this edition was on sustainability highlighted on the front cover and throughout the magazine, an issue is therefore also being represented in the magazine communicating an ideology and placing the magazine in a social and cultural context. The reader is positioned to feel they can make a difference and should be responsible.
  - In January 2021 the front cover featured fashion model Aweng Ade-Chuol kissing her wife Lexy. The magazine used the front cover and the inside feature article, '*Inside A Supermodel Marriage*', to discuss their relationship and to also highlight the homophobic abuse she received after her marriage and her subsequent mental health issues. The feature article constructed representations of the two women and their story through images, headlines and text. Find the issue online to read the headline and sub-headline.
  - The website for this issue of the magazine used the black and white style of the front cover and included an audio-visual interview with the two women.

Audience

- Another relevant research example is *GQ* magazine. This men's lifestyle magazine produces a media kit which will be useful if you are considering creating this style of magazine. *GQ*, as a publication, fits the brief of 25–44 year old affluent 'aspirers' and so is relevant for research. The 2022 kit, which can be found at: https://cnda.condenast.co.uk/static/mediapack/gq_media_pack_latest.pdf, gives very detailed information about its perceived readers and the role of the magazine in their lives: '*As masculinity evolves and men's fashion has moved to the centre of the global pop-culture conversation, GQ's authority has never been broader or stronger.*'

Tip

Consider how the magazine double-page spread you have researched fulfils some of the requirements of the sample brief, for example:

- A headline, subheadings and columns.
- One main image and at least two smaller/minor images (all original and different from the images on the front cover and the contents page).
- Representations of at least one social group, for example women. There may also be representation of a social issue.
- There is a feature article of the required word length relating to a cover line on the front cover.
- Pull quotes are included and used for emphasis.

Tip

Consider how your additional pages, for example a double-page feature article, can reinforce the magazine's branding and construct appropriate and insightful representations as required by the brief.

Tip

When you are constructing your magazine pages consider how you can use language and mode of address to engage the intended audience.

- It also provides specific data about its audience, which will be useful for selling space to advertisers, for example:

  - The readership is 212k
  - 61% of its audience are from the ABC1 demographic
  - The magazine has 1.8m social followers
  - GQ readers in total spend on average £7.7k on fashion and £1.2k on beauty
  - 5.3m readers are **digital uniques**

Audience

The target audience specified by the production brief may change from year to year and it could be the case that this audience is one with which you may not be familiar. It is therefore important that you develop an understanding of the target audience in relation to the product when you are conducting your research. In the case of magazines, **press packs/media kits** are invaluable resources.

- The target audience for the sample brief is 25–44 year old affluent 'aspirers'. The existing example of *Elle* magazine, explored here, targets this audience. The tagline used by the publication in its marketing information and website reinforces the idea of the link between the magazine as a lifestyle guide and the reader: *'You can tell she reads Elle'*. Circulation figures for most magazines are produced by **ABC** and can be found at https://www.abc.org.uk.
- The media kit for Elle magazine gives more information about its audience and can be found here: www.ellemediakit.com.

Tip

Accessing the media kit/press pack for a magazine similar to the one you intend to produce may give you an insight into what the magazine thinks about its readers as well as the actual reader demographic.

Rapid Recall 7.2

Which theoretical perspective groups audiences into categories, one of them being 'aspirers'?

Key Terms

Digital uniques
Individual users to a website over a given time period.

Press packs/media kits
Known by either name, these are compiled by the magazine publishers and their purpose is to give information to advertisers about the publication and its readers. They provide details about the target demographic and usually include a **pen portrait** of the reader or a graphic representation of their interests. There is also information about the reach of the magazine across different media platforms.

Pen portrait
A marketing technique for defining an audience. It is an informal description of a person or group. It can cover factual aspects as well as attitudes and lifestyle.

Key Figure

ABC
The Audit Bureau of Circulations (ABC) compiles and verifies data for media owners, agencies and advertisers. It provides information about the digital reach and circulation of the publication that can be used to attract advertisers.

Tip

Although only key pages of the existing magazine have been mentioned here, it is useful to look at the whole publication as this will give you a better understanding of the target audience and how the publication appeals to them.

Link

You will find analysis of other mainstream magazine products on pages 205–207 of the Year 1 book.

Stretch and Challenge 7.6

For how Hearst cross-market to similar demographics read 'About Us', https://www.hearst.co.uk/about-us.

Tip

Seemingly small elements, such as the price of the magazine, are important in giving clues to the magazine's target audience and their disposable income.

Tip

Consider how you can reflect the industry content of your magazine in the pages you create.

Link

Details of the key features of an online magazine can be found on pages 208–209 of the Year 1 book.

Stretch and Challenge 7.7

Read more about the changes to the *Elle* brand and the reasons behind it in the online article 'Hearst Magazines UK Refreshes Elle UK, with Innovative Distribution Strategy, Bold New Look and New Editorial Content' (Hearst, 2016).

Industry

- *Elle* is published and distributed by Hearst Magazines, a mainstream publisher with other high-profile brands including *Men's Health*, *Cosmopolitan*, *Esquire*, *Good Housekeeping* and *Red*. The fact that many of the brands in its output are in a similar genre enables Hearst to cross-market to a similar demographic.
- *Elle* is a successful magazine with a cross-platform presence. It also has a spin-off magazine *Elle Decoration*, reinforcing the aspirational nature of the brand and its importance as a style influencer and opinion leader for the reader 'ELLE Decoration's *audience is luxury-focused and style-savvy, with a desire to be at the cutting-edge*' (Hearst, n.d.a).
- *Elle* is published monthly, at time of writing costing £4.99, it is also available on subscription and has an online presence.
- The magazine is also a global brand with 45 editions across 80 countries and reaching 175 million readers across digital platforms (Hearst, n.d.b)

Cross-Media Products

At A Level you will need to demonstrate your ability to produce two products and to illustrate cross-media links. In order to do this, it will help, when analysing existing similar products, to explore the links made by the creators of these media products to establish a cross-media brand identity. Consider the links the website for *Elle* make to the print product as well as what makes it different.

- In February 2023 the choice of colour for the website banner and the chosen image link to the front cover of the print magazine featuring Emma Corrin, so establishing cross-media branding.
- The font style matches that of the magazine's masthead, establishing the identity of the brand and making it recognisable for audiences.
- A second page on the website relates to the main topic of the print magazine, sustainability, and, similar to the magazine, positions the audience to feel responsible for the choices they make.
- The website is obviously more interactive than the print product. Navigational features facilitate movement around the website and allow the audience to make choices about which elements of the site are relevant to them.
- The titles in the navigation bar reflect the sub-genre of the magazine, with a focus on fashion and beauty, as would be expected from a women's lifestyle magazine. However, the inclusion of 'Life + Culture' suggests that the magazine will offer something more and reflects a broader discourse, suggestive of the slightly older demographic of women readers.
- The sample brief requires that you incorporate 30–45 seconds of audio/audio-visual material into your own website. There is regularly a range of examples of short audio-visual pieces on the *Elle* website, including in February 2023 a feature on the *Bridgerton* prequel *Queen Charlotte: A Bridgerton Story* incorporating an audio-visual Q&A session with Nicola Coughlan and an exclusive clip from the new series. These videos usually reflect both the aspirational style guide element of the magazine as well as its more serious side where the content often addresses more pertinent issues of interest to the more discerning female audience.

- The layout and design of the website is sophisticated and uncluttered, and the topics included are relevant to the educated, style conscious, female target audience. The brand was refreshed in 2016 with a new look and distribution strategy. This included enabling readers to pre-order copies of the September 2016 issue with a choice of five covers to appeal to different elements of the magazine's community:

  The ELLE team will dissect and analyse news and trends, with the aim of delivering insightful content to its loyal audience. (Hearst, 2016)

Tip

When you are engaging in your research consider how the decisions made by the producers of *Elle* reflect the target audience and how you can replicate this in your production.

Audio/Audio-Visual Option

For this option from the magazine brief you will need to engage in research of culture programmes and consider how you will build in cross-media links, for example:

- Research a programme in a similar genre, for example BBC Radio 4's *Front Row* or BBC Two's *The Culture Show*.
- Research a programme that reflects the target audience, for example Radio 4's *The Media Show*.
- Consider the codes and conventions of the programmes you research. Listening to relevant podcasts will prepare you for the audio option. For example 'A Day in the Life of Elle's Deputy Digital Editor', which can be found here: https://www.elle.com/uk/life-and-culture/elle-voices/a37606357/huawei-elles-deputy-digital-editor/.
- In your research into existing products, consider how the different audio elements work together to engage an audience, for example sound beds, music and dialogue.
- Consider how you will make cross-media links to your magazine and fulfil the requirements of the brief by including an introduction to the magazine item by the presenter and an interview with the editor.

Quickfire 7.5

Why is it important to refresh magazine brands?

Link

Detailed information related to construction audio-visual products can be found on pages 224–226 of the Year 1 book.

An interview with the new magazine's editor is one of the requirements of the sample brief.

Planning for the Cross-Media Magazine Brief

Once you have completed your research into cross-media products similar to the ones you want to produce, you need to use your findings to influence your decisions regarding the planning tasks you must undertake. These could include the following.

A Pitch or a Treatment

This allows you to set out your ideas and ensure that you are adhering to the requirements of the brief and that you have taken into consideration:

- the cross-media elements of the brief
- how you will use your research into similar products
- media language, including establishing the codes and conventions of your chosen sub-genre
- the construction of representations
- industry aspects, including reflecting the ethos of the magazine and the production, distribution and marketing of your product
- how to target, appeal to and attract your audience.

Tip

Look back at the section on television documentary, page 244. Some of the elements of media language discussed will be relevant to this sub-genre.

Tip

Use the requirements of the brief to guide you in your construction of this product.

Tip

Refer to the work you did when studying *Woman's Hour* or *Have You Heard George's Podcast?* These programmes target a similar audience and include codes and conventions relevant to your set brief.

Link

There is an example of a treatment for a magazine matching the print element of the A Level sample brief on page 210 of the Year 1 book.

Mock-Ups and Draft Designs of Your Pages

Use what you have found in your research to influence your decisions about the look of your magazine and website. Remember you are not required to create websites through programming languages such as HTML; it is acceptable to use web design software or templates. In creating your print magazine and website pages you must ensure that you establish a house style across the pages in each form and make links across the two forms. Careful planning will help you to achieve this inter-relation between your products.

Consider how and where you want to photograph your subject to reflect the sub-genre of your magazine and your target audience.

Planning and Taking Photographs

Still images are an important element of the print and online element of this brief and must be given careful consideration. You will need to construct photographs that reflect the style and target audience of the magazine as well as fulfilling the requirements of the brief. The print product from the sample brief requires that you include at least eight images. All the images must be original and must not be replicated across the different products.

Scripts and Storyboard

For the audio/audio-visual option of this brief you are required to produce a sequence from a radio or television culture programme. As part of your planning for the audio-visual option you will need to produce a storyboard of your sequence ensuring that you are fulfilling the requirements of the brief, for example filming in at least two locations. Similarly, for the audio option you will need a script/running order. Although radio interviews and podcasts frequently seem as if they are unscripted, it will be helpful for your participants to know what you want them to say and how you want them to say it, as they will be playing a role. Both the audio and audio-visual sequences should reflect the codes and conventions of the form and construct appropriate representations.

Tip

Look back at page 249 which covers scripts and storyboards for the Television brief.

Producing a Cross-Media Magazine Production: Tips

- Ensure that what you intend to produce adheres closely to the brief and that there are links between the two forms to establish the brand identity. You need to consider how you will create a house style that will be recognisable in both of your production pieces. You also need to ensure that the pages you produce link together as part of the same publication.
- Use your knowledge and understanding from the other components in the course and your research into existing products to ensure that you demonstrate the elements of media language relevant to your chosen form. This should include, for example, font styles, codes of colour, language, discourse and specific conventions related to your chosen sub-genre.
- Remember that all the work must be your own and the images you use must be original. Plan your magazine photoshoot carefully so as to achieve the best results. This may include a recce to find the best locations for the photographs. Take more photos than you need so that you can select the most appropriate, bearing in mind the amount specified in the brief.
- Consider how you will construct your photographs in order to reflect the representations required by the brief.
- If you want a studio look to your front cover or inner pages then you need to give some thought to location and lighting. You will also need to advise your model on their clothing and appearance to ensure a professional looking product.

Tip

Although you have engaged in research of existing products and will replicate some of your findings in your own productions, also think about what may be different about your product that will appeal to your target audience.

Cross-Media Magazine Production: Examples of Student Work

When you have researched and planned your production ideas you are ready to start your cross-media production, as you will now have a clear idea of how to make your two products inter-related, yet different. You will also be more informed regarding how to reflect the theoretical framework in your own production. The following magazine pages, created by a sixth form student, did not completely follow the sample brief but do illustrate some of the key points to bear in mind when creating a media product in this form. Consider how this student has interpreted some of the elements of the sample brief and has clearly been influenced by the research undertaken and her knowledge and understanding of the theoretical framework.

- The front cover has established a clear house style, which is replicated across all the pages. This is communicated through the masthead, font style and choice of images. The choice of a more subdued colour scheme, used across all the pages, reflects the more sophisticated style of the magazine.
- The sub-genre of fashion is clear and is reinforced through the cover lines on the front page, there are at least five, as required by the sample brief, and the strapline *'Gucci Runway: Cruise 2018 Overview'* establishes the lifestyle sub-genre.
- The choice of models on the front cover and subsequent pages constructs a representation of young people from a specific ethnic group. The audience are encouraged to engage through the headline, *'Started from the Streets Now We're on the Runway'*. The use of the low camera angle, the visual codes of clothing and the location choice employed on the contents page creates a more edgy look, appealing to the target audience and reinforcing the magazine's style and brand.

Tip

You are allowed to use unassessed participants to appear in your media production but they must be under your direction. Here the student will have advised the models on what to wear, code of expression and gesture in order to construct the desired effect.

ESTHETIC

CONTENTS MARCH 2018

REGULARS

20
EDITOR'S LETTER

21
ESTHETICS.COM

FASHION

25
17 SPRING STYLES

47
ON THE GO FASHION
For those lazy and busy days you still want to look FIRE.

35
SHOE UPGRADE!
Get the latest looks from high street, online and designer.

71
FASHION FORWARD > DETAILS. DETAILS. DETAILS.

88
GUCCI RUNWAY: CRUISE 2018 OVERVIEW
'I like popular culture and this is the reason why I like the Renaissance because it is super pop. Pop means we all understand it and admire it' – Alessandro Michele, Gucci Creative Director.

94
GV X SJ TAKEOVER
From street fashion to runway, what is it like managing a fashion empire?

109
JEAMS X LOUIS VUITTON
EXCLUSIVE INTERVIEW! Take a look at what Jeams has been up to in the ultimate fashion collaboration with Louis Vuitton.

117
BTS REVEAL THEIR FAVOURITE FASHION BRANDS.
Includes A LOT of Gucci

BEAUTY

26
MONOLID MAGIC
Tips and tricks to stop the smudging and more!

60
ITEMS YOU MUST INCLUDE IN YOUR EVERYDAY SKIN ROUTINE
Let's not skip the moisturiser!

77
BEAUTY BITES:
ESTHETICS Beauty Editor, Natalia Ruiz, answers your FAQs

96
SJ'S EVERYDAY MAKEUP TIPS
SJ takes us through her beauty routine to get her effortless glow.

128
THIS MONTHS BOLD COLOUR: VIOLET
How to rock a bold, purple smokey eye or a plum pout

152
TAKE CONTROL OF THE FRIZZ
No more bad hair days with these must have products!

HEALTH

64
10 DAYS, 10 EXERCISES, 10 SECONDS

115
HEALTHY FATS YOU NEED:
From Almonds and Avocados to Tuna and Tofu

158
IS DRINKING TEA A GOOD WAY TO CLEANSE YOUR BODY?
Dr. Alexander gives you the rundown

LIFESTYLE

148
ADIDAS: EVERY. BODY. CAMPAIGN
Putting the spotlight on the beauty of diversity

151
3 HELPFUL APPS TO HELP ORGANISE YOUR LIFE

177
WHERE TO NEXT? PHILIPPINES.
Explore the clearest waters and white sand beaches...

Pages from *Esthetic* magazine courtesy of Kelly Joves of Peter Symonds College.

Tip

A 'contents' page is more than just a list of the contents in the magazine. It is a way for the magazine to communicate its style and suggest its discourse through the topics and features listed. In your production you need to give consideration as to how you will lay out your page and how you will use media language to establish the style of your magazine and appeal to your target audience.

Tip

You will have had opportunities during your course to practise projects like this using the editing packages available in your centre. You will then be able to apply this knowledge to the editing of your own production. Make sure you leave enough time to complete the editing process.

- There is a relatively full list of contents and the use of topic-specific lexis and mode of address reinforces the sub-genre: *'SHOE UPGRADE!'* and *'TAKE CONTROL OF THE FRIZZ'*.
- There is a clear attempt to appeal to a younger demographic through choice of articles, the models and the mode of address. The use of language creates a community who understand the references and are addressed directly.
- Important details related to the industry context are included on the front cover, for example the barcode, date and price.
- The double-page spread carries through the house style in the use of colour, font style, the topic of the article and the representation of the subject. It is clear the student has researched and been inspired by similar products and their layout and design. As required by the brief, there is a headline and sub-headings and the feature article related to one of the cover lines *'Ultimate Collab Jeams X Louis Vuitton'*. There is one main image and two smaller images and the student has clearly considered location and other visual codes, including clothing and expression, when constructing these images.
- The layout and design clearly adhere to the codes and conventions of this style of magazine and it has been competently edited in order to achieve a professional look.
- Pull quotes are included, which are used to develop the representation of the fictional character.

Link

Look at the sections in this chapter related to creating websites and audio-visual production for the television and music marketing briefs. These will help you to produce those elements of this brief.

LOUIS VUITTON

JEAMS
X EXCLUSIVE INTERVIEW WITH JEAMS
LOUIS VUITTON

HOW DID YOUR LOUIS VUITTON COLLECTION COME TOGETHER?

"WHEN YOU THINK YOU KNOW IT ALL, IT TURNS OUT THERE'S MORE TO DISCOVER."

WHAT INSPIRED YOU TO DO THIS COLLABORATION?

"I THOUGHT I ALREADY HIT THE JACKPOT BEING AN AMBASSADOR."

HAS IT ALWAYS BEEN A DREAM TO WORK WITH LOUIS VUITTON?

ARE THERE ANY FUTURE COLLABORATIONS LATER DOWN THE LINE?

YOU MENTIONED THAT BEING GERMAN-FILIPINO HAS INFLUENCED YOU, IN WHAT WAYS HAS IT IMPACTED YOUR CAREER?

"I HAD NO IDEA THAT ALL THESE REJECTIONS WOULD LEAD ME TO BURBERRY."

Researching Specific Forms and Products: Film Marketing

Example brief:

A cross-media production to market and promote a new film in a genre (or sub-genre) of your choice.

Create a DVD front and back cover, a teaser poster and a main theatrical release poster for a new film and associated audio/audio-visual or online material to promote the same film.

Your cross-media production should be produced for an independent UK film company (such as Warp or DNA) targeting an audience of 16–34 year old fans of your chosen film genre.

The cross-media production must not include a compete short film, film sequence or trailer.

> **Key Term**
>
> **Teaser poster**
> Also known as an 'advance' poster as it appears before the main marketing campaign is launched. These posters purposely contain limited information; the aim is to use enigmas to hook the audience, for example a tagline or a single image.

Task	Details	The production must include as a minimum:
Print AND	**An original DVD front and back cover, a teaser poster and a main theatrical release poster** Length: four pages (note: the front and back DVD cover count as one page each)	**DVD front and back cover, teaser poster and a main theatrical release poster to include:** • A minimum of ten original images in total • At least three different locations for photography • At least three different characters representing at least two different social groups **DVD front cover:** • At least one main image • Original title for the film • Age rating, names of director and actors **Spine:** • Title, production company logo, age rating **DVD back cover:** • Background image and main image • Four thumbnail images depicting different scenes from the film • Promotional blurb for the film (approximately 200 words), including reference to narrative conflict/equilibrium • **Billing block** • Production company logo, age rating and technical information **`Teaser poster' (portrait format):** • At least one main image (different from the images on the DVD cover) • Written text: tagline/title/release date as appropriate • Narrative enigma **Main theatrical release poster (landscape format):** • Original title for the film and tagline • At least one main image (different from images on DVD and teaser poster) • Release date, billing block and production company logo • Details of awards/quotes from critics

> **Key Terms**
>
> **Spine**
> The thin strip that is placed between the back and front of the DVD cover and is on show when the DVD is stored on the shelf. It reads from top to bottom and usually includes the name of the film, replicating the font style used on the cover. It also can include the production company name and logo, and the certification logo.
>
> **Billing block**
> Usually appears at the bottom of a film poster or the back of a DVD cover, It includes the credits and industry information.

Tip

The specific detail of the production brief will change each year, for example the industry element or the target audience. The audio-visual task for this brief may detail a different type of form or television genre. It is very important that you check you are following the correct brief for your year of assessment.

This film marketing brief includes a lot of detail, which is the minimum that you must include. You must ensure that you adhere to all the requirements of the brief.

Either: Option (a) online	**A new functioning website to include a working homepage and one other linked page to promote the same film to its target audience** Length: two pages, including 30–45 seconds of embedded audio or audio-visual material related to the topic	**Homepage:** • Original title and logo for the film (same as above) • Menu bar • Main image plus at least two other images (all original) to establish the locations, characters/social groups and narrative of the film • Written text, including a synopsis, to promote the film (approximately 200 words in total) • An original audio or video 'blog' (approximately 30–45 seconds) by the director detailing either the research undertaken for the film or a production diary **Working links to one further page from the website:** • Either a 'Characters' or 'Locations' page **The cross-media production must not include a complete short film, film sequence or trailer**
OR Option (b) audio/audio-visual	**A sequence from a new TV or radio arts/culture programme to promote the same new film to its target audience** Length: 2–2.30 mins	• Introduction/overview of the item by a presenter • Filming or recording in a studio and at least one other location (e.g. a location from the film) • Interview with the film director detailing the concept for the film and the production process • Diegetic sound (including dialogue and narration) and non-diegetic sound (including soundtrack) • Editing of sound (including narration, dialogue, music) and visual images as appropriate • Review by a critic or audience responses to the magazine (audio only) • Range of camera shots, angles and movement (audio-visual only) **The cross-media production must not include a complete short film, film sequence or trailer**

Tip

You must give close consideration to the cross-media elements of the brief and think about how you will demonstrate this in your own production.

Stretch and Challenge 7.8

Consider the techniques you can use to establish a relationship between the different forms you create. For example, the choice of images, the colour codes and font style.

Responding to the Brief

When you have chosen which brief you want to follow you will have some decisions to make:

- the genre, sub-genre or hybrid elements of your film
- the theme/subject/topic of your film
- which independent film company would produce and distribute your film
- which second option to choose
- how you will incorporate cross-media elements into your production
- which existing products to research
- the facilities and equipment you will need to realise your ideas. Are they achievable?

Analysing Similar Products

As the A Level Component 3 production is cross-media, it is important that when you have decided which second option to choose, you explore how similar products are inter-related and how they work together to promote the film. It is very important that you make clear links between the different forms you are producing, while showing their distinctive conventions.

Regarding the briefs, you must take particular note of the industry element, for example the suggested film company and the target audience. In the sample brief you are required to produce a new film produced by an independent film company and targeting a 16–34 year old audience. It is therefore important that the existing examples you explore fulfil these requirements.

Link

An analysis of other examples of marketing materials for *Submarine*, an independent film produced by a different film company, can be found on pages 226–229 of the Year 1 book.

Print Products: DVD Cover

Choose products that are similar to the ones you want to create and focus on how they incorporate aspects of media language, construct representations, demonstrate industry elements and target their audience.

A DVD cover is constructed to market the film to an audience, so will therefore communicate messages about the sub-genre.

Ex_Machina (2015) is a feature film written and produced by DNA films, a British independent film company. It is a hybrid genre, incorporating elements of science-fiction, thriller and drama. It was given a 15 certificate in the UK.

Find the DVD cover for *Ex_Machina* here: https://www.covercity.net/cover/dvd-covers-ex-machina-45871. Consider how the cover demonstrates the codes and conventions of an independent film.

Media Language

As a marketing device, the DVD cover and related posters use media language to communicate the sub-genre of the film. With *Ex_Machina* this is done through the visual codes of colour and iconography. The use of black, white and silver tones is cold and clinical and has connotations of the science-fiction genre. This is further reinforced by the appearance and clothing of the girl robot, which suggests she is alien, not human, conforming to the conventions of the sub-genre.

The blurb and the tag line on the DVD cover reinforce the sub-genre and give clues to the narrative. The taglines, '*There Is Nothing More Human Than the Will to Survive*' on the teaser poster and '*To Erase the Line Between Man and Machine is to Obscure the Line Between Men and Gods*' on the DVD cover create narrative enigmas suggesting the film's theme of artificial intelligence and the conflict between humans and the girl robot. The blurb uses lexis appropriate to this sub-genre, for example *'artificial intelligence'* and *'Robot girl'*, and creates enigmas through narrative conflict *'remote location'* and *'fascinating experiment'*.

The characters are clearly established and the ordinariness of the male characters is in stark contrast to the otherness of the female character. This again is established through codes of clothing and expression. The teaser poster contains minimal information, but the way in which the image of the woman has been constructed is intriguing and the code of gesture suggests vulnerability, a human emotion not usually associated with robots, thus echoing the film's theme of interaction. The teaser poster introduces us to the character of Ava and, as the audience have a restricted view of her, an enigma surrounding her role is established.

Tip

The thumbnail images on the back of DVD covers convey aspects of the film's narrative and further develop characters. They may be required as part of the brief and will help you to convey messages about your film and show your understanding of the theoretical framework, for example, the construction of representations

Tip

It is possible, through careful direction and consideration of clothing, expression and iconography, to communicate multiple messages about a film through the DVD cover and posters.

Tip

Consider how you could apply your research findings to your own production.

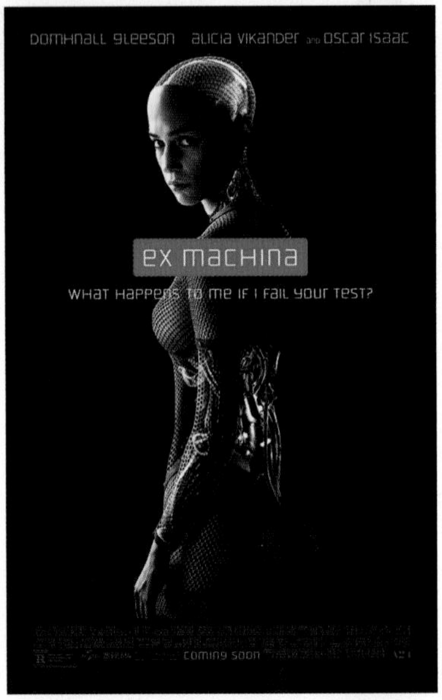

This is then developed more fully in the theatrical poster, where the character is engaging in direct mode of address with the audience. Her clothing and expression are similar to those on the DVD cover, creating a brand identity for the film. This poster contains more information, including the mark of quality, expert witnesses and the names of the actors.

The DVD cover includes other characters and their images, and the mention of Caleb in the blurb suggests his role in the film. Ava, the female robot, and Nathan, the scientist, directly address the audience, while Caleb is looking specifically at the robot, suggesting a possible narrative strand involving their relationship. Relationships are also suggested through the thumbnails on the back cover, which create further narrative enigmas and reinforce the sub-genre through media language, including iconography and visual codes.

As this is a low-budget, independent film, the focus of the marketing, as is evident here, is on the characters and their narrative, as there are no high-profile stars to draw the attention of the audience.

Quickfire 7.6

What cross-media links are there between the DVD cover and the teaser poster?

Rapid Recall 7.3

What is meant by a mark of quality?

Rapid Recall 7.4

What are expert witnesses?

Stretch and Challenge 7.9

Consider how well the different elements of the *Ex_Machina* film inter-relate to create a brand for the film that is recognisable to audiences. How could you replicate this in your production pieces?

Stretch and Challenge 7.10

Consider how you could use your understanding of semiotics and structuralism to help both in the analysis of your chosen existing products and the production of your own pieces.

Representation

The marketing materials for *Ex_Machina* construct representations of gender, age and an issue in order to appeal to the target audience.

The visual codes of clothing, expression and gesture contribute to the representation and, unusually for this genre, the main character is Ava, the robot girl. She is not only presented as strong, powerful and a possible threat but also as vulnerable and a possible love interest.

Caleb and Nathan are represented as binary opposites to Ava and are positioned in the background suggesting their possible secondary importance. Their clothing and expression represent them realistically and as serious characters within the narrative. Nathan, who is in charge of the experiment, is older and his code of gesture represents him as more dominant and powerful.

Media Industries

- *Ex_Machina* was produced by the British independent film company DNA Films, known for making other successful independent films including *28 Weeks Later* (2007), *Dredd* (2012), *Sunshine on Leith* (2013) and *T2 Trainspotting* (2017).
- The film company is run by Andrew Macdonald and his producing partner Allon Reich. It is is one of the UK's most successful production companies. DNA also has links to Hollywood and partnered Fox Networks Group to create DNA TV Ltd.
- Funding is often an issue for independent film companies. *Ex_Machina* is a low-budget film costing $15,000,000 to make. Compare this to the $250 million budget for *Avatar: The Way of the Water*. In order to secure funding for the project there was a collaboration between DNA Films, Film4 and Universal Pictures International, which together were responsible for the production and distribution of the film. *Ex_Machina* had its UK premiere at the BFI in London, reinforcing its status as an independent film.
- It received critical acclaim, which aided the marketing of the DVD and Blu-ray release and won a range of awards at the Independent Film Awards, including Best British Independent Film, Best Director and Best Screenplay for Alex Garland, and Outstanding Achievement in Craft for visual effects.
- The film was given a certification of 15 by the BBFC.

Rapid Recall 7.5

The collaboration between DNA Films, Fox Networks and other TV and film companies is an example of what industry practice?

Audience

- As the actors in the film are less well known the marketing needed to focus on other elements of the film, including the director and his previous films, the sub-genre and the narrative. As can be seen in the marketing material, the characters and the narrative are central to the promotion of the film.
- There is a clear attempt to appeal to the younger female audience with the central positioning of Ava as the focus of the narrative and the marketing material.
- The iconography and other conventions of a science-fiction film will attract fans of the genre. The narrative enigmas included in the marketing material will target the audience along with the inclusion of 'Special Features' on the DVD cover.
- The certification of 15 suggests the 16–34 target audience required by the sample brief.
- As part of the marketing, the distribution company launched a viral marketing campaign. They created a fake profile for Ava the robot on Tinder, asking anyone who was interested a series of questions about what it meant to be human. Interested 'swipers' were then directed to an Instagram page promoting the film. This was an innovative marketing stunt, which also linked to the theme of the film, and the interaction between robots and humans.

Cross-Media Products

At A Level you will need to demonstrate your ability to produce two products and to illustrate cross-media links. In order to do this it is important to explore how your research products appeared on different platforms and what were seen to be the important cross-media links to be made to establish the brand. As one of the options in the brief is to create a new, functioning website to promote the film, exploring examples of existing film websites will prepare you for this option. The website for *Ex_Machina* made clear links to the print marketing products for the film, but also incorporated new experiences.

- The website used similar dark codes of colour to the other print marketing products, clearly establishing the science-fiction genre. This was reinforced through the choice of font style and the graphics, which had connotations of cyber elements in the film.
- Images of Ava made close links to both the DVD cover and the teaser trailer, reinforcing the powerful, enigmatic and vulnerable aspects of her character. Other characters were also profiled on the site.
- The construction of the title of the film in the red box is part of the branding used across all marketing platforms.
- There was an interactive element to the website: *Ava Sessions*. Here the audience could converse with the robot, Ava, who asked a series of questions and then analysed your emotions and sketched your portrait using face recognition software. This action closely mimicked her drawing style in the film.

Rapid Recall 7.6

What is involved in the distribution of a film?

Tip

Researching the industry information for existing products will help in the construction of the billing block for your production and in deciding which logos you need to include.

The marketing and promotion of the film must appeal to the target audience.

Stretch and Challenge 7.11

Consider how Steve Neale's theory can be applied to *Ex_Machina*, which is recognisable as science fiction belonging to the AI sub-genre, but also has differences in order to appeal to a broader demographic.

Tip

Remember that, in order to avoid any overlap with the Film Studies specification, the cross-media production must not include a complete short film, film sequence or trailer. The audio-visual element of the website will be specified in the brief.

Tip

One of the aspects of the brief that will change each year will be the website pages you are required to produce. Make sure that you look at these closely and that you engage in relevant secondary research to prepare you to create your own pages.

Tip

The inclusion of a feature such as a location report in your audio/audio-visual option allows you to demonstrate your knowledge and understanding of industry issues, for example casting and budget.

Link

Look back at the chapter on television documentary in this book. Some of the elements of media language discussed will be relevant to this aspect of the Film Marketing brief.

Tip

Refer to the work you did when studying *Woman's Hour* or *Have You Heard George's Podcast?* for Component 1 of the course. These programmes demonstrate relevant codes and conventions of the audio format detailed in this brief.

Tip

Mock-ups can be hand drawn or produced digitally and adapted as your ideas develop.

Tip

Remember to keep referring to your Statement of Aims and Intentions to ensure that you are demonstrating your knowledge and understanding of the relevant elements of the theoretical framework.

Audio/Audio-Visual Option

For this option from the film marketing brief you will need to engage in research into culture programmes and consider how you will build in cross-media links, for example:

- Research a programme in a similar genre, for example BBC Radio 4's *The Media Show* or BBC Two's *The Culture Show.*
- Research a programme that reflects the target audience, for example *Kermode and Mayo's Film Review* on Radio 5 live.
- Consider the codes and conventions of this genre of programme. Listening to relevant podcasts will prepare you for the audio option. For example, Anna Smith's *Girls On Film* podcast.
- Consider how you will make cross-media links to your film in this option. For example, a review of the new film followed by an interview with the fictional director discussing their inspiration and the concept for the film. A location report showing aspects of the production values of the film.

Link

Page 231 of the Year 1 book has an example of a film marketing treatment with similar elements of the A Level sample brief.

Planning for the Cross-Media Film Marketing Brief

Once you have completed your research into cross-media products that are similar to the ones you want to produce, you need to use your findings to influence your decisions regarding the planning tasks you must undertake. These could include the following.

A Pitch or a Treatment

This allows you to set out your ideas and ensure that you are adhering to the requirements of the brief and that you have taken into consideration:

- the cross-media elements of the brief
- how you will use your research into similar products
- media language, including establishing the codes and conventions of your chosen sub-genre
- the construction of representations of social groups
- industry aspects, including the production, distribution and marketing of your product
- how to target, appeal to and attract your audience.

Mock-Ups and Draft Designs

Use what you have found in your research to influence your decisions about the visual appeal of your film marketing products. Remember, you are not required to create websites through programming languages such as HTML; it is acceptable to use web design software or templates. In creating your DVD cover, posters and website pages you must ensure that you establish the film's brand across the pages in each form and make links across the two forms. Careful planning will help you to achieve this inter-relation between your products.

The design of your products should be influenced by your research into examples of existing products. This will guide you with regard to demonstrating elements of media language and constructing representations.

A Recce

Visit the different locations you may want to use in your film marketing production pieces and take photographs. Your research will help you to select locations that reflect your chosen sub-genre. You will need to take into account other considerations, for example the time of day, lighting and access. The images you collect will help to construct the pages. After further planning you can then re-visit your locations with your characters.

A Storyboard

A storyboard is an essential planning device used by the creators of film and television products. It allows you to plan in advance the range of shots you want to include and to show your understanding of media language. Consider what you have learned through your research about the codes and conventions of the sub-genre you want to produce and ensure that you use them in your planning.

Consider the elements of media language that you can use in your production, for example the narrative structure of the sub-genre. Your research will have informed you of the typical codes and conventions of a TV or radio arts/culture programme, including locations and mode of address. You must also adhere to the requirements of the brief regarding the content of the programme.

A Script

A script is another planning option and should be influenced by your research and reflect the conventions of the sub-genre. Not all the elements of your arts/culture programme extract may need to be scripted; it may seem more realistic, for example, if your director and the interviewer improvise a conversation guided by you regarding what you want them to say. Other people, for example your presenter or film reviewer, may need a more formal script.

Film Marketing Brief: Examples of Student Work

Once you have researched and planned your production ideas, you are ready to start your cross-media production as you will now have a clear idea of how to make your two products inter-related, yet different. You will also be more informed regarding how to reflect the theoretical framework in your own production. The following DVD cover and film poster were created by a sixth form student and illustrate some of the key points to bear in mind when creating media products in this form. Consider how this student has interpreted some of the elements of the sample brief and has clearly been influenced by their research.

The application of knowledge and understanding of the media theoretical framework is clear through the inclusion of the conventions of a DVD cover from the horror genre. The choice of visual codes, including colour, reflects the sub-genre. The front cover, as required by the sample brief, includes a main image that has been digitally manipulated and, combined with the title and choice of font style, communicates meaning and creates audience expectations. The inclusion of the expert witness and use of lexis also establishes the sub-genre.

Tip

Always bear in mind the target audience of your set brief. Some arts/culture programmes are aimed at an older audience. The audience in the sample brief is 16–34 year olds. Consider how you will construct your programme extract to appeal to this demographic.

Link

Look back at the section in this chapter for the television brief, where you will find more information about constructing a storyboard.

Link

'Tips for Writing a Script' can be found on page 220 of the Year 1 book, along with an example.

Stretch and Challenge 7.12

Research examples of scripts related to your chosen sub-genre. These are often related to the channel and will have a house style.

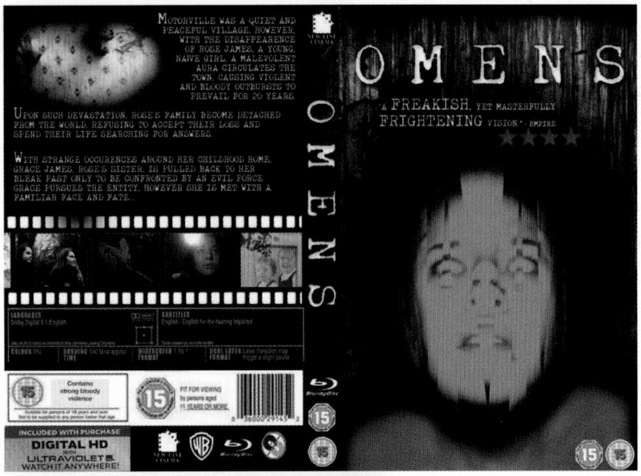

Work courtesy of Sophie Burman of St Cyres School

The back cover incorporates four thumbnail images that depict scenes from the film and establish the characters and narrative enigmas. The choice and representation of the characters reflects the target audience of the film, as does the 15 certificate. The inclusion of iconography related to the sub-genre adds appeal for fans of the genre.

The lack of star billing and focus on the sub-genre and narrative illustrates that the film is from an independent producer and has a low-budget feel to it.

The blurb establishes a narrative typical of this sub-genre and uses appropriate language '*malevolent aura*', '*strange occurrences*' and '*an evil force*'. It also refers to an equilibrium, '*Motorville was a quiet and peaceful village*', and leaves the audience on a cliff-hanger, a persuasive device to encourage them to purchase the DVD.

This teaser poster makes clear cross-media links with the DVD cover in order to establish the brand identity of the film. This includes the central image, the colour codes, background image and font style. The font style is replicated in the release date creating an overall style to the poster.

There is a minimal amount of information, as is typical of a teaser poster, giving only the clues to the sub-genre, which are communicated through elements of media language, along with the release date.

The image is clearly original and has been manipulated post-production in order to achieve a look that replicates the conventions of the sub-genre and attracts the target audience.

It is important to think about how the film's brand identity created in these two products could be replicated in other options within the sample brief.

Quickfire 7.7

How could the front cover of the DVD have more effectively constructed representations to fulfil the requirements of the brief?

Quickfire 7.8

What aspect of this film poster does not conform to the sample brief?

Quickfire 7.9

What further information should appear on a theatrical poster for this film?

Stretch and Challenge 7.13

Consider how the cross-media elements incorporated into the DVD cover and film poster can be integrated into the website.

Researching Specific Forms and Products: Music Marketing

Example brief:

A cross-media production for a new artist or band in a genre (or sub-genre/hybrid) of your choice. Create an original music video and associated print or online material to promote the same artist or band.

Your cross-media production should be produced for a major record label targeting an audience of 16–25 year olds, who have a specific interest in your chosen genre of music.

Task	Details	The production must include as a minimum:
Audio-visual AND	**An original music video** Length: 3–3.30 mins	**Promotional music video in the chosen genre that interprets the music and lyrics of the song:** • At least three locations (e.g. studio, rehearsal or live venue, or other locations) • Wide range of camera shots, angles and movement to interpret/amplify the music and lyrics • Shots of the artist or band to establish a clear identity • Performance footage (rehearsal and/or live) • Clear structure and an element of narrative conflict and equilibrium • Representations of at least one social group • Editing of original footage to the music track • Original name of artist or band, track title

Tip

The specific detail of the production brief will change each year, for example the industry element and the target audience. The print task may detail a different type of publication. It is very important that you check that you are following the correct brief for your year of assessment.

Tip

Depending on the policy in your centre, you may be given all of the briefs to choose from, or a selection. This may be influenced by, for example, group size or availability of equipment.

Tip

You will need to study the briefs you are given and make a considered decision about which is the best one for you to choose. Consider your interests and the production skills you have acquired during the course.

Tip

Remember you may use an existing song for your music video (this does not need to be copyright-free), but the song must not have an existing official music video.

Tip

If the track you choose is longer than 3.30 mins you will need to fade it out at the required time.

Either: Option (a) online	**A new, functioning website to include a working homepage and one other linked page to promote the same new artist or band** Length: two pages, including 30–45 seconds of embedded audio or audio-visual material related to the band/artist	**Homepage:** • Menu bar • Main image plus at least two other images (all original) to establish the identity of the new artist or band and promote the music • Original logo for the artist or band name **Working link to one further page from the website:** • Either a 'News' or 'Biography' page These pages must include: • Written text promoting the band or artist and their music (approximately 200 words in total) • An original audio or video 'blog' (approximately 30–45 seconds) by the artist or a band member detailing the production process of the music video
OR Option (b) print	**A front cover and a double-page spread feature article for a new mainstream music magazine to promote your artist or band to the target audience** Length: three pages	**Front cover:** • Original title and masthead for the magazine; strapline • Cover price and barcode • Main cover image to establish the identity of the new artist or band plus at least one smaller/minor image (both original) • Main cover line relating to the new artist or band plus at least 3 further cover lines **Double-page spread:** • Feature article (approximately 300 words) to promote the music; this should include an interview with the artist or band • Headline and standfirst, sub-headings, columns • One main image and at least two smaller/minor images (all original and different from the images on the cover) • Pull quotes and/or sidebar

Responding to the Brief

When you have chosen which brief you want to produce you will have some decisions to make:

- the music genre
- the choice of music track
- which second option to choose
- which existing products to research
- the facilities and equipment you will need to realise your ideas. Are they achievable?

Analysing Similar Products

As the A Level Component 3 production is cross-media, it is important that once you have decided which second option to choose, you explore how similar products are inter-related and how they work together to promote the artist or band. It is very important that you make clear links between the different forms you are producing.

Audio-Visual Products

Choose products that are similar to the ones you want to create and focus on how they incorporate aspects of media language, construct representations, demonstrate industry elements and target their audience.

Despite predictions of its demise, the music video remains a strong visual form and a dominant source of music consumption. While evolving over time, the music video has always as a form presented social and political issues, given visibility and attention to important subjects, and offered a representation of the artist and the genre. Consider how music videos have documented recent social and cultural events in the wake of the Black Lives Matter and Me Too movements and how artists like Taylor Swift and Harry Styles continue to use the music video form, at times like short films, to tell a story and construct representations of themselves and their changing persona.

Music videos produced by mainstream labels are high budget productions

Music videos produced by mainstream record labels tend to be high budget intended for a broader, mainstream demographic with the aim of promoting the artist and constructing a representation. The high production values may be evident in, for example, the range of settings and the different mise-en-scéne which may incorporate props, lighting, costume and hair. It may also be evident through the more sophisticated filming and editing techniques.

Tip

Consider how you can recognise that the music videos you studied for Component 1 are high budget, for example *Formation* by Beyoncé and *Turntables* by Jonelle Monáe.

Media Language and Representation

In your research of existing music videos, consider how media language is used to establish the music genre and construct a representation of the artist. Codes of clothing and settings form a rapid way of conveying messages about the artist and their persona. Consider how artists like Harry Styles and Taylor Swift use clothing and visual motifs in their music videos that are then incorporated into other marketing products.

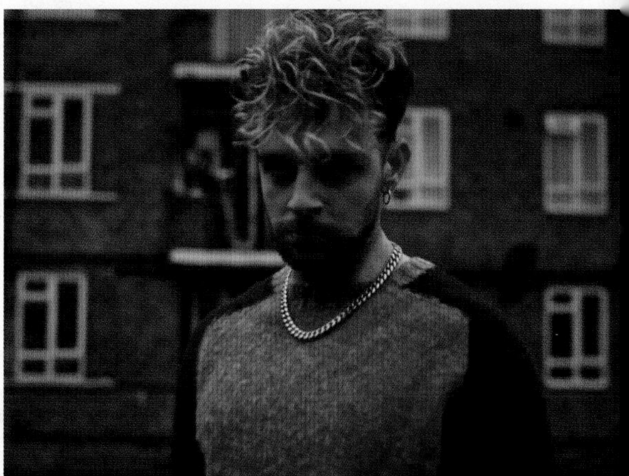

In some music videos the artist is shown performing and is established through the narrative as an integral part of their music, other musicians may distance themselves from the actual narrative and other artists employ a combination of the two, combining a narrative with shots of performance. Representations are often constructed through a range of technical codes, establishing the role of the artist within the music video. Very often the music video focuses on the identity of the artist and their music.

The representation of the artist and other social groups or issues are constructed through technical codes, including the choice and range of shots, lighting, pace and editing. The construction also encompasses codes of clothing, gesture and expression.

Consider how Tom Grennan's music video *Little Bit of Love* (https://www.youtube.com/watch?v=SsdkvYdSzlg\) uses close-up shots to convey emotion and engage with the audience, and also to rapidly convey narrative information, for example the shot of the bag of money which becomes a recurring motif in the video. Establishing shots are used to show the urban environment and to create a sense of realism through setting. Grennan uses clothing and iconography to represent different representations of masculinity and to challenge stereotypes. In the music video Grennan is both the artist in performance engaging in direct mode of address with the audience and an integral part of the narrative.

Audience

Your research should be led by the intended audience specified in the Music Marketing brief you are following. In the sample brief it is 16–25 year olds. You will need to ensure that the cross-media production you create is relevant and appropriate for this demographic. Consider how you will engage the target audience through, for example, direct mode of address, intertextual references or issues that will resonate with the audience. Use what you have learned when studying the set music video products in Component 1 and the additional examples you have studied in preparation for the unseen element of this component. In your own independent research, look at examples that aim to appeal to the target demographic.

Tip

If you choose to produce a website for your new artist or band as part of your production submission, you will need to research the websites of similar artists or their record labels, where pages will be devoted to different artists.

Tip

Consider how you could incorporate a theme or a motif into your own music video to help to construct the representation of the artist.

Stretch and Challenge 7.14

Consider how you can apply your understanding of the theoretical framework when you are conducting your research and creating your own products. For example, Judith Butler's theories of gender performativity and Gauntlett's perspective on identity are both relevant to this music video.

Industry

The briefs will often suggest examples of record labels to illustrate the industry context. For example, the briefs for 2022 set a major record label (such as Atlantic Records or Capitol Records). This will help you to focus your research by looking at the artists signed to these labels and how they are marketed across different media platforms.

Tip

When you are engaging in secondary research, consider how the artist has constructed their representation, for example through clothing, gesture, etc. Consider how you could replicate this in your music video.

Cross-Media Products

One of the main differences from the AS course is the cross-media element of the A Level production work. It is essential that you demonstrate your understanding of the media theoretical framework and the digitally convergent nature of the media through your creation of a production in two media forms. It is therefore important that in your research you explore cross-media products. Your findings will help you to see how you can make links across different platforms, while developing your knowledge and understanding of the codes and conventions of different media forms.

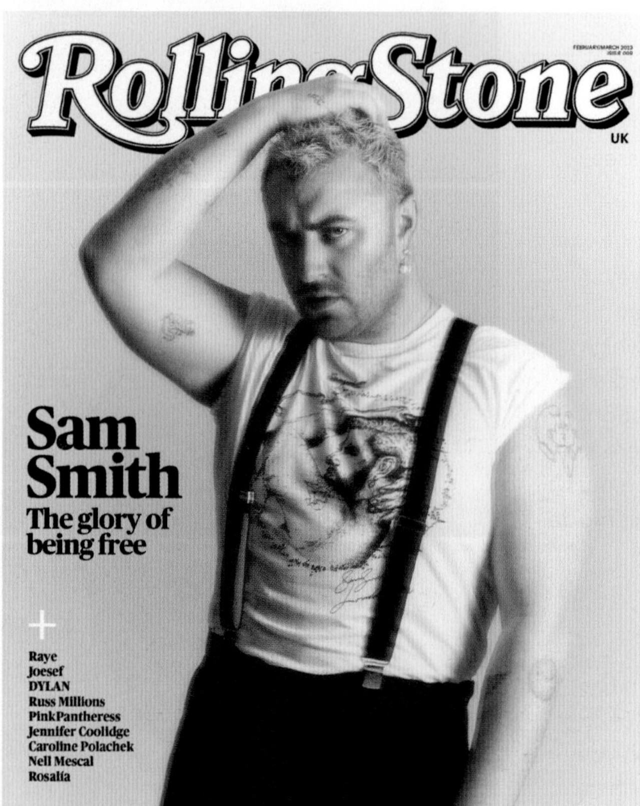

It is important for music artists to have exposure across different platforms, particularly when promoting a new album. Sam Smith is a mainstream music artist who appeared on the front cover of *Rolling Stone UK* magazine in February/March 2023. This coincided with the launch of their new album *Gloria*, so is an important marketing strategy for the artist.

The example brief requires that you produce a front cover and double-page spread feature article for a new mainstream music magazine. *Rolling Stone UK* is published by Stream Publishing in the UK. It is a mainstream music magazine that also covers film, television, politics and culture. It is a US publication but in 2021 was re-launched in the UK after 50 years; the publishers saw a gap in the market for a music magazine with a British perspective. It is therefore useful to consider the codes and conventions used and how the magazine represents the artists in the publication. Recent front cover music artists that have appeared on the front cover have included Harry Styles, Little Simz, Yungblud and Florence and the Machine.

The visual codes used on the front construct representations of the artist that will be reinforced across other platforms, for example their music videos. Their code of gesture, and their moody, serious code of expression with a direct mode of address, present them as strong and powerful, and reinforce their star persona. The direct mode of address engages the audience but also distances them, as they seem unapproachable. The cover lines and quote reinforce this representation of the artist as confident in their own skin, a theme echoed in representations of Sam Smith in other media products at the time of writing. This is reinforced through the choice of language in the cover line '*The glory of being free*'.

The front cover of *Rolling Stone UK* magazine displays some of the requirements of the sample brief:

- Original title and masthead of the magazine.
- Main cover image to establish the identity of the new artist or band.
- Main cover line relating to the new artist or band plus at least three further cover lines.

If you research other front covers of *Rolling Stone UK* magazine you will see that other elements of the brief are included, for example a cover price and barcode.

This example of a double-page feature article from *Rolling Stone UK* magazine uses media language and constructs a representation of the artist, Nell Mescal. It also demonstrates several of the conventions of the format and fulfils many of the requirements of the sample brief:

- It is a feature article of approximately 300 words promoting Nell Mescal, which includes an interview with the artist.
- There are key conventions of magazine feature articles evident, including a headline, standfirst and columns.
- There is one main image of the artist and two smaller, different images constructing a representation.
- There is a pull quote.

Tip

Use what you have learned during the course to help you in your research. For example, your study of the set magazine products in Component 2 has developed your understanding of this form. You can use this knowledge to help you construct your own print products.

Tip

Consider how the research you do will influence your own production. You will need to decide how you want to represent the new artist you create, considering clothing, expression and how they relate to the publication you have chosen to produce.
For your research, try to find examples of products that contain elements similar to the requirements of the brief. This will help you to construct your own production more effectively.

The Mix

'AT THE START of 2022, I did a video saying I wanted to go on tour, but that idea just felt so far away from me," says 19-year-old Nell Mescal.

"Now I've done two tours. I feel like anything is possible, I'm just manifesting the idea of more collaborations for 2023."

When we talk, the Kildare-born singer has just finished an extensive tour of the UK, supporting Manchester art-pop star Phoebe Green in what has been the latest step in a whirlwind journey since Mescal released debut single 'Graduating' back in July.

At the time, she told Rolling Stone UK how her emotionally charged debut effort channelled the struggles she experienced during school, which eventually led her to drop out without graduating. The song, rooted in indie folk, sees Mescal's bleak experience laid bare. It clearly struck a chord. Within a week she was contacted by fans who thanked her for reflecting their own similar, lived experiences.

"When I released 'Graduating', I got a lovely message off someone saying that they were supposed to graduate but didn't want to go because someone was bullying them," she recalls. "To have that reaction in the first week of release was lovely, but also extremely cathartic for the situation I'd been through."

In fact, the honesty within Mescal's music is one of its biggest strengths, even if it isn't always as solemn as the sound of 'Graduating'. Despite the title, her follow-up track 'Homesick', released in January, is a perky slice of indie pop that offers solidarity with outsiders.

"I wrote it in LA. One of the lines is about sitting in a hotel lobby and just being jealous of everyone else's outfits. When I leave my house in London too, everything just feels like a fashion show," she says.

She moved to the capital from Ireland – the place where she forged her musical beginnings – last year. "My first musical memories were listening to Mary Chapin Carpenter and a lot of country albums," she explains. "I'd perform in an Irish talent show and I'd sing Dougie MacLean's 'Caledonia' with my dad every year. I'd sing at every opportunity and then began writing at 12, but I started saying it'd be my career when I was 14. I'd had back surgery and just spent a lot of time at home writing every day and that was the start."

Five years later, Mescal occupies a unique position as one of Ireland's most unusual musical voices. If you've clocked the surname by now, you'll realise that her older brother Paul – whose breakout role came in lockdown smash hit *Normal People* – is one of the world's hottest screen prospects.

The siblings' close relationship, Mescal explains, has seen her brother become a valuable sounding board for her upcoming releases. "We're both too similar, we'll have exactly the same ideas and when I think it's not great, I always think he'll have the same reaction as me, which is daunting!" she says.

Another person Mescal has played her songs to is the US singer Phoebe Bridgers, Paul's girlfriend (although at the time of writing a question mark hangs over whether they remain together). In what Mescal admits to being her biggest pinch-me moment of the past 12 months, she joined Bridgers on stage at Brixton Academy last summer to perform her 2017 track 'Georgia'.

"I just got a text from Phoebe and immediately thought it was a joke. I called my mum and she started screaming," she recalls. "I said yes immediately and then was frantically trying to convince myself I knew all the words and getting ready. It was a quick thing, but the best experience."

Although that brief cameo with Bridgers marked one of Mescal's biggest live experiences to date, she says that hitting the road with Phoebe Green has allowed her to work on the performance side of her craft while also changing the relationship she has with some of her more emotional songs.

"My drummer Meg was recently saying the difference between me on the first day of tour and [the] last day was just incredible. It's been such a catalyst for me to just be like, 'I wrote these for a reason and I'm singing them for a reason.'"

In turn, it has also helped liberate her from the personal pain that inspired tracks like 'Graduating'.

"It does take a while but you feel that click eventually happen. It happened during this live tour, it stopped feeling like a chore and I could have more fun with it."

She is also under no illusion that some fans will attend her shows purely because of the Mescal name, but she is entirely confident that she'll win them round as new members of her fanbase. "I've been singing my whole life. Paul is incredible and it's been amazing to see what's happened for him in the past few years. People might come because of his name, but if they stay then it's because they like the music."

And although her brother might be carving out a career as a Hollywood regular, Mescal has conclusive proof that she – as the youngest of three talented siblings – is in fact their parents' favourite. "I'm on both my parents' lock screen," she jokingly admits. "I'm the baby girl."

For 2023, Mescal promises more music and a string of buzzy performances – including slots at the industry-heavy Great Escape.

"I've been listening to a lot of music that has been all over the place and I don't want to be tied down," she says. "I just can't wait to release 'Homesick' straight after 'Graduating', because it shows an entirely new spectrum to my sound. That's what I'm aiming for."

NICK REILLY

"The tour has been a catalyst for me: 'I wrote these for a reason"

ON COURSE Life has been a whirlwind for Nell since she dropped out of school and released her debut single

IN SYNCH Nell trusts her famous brother's opinion on her music

FAST FACTS

FAMILY TIES Nell's older brother Paul played Connell in the BBC series *Normal People*. They have another brother, Donnacha

WRITE ON She has been writing music for as long as she can remember, but 'Graduating' took just an hour

24 | Rolling Stone | February/March 2023

February/March 2023 | Rolling Stone | 25

Quickfire 7.10

How does the double-page spread article construct a representation of the artist?

Tip

Make sure that the style of writing and the mode of address of your product match the target audience detailed in the brief.

Writing 300 words is a requirement of this brief; it is therefore important that you study the style of writing of the products you research and ensure that what you write for your production reflects the age of the target audience. The article above about Nell Mescal is informal and chatty, as can be seen in the caption for the central photograph: '*Life has been a whirlwind for Nell since she dropped out of school and released her debut single.*' The feature article also includes 'Fast Facts' and lots of conversational quotes from the artist about her life. Accessing the press pack/media kit of magazines similar to the one you want to produce will provide you with some useful information about the target audience.

Tip

Consider how you would construct a representation of Nell Mescal if she was the front cover artist on this magazine. This will allow you to focus on how you would represent this artist through, for example, clothing, gesture and expression which adheres to the codes and conventions and the style of the magazine.

You will need to consider how you want to construct the representation of your artist or band.

Tip

Use the brief as a checklist to ensure you have included all of the required elements.

Link

There is an example of a treatment for a magazine production on page 210 of the Year 1 book, for reference.

Link

Additional information about constructing a storyboard can be found in the Year 1 book, page 238.

Rapid Recall 7.7

What is a treatment?

Planning for the Music Marketing Brief

Once you have completed your research you will need to consider how your findings will impact upon the decisions you make for your production. To do this you will need to plan:

- How you will apply the codes and conventions of your chosen genre identified in your research, including the selection and combination of elements of media language, the use of intertextuality or aspects of hybridity and how you will communicate meaning through, for example, semiotics.
- How you will construct the representation of your artist or band through the use of visual and technical codes. Will you challenge or reflect stereotypical representations of, for example, gender, age or ethnicity? Will your products allow you to show representations of issues or events? Does your artist or band have an ideological perspective you can show through the music video?
- How might the way in which you construct representations reflect contexts, for example social and cultural or political?
- How you will inter-relate your two products to emphasise the cross-media elements. For example, consider how the music video and the magazine article, although they are in different forms, can share distinct elements related to the construction of the artist.
- How you will reflect the industry context in your two products and the ideology of the organisation, in this case the mainstream music artist and record label.

Planning Tasks

- Construct a profile of your target audience. Refer to this profile as you start to construct your production pieces and consider if they will attract and appeal to this target audience.
- Create a pitch or treatment that could be written or presented to the class or a smaller group of your peers. This should outline your main ideas and plan for how you will demonstrate your knowledge and understanding of the theoretical framework. It should also clearly highlight how you intend to address the cross-media elements.

- Conduct a recce of the different locations you intend to include in your music video and photoshoot for your magazine pages or website. For the sample brief you must have at least three locations and a range of images of your artist or band. Your choices of locations should reflect the genre and industry elements of your production. You also need to consider continuity, for example changes in lighting at different times.
- Create a storyboard and mock-ups for your music video, magazine pages or website. These are essential planning devices to aid you in visualising your final products.
- You also need to carefully consider how you will reflect your understanding of the theoretical framework through, for example, genre codes and conventions, technical codes, visual codes, the narrative structure and the use of intertextuality. Ensure that your storyboard and mock-ups encompass the requirements of the brief, for example a range of locations and different shots of your artist or band.
- Produce any other planning tasks you require for this project to help you manage your time and resources, for example a timeline, equipment list, permissions, and health and safety considerations.

When you have completed all your research and planning, and before you start your production, you need to complete your Statement of Aims and Intentions. This aspect of the production is covered in more detail in Chapter 8 of this book.

Consider how the choice of settings contributes to the construction or representations in this music video. Images courtesy of George Francis of Peter Symonds College.

Cross-Media Music Marketing Production: Examples of Student Work

When you have completed your research and planning you are ready to start your cross-media production, as you will now have a clear idea of how to make your two products inter-related, yet different. You will also be more informed regarding how to reflect the theoretical framework in your own production. The screenshots on this and the following page are taken from music videos created by sixth-form students responding to the Eduqas set brief and illustrate some of the key points to bear in mind when creating a media product in this form. Consider how these two students have interpreted elements of the sample brief.

Both students clearly adhere to the requirements to produce a music video for a mainstream artist, this is evident in the construction of the artist's representation and the filming and editing techniques employed. The students have chosen tracks from different music genres and it is clear to see from the stills that they have researched their music genres in detail and have applied their findings to their own production.

Music video stills of *Cruel World* courtesy of Amber Bishop, Peter Symonds College.

Link

Another example of a student music video is shown on page 240 of the Year 1 book.

Tip

Remember that you cannot just film or take photographs anywhere; some locations will require you to ask for permission. This is the case for many public areas, including shopping centres, cemeteries and public buildings. You need to plan your work well in advance, so you can ask for permission.

Consider how they have:

- Included a **range of locations** that are relevant to the chosen genre and reinforce the style of the artist. In *Night Crawling* the settings contrast with each other to create the desired aesthetic, the urban setting with the use of subways and graffiti constructs an edgy feel to the music video and contributes to the powerful representation of the female artist and reflects the chosen music genre. The shots of the graveyard and the church in washed-out colour adds the gothic feel. In *Cruel World* the settings similarly reinforce the music genre. Here there are broad, naturalistic shots of a desolate coastline with the sea and hills creating a sense of space and freedom, contrasted with the personal, more intimate location of the artist's bedroom. Both music videos include the required **performance footage** and use bright lighting for the studio shots, which offers a further chance to construct the artist's representation.

Music video stills of *Night Crawling* courtesy of Diana Zaletova, Peter Symonds College.

Link

Revisit the 'Tips for Success' in creating a music video on page 239 of the Year 1 book.

Tip

There is a range of options regarding how you can present your artist in the music video. They can, as is evident here, be an integral part of the whole video, featuring in the narrative and performing. Alternatively, you can cut between the artist/band performing and the narrative, which may focus on a different set of characters and focus on interpreting the lyrics.

- **A range of technical codes** are employed by both students including establishing shots of the setting, for example the shot of the city at night from the motorway bridge in *Night Crawling* and the natural surroundings in *Cruel World*. Close-ups and direct mode of address are used for the performance shots demonstrating an understanding of the conventions of the form and allowing the artist to engage with the audience. The focus on the guitar being played in *Night Crawling* contributes to the authenticity of the artist.
- In both music videos the **representation of the artist/artists** are very effectively constructed through media language including costume, iconography, expression and gesture. In *Cruel World* the artist's construction is multifaceted. Clothing is employed in the external shots to establish a retro look to the music video supported by props, for example the telephone and the retro car, while the shots of the artist as part of the landscape and the performance footage show another aspect of the performer. The women with the artist who are dressed similarly create a narrative enigma and these sections of the video construct a notion of the surreal to engage the target audience. In *Night Crawling* the clothing and expressions of the artists help in establishing the more edgy feel of this music video, reflecting the chosen genre.

Cross-Media Elements

An option in this brief is to create a functioning website promoting the same new artist and band, and including a homepage and one other linked page. While the student work featured here is not for the same artist as the music video, the website for a music magazine does include some of the requirements on the brief and is for an independent artist, and is therefore useful for illustration.

There is a homepage establishing the music genre, suggesting the focus is independent music artists. This is illustrated by the original animated image of an artist playing a guitar. The simple, minimalist style of the website also has the connotations of less mainstream artists who are credible performers.

One of the linked pages is to an interview with an artist including 200 words of written text and some original images (below). There is also some audio-visual footage of a band in performance.

Quickfire 7.11

What else would need to be included on this website to fulfil the requirements of the brief?

Extracts from the music magazine website courtesy of Michael Shenton of Oldham Sixth Form College.

Cross-Media Products

The second option for the music marketing brief is to create a front cover and double-page spread feature article for a new mainstream music magazine to promote the artist/band you have created. The front covers shown here are student productions that reflect the requirements of the brief and effectively show knowledge and understanding of the media theoretical framework.

The two magazine production pieces shown here are the print options created by the students who produced the music videos *Night Crawling* (*Paradox* magazine) and *Cruel World* (*Split* magazine) featured earlier. Consider how these students have:

- Made very clear links between the two products and forms.
- Demonstrated evidence of research into existing products that has then been applied to their music videos.
- Reflected the codes and conventions of a mainstream music magazine through the layout and design.
- Clearly targeted the intended audience, for example 'Youngest Artists of 2021'.

- Established the link between the products by the use of the music artist featured in the video on the front cover, reinforcing the representation.
- The students have further explored and developed the representation of the artist through the images used on the double-page spread. The direct mode of address of the female artist in the full-page image in *Paradox* accompanied by the handwritten style font echoes the edgy image constructed in the music video. The images in *Split* reinforce the quirky, eccentric persona of the artist in *Cruel World* through the use of clothing and expression.
- In *Split*, the choice of the double-page feature article allows the student to demonstrate their research into similar products as evidenced by the appropriate mode of address and the use of the Q&A format which further develops the star persona of the artist and appeals to the intended audience. The article also references decisions made in the music video, establishing a clear link between the two products.
- Pull quotes contribute to the construction of meaningful representations in both magazines; *'Women Can Achieve Just as Much as Men'* and *'When People Want to Escape Reality, This Song is for Them'*.

Tip

Consider how these students have demonstrated the codes and conventions of a mainstream music magazine in their productions.

Tip

Consider how you could exploit all the opportunities to construct representations in the print production through, for example, cover lines, choice of topic for the feature article, copy and pull quotes.

Tip

Look back at the stills from the music video on page 279. Consider how you can tell the *ERA* magazine and the video at the top of page 279 are part of the same cross-media production.

Component 3 Summary

- This component is the non-exam assessment. It is 30% of the final A Level qualification and is worth 60 marks. It is internally assessed in your centre and externally moderated by WJEC.
- This component synthesises your knowledge and understanding of the media theoretical framework you have gained throughout the course and requires you to apply this to a practical production.
- The A Level production is cross-media and must be based on two media forms.
- A set of production briefs will be released each year on 1 March in the year prior to your assessment and will be published on the WJEC/Eduqas website. The details of the brief will change each year, including the intended audience and the industry context, but the following briefs will always be set:

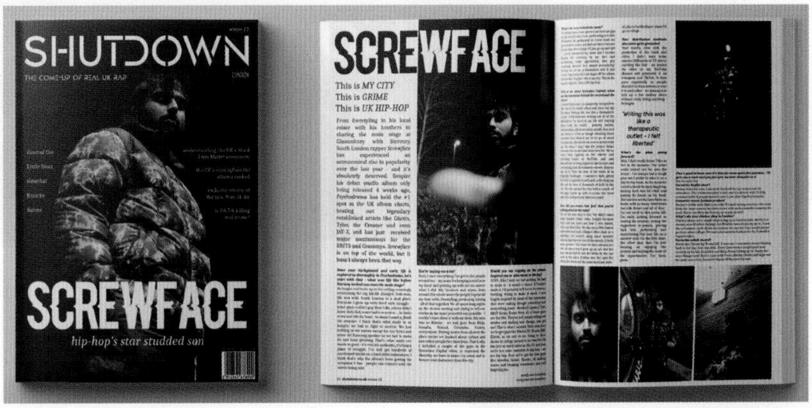

- **Television**: a cross-media production to include a sequence from a new television programme and related print or online products.
- **Advertising and marketing: music**: a cross-media production to include an original music video for a new or local/ unsigned artist or band and related print or online products.
- **Advertising and marketing: film**: a cross-media production to include a print marketing campaign for a new film, and related audio-visual or online products.The cross-media production must not include a compete short film, film sequence or trailer.
- **Magazines**: a cross-media production to include a new print magazine and related audio-visual or online products. You are not required to create websites through programming languages such as HTML. It is acceptable to use web design templates but the content must be original.

- All images used in the production work must be your own.
- You must complete an individual media production, group work is not permitted. However, you can use unassessed people who will be under your sole direction.
- The focus of the assessment is your ability to demonstrate your knowledge and understanding of media language, representation, media industries and audiences.
- You should not spend longer than 16 weeks on this component.

You must complete a Statement of Aims and Intentions **before** you embark upon your production. This gives you the opportunity to outline your aims and intentions for the cross-media production and requires you to explain how you have applied the media theoretical framework.

- You must also complete a cover sheet to accompany your production, detailing further information, for example the unassessed people in your production and the software packages you have used.
- You will be monitored by your teacher at key stages in the production process.

Tip

Consider how the student who produced *Screwface* has addressed the Assessment Objective by meeting the requirements of the print option of the brief using media language to communicate meanings and construct representations.

Tip

When you are constructing your production pieces, consider how you are going to reflect your knowledge and understanding of representation. You need to decide whether you want to conform to, or challenge, the typical stereotypes of your chosen sub-genre.

Component 3: How Will I Be Assessed?

This component assesses your ability to:

- Create media products for an intended audience, by applying knowledge and understanding of the theoretical framework of media to communicate meaning. It is worth 30% of the overall assessment and 60 marks. You are required to:
  - Produce a statement of aims and intentions to create a cross-media production for an intended audience. [10 marks]
  - Create a cross-media production that meets the requirements of the set brief, including suitability for the chosen form, genre, industry context and target audience. [20 marks]
  - Create a cross-media production that uses media language to communicate meanings and construct representations. [30 marks]

Tip

Consider how you could apply any of the theories or theoretical perspectives you have studied, for example feminist theories, to the products you create and how you can highlight this in your Statement of Aims and Intentions.

Tip

There is a pro-forma Statement of Aims and Intentions available on the WJEC/ Eduqas website, which must be submitted with your production.

8 Component 3: Statement of Aims and Intentions

The Statement of Aims and Intentions is a requirement of the non-exam assessment and is worth 10 marks. It allows you to outline the ways in which you have applied the theoretical framework in response to the cross-media production brief and how you have targeted the intended audience.

It should be completed after you have decided how to interpret the production brief and **after** the research and planning stages but **before** the production stage, and you should submit it to your teacher.

The Statement of Aims and Intentions must be approximately 500 words in length. Its purpose is to enable you to outline your plans for meeting the requirements of the cross-media brief and to demonstrate the ways in which you will apply your knowledge and understanding of the media theoretical framework.

The Statement of Aims and Intentions must be submitted to your teacher before production work commences. You will use the template on the cover sheet provided by WJEC/Eduqas to guide you and you will be required to explain the following where relevant.

Tip

The Statement of Aims and Intentions must be closely linked to the two forms you have chosen for your production brief.

Tip

This task is not reflective or an evaluation, it must be completed **before** you embark upon the chosen production.

How and Why Will You Use Media Language in Your Cross-Media Production?

- The choices you make about the selection and combination of elements of media language you intend to use in your product.
- Your use of any intertextual references or genre hybridity.
- How you intend to use the codes and conventions of the chosen sub-genre to communicate meaning.
- The message you intend to communicate in your product. This may show your understanding of semiotics and the ideology of your product.

The Statement of Aims and Intentions helps you to formalise your planning.

How and Why Will You Construct Representations of Individuals, Groups and Issues/Events?

The specific techniques you intend to use to construct representations including:

- Visual codes, technical codes and language.
- How the representations construct versions of reality.
- The inclusion of under-represented or misrepresented groups or individuals.
- How the way in which you construct the representations communicates meaning.
- The reinforcing or challenging/subverting of stereotypes.
- How the representations you have constructed will relate to context, for example social, cultural, historical or political.

How Will You Target Your Intended Audience?

The methods you intend to use to position/appeal to the target audience, for example:

- The elements of media language you will incorporate and how this will target your audience.
- The mode of address that will suit your audience – formal or informal?
- How you will reflect the industry context in order to target the intended audience.

How Will Your Production Conform to its Industry Context?

The production processes, distribution and marketing, scheduling or regulatory issues, including:

- How the product reflects the values of the organisation, for example if it is a television sequence for the BBC as a public service broadcaster or a music video for an artist signed to an independent record company.
- How the production context and processes shape the media product.
- The demographics and psychographics of your target audience in relation to the industry context.

How Will Your Cross-Media Production Demonstrate Digital Convergence?

- As this is a cross-media production, the two forms you choose must demonstrate their links across different media platforms.
- You should use subject-specific terminology to demonstrate your knowledge and understanding of the chosen form.

Your teachers will check your research and planning work and the Statement of Aims and Intentions, and sign the relevant authentication statement on the cover sheet.

Tip

It is very important that you reflect the aims and intentions you have written in your statement in what you create for your production. Your teacher will assess your production in the light of what you say in your statement.

Tip

It is also important that you complete your cover sheet in as much detail as possible, as this will help the moderator who may look at your work.

The Cover Sheet

The Statement of Aims and Intentions is completed as part of a cover sheet that will be submitted with your production.

One part of the cover sheet will be completed by you and will give details of key aspects of your production work including:

- The software you used in constructing your production.
- Information about any non-original music you have used.
- Details of any non-assessed participants you have used in your production.

You and your teacher are required to sign the cover sheet to authenticate your work at three key stages during the process. This will be firstly when you have completed your planning and subsequently at two further times where you will be required to discuss details of your audio-visual footage or show any draft work you have produced. Your teacher will also complete a section with their comments and marks.

The cover sheet will be completed by you and your teacher to authenticate the work you have produced.

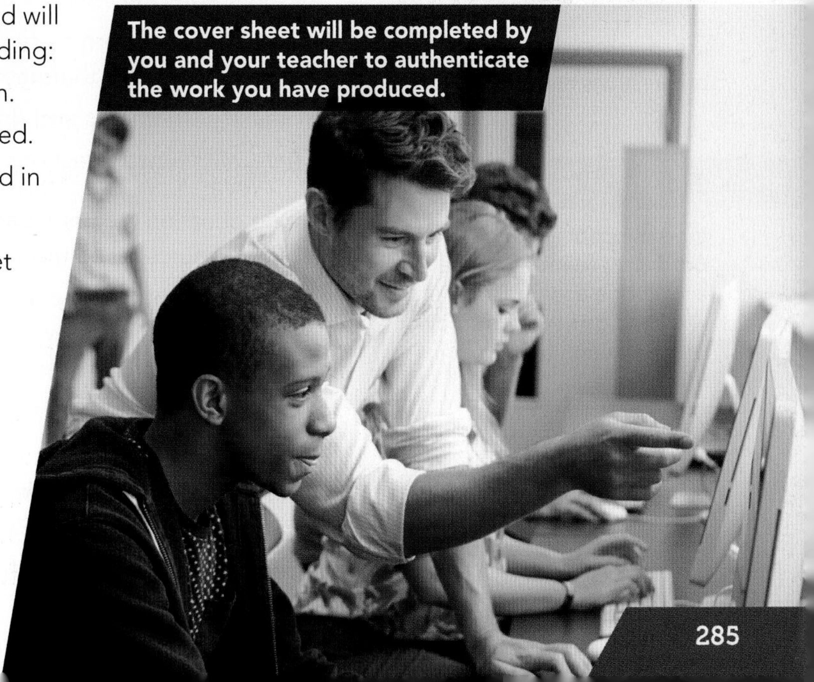

9 Examination Preparation and Tips

Component 1: The Media Products, Industries and Audiences

OVERVIEW

In this assessment you are expected to:

- Analyse critically and compare how media products, including products outside the commercial mainstream, construct and communicate meanings through media language.
- Use a range of complex theories of media studies and use specialist subject-specific terminology appropriately in a developed way.
- Debate key questions relating to the social, cultural, political and economic role of the media.
- Construct and develop a sustained line of reasoning that is coherent, relevant, substantiated and logically structured in an extended response.

Tip

Across Section A as a whole, there will always be one unseen audio-visual resource and one unseen print-based resource.

Tip

The audio-visual unseen resource will always be the first question, the resource may link to the media language or representation question. It is important to read the questions carefully at the start of the examination; you will be given 1 minute to do this. This will allow you to see the order of questions and their focus.

Tip

In your response to the unseen products you must use the knowledge and understanding you have gained from studying related examples from the set forms in class.

Section A: Analysing Media Language and Representation

This section assesses media language and representation in relation to two of the media forms studied for Section A: advertising and marketing, music video **or** newspapers.

> Section A assesses Assessment Objective 2: Apply knowledge and understanding of the theoretical framework of media to:
>
> - analyse media products, including in relation to their contexts and through the use of academic theories
> - make judgements and draw conclusions
>
> There will be two questions in Section A

- One question will assess **media language** in relation to an unseen audio-visual or print resource taken from any of the forms studied in this section.
- One question will assess **representation** through comparison of one set product and an unseen audio-visual or print resource from any of the forms studied for this section. You may be required to compare products from the same or different media forms. This is an extended response question and reference to media contexts will be required.

In the question with an unseen audio-visual resource you will see it three times:

- **First viewing**: watch the unseen resource.
- **Second viewing**: watch the unseen resource and make notes.

You will then have 5 minutes to make further notes:

- **Third viewing**: watch the unseen resource and make final notes.

Tip

At A Level you are expected to apply the theories you have learned in relation to the media products to be analysed.

Tip

Taking effective notes is a skill that can be learned. It is important to develop a strategy of taking notes that works for you. Page 245 of the Year 1 book has tips on taking notes.

Tip

Read the questions carefully so that you can focus your note taking more effectively.

Sample Questions

The following questions are taken from the A Level Sample Assessment Materials (SAMS) booklet which includes an example paper and mark scheme. The SAMS has not been updated to include new set products as the aim is to give an indication of the types of questions that may appear in the examination and an indication of possible responses (Indicative Content). The questions here are accompanied by the general information about what you may include in a response and can be applied to the new set products you are studying.

Question 1: Sample Question

1 0 Compare how audiences are positioned by the representations in this *Save the Children* advertisement and the *WaterAid* advertisement you have studied.
[30 marks]

In your answer you must:

- consider how the representations construct versions of reality
- consider the similarities and differences in how audiences are positioned by the representations
- make judgements and draw conclusions about how far the representations relate to relevant media contexts.

This question assesses AO2 1 and 3: Apply knowledge and understanding of the theoretical framework to:

- analyse media products, including in relation to their contexts
- make judgements and draw conclusions

In an extended response question you must spend time thinking about what the question is asking, looking carefully at how it is constructed and the words and phrases used. The *Save the Children* unseen resource *Most Shocking Second a Day* can be viewed here: https://www.youtube.com/watch?v=RBQ-IoHfimQ.

Tip

In extended response questions, you are required to construct and develop a sustained line of reasoning. Your argument must be logical, coherent and relevant and you need to make sure that the points you make are fully substantiated and that you refer in detail to the products.

If you understand the requirements of the examination paper you will be able to plan your preparation.

Develop a note-taking strategy that works for you.

Tip

From Summer 2023 a new question numbering system will be introduced and the questions in this chapter have been amended accordingly.

Tip

The audio-visual unseen resource, *Save the Children*, can be viewed at: https://www.youtube.com/watch?v=RBQ-IoHfimQ.

Tip

Notice the mark tariff for the question; this will guide you on how much you need to write.

Key Term

Command words
These are the key words you need to look out for in examination questions, which will guide you in what you need to include in your response.

- **Compare**: this is an AO2 **command word** requiring you to consider the similarities and differences between products and make judgements and draw conclusions.

Addressing the Bullet Points

Here you will be required to compare how the two advertisements are mediated through selection and construction in order to construct a particular representation and position audiences including through:

- technical and audio codes
- editing
- use of visual codes.

The following Indicative Content is a general response to the question to allow you to apply the points to any unseen or set product.

Analyse how the representations construct versions of reality.

- Representations in advertisements are constructed to encode a viewpoint and position audiences in a particular way. Different advertisements will construct different versions of reality in order to engage the audience. For example, advertisements for beauty products and others with a consumerist ideology tend to be aspirational, selling a lifestyle that is not a reflection of reality.
- Charity campaigns and those seeking to raise awareness of an event or issue will create a specific version of reality in order to reach the audience. In the *Save the Children* advertisement the world is created as realistic in order to shake audiences out of their complacency.

Tip

Consider how you could use the theories of Stuart Hall in analysing these products.

Tip

It is important to produce a specific rather than a general response and support your points with examples from both the resources.

Analyse the key **similarities** in how audiences are positioned by the representations. Consider the following in relation to a discussion of advertising products:

- The aim of the advertisement is to establish a relationship with the audience, this is particularly the case in those that are raising awareness and may want the audience to respond actively.
- The audience may be positioned emotionally by the advertisements as they may include situations and characters that are relatable to the audience with whom they may feel empathy. They create a social discourse within the parameters of the advertisement in order to position the audience.
- Technical and audio codes position audiences within the world of the product. For example, the use of close-ups can be both engaging and uncomfortable where the producers may want the audience to examine their preconceptions, for example in *Super. Human*. Audio codes are powerful in positioning audiences where they may, for example, have associations with a particular soundtrack or the choice of the voiceover narrator. Consider how you can support your points with specific examples of similar technical codes used for the same effect in the two products you are comparing.
- There is usually a key character/characters in the advertising products that position the audience, encouraging identification and empathy. This use of personalisation is effective in establishing a relationship between the brand and the audience. The construction of these representations and their effect on the audience may be similar.
- Some advertisements may position audiences through the use of locations and settings. In *Save the Children* the narrative is completely located in London, a familiar location, however both the mise-en-scène and the narrative situation change as the child's secure, familiar environment is affected by war. Other advertisements may challenge accepted ideas of locations, for example charity advertisements focusing on other countries. Charity and raising awareness campaigns tend to use 'real' locations that are relatable to audiences, while advertisements for high end consumable products may use more aspirational, escapist settings to appeal to audiences.

- The construction and mediation of the product can be effective in positioning the audience. An advertisement has limited time to construct its narrative and hook the audience. The elements of the narrative, for example the disruption and resolution, are important and a common convention of some advertisements whose aim is to raise awareness, is to end with a more positive message to make the audience feel good and more inclined to respond positively. Consider how you can develop your analysis of the construction of the products through the inclusion of specific examples, for example the disruption or resolution and its possible effect on the audience, for example the more upbeat ending of *Super. Human.*
- The ideology of the product's message may be similar. For example, some advertisements aim to make the audience feel privileged and therefore engender a sense of responsibility for helping or donating. Other campaigns may challenge audiences' preconceived ideas about issues or social groups through the encoding of ideas associated with the brand.

Tip

You must discuss similarities and differences as indicated by the bullet points but there is no requirement for these to be covered equally. There may be more similarities than differences for example.

Analyse the key **differences** between how audiences are positioned by the representations. Consider the following in relation to a discussion of advertising products:

- The way in which the audience is positioned may differ. Some advertisements, particularly those whose producers feel that audiences may have compassion fatigue, may use more positive representations or humour to position audiences. In contrast, in *Save the Children* the aim is to shock the audience; the girl's situation gradually deteriorates making the audience feel helpless.
- The purpose of the advertisement may mean the audience is positioned differently. The *Save the Children* advert's aim is to place the audience in the position of a child caught up in war, specifically, in this case, the Syrian war, by setting the advertisement on the streets of London. The young girl is part of a secure community of family, friends and school; her vulnerability and innocence are emphasised as her world falls apart. An advertisement for a consumable product, for example a fragrance or beauty product whose aim is to make the audience want to purchase the product, has a different focus and will therefore employ different strategies to engage and position the audience, for example bright colours, high key lighting, attractive models and the construction of an aspirational world and lifestyle.
- The construction of representations may differ from those that are more realistic as the advertisement is concerned with portraying real-life issues and events, to those that are more constructed to create a world of aspiration and escapism.

Make judgements and draw conclusions about how far the representations relate to relevant **media contexts**.

Making judgements and drawing conclusions is a key element of the Assessment Objective in this question. The clue is in the command words 'how far', which encourages you to make a judgment in your response. You may want to refer to the following in relation to this question with a focus on advertisements in relation to contexts.

Social and Cultural Contexts

- Advertisements reflect society and are key indicators of social and cultural change. This will have been evident in your study of historical and contemporary advertisements in preparation for this examination. The representations constructed by media producers evolve to more accurately reflect society. In contemporary examples of the form, representations are generally more diverse than in the past. Audiences expect to see representations of themselves in advertisements, for example make-up for all skin colours and to see sections of society previously under-represented, for example disability (*Super. Human.*).

- Some advertisements use representations to encourage audiences to examine preconceived ideas they may have about gender, age, other social groups and issues. Consider how you could demonstrate this understanding with reference to the products you are required to analyse in the examination.
- There is a range of possible audience responses linked to cultural context, such as where audiences live, political views, social class, gender and age. Some advertisements shock audiences into re-examining their viewpoints and beliefs.

Tip

The unseen products chosen link to the study of the *Daily Mirror* set product, the expectation is that you will transfer your knowledge and understanding of the form when you are analysing the unseen products.

Question 2: Sample Question

In this sample paper, Question 2 is the unseen media language question where you will be given an unseen resource from a media form you have studied for Section A. The form selected here is newspapers.

Question 2 0 is based on Resource A, the front page of *The Sun* newspaper (November 2016) and the front page of *The Daily Mail* newspaper (November 2016). Study Resource A carefully an use both front pages when answering the question.

2 0 How does media language incorporate viewpoints and ideologies in these front pages of *The Sun* and *The Daily Mail*?

Note: Both front pages referred to in the question can be found here:

https://www.theguardian.com/us-news/gallery/2016/nov/10/newspaper-front-pages-cover-aftermath-of-trumps-victory-in-pictures. **[15 marks]**

Tip

Although here the requirement is to analyse two front pages, it may be that in some cases there will be only one unseen newspaper front page to analyse.

This question is assessing AO2 1: Apply knowledge and understanding of the theoretical framework of media to analyse media products

In this question both products must be analysed. The command word is 'How', asking you to apply your knowledge and understanding of the theoretical framework of media.

Tip

In this type of question, where the focus is media language, you can demonstrate your understanding of the theoretical framework by applying theories, for example semiotics, and theoretical perspectives.

The focus of your response should explore examples of how media language constructs viewpoints and ideologies in the newspaper front pages, such as:

- Both UK newspapers covered this event suggesting their viewpoint is that the US election result is significant to Britain, reflecting the importance of the relationship between Britain and the USA in the post-Brexit context.

The Sun front page

- How the combination of visual codes communicates messages and constructs viewpoints. For example, in *The Sun*, how the juxtaposition of Homer and a cartoon Donald Trump and the headline 'D'oh' synonymous with Homer, signifies the surreal nature of the election outcome and the viewpoint that things have turned out badly.
- The iconography of the stars and stripes is a recognisable visual signifier of the USA, which is here being ridiculed by the newspaper.
- The use of **language** to convey a viewpoint, for example the use of informal language, for example, the subheading reinforces the viewpoint that the result is not being taken seriously.
- The **copy** on the front page references *The Simpsons* predicting that a Trump presidency would be problematic for the USA, implying a viewpoint that the outcome is negative and previously unbelievable.
- The combination of these elements of media language conveys a less serious tone and potentially reflects a belief that the result will have a less ominous impact than some newspapers were predicting.
- Viewpoints are constructed through **intertextuality**. The front page is constructed around an intertextual reference to a popular TV text (*The Simpsons*) that is associated with humour and satire, incorporating a sense of mockery of the election outcome.

The Daily Mail front page

- The use of **hyperbolic language** in the headline establishes a clear viewpoint that the election result is of extreme importance and will have a dramatic impact on Britain as well as the USA.
- The selection of the main headline, '*Trumpquake*', sensationalises the event and adopts an informal **mode of address**, reflecting the pre-election image of Trump as a populist businessman. The use of an extended metaphor ('*seismic*', '*shockwaves*', '*quake*', '*swept*') reinforces the significance of the event, likening Trump's victory to a force of nature.
- The use of **emotive language** ('*electrifying human drama*', '*revolt by America's forgotten white working class*') engages the audience by humanising the political event, presenting the viewpoint that this is seen by some as a positive outcome.
- The selection of the **main image** anchors the use of language by representing Trump as a powerful, statesmanlike politician. This choice of a strong and positive central image resonates with the *Daily Mail's* right-wing ideology and implicit support of Donald Trump as a Republican.
- This is reinforced by the **technical codes** used, for example the slightly low-angle camera shot, the light shining on Trump's face and the dominant position of the clenched fist.
- The viewpoint that Trump won because he appealed to the USA's forgotten working-class white people also positions the *Daily Mail* ideologically as supportive of this demographic, arguably appealing to their target audience.

Tip

In your response you are expected to explore examples from both front pages, but it is not expected that these are analysed equally. However, responses in the higher bands will cover both products in an even way, will explore media language, viewpoints and ideologies in detail, and may be informed by relevant theories.

Tip

Although the bullet points are related to the specific unseen newspaper products used in this question, the points suggested for inclusion in a response can be transferred to other media language questions focusing on newspapers.

Section B: Understanding Media Industries and Audiences

This section will assess knowledge and understanding of media industries, audiences and media contexts in relation to any of the forms studied for this section: advertising, film, newspapers, radio and video games.

Tip

Although Question 3 will always be a stepped question, the amount of steps and the mark distribution between parts of questions may differ.

> This section assesses AO1: Demonstrate knowledge and understanding of:
> - the theoretical framework of media
> - contexts of media and their influence on media products and processes

Question 3: Sample Question

This is a stepped question assessing knowledge and understanding of media industries in relation to one form studied.

3 1 Briefly explain what is meant by distribution. [2 marks]

> This question assesses AO1 1a: Demonstrate knowledge of the theoretical framework

Tip

In this section there will be lower tariff questions that will only assess knowledge or knowledge and understanding. Look out for these and make sure you do not spend too long answering them. Although Question 3 1 has a low tariff, you must complete a response in enough detail to be awarded full marks.

Two marks are awarded for a good, accurate explanation evident through exemplification and/or detail, for example:

- The process of making a media product available to audiences/users so that they can consume it, which includes aspects of marketing such as creating a campaign, etc.

The marker will credit all valid responses to this question.

One mark is awarded for a basic explanation, which may be incomplete or contain some inaccuracy, for example:

- Supplying a media product.
- Marketing a media product.

Tip

The command word for Question 3 1 is 'explain', which tells you the question is assessing AO1 and you should give specific information to demonstrate your understanding of an aspect of the theoretical framework.

3 2 How have recent technological changes had an impact on the production and distribution of newspapers? [10 marks]

This question assesses AO1 1a and b: Demonstrate knowledge and understanding of the theoretical framework of media

Responses will demonstrate knowledge and understanding of recent technological changes in the newspaper industry and the production and distribution of newspapers, such as:

- How technology has impacted on traditional methods of production and distribution.
- Traditional newspaper distribution still exists with physical print copies distributed via retail outlets, although numbers are declining.
- The impact of recent technological change, such as:
  - print readership and the traditional newspaper industry being in steady decline; slumping sales; declining audiences – the newspaper being less popular than broadcast and online media
  - increased use of online search, including Google, which has changed the habits of readers of news
  - more consumer interest in online news sites and apps able to provide news 'as it happens' across a range of digital platforms (e.g. BBC News, Twitter)
  - attempts to combat decreasing trends in popularity by increasing use of online media, including official newspaper websites (such as *Mirror Online*) and social media
  - social media has created greater opportunities for citizen journalism and different versions of news.

Tip

In higher tariff questions like 3 2, you will be expected to demonstrate your understanding of media industries and then support this with reference to your set product. For example, in some questions a second stem of the question may say: Refer to (set product) to support your points. This can be seen in question 3 4.

Tip

Read the instructions related to the questions carefully, you will be told when you are expected to draw together your knowledge and understanding from across the whole course.

3 3 What is a media conglomerate? [1 mark]

This question assesses AO1 1a: Demonstrate knowledge of the theoretical framework of media

One mark is awarded for a correct definition, for example:

- A company or group that owns numerous companies involved in media production or distribution.

3 4 Explain how ownership shapes media products. Refer to *The Daily Mirror* to support your points. [12 marks]

This question assesses AO1 1a and b: Demonstrate knowledge and understanding of the theoretical framework of media

This question provides you with the opportunity to draw together knowledge and understanding from across the full course of study. In addition to points related to media industries, responses should be rewarded for drawing together knowledge and understanding of other areas of the theoretical framework such as media language, representations and audiences, or of media contexts.

Responses should demonstrate knowledge and understanding of media ownership and how it may shape products, such as:

- the nature of media ownership – for example, conglomeration, vertical integration and diversification
- the economic and commercial benefits of this kind of ownership
- the ideological implications of this kind of ownership
- the importance of funding to media products

Tip

Notice the two stems of Question 3 4. The first stem guides you to discuss what you know about the newspaper industry. The second stem asks that you apply this knowledge and understanding to your set product. This question is not asking for just an analysis of the *Daily Mirror*, it is a broader question.

- issues of political bias and editorial control
- theoretical approaches such as power and media industries.

Responses should refer to the *Daily Mirror* to support points made and show an understanding of how ownership may have shaped the product, such as:

- the *Daily Mirror* is owned by parent company Reach plc – the biggest newspaper publisher in the UK
- this ownership by a media conglomerate means the newspaper has a commercial imperative to achieve high circulation and make profit as a populist, tabloid newspaper
- the newspaper has a 'centre-left' stance and political bias towards the Labour party, evident in, for example, its concern over the future of the NHS and the reporting of the accusations of the breaking of lockdown rules by Conservative MPs
- the newspaper markets itself as *'the intelligent tabloid'*, that aims to *'inform and analyse'*.

Responses in the higher bands are likely to draw together knowledge and understanding of other areas of the theoretical framework and/or media contexts, for example:

- news values shape the representations and ideologies in the newspaper as much as ownership, for example the *Daily Mirror* often uses personalisation to highlight social issues of concern to its readership
- the need to target and appeal to its working-class, mass audience shapes the content and style of the newspaper as much as ownership, for example the paper's emphasis on sport and human interest stories
- the purchase in 2018 of the Express newspaper group and the renaming of the company as Reach plc
- ownership by a media conglomerate shapes the newspaper in terms of its tendency to reinforce dominant discourses and ideologies around, for example, law and order
- the political context of contemporary Britain shapes the newspaper's agenda, for example the reporting of tax cuts for funders of the Conservative party reflects contemporary concerns around equality in society and transparency in politics.

Tip

In Question 3 4 you are expected to refer to the pages of the *Daily Mirror* that have been chosen for study in your centre. This will be a different edition of the newspaper from the one studied for Section A.

Question 4: Sample Question

This will be a stepped question assessing knowledge and understanding of audiences in relation to a different media form from that assessed in Question 3.

4 1 Explain how national and global audiences can be reached through different media technologies and platforms. Refer *to Late Night Woman's Hour* to support your points. [8 marks]

This question assesses AO1 1a and b: Demonstrate knowledge and understanding of the theoretical framework of media

Responses will demonstrate knowledge and understanding of media audiences and how national and global audiences can be reached through different media technologies and platforms, such as:

- the meaning of and differences between national and global audiences
- the role of the BBC historically in providing content for both audiences, for example through the World Service

Tip

Responses to Question 4 1 may refer to Shirky's audience theories.

- the importance of radio as a global medium, easily distributed globally. This has further developed with the progress of digital technology facilitating the distribution of content across different digital platforms to reach different audiences more effectively, through, for example, BBC Sounds
- radio as a portable medium that can be accessed in a range of locations and via a range of devices to suit the lifestyle of different audiences
- podcasts, a relatively recent development, have broadened the reach of radio and in particular appeal to younger listeners
- for most radio programmes there are opportunities for audiences to listen across different platforms – the live broadcast, on the specially created podcasts and via the BBC website and BBC Sounds
- radio programmes also use social media, for example Twitter, to access and engage audiences, thus broadening the national and global reach of content.

Tip

Remember that Question 4 will assess a different form from that assessed in Question 3 and may assess more than one form.

Tip

In response to Question 4 2 you may refer to fandom as a theoretical perspective to support your analysis.

4 2 How do media organisations meet the needs of specialised audiences? Refer to *Late Night Woman's Hour* to support your points. [12 marks]

This question assesses AO1 1a and 1b: Demonstrate knowledge and understanding of the theoretical framework of media

Responses will demonstrate knowledge and understanding of some of the following:

- the difference between mass and niche/specialised audiences
- an understanding that the BBC, the producer of the set radio products, is a public service broadcaster and as such has a remit to cater for specialised audiences
- the role of a public service broadcaster, for example in terms of educating and informing, as well as entertaining
- Radio 4 as a speech-led broadcasting channel and its schedule, which caters for specialised audiences
- measures the BBC has taken and outlined in its report to target a younger specialised audience.

Responses should give examples from the set radio products for how they meet the needs of specialised audiences, which may include reference to:

- the choice of presenter
- language and mode of address, which may be aimed at a younger and/or more specialised audience
- scheduling time for those audiences listening live
- availability of the programme across a range of digital platforms to meet the needs of more diverse audiences with different listening habits
- the subject of the programme/podcast, and its interest to a specialised audience. In the case of a podcast, this may include content that would not be appropriate for mainstream broadcast and this may appeal to more specialised audiences
- guests that may appeal to a more specialised audience.

Tip

Consider what specific examples you would give from the radio set product you have studied to support your points in Question 4.

Additional Example Paper

This additional example paper was produced by WJEC/Eduqas to provide further examples of questions. The products referred to may have changed since writing so may not include the new set products you are studying but the media forms will be the same. The questions can therefore be used as a guideline for what to expect in the examination.

Section A: Analysing Representation and Media Language

Representation

Question 1 0 is based on the unseen audio-visual resource and the music video you have studied: *Formation* or *Dream.*

The audio-visual resource consists of the *Guinness: Compton Cowboys* television advertisement, released in 2017, which can be watched on YouTube.

1 0 Compare the ideologies conveyed through the representations in this television advertisement and the music video you have studied.

In your answer, you must:

- **consider how representations convey ideologies**
- **consider the similarities and differences in the ideologies conveyed**
- **make judgements and draw conclusions about how far social and cultural contexts affect the representations. [30 marks]**

Stretch and Challenge 9.1

Use this additional example paper to practise writing under timed conditions. Remember that in the exam you will have 2 hours and 15 minutes to complete the whole paper.

Stretch and Challenge 9.2

Using the previous sample paper as a guide, work out which Assessment Objectives are being targeted in the questions on this additional paper.

Media Language

Question 2 is based on an unseen film poster for *Let Me In,* released in 2010. Study the film poster carefully before answering the question.

2 0 Explore how codes and conventions create meaning in this film poster. [15 marks]

Section B: Understanding Media Industries and Audiences

3 1 Briefly explain what is meant by diversification in media industries. [2 marks]

3 2 Explain the impact of recent technological changes on the video games industry. Refer to *Assassin's Creed III: Liberation* to support your points. [8 marks]

3 3 Explain how the producers of video games ensure their financial success. Refer to *Assassin's Creed III: Liberation* to support your points. [15 marks]

4 1 Explain how advertisements target audiences. Refer to the *WaterAid* advertisement you have studied to support your points. [8 marks]

4 2 Explain how historical contexts influence audience interpretations of media products. Refer to the *Tide* advertisement you have studied to support your points. [12 marks]

Tip

In Question 3 3, you will be rewarded for drawing together knowledge and understanding from across your full course of study, including different areas of the theoretical framework and media contexts.

Component 2: Media Forms and Products in Depth

OVERVIEW

In this assessment you are expected to:

- Analyse critically how media products construct and communicate meanings through the interaction of media language and audience response.
- Use and reflect critically upon a range of complex theories of Media Studies, and use specialist subject-specific terminology appropriately and in a developed way.
- Debate critically key questions relating to the social, cultural and economic role of the media through sustained discursive writing.
- Construct and develop a sustained line of reasoning that is coherent, relevant, substantiated and logically structured in an extended response.

Tip

As the total number of marks available in each section of the exam is the same, you should divide your time evenly across the three sections of the paper, spending about 50 minutes on each.

Tip

Make sure you spend a few minutes planning your response. A mindmap or a short essay plan comprising a few bullet points is a useful way of organising your ideas. Leave enough time at the end of the exam to go back over your answers too. Check that you have answered the question and that you have used relevant theories and subject-specific terminology where appropriate.

Tip

Check which theories you need to be able to apply to the products you have studied. This information is provided at the end of each section in Chapter 5 and in the grid on page 240 of Chapter 6. You can also cross-reference this by looking at the A Level Media Studies specification in the Eduqas section of the WJEC website.

The examination assesses your knowledge and understanding of media language, representation, media industries, audiences and media contexts in relation to television, magazines and online media.

As discussed in Chapter 6, the exam paper is divided into three sections – one for each of the media forms that you have studied in depth:

- Section A is on Television
- Section B is on Magazines
- Section C is on Online media.

In each section, there will be **either** one two-part question **or** one extended response question on the set products you have studied for that particular media form. Each part of a two-part question will be on a different set product.

Preparing for the Exam

In order to prepare for the Component 2 exam, you will need to go back over the set products you have studied for each of the three media forms.

Although you will need to look at all four areas of the theoretical framework, the specific aspects of media language, representation, media industries and audiences that you need to revise for each media form and product will vary. Information regarding the specific aspects of the theoretical framework that need to be covered for each of the set products can be found in the A Level Media Studies specification, which is available in the Eduqas section of the WJEC website.

Sample Assessment Materials

Section A: Television in a Global Age

Although there are three options in Section A, the questions are all the same except for the television products that they refer to. Which question you answer will depend on the set products you have studied.

The sample question shown here is in two parts. You need to make sure that you answer both parts of the question. It is also important to note that you cannot mix and match options; if you use Option 1 for the first part of the question you cannot then switch to Option 2 or Option 3 for the second part.

Remember that two-part questions could feature in any of the three sections of the Component 2 exam paper.

Option 1: *Peaky Blinders* and *The Bridge*

11. To what extent can the set episode of *Peaky Blinders* be seen as postmodern? [15 marks]

12. Television production takes place within an economic context. Discuss the influence of economic factors on *The Bridge*. [15 marks]

Option 2: *Black Mirror* and *The Returned*

21. To what extent can the set episode of *Black Mirror* be seen as postmodern? [15 marks]

22. Television production takes place within an economic context. Discuss the influence of economic factors on *The Returned*. [15 marks]

Option 3: *Killing Eve* and *Tehran*

31. To what extent can the set episode of *Killing Eve* be seen as postmodern? [15 marks]

32. Television production takes place within an economic context. Discuss the influence of economic factors on *Tehran*. [15 marks]

Tip

The questions shown here are taken from the Sample Assessment Materials published on the Eduqas website in 2017. While the questions themselves are the same, the set products referred to in the questions have been changed to reflect subsequent updates to the specification.

Assessment Objectives

The first part of this sample question is addressing two assessment objectives:

- **AO2 1**: Apply knowledge and understanding of the theoretical framework of media to **analyse media products**, including in relation to their contexts and through the use of academic theories
- **AO2 3**: Apply knowledge and understanding of the theoretical framework of media to **make judgements and draw conclusions**

More specifically, the question is assessing your ability to apply knowledge and understanding of postmodern theory to the set television product you have studied, and to make judgements and draw conclusions about the extent to which it is postmodern.

To be awarded a mark in the upper band:

- your analysis of the set episode should be perceptive, insightful and informed by a detailed knowledge of postmodern theory
- the judgements and conclusions you make should be fully supported with detailed reference to specific aspects of the set episode.

Tip

Questions that use phrases such as 'To what extent ...?', 'How far can ...?' or 'How important is ... ?' require you to make judgements and draw conclusions. It is important that you engage explicitly with this aspect of the question, making sure that your response leads to some form of judgement or conclusion.

AO2 3: Making Judgements and Drawing Conclusions

For this particular question, there are a number of possible conclusions that you could draw. Having applied your knowledge and understanding of postmodern theory to your set television product, you might conclude that:

- the set episode *is* postmodern, or
- the set product is only postmodern to a certain extent, or
- the set product is not postmodern at all.

There are, therefore, a range of valid responses to this question, all of which are perfectly acceptable provided you **substantiate** your answer by making detailed reference to specific aspects of the set episode you have studied. The key is making sure that you support your points and that your analysis of the set product demonstrates your ability to apply knowledge and understanding of postmodern theory.

Key Term

Substantiate
To provide evidence to support or illustrate a point, idea or argument – for example, supporting the idea that a television product is postmodern by referring to a specific technique that is used in the set episode.

AO2 1: Analysing Media Products Through the Use of Academic Theories

This question requires you to do more than just demonstrate your knowledge and understanding of postmodern theory; it requires you to *use* that knowledge and understanding to *analyse* the set product. In other words, postmodern theory needs to be *applied* to the set episode rather than discussed in isolation.

In discussing the extent to which *Peaky Blinders* can be seen as postmodern, you could discuss:

- the extent to which the set episode blurs the boundaries between fiction and reality (e.g. by placing real historical characters such as Winston Churchill in a fictional narrative)
- the way in which the set episode combines the conventions of the gangster drama with those of the western and the period drama, exhibiting genre hybridity
- the extent to which the world of *Peaky Blinders* could be seen as a simulacrum.

In discussing the extent to which *Black Mirror* can be seen as postmodern, you could discuss:

- the extent to which the set episode blurs the boundaries between fiction and reality (e.g. whether Kelly and Yorkie's virtual selves can be seen as examples of the hyperreal)
- the way in which the set episode parodies popular films of the 1980s such as *Pretty in Pink*
- the extent to which the world of San Junipero could be seen as a simulacrum.

In discussing the extent to which *Killing Eve* can be seen as postmodern, you could discuss:

- the extent to which the set episode blurs the boundaries between fiction and reality (e.g. by combining references to real organisations such as MI5 and fictional ones such as The Twelve)
- the extent to which the programme depicts a postmodern, hyperreal world where images have displaced reality (e.g. through the references to CCTV in the set episode)
- the extent to which the set episode uses reflexivity and intertextuality to draw attention to the programme's own status as a fictional construct (e.g. through the intertextual references to thriller writers such as Lee Child and John Le Carré, whose books are shown on Eve's desk).

Assessment Objectives

> The second part of this question is addressing the following assessment objective:
>
> **AO1 2:** Demonstrate knowledge and understanding of **contexts** of media and their influence on media products and processes

More specifically, it is assessing your knowledge and understanding of economic contexts and their influence on television production.

To be awarded a mark in the upper band:

- you should demonstrate excellent knowledge and understanding of economic contexts and their influence on television production, drawing perceptive and insightful links between the set television product and the economic context in which it was produced
- you should show a detailed understanding of the significance of relevant economic factors.

AO1 2: Demonstrating Knowledge and Understanding of Media Contexts and Their Influence on Media Products and Processes

You could demonstrate your knowledge and understanding of economic contexts and their influence on television production by referring to any of the following:

- the significance of different ownership and/or funding models in the television industry (i.e. whether media companies are privately or publicly owned, whether they are publicly or commercially funded, etc.)
- the growing importance of co-productions (including international co-productions) in the television industry today
- the way in which production values are shaped by economic factors
- the impact of risk aversion on television production (e.g. in terms of the commissioning and financing of programmes)
- the different sources of funding available to producers working in the television industry today.

In discussing the influence of economic factors on *The Bridge* you could discuss:

- how the transnational settings, cast and crew reflect the programme's economic context as it was co-financed and co-produced by Sveriges Television and Danmarks Radio
- the significance of the grant received from the Copenhagen Film Fund for the third season of *The Bridge* (e.g. the way in which this led to more Danish crew members being employed on the third season)
- the importance of the €1 million grant received from Creative Europe MEDIA in terms of the programme's production values.

In discussing the influence of economic factors on *The Returned*, you could discuss:

- the need for Canal+, as a premium pay channel, to provide high-quality original programming to attract and satisfy subscribers
- the importance of the grant received from Creative Europe MEDIA in terms of the programme's production values
- the way in which the producers were able to secure funding through the Ile-de-France Regional Fund and the Rhône-Alpes Regional Fund because of the locations they filmed in.

In discussing the influence of economic factors on *Tehran*, you could discuss:

- the significance of the funding secured from UK distribution company Cineflix Media, who provided 40% of the production costs, and the way in which this is reflected in the production values of the show
- the significance of the decision to film the scenes set in Tehran in Athens (e.g. enabling the producers to secure cash rebates and tax relief from EKOME – the body responsible for supporting the Greek audio-visual industry)
- the significance of the decision to cast Navid Negahban in one of the lead roles (e.g. his previous role in the globally popular American spy thriller *Homeland* could be seen to help open the programme up to wider international markets).

Section B: Magazines: Mainstream and Alternative Media

As with Section A, there are three options in this section. The questions are the same except for the set magazine products that they refer to.

The sample question shown here is an extended response question.

Tip

In extended response questions, you are required to construct and develop a sustained line of reasoning. Your argument should be logical, coherent and relevant and you need to make sure that the points you make are fully substantiated. The extended response questions on the A Level Component 2 paper are those that are worth 30 marks.

Option 1: *Woman* and *Adbusters*

40. Compared with the past, David Gauntlett argues that in the media today 'we no longer get singular, straightforward messages about ideal types of male and female identities'.

Evaluate the validity of this claim with reference to the set editions of *Woman* and *Adbusters* and the historical contexts in which they were produced. [30 marks]

Option 2: *Woman's Realm* and *Huck*

50. Compared with the past, David Gauntlett argues that in the media today 'we no longer get singular, straightforward messages about ideal types of male and female identities'.

Evaluate the validity of this claim with reference to the set editions of *Woman's Realm* and *Huck* and the historical contexts in which they were produced. [30 marks]

Option 3: *Vogue* and *The Big Issue*

60. Compared with the past, David Gauntlett argues that in the media today 'we no longer get singular, straightforward messages about ideal types of male and female identities'.

Evaluate the validity of this claim with reference to the set editions of *Vogue* and *The Big Issue* and the historical contexts in which they were produced. [30 marks]

Assessment Objectives

This question is addressing AO1 2 and AO2 2:

AO1 2: Demonstrate knowledge and understanding of **contexts** of media and their influence on media products and processes

AO2 2: Apply knowledge and understanding of the theoretical framework of media to **evaluate academic theories**

More specifically, the question is assessing your knowledge and understanding of historical contexts and their influence on the set magazine products, and your ability to evaluate Gauntlett's theory of identity.

To be awarded a mark in the upper band:

- you need to demonstrate excellent knowledge and understanding of historical contexts and their influence on the set magazine products
- the links you draw between the representations in the set magazine products and the contexts in which they were produced should be perceptive and insightful, showing a detailed understanding of the significance of relevant contextual factors
- your evaluation of Gauntlett's theory should be insightful, thorough and critically informed
- your arguments about the validity of Gauntlett's theory should be fully supported with detailed reference to specific aspects of the set magazine products.

Tip

Make sure that you have a detailed knowledge of your set magazine and that you are able to refer to specific features, articles, adverts, cover lines and images to support the points you make. Remember that it is not the entire magazine that you have to be familiar with – it is only specified extracts. You can access the extracts from the historical magazines via the WJEC Eduqas website. A list detailing the specific extracts from the contemporary magazines that you need to study can also be found there.

AO1 2: Demonstrating Knowledge and Understanding of Media Contexts and Their Influence on Media Products and Processes

In order to demonstrate your knowledge and understanding of the influence of historical contexts on the set magazine products, you should consider:

- the extent to which the representations of gender found in the set editions of the two magazines reflect the norms and values of the historical periods in which they were produced

- the extent to which any differences in the representations of gender in the two set magazine products are due to the respective historical contexts in which they were produced.

AO2 2: Evaluating Academic Theories

This question also requires you to evaluate an academic theory, which means assessing its potential strengths and limitations, and making a judgement about its validity, value or relevance. One question on the A Level Component 2 paper will always be an evaluation of theory question.

In evaluating Gauntlett's theory, you may find it useful to discuss:

- the extent to which the representations of gender in the two set magazine products differ
- the extent to which the messages about ideal types of gender identity offered in the historical magazine from the 1960s are singular and straightforward
- the extent to which the representations of gender in the contemporary magazine are diverse, pluralistic and complex
- the extent to which any differences in the representations of gender in the two set magazine products are due to the respective genres of the two magazines, their particular target audiences and/or their relationship to mainstream culture.

If you are studying Option 1, you could discuss:

- the extent to which *Woman* offers singular and straightforward messages about domesticity and female beauty (e.g. in the *'Are You an A-Level Beauty?'* feature)
- the extent to which the advertisement for the Women's Royal Army Corps in *Woman* introduces a degree of diversity in terms of the representation of gender
- the extent to which *Adbusters* offers more nuanced, complex and pluralistic representations of gender (e.g. through the cover image)
- the extent to which *Adbusters* subverts hegemonic messages about ideal male and female identities through parodies and culture jams such as the mock advert for 'Louibouton' (sic) shoes.

If you are studying Option 2, you could discuss:

- the extent to which *Woman's Realm* offers singular and straightforward messages about domesticity and female beauty (e.g. in the *'Bottled Beauty'* feature)
- the extent to which love and romance are constructed as stereotypically female interests in *Woman's Realm* (e.g. in the opening editorial about Valentine's Day)
- the extent to which *Huck* can be seen to offer a more diverse and pluralistic range of gender representations (e.g. through the main cover image which features an armed Kurdish woman)
- the extent to which *Huck* challenges binaristic understandings of gender (e.g. in the *'Beyond Binary'* feature on genderqueer identities).

If you are studying Option 3, you could discuss:

- the extent to which *Vogue* reinforces hegemonic cultural ideals of femininity through its emphasis on narrowly defined notions of female beauty
- the extent to which the representations of gender that *Vogue* offers are determined by the genre conventions of the fashion magazine
- the extent to which features in *The Big Issue* such as 'Letter to My Younger Self' with Grayson Perry challenge singular, straightforward messages about ideal gender identities and reflect shifting cultural values

Tip

The evaluation of theory question could feature in any of the three sections in Component 2. Check the grid on page 240 of Chapter 6 to see which theories you need to study for each section.

Tip

Although you need to refer to the products you have studied when evaluating the prescribed theories, it is important not to place too much weight on isolated examples. For instance, if either or both of the set products do not appear to support a particular theory or hypothesis, this does not necessarily mean that the entire theory or hypothesis is invalid. It is important to consider how typical the set products are of broader trends across the media.

- the extent to which the 'Moving On' feature and the 'My Pitch' section in *The Big Issue* can be seen to offer a more diverse and pluralistic range of gender representations.

Section C: Media in the Online Age

Like the sample question in Section B, this is an extended response question. This means that you will need to construct and develop a sustained line of reasoning.

7 0 How far can aspects of identity be seen to affect the way in which audiences use online media? Discuss, with reference to **both** of your set online products.

You should refer to relevant academic theories in your response. [30 marks]

Group 1	Group 2
JJ Olatunji/KSI	The ***gal-dem*** website
or	or
Zoe Sugg	The ***Attitude*** website

Assessment Objectives

This question is addressing AO1 1 and AO2 3:

AO1 1: Demonstrate knowledge and understanding of the theoretical framework of media

AO2 3: Apply knowledge and understanding of the theoretical framework of media to **make judgements and draw conclusions**

More specifically, the question is assessing your knowledge and understanding of audiences and audience theories, and your ability to make judgements and draw conclusions regarding how far aspects of identity can be seen to affect the way in which audiences use online media products.

To be awarded a mark in the upper band:

- you should make detailed reference to relevant audience theories
- your discussion of the set products should be perceptive, insightful and critically informed by a detailed knowledge and understanding of audiences and how they use online media products
- the judgements and conclusions you make need to be perceptive, insightful and fully supported with detailed reference to specific aspects of the set products.

AO1 1: Demonstrating Knowledge and Understanding

In demonstrating your knowledge and understanding of audiences, you could refer to relevant demographic and/or psychographic factors and academic theories such as:

- Gauntlett's theory of identity
- Shirky's 'end of audience' theory
- Hall's reception theory
- Jenkins' theory of fandom.

AO2 3: Making Judgements and Drawing Conclusions

In making judgements and drawing conclusions about how far aspects of identity affect the way in which audiences use online media, you could discuss:

Note

Make sure you double check the WJEC/Eduqas website or Illuminate (https://bit.ly/3r1d7at) for the most up-to-date information on which set products you should be studying.

Tip

For tips on how to structure an extended response, see page 254 of the Year 1 book.

Tip

This is another example of a question that requires you to make judgements and draw conclusions. If a question uses the phrase 'How far ...?' or 'To what extent ...?' you know that this is something you need to include in your answer.

- the extent to which the uses and meanings of online media products are determined by their producers
- the extent to which audiences are active participants in the production of textual meaning
- the extent to which demographic factors such as age, gender, ethnicity and social class, and psychographic factors such as values, attitudes and lifestyle, can be seen to affect the way in which audiences use online media products.

If you are studying the ***gal-dem*** *website*, you could discuss:

- the extent to which gender and ethnicity may affect the way in which audiences use articles on the *gal-dem* website such as 'The Architect Inspiring Muslim Girls Everywhere' (whether they see the Muslim architect Sumayya Vally as a role model or aspirational figure and use the article as a resource for what Gauntlett refers to as 'identity work' or whether they use it simply to broaden their knowledge and understanding, for example)
- the extent to which culture, ethnicity, sexuality and personal experiences may affect the way in which audiences use articles on the *gal-dem* website such as 'How I Reclaimed my Identity as a Queer Bengali Muslim'.

If you are studying the ***Attitude*** website, you could discuss:

- the extent to which an audience member's own experiences of prejudice or discrimination may affect the way in which they use articles on *Attitude's* website such as 'Iraqi LGBT Activist Amir Ashour Tells Attitude About His Ongoing Fight for Equality'
- the extent to which body image may affect the way in which audiences use articles in the 'Active' section of *Attitude*'s website such as 'It was only after coming out that I started getting body confidence issues'.

If you are studying **JJ Olatunji/KSI** you could discuss:

- the extent to which body image may affect the way in which JJ Olatunji's audiences use YouTube videos such as 'HOW STRONG IS KSI?' (e.g. whether some may use this as an aspirational ideal)
- the extent to which personal experiences and mental health may affect how audiences use videos such as 'I Was Feeling A Bit Down'.

If you are studying **Zoe Sugg**, you could discuss:

- the extent to which self-esteem and self-image may affect the way in which Zoe Sugg's audiences use blog posts such as 'Just Say Yes' or 'Panic Attacks'
- the extent to which age and life experiences may affect the way in which audiences use YouTube vlogs such as 'My First Trimester | Fear of Sickness/Emetophobia | First Signs and Symptoms'.

Additional Sample Assessment Materials

Here is an additional example paper for Component 2:

Section A: Television in the Global Age

Answer **one** question in this section.

Either,

Option 1: *Peaky Blinders* and *The Bridge*

10. According to Claude Lévi-Strauss, texts convey their meanings through a system of binary oppositions.

    Evaluate this structuralist theory. Refer to the set episodes of *Peaky Blinders* and *The Bridge* in your response. [30 marks]

Stretch and Challenge 9.3

Use this additional example paper to practise writing under timed conditions. Remember that in the exam you will have two-and-a-half hours to complete the whole paper.

Tip

The questions shown here are taken from the additional Sample Assessment Materials provided by Eduqas. As before, while the questions themselves are the same, the set products referred to in the questions have been changed to reflect subsequent updates to the specification.

Or,

Option 2: *Black Mirror* and *The Returned*

20. According to Claude Lévi-Strauss, texts convey their meanings through a system of binary oppositions.

    Evaluate this structuralist theory. Refer to the set episodes of *Black Mirror* and *The Returned* in your response. [30 marks]

Or,

Option 3: *Killing Eve* and *Tehran*

30. According to Claude Lévi-Strauss, texts convey their meanings through a system of binary oppositions.

    Evaluate this structuralist theory. Refer to the set episodes of *Killing Eve* and *Tehran* in your response. [30 marks]

Section B: Magazines: Mainstream and Alternative Media

Answer **one** question in this section.

Either,

Option 1: *Woman* and *Adbusters*

40. How significant are economic factors in the magazine industry? Refer to *Woman* and *Adbusters* in your answer. [30 marks]

Or,

Option 2: *Woman's Realm* and *Huck*

50. How significant are economic factors in the magazine industry? Refer to *Woman's Realm* and *Huck* in your answer. [30 marks]

Or,

Option 3: *Vogue* and *The Big Issue*

60. How significant are economic factors in the magazine industry? Refer to *Vogue* and *The Big Issue* in your answer. [30 marks]

Section C: Media in the Online Age

The question in this section is in two parts. Answer **both** parts of the question.

71. Explain how social and cultural contexts influence responses to online media products. Use JJ Olatunji/KSI to support your response. [15 marks]
72. Explore how the representations on the *gal-dem* website position audiences. [15 marks]
81. Explain how social and cultural contexts influence responses to online products. Use Zoe Sugg to support your response. [15 marks]
82. Explore how the representations on the Attitude website position audiences. [15 marks]

Quick Guide to Theoretical Approaches

10

Media Language

Semiotics: Roland Barthes

Semiotics is the study of signs and meaning. Roland Barthes is a key semiotic theorist whose ideas you will need to be familiar with. The main principles of his theory of semiotics, which are outlined in his book *Elements of Semiology* (1964), include:

- the idea that texts communicate their meanings through a process of signification
- the idea that signs can function at the level of denotation, which involves the 'literal' or common-sense meaning of the sign, and at the level of connotation, which involves the meanings associated with or suggested by the sign
- the idea that constructed meanings can come to seem self-evident, achieving the status of myth through a process of naturalisation.

Narratology: Tzvetan Todorov

Narratology is the study of narrative. A particularly influential narrative theorist is Tzvetan Todorov. The main principles of his theory of narrative include:

- the idea that all narratives share a basic structure that involves a movement from one state of equilibrium to another
- the idea that these two states of equilibrium are separated by a period of imbalance or disequilibrium
- the idea that the way in which narratives are resolved can have particular ideological significance.

Tzvetan Todorov

Genre Theory: Steve Neale

Genre theory is concerned with the way in which media products are classified and categorised. Steve Neale was a theorist who wrote extensively on genre. Although his work focuses primarily on film, his ideas can be applied to other media forms. The main principles of Neale's genre theory include:

- the idea that genres may be dominated by repetition, but are also marked by difference, variation and change
- the idea that genres change, develop and vary, as they borrow from and overlap with one another
- the idea that genres exist within specific economic, institutional and industrial contexts.

Structuralism: Claude Lévi-Strauss

Structuralism is concerned with the underlying systems and structures through which meanings are produced. The cultural anthropologist Claude Lévi-Strauss is one of the most significant figures associated with this theoretical approach. The main principles of his structuralist theory include:

- the idea that texts can best be understood through an examination of their underlying structure

- the idea that meaning is dependent upon (and produced through) pairs of oppositions
- the idea that the way in which these binary oppositions are resolved can have particular ideological significance.

Postmodernism: Jean Baudrillard

The term postmodernism has a number of different uses and meanings. It refers to both a cultural movement that emerged in the mid-20th century in fields such as literature, architecture, media and the arts, and a critical approach that has been used in a wide variety of academic disciplines, including philosophy, sociology and cultural studies as well as media studies. A particularly notable postmodern thinker is the French cultural theorist Jean Baudrillard. The main principles of his postmodern theory include:

- the idea that in postmodern culture the boundaries between the 'real' world and the world of the media have collapsed and that it is no longer possible to distinguish between reality and simulation
- the idea that in a postmodern age of simulacra we are immersed in a world of images that no longer refer to anything 'real'
- the idea that media images have come to seem more 'real' than the reality they supposedly represent (hyperreality).

Representation

Theories of Representation: Stuart Hall

Stuart Hall was a cultural theorist whose research encompassed a wide range of topics, including how representations are constructed and the ways in which audiences may respond to these constructions. The main principles of Hall's theory of representation include:

- the idea that representation is the production of meaning through language, with language defined in its broadest sense as a system of signs
- the idea that the relationship between concepts and signs is governed by codes
- the idea that stereotyping, as a form of representation, reduces people to a few simple characteristics or traits
- the idea that stereotyping tends to occur where there are inequalities of power, as subordinate or excluded groups are constructed as different or 'other' (e.g. through ethnocentrism).

Theories of Identity: David Gauntlett

David Gauntlett is a theorist who has published widely on a range of topics, including media and identity, everyday creativity and the use of digital media. The main principles of his theory of identity include:

- the idea that the media provide us with 'tools' or resources that we use to construct our identities
- the idea that while in the past the media tended to convey singular, straightforward messages about ideal types of male and female identities, the media today offer us a more diverse range of stars, icons and characters from whom we may pick and mix different ideas.

Feminist Theory: Liesbet van Zoonen

Feminist theory is concerned with identifying, critiquing and challenging gender inequalities. Liesbet van Zoonen is a feminist academic whose work focuses on gender, popular culture and the media. The main principles of her theory include:

- the idea that gender is constructed through discourse, and that its meaning varies according to cultural and historical context
- the idea that the display of women's bodies as objects to be looked at is a core element of Western patriarchal culture
- the idea that in mainstream culture the visual and narrative codes that are used to construct the male body as spectacle differ from those used to objectify the female body.

bell hooks

Feminist Theory: bell hooks

bell hooks was a renowned feminist theorist and cultural critic who wrote extensively on racial and sexual politics in film, music and popular culture. The main principles of her theory include:

- the idea that feminism is a struggle to end sexist/patriarchal oppression and the ideology of domination
- the idea that feminism is a political commitment rather than a lifestyle choice
- the idea that race and class as well as sex determine the extent to which individuals are exploited, discriminated against or oppressed.

Theories of Gender Performativity: Judith Butler

Judith Butler is an American academic and cultural theorist. Their theory of gender performativity is outlined in the books *Gender Trouble: Feminism and the Subversion of Identity* (1990) and *Bodies that Matter: On the Discursive Limits of Sex* (1993). The main principles of this theory include:

- the idea that identity is performatively constructed by the very 'expressions' that are said to be its results (it is manufactured through a set of acts)
- the idea that there is no gender identity behind the expressions of gender
- the idea that performativity is not a singular act, but a repetition and a ritual.

Judith Butler

Theories Around Ethnicity and Postcolonial Theory: Paul Gilroy

Postcolonial theory explores the legacy of colonialism and imperialism, and the continuing impact this can be seen to have on contemporary culture. Paul Gilroy is an academic who has published widely in the field of postcolonial studies. The main principles of his theory include:

- the idea that colonial discourses continue to inform contemporary attitudes to race and ethnicity in the postcolonial era
- the idea that civilisationism constructs racial hierarchies and sets up binary oppositions based on notions of otherness.

Industry

Power and Media Industries: James Curran and Jean Seaton

James Curran and Jean Seaton are academics whose work focuses mainly on media history and the political economy of the media. Their theory of power and media industries is outlined in the book *Power Without Responsibility* (2009), which provides a broad overview of the history of British media. The main principles of this theory include:

- the idea that the media is controlled by a small number of companies primarily driven by the logic of profit and power
- the idea that media concentration generally limits or inhibits variety, creativity and quality
- the idea that more socially diverse patterns of ownership help to create the conditions for more varied and adventurous media productions.

Regulation: Sonia Livingstone and Peter Lunt

Sonia Livingstone and Peter Lunt are academics who have published widely on media policy, media audiences and regulation. Their theory of regulation is outlined in the book *Media Regulation: Governance and the Interests of Citizens and Consumers* (2011). The main principles of this theory include:

- the idea that there is an underlying struggle in recent UK regulation policy between the need to further the interests of citizens (by offering protection from harmful or offensive material) and the need to further the interests of consumers (by ensuring choice, value for money and market competition)
- the idea that the increasing power of global media corporations, together with the rise of convergent media technologies and transformations in the production, distribution and marketing of digital media, have placed traditional approaches to media regulation at risk.

Cultural Industries: David Hesmondhalgh

David Hesmondhalgh

David Hesmondhalgh is an academic whose work focuses primarily on media policy and the creative industries. A fourth edition of his book *The Cultural Industries*, which charts the evolution of the cultural industries since the 1980s, was published in 2018. The main principles of his theory of cultural industries include:

- the idea that cultural industry companies try to minimise risk and maximise audiences through vertical and horizontal integration, and by formatting their cultural products (e.g. through the use of stars, genres and serials)
- the idea that the largest companies or conglomerates now operate across a number of different media industries
- the idea that the radical potential of the Internet has been contained to some extent by its partial incorporation into a large, profit-orientated set of cultural industries.

Audiences

Media Effects: Albert Bandura

Media effects theories are concerned with the effects that the media may have on audiences. Albert Bandura was a psychologist whose research explored the way in which the media can influence social behaviour. The main principles of his 'social learning theory' include:

- the idea that the media can implant ideas in the mind of the audience directly
- the idea that audiences acquire attitudes, emotional responses and new styles of conduct through modelling
- the idea that media representations of transgressive behaviour, such as violence or physical aggression, can lead audience members to imitate those forms of behaviour.

Albert Bandura

Cultivation Theory: George Gerbner

George Gerbner is another theorist whose research was concerned with the effect that the media can have on audiences. His work explored the way in which the media can influence people's perceptions of social reality. The main principles of his cultivation theory include:

- the idea that exposure to repeated patterns of representation over long periods of time can shape and influence the way in which people perceive the world around them (i.e. cultivating particular views and opinions)
- the idea that cultivation reinforces mainstream values (dominant ideologies).

George Gerbner

Reception Theory: Stuart Hall

Stuart Hall's reception theory is outlined in the essay 'Encoding, Decoding', which features in his book *Culture, Media, Language* (1990). The main principles of this theory include:

- the idea that communication is a process involving encoding by producers and decoding by audiences
- the idea that there are three hypothetical positions from which messages and meanings may be decoded:
  - the dominant-hegemonic position: the encoder's intended meaning (the preferred reading) is fully understood and accepted
  - the negotiated position: the legitimacy of the encoder's message is acknowledged in general terms, although the message is adapted or negotiated to better fit the decoder's own individual experiences or context
  - the oppositional position: the encoder's message is understood, but the decoder disagrees with it, reading it in a contrary or oppositional way.

Henry Jenkins

Fandom: Henry Jenkins

Henry Jenkins is an academic and theorist whose work focuses primarily on fandom, media convergence and participatory culture. His theory of fandom is outlined in the book *Textual Poachers: Television Fans and Participatory Culture* (1992). The main principles of this theory include:

- the idea that fans are active participants in the construction and circulation of textual meanings
- the idea that fans appropriate texts and read them in ways that are not fully authorised by the media producers ('textual poaching')
- the idea that fans construct their social and cultural identities through borrowing and inflecting mass culture images, and are part of a participatory culture that has a vital social dimension.

Clay Shirky

'End of Audience' Theory: Clay Shirky

'End of audience' theories are concerned with the changing relationship between media production and consumption in the digital age. Clay Shirky is a social media theorist who studies the effects of the internet on society. The main principles of his 'end of audience' theory include:

- the idea that the internet and digital technologies have had a profound effect on the relations between media and individuals
- the idea that the conceptualisation of audience members as passive consumers of mass media content is no longer tenable in the age of the internet, as media consumers have now become producers who 'speak back to' the media in various ways, as well as creating and sharing content with one another.

Glossary of Key Terms

Above the fold The portion of a webpage that is immediately visible to the user without the need for scrolling. That which can only be viewed via scrolling is said to be below the fold. The terms are borrowed from the newspaper industry, as newspapers would traditionally be folded in half before being put on display on newsstands. Therefore, passers-by would only be able to see material that appeared above the fold.

Absolute truth A truth that is not subject to interpretation and cannot be questioned. Postmodernists challenge the idea of absolute truth as they suggest that all truths are relative and vary according to perspective.

Activist magazine A magazine that seeks to bring about social or political change through direct action.

Aesthetic The look, style or feel of a media product.

Alternative media Media products that differ in their content, production and distribution from more mainstream media forms.

Anachronism Something that is placed in the wrong time period, for example a reference to a book or a song in a period drama that had not yet been written at the time the period drama is set.

Analyse critically This phrase is specific to the A Level/Year 2 element of the specification, as the ability to analyse critically is an advanced skill involving expressing opinion through subjective writing. It also refers to the careful exploration and analysis of the set products.

Anthology series A series that is comprised of entirely separate, self-contained stories. The individual episodes may be connected by a common, over-arching theme but they generally feature different characters.

Appropriation A process that involves taking or claiming something for one's own use. Fans may appropriate images, characters or ideas from popular television programmes, for example, using them as the basis for their own artwork or fanfiction.

Arbitary signs Signs that bear no obvious resemblance to the thing signified, the meanings of which have been accepted through repetition over time.

Backward compatibility The property of the system that allows interoperability with an older system. It allows gamers to play video games that were developed for previous versions of the console.

Bathos The effect that is produced when there is an abrupt switch from something that is serious, grand or important to something that is trivial, commonplace or ludicrous. A sense of anticlimax. This technique is often used for comic effect.

BBC World Service This is the largest international broadcaster, distributing content in over 30 languages.

Biannual A magazine that is published twice a year.

Billing block Usually appears at the bottom of a film poster or the back of a DVD cover, It includes the credits and industry information.

Bimonthly A magazine that is published every two months.

Binary opposites When people, ideas, concepts or values are set up in conflict with one another.

Body shaming The practice of criticising, humiliating or ridiculing someone on the basis of their body size or shape.

Bylines A line in a newspaper story naming the writer or contributor.

Candid photograph A photograph that appears natural or spontaneous rather than posed. The subject is often unaware that their picture is being taken.

Casual gamers Gamers who play more spontaneously and may only play a few games a year. They tend to choose games that are less challenging and lacking in complexity.

Celtic noir A sub-genre similar in style, mood and aesthetic to Nordic noir, but which is set in Celtic- or Gaelic-speaking regions of Wales, Scotland and Ireland.

Centre-left Describes a person, organisation or political party that has political views which are closer to socialism than to capitalism and leans to the left.

Centre-right Describes a person, organisation or political party that has political views which are closer to capitalism and conservatism than to socialism, but are not as extreme as some political viewpoints and therefore is closer to the centre.

Character functions Refers to the structural reason the character is in the narrative. All characters have a key role to play in extending the plot.

Character typology A system that defines the characteristics of different types of people or characters across a range of different narratives, for example the hero and the villain.

Chiaroscuro lighting Chiaroscuro is an Italian term used in the visual arts to describe a dramatic contrast between darkness and light. In film and television products, this effect is produced through particular lighting techniques.

Citizen journalism The collection, dissemination and analysis of news by ordinary members of the public, usually via the internet.

Civilisationism Refers to Gilroy's idea that geopolitics will always be centred on cultural differences rather than similarities. He associated civilisationism with ethnocentrism, as, in his opinion, it reproduces racial hierarchies and colonial attitudes by constructing certain, usually non-Western cultures as 'other'.

Colonial Refers to the practice of acquiring political control of another country.

Colonisers People who settle in and assume control over another country. Those whose countries are occupied and taken over are the colonised.

Command words These are the key words you need to look out for in examination questions, which will guide you in what you need to include in your response.

Commercial mainstream With regards to the media, refers to traditional forms of mass media with a broad audience and powerful influence.

Commercial radio station A station that generates revenue through advertising and sponsorship. This is particularly true of local commercial stations that will provide a platform for local business advertising.

Commutation test A structuralist, analytical technique used in the paradigmatic analysis of any text. It determines if a change of sign/signifier leads to a change in meaning.

Consciousness-raising A form of activism that aims to heighten public awareness of an issue.

Contemporary and emerging media Refers to all types of communications based on digital technology, including those platforms that facilitate communication, disseminate information and include interactive elements.

Content marketing Defined by the Content Marketing Association (2018b) as '*the discipline of creating quality branded content across media channels and platforms to deliver engaging relationships, consumer value and measurable success for brands*'.

Continuity editing Editing that combines a series of shots into a seamless sequence in order to effectively convey the narrative.

Convergence A process through which different media forms merge or overlap with one another. Defined by Henry Jenkins (2006) as a '*move from medium-specific content toward content that flows across multiple media channels, toward the increased interdependence of communication systems [and] toward multiple ways of accessing media content*'.

Co-opt To adopt or appropriate something for one's own uses. In Media Studies, the term is often used to describe the way in which aspects of alternative culture are exploited and incorporated by mainstream media to make a profit.

Core gamers Players with a wide range of gaming interests, who actively engage with different types of games but do not have the intensity of a hardcore gamer.

Cosplay A shortened version of the term costume play, this is a performance art in whereby fans dress up and assume the roles of characters from video games, television and film, usually at organised events for fan communities.

Critical analysis Refers to your ability to apply your knowledge and understanding of the theoretical framework in a sophisticated way, informed by your learning. For example, exploring the relevance of a particular media theory in relation to one of the set products.

Cross-media production At A Level your production must cover more than one form. For example, a DVD cover and poster for a film **and** online promotional material.

Cross-demographic appeal The capacity of a media product to simultaneously appeal to more than one audience.

Cultivation theory The idea that constant exposure to the media influences (or cultivates) particular attitudes and beliefs that shape our perception of the world around us.

Cultural capital A form of cultural knowledge that endows those who possess it with power or social status. The ability to speak knowledgeably about media products, to identify intertextual references, or to distinguish between the 'good' and the 'bad' are all forms of cultural capital.

Cultural industries Defined by David Hesmondhalgh (2013) as industries that '*deal primarily with the industrial production and circulation of texts*'. Examples include the film, television, magazine and music industries.

Cultural verisimilitude A form of realism that is established when a media product corresponds with what we know about the social and cultural world that exists outside the text.

Culture jamming Defined by Naomi Klein (2000) as '*the practice of parodying adverts and hijacking billboards in order to drastically alter their messages*'. Subvertising (a portmanteau word combining 'subvert' and 'advertising') is another term commonly used to describe this cultural practice.

Culture lag The idea that changes in media representations may lag behind changes in the wider society within which those representations are produced.

Data harvesting The process of extracting large amounts of data from a website to use for other purposes.

Deepfake A video that has been digitally manipulated using a form of artificial intelligence called deep learning in order to produce a fake image of a person or event. This often involves replacing the face or voice of one person with that of someone else. Due to the sophisticated nature of these artificial intelligence systems, deepfake videos can appear highly convincing.

Deregulation A process that involves the loosening of regulatory constraints that are seen as hurdles to economic growth. This is generally associated with marketisation or privatisation. For example, Watson and Hill (2015) suggest that deregulation typically involves a shift '*from public to commercial, largely corporate, control*'.

Desaturation A process through which colours are made to appear more muted. In film and television programmes, this is typically achieved through colour grading, as more white, black or grey is added to the image.

Desktop publishing (DTP) The use of computers and software programs to design, create and publish books, newspapers or magazines.

Diaspora Defined by Chris Barker (2008) as '*a dispersed network of ethnically and culturally related peoples*'. For example, the Asian or South Asian diaspora refers to people of Asian descent who live outside of their ancestral homeland in different parts of the world. British Asians are therefore said to be part of the Asian diaspora, along with other people of Asian descent such as Asian-Americans. A significant factor in the formation of the Asian diaspora was the Partition of India in 1947, which saw millions of people displaced.

Digital-first A policy in which media content is first created in digital form and then adapted for other mediums. For example, in the case of a digital-first magazine, content is generally published online before it appears in print.

Digital natives People born or brought up during the age of digital technology who therefore have a high level of digital literacy when it comes to using computers and the internet.

Digital optimists Those who believe that the internet and digital technologies have a positive impact on culture and society. David Hesmondhalgh (2013) defines digital optimism as '*the view that digitalisation and the Internet have democratized cultural production and consumption*'. He cites Clay Shirky and Henry Jenkins as two notable proponents of digital optimism.

Digital uniques Individual users to a website over a given time period.

Digitally convergent The ability of audiences to view multimedia content across different platforms and devices.

Digitally convergent platforms Where different media platforms merge with one another as a result of advances in technology. For example, the smartphone brings together different functions in one device: users can make phone calls, browse the internet, facetime, play games, watch films and listen to music. All of these would have previously existed on separate platforms.

Direct action A means of achieving change that advocates action over discussion. This can take many forms, from protesting, demonstrating and going on marches, to boycotting goods or companies.

Discourse A particular way of talking and thinking about a topic; a system of representation. For example, when looking at the representation of gender or ethnicity in a media product, it may be useful to think about the discourses that are used – the ways in which gender or ethnicity are talked about, and the ideas and values that this system of representation conveys.

Disjuncture Lacking unity, thus creating a separation or disconnection, for example between the lyrics and the visuals in a music video.

Disruptive-display advertising Advertising content that appears in unexpected places, for example in the plug of a daily newspaper, which arrests attention because it challenges the expectations of what is typical.

Diversification The process through which a company expands its operations into new or different areas of business.

Dominant ideology Refers to how those in positions of power present, repeat and reiterate a particular viewpoint that then appears to be 'dominant' or the norm. This is then accepted by the audience.

Eclecticism A practice that involves combining or drawing on a wide range of sources or styles. Eclecticism is concerned with plurality and diversity as opposed to singularity and similarity. Postmodern products are often highly eclectic, as they reference a diverse array of cultural forms and styles.

Edition-based digital format An online newspaper distributed in electronic form but formatted identically to the print version.

Ellipsis The use of three dots at the beginning, middle or end of a sentence to attract attention and interest through the withholding of information.

Essentialism The belief that gender and other aspects of identity are innate, natural or biologically determined rather than socially constructed. The idea that social groups such as men and women are inherently different because they are born with certain traits, for example.

Ethnicity A person's cultural identity, which may be indicated through customs, clothing or food. Your ethnicity suggests an identity that is based on a sense of place, ideology or religion.

Ethnocentrism The attitude that one's own ethnic group, culture or nationality is superior to others.

Exposition With regard to the documentary form, this refers to the elements of the narrative that are revealed to the audience, allowing them to more fully understand characters. It also serves to mediate a message for the audience, persuading them of a particular viewpoint.

Extended metaphor A comparison between two dissimilar ideas in order to amplify meaning, which may extend throughout the text. For example, in *Hallelujah* the use of a religious narrative to explain the romantic relationship.

Extended response question A question with a higher mark tariff, which is more demanding. It requires the ability to construct and develop a sustained line of reasoning that is coherent, relevant, substantiated and logically structured.

Fanfiction Stories or works of fiction that are based on existing films, television programmes or literary works, and which are produced by fans rather than the original creators of those products. Sometimes referred to as fanfic.

Features Items in the newspaper that are typically longer than a hard news story. They cover topics of interest to the audience range of the newspaper and offer a contrast to the more serious items inside.

Film noir A mode of filmmaking that emerged in the USA in the 1940s and which featured a distinctive visual style, characterised by low-key or chiaroscuro lighting, claustrophobic framing and unsettling camera angles.

Fly-on-the-wall filming Refers to a style of documentary filming whereby the cameras are unobtrusive, and the subjects are observed in everyday situations unaware that they are being filmed. The technique is used to portray realistic representations of people and institutions. The production team filmed for a year in the schools featured in the *Educating ...* series.

Format A term used in the television industry to refer to the concept of a programme. David Hesmondhalgh (2013) pointed out that this is frequently developed in an initial market, then sold as a copyrighted idea to overseas markets.

Formatting A term used by theorists such as David Hesmondhalgh and Bill Ryan to describe the way in which cultural industry companies use market research to deal with '*the uncertainties of the cultural marketplace*' (Ryan, 1992). Formatting a product may involve the use of genre or stars to deliver an audience, for instance.

Generic verisimilitude The degree to which a media product conforms to the rules of its genre, facilitating a willingness to suspend disbelief on the part of the audience.

Genre hybridity The result of combining conventions from different genres. Genre hybridity may be produced by combining the conventions of a western with those of a crime drama, for example.

Ghettoisation The treatment of particular social groups as if they are different and separate from other parts of society and therefore not as important.

Gif An image format that is commonly used for simple animations and low-resolution videos.

Global village This phrase was coined by Marshall McLuhan and refers to the metaphoric shrinking of the world due to advances in technology.

Gonzo journalism A highly personal or subjective style of journalism in which the reporter or photographer is fully immersed in the world that they document rather than maintaining a sense of objectivity or critical distance. One of the figures most commonly associated with gonzo journalism is Hunter S. Thompson. His articles on the 1960s counterculture, many of which were published in *Rolling Stone* magazine, played a pioneering role in its development.

Grand narrative A term used for '*any theory claiming to provide universal explanations and to be universally valid*' (Sim, 2011).

Grassroots campaign A marketing strategy that targets a smaller, niche group, often a particular community, in the hope that they will spread the word to a broader audience.

Grid A tool used in the newspaper and magazine industry to organise or format page layouts. The grid typically dictates the size of the margins, the number and width of the columns, the placement of images on the page and the use of white space, hence providing a sense of order and structure.

Hard news '*"Hard" news is typically used to refer to topics that are usually timely, important and consequential, such as politics, international affairs and business news*' (digitalnewsreport.org, 2018).

Headshot A photograph of a person's face or their head and shoulders. Headshots are conventionally used in portrait photography and often feature on magazine covers.

Hegemonic Something that is dominant – a dominant set of values or ideas, for example.

Heteronormativity A set of assumptions or presuppositions that treat heterosexuality as normal and natural.

Homogeneous Being composed of elements that are all the same or broadly similar. The opposite of this is heterogeneous, which means being composed of diverse or varied elements.

Horizontal integration When different companies producing and selling similar products join together.

Hyperlink A word, phrase or image in an electronic document or webpage that the user can click on to navigate to a different part of the document or a different page.

Hypermodality A term used to describe the way in which the linkages in online media products such as webpages '*go beyond the default conventions of traditional multimodal genres*' (Lemke, 2002). For example, while there may be links between images and text in a film poster or print advertisement, a webpage also provides links to other pages or documents, introducing another layer of connectivity.

Hyperreality A state or condition in which images or simulations may be accepted as 'real' as they come to seem more real than reality itself.

Iconic representation A sign that has a physical resemblance to the thing that it stands in for or represents. For example, marketing materials often feature iconic representations of the products they advertise or promote.

Ideology A set of attitudes, values and beliefs; a way of looking at the world.

Idiom A well-known phrase with a figurative, not literal, meaning.

Implosion A process in which things collapse in on themselves (as opposed to explosion which involves an outward dispersal of energy). In postmodern theory, the term is commonly used to describe the way in which the boundaries separating the 'real' world from the world of the media have collapsed in on one another.

Independent magazine A magazine that is produced outside the control or ownership of the major publishing houses.

Industry context Refers to elements of the production, for example the media organisation, production processes, distribution, marketing and regulation.

Interpretive communities Initially used by Stanley Fish, a literary critic, to explain how different groups of people, i.e. readers or audiences, interpret texts similarly due to their shared social and cultural positions and their experiences.

Intersectional feminism A particular body of feminist thinking which recognises that women's identities and experiences of oppression differ. More specifically, intersectional feminism explores the way in which different forms of discrimination, such as sexism, racism, classism and homophobia, overlap or intersect with one another, impacting on different women in different ways, according to their race, class and sexuality as well as their gender.

Intertextuality The process by which one text makes reference to another.

Irony A knowingness or acute self-awareness. This is a common characteristic of postmodern media products.

Islamophobia The irrational fear or hatred of Islam and Muslims.

Lexis The specific words used in a product which may relate to the genre of the product and include terminology that is understood by the target audience.

LGBT An acronym that stands for lesbian, gay, bisexual and transgender. Other variations include LGBTQ and LGBTQ+. The Q in these variations stands for 'questioning' or 'queer', while the addition of the '+' is intended to make the category more inclusive by encompassing other related groups such as those who identify as pansexual or asexual.

Libel The defamation of a person's character through written or printed word or images.

Lifestyle magazine A genre of magazine that relates to how people live their lives and what interests them. These are usually popular men's and women's magazines.

Low-key lighting A technique that leaves significant areas of the shot in shadow. In low-key lighting set-ups, the fill light (a secondary light source that is typically used to eliminate areas of shadow) is removed or reduced.

Magazine design Jenny McKay suggests that: '*At its simplest magazine, design is the way in which words and images and physical elements such as paper and binding work together*' (McKay, 2000). Magazine design plays a crucial role in establishing the brand identity of a magazine as well as creating audience appeal.

Mainstream publisher A publisher that publishes popular magazines that have a wide, rather than niche, appeal and have high circulation figures. These magazines are termed 'mainstream' as they are generally conventional in style and content and reflect the attitudes and interests of the majority of people.

Male gaze A term used by Laura Mulvey to describe the way in which the media position us to view women's bodies as objects of visual pleasure, adopting a heterosexual male perspective, regardless of our own gender or sexual orientation.

Masculinity The state of 'being a man', which can change as society changes. It is essentially what being a man means to a particular generation. This will then be reflected in the contemporary media.

Mass audiences Large groups of people that are targeted by media products. This is made much easier due to technological progress.

Media democracy Refers to the way in which developments in technology have empowered citizens and promoted democratic ideals. Technology has given individuals the opportunity to participate in the media and journalism by creating content that allows them to report on current affairs and express opinions.

Mediated Refers to the way in which the media present aspects of the world to the audience. Newspapers act as a mediator, constructing stories and, in the process, encoding meaning.

Meme An image, phrase, idea or video disseminated by internet users – a screenshot from a television programme which has an amusing quote or phrase added to it before it is posted online, for example.

Metanarrative Refers to an accepted account or interpretation of events on which people have come to base their beliefs, for example the narratives associated with historical truths and those related to religion. It is a term used for '*any theory claiming to provide universal explanations and to be universally valid*' (Sim, 2011).

Microtargeting A marketing strategy in which personal data are used to identify the particular interests of an individual or small group, enabling them to be targeted more effectively. This is sometimes referred to as psychographic microtargeting.

Motif A dominant or recurring theme or idea in literary, artistic or musical work.

Multimodality Defined by Theo van Leeuwen (2005) as '*the combination of different semiotic modes – for example, language and music – in a communicative artefact or event*'. For example, websites are multimodal as they combine images, text and sound.

Myth Dominant ideas and beliefs that are not necessarily true but have been accepted by a culture.

Narrative trope Describes commonly recurring elements in a narrative, including literary devices, clichés and conventions.

Nordic noir A sub-genre constructed for marketing purposes and defines a type of Scandinavian crime drama featuring bleak, cold settings, troubled characters and dark storylines.

Open world play Refers to the type of game where the player is given freedom to explore a virtual world and can make choices that determine the next moves. This gives the player a feeling of control in contrast to linear game play.

Opinion leaders Those in positions of power, for example newspaper owners and editors, who aim to persuade an audience of their point of view.

Othering The process of treating someone or something not only as fundamentally different from one's own group but also as inferior or subordinate on the basis of those perceived differences.

Paradigm A set of related signs from which the encoder can choose. In choosing one sign rather than another, the encoder of the product makes a paradigmatic choice.

Parody An imitation or copy of a particular product or style using deliberate exaggeration for comic or satirical effect.

Participatory culture The opposite of consumer culture, as it is a culture in which private individuals are not only consumers but also contributors and producers (prosumers). This has been made easier by new technologies. Jenkins' research showed that members of this culture believed their contributions mattered and they felt connected to each other.

Pastiche A form of imitation. Unlike parody, which mocks or satirises the object of imitation, pastiche is a neutral form of mimicry as it simply reproduces that which it copies or imitates.

Paywall A method of restricting access to a website other than by a subscription payment. Some newspapers introduced this as a way of creating revenue to make up for losses from print newspapers and advertising.

Pen portrait A marketing technique for defining an audience. It is an informal description of a person or group. It can cover factual aspects as well as attitudes and lifestyle.

Performativity The idea that identity is constructed through a series of performative acts.

Phatic internet technologies According to Wang, Tucker and Haines (2012), these are '*special forms of communications technologies devoted to personal and social needs and goals*'.

Photo essay A set of photographs that present an argument or narrative about a given topic or theme.

Pluralist pattern Describes the way in which some media content is shaped by consumer demand with the idea of giving people what they want rather than the content being dictated by the editor or owner. This concept of the reader wanting to know, was used by Rupert Murdoch to explain some of the more controversial stories in the *Sun*.

Polemical Opinionated, controversial, argumentative or strongly critical. Polemical magazine articles are commonly found in activist magazines and current affairs magazines.

Popular press Refers to the cheaper newspapers with a mass circulation. They are also commonly known as the tabloid press.

Postcolonial Refers to the time after the end of colonial rule. Postcolonial studies explore the lasting impact of colonial rule on people, countries and culture.

Pragmatics Relating to practical considerations, for example the importance of the generic elements of a media product in its marketing.

Press packs/media kits Known by either name, these are compiled by magazine publishers and their purpose is to give information to advertisers about the publication and its readers. They provide details about the target demographic and usually include a pen portrait of the reader or a graphic representation of their interests. There is also information about the reach of the magazine across different media platforms.

Profile A term used in the newspaper and magazine industry for a short biographical sketch of an individual or organisation.

Prosumers Derives from the marketing term 'production by consumers' and is used to describe those individuals who comment on, create or adapt existing content and then distribute it through the internet and social media.

Publisher-agency A media company that combines the functions of a magazine publisher with those of a content marketing agency. TCO is an example of a company that uses this business model.

Quality press Refers to newspapers that are distinguished by their seriousness. They cover the news in more detail and international stories. They were previously known as broadsheet newspapers.

Quarterly A magazine that is published four times a year.

Race Defined by racial characteristics, for example skin colour and facial features.

Realism A mode of representation that conceals the processes of construction, creating the illusion that the product offers a window onto the real world.

Reality television A sub-genre of television that is largely unscripted and focuses on the lives of ordinary people. The intention of the programmes in this genre is to present everyday life or, alternatively, 'real-life' situations created by the producers. The programmes tend to be entertaining rather than informative.

Reflexivity Defined by Tim Woods (2009) as the '*self-conscious incorporation of the processes of production, construction or composition*'. A reflexive media product will therefore reveal rather than conceal the ways in which it has been constructed. Also described as self-reflexivity or self-referentiality.

Reformers One of the psychographic groups in the 4Cs system of consumer classification developed by advertising agency Young and Rubicam. Reformers tend to be tolerant, socially aware and anti-materialistic. Their core need is for enlightenment.

Repertoire of elements The key features or conventions that are recognisable to an audience and as such distinguish one genre or sub-genre from another.

Reuters An international, independent news agency formed in 1850. It sells news, including written stories, photographs and video footage, to media industries. Clients pay a subscription which entitles them to use Reuter's news stories, pictures or video footage in their papers, magazines, websites or news bulletins.

Rolling news A 24-hour, continuously updated news service, broadcast on television and online.

Royal Charter This initially established the BBC and is its constitutional basis. Until 2016 it was reviewed before renewal, every ten years, by the government. Since 2016 it is every 11 years. The Charter sets out the public purpose of the BBC, guarantees its independence and outlines the duties of the BBC Trust.

Semantic field A set of inter-related words that refer to the same general area or topic. The language in a magazine such as *Kerrang!* is likely to draw on the semantic field of that particular genre rock music, for example.

Semantics Relates to the branch of linguistics concerned with how meanings are created. In a study of the media this applies to the meanings of the words or objects contained within a product.

Simulacra Postmodern concepts used to describe signs that simply refer to another sign rather than anything 'real'. Simulacra are commonly understood as copies of copies. The singular is simulacrum.

Simulacrum A term used by postmodern theorist Jean Baudrillard to describe a copy without an original (a copy of a copy) or a copy that has taken the place of the original.

Simulation An imitation of something; a fake.

Slash fiction A genre of fanfiction that depicts two fictional characters or famous people of the same sex in a romantic or sexual relationship with one another. Slash fiction focusing on female characters is often called femslash.

Social construct An idea or concept that is created, developed and accepted by society. These ideas are reinforced through repetition and practice.

Social realist genre Refers to films that give an indication of what life is really like. Often explore wider social issues through the creation of emotional personal stories.

Social semiotics A critical approach that addresses the perceived limitations of mainstream semiotics by acknowledging and exploring the social contexts in which meaning-making takes place.

Soft news Refers to items that are primarily entertaining or of personal interest to the reader, for example celebrity and lifestyle.

Specialised audience An audience with specific interests and needs which requires targeting in a particular way.

Spine The thin strip that is placed between the back and front of the DVD cover and is on show when the DVD is stored on the shelf. It reads from top to bottom and usually includes the name of the film, replicating the font style used on the cover. It also can include the production company name and logo, and the certification logo.

Standalone images Arresting images with no story attached. They may be used as a hook to attract an audience.

Statement of Aims and Intentions An assessed element of Component 3. It must be completed before you embark upon your production. It facilitates your planning, ensuring you have considered how to address the main elements of the theoretical framework.

Stepped question Refers to when an examination is split into different sub-parts with the mark tariffs usually increasing as the question parts become more difficult. In Component 1 Section B there are some questions that test your knowledge and are lower in tariff than those that require you to discuss and explain.

Street vendors Those who sell goods or services to members of the public from the street. For example, magazines such as *The Big Issue*, which are commonly referred to as street newspapers, are purchased from street vendors rather than from newsagents or supermarkets.

Structuralism A critical approach used to analyse the underlying structures or patterns of meaning within a text or culture.

Subculture A smaller cultural group that differs in some way from the larger, dominant culture under which it exists.

Subordinate A group that is disadvantaged compared with other groups and may face unequal treatment or discrimination.

Subsidiary A company that is owned by a larger company. The company that owns the subsidiary is often referred to as the parent company or the holding company.

Substantiate To provide evidence to support or illustrate a point, idea or argument – for example, supporting the idea that a television product is postmodern by referring to a specific technique that is used in the set episode.

Surface realism A particular form of realism in which aspects of mise-en-scéne such as costumes and props are used to convey an impression of authenticity. This technique is widely used in period dramas.

Sustained line of reasoning Refers to writing that is logically developed. Points are clearly identified and then developed using appropriate evidence. This then leads to a clear conclusion.

Symbolic annihilation The idea that the under-representation of particular social groups works to maintain social inequalities by denying those groups any meaningful presence, thereby rendering them silent or invisible.

Syntactic In linguistics, this refers to the way in which words are ordered in a sentence in order to create meaning. When applying this to media products, it refers to the structure of the product and how the construction of the semantic elements in any given genre create meanings.

Syntagm A combination of signs that, when linked together in a particular way, produce meanings.

Teaser campaign Posters or trailers that are part of the marketing campaign for a new film. They are released before the main campaign and their aim is to create a 'buzz' around the film through the creation of enigmas which catch the attention of the audience.

Teaser poster Also known as an 'advance' poster as it appears before the main marketing campaign is launched. These posters purposely contain limited information; the aim is to use enigmas to hook the audience, for example a tagline or a single image.

Technological convergence The ability to distribute content across different platforms, thus increasing commercial potential. For example, the BBC radio and television audience is no longer restricted to live watching and listening as they can access content through a range of digital platforms to suit their needs.

Textual determinism The idea that the meaning of a text is inherent within and determined by the text itself. Structuralist approaches such as semiotic analysis are often criticised for their textual determinism, as they are said to neglect the role of the audience in determining textual meaning.

Textual poaching A term used by Henry Jenkins to describe the way fans may appropriate a text and read it in a way that was not originally intended by its producer. In this way, media texts are reinterpreted and given new meanings.

The uncanny A sensation commonly produced in the supernatural genre, whereby the familiar is made to feel strange or unfamiliar. In Freudian theory, the uncanny is often associated with the return of something that has been repressed.

Theoretical approaches The academic framework related to the study of a particular discipline, for example Media Studies, which underpins understanding.

Three clicks user The three-click rule is related to website navigation and suggests that this is the optimum number of clicks to access information or make a purchase on the internet.

Trans-historical While some ideas and beliefs are initially relevant to a particular time period, certain ideas embody universal truths that cut across different time periods and forms of expression.

Transmedia storytelling Defined by Henry Jenkins (2007) as *'a process where integral elements of a [story or narrative] get dispersed systematically across multiple delivery channels for the purpose of creating a unified and coordinated entertainment experience'*.

Tribe An advertising tribe is a group of people who together identify themselves with a particular lifestyle and set of behaviours. They will also identify with particular products and share similar views about specific brands. These tribes are important to advertisers as they can be influential and play a role in marketing the product and raising brand awareness.

Trope A significant recurring device, motif or theme.

Tumblr A blogging or social networking site that enables users to share music, art, photos, videos and various other types of content.

Verisimilitude Having the appearance of truth ('verity' means truth, while 'similitude' means having a similarity or resemblance to something).

Vertical integration In terms of the film industry, this refers to a film company that owns other companies across different stages of the process, for example a production company that owns a distributor. This facilitates their ability to distribute and exhibit their films.

Virtual costuming Where new costumes or skins can be bought for characters in the virtual world of the game. Gamers can be involved in making choices about how they want their characters to be represented and the games' publishers can add to their revenue from the cash used to do this.

Virtue signalling The act of posting online content that suggests the person is good and virtuous.

Watershed The time when it becomes permissible to broadcast programmes that are unsuitable for younger audiences. In the UK this is after 9pm.

Whip pan When the camera pivots across a scene at speed creating a blurred shot. It is used to show passages of time, movement between locations and to suggest frenetic action.

Zombie drama A sub-genre of horror and the supernatural that focuses on the 'undead'.

Index

Acknowledgements

p1 Only Background/Shutterstock.com; p6 ESB Professional/ Shutterstock; p7(t) Stokkete/Shutterstock; p7(m) Mark Thomas/Alamy Stock Photo; p7(b) Courtesy Channel 4; p8 ADDICTIVE STOCK CREATIVES/Alamy Stock Photo; p9 PhotoHouse/Shutterstock; p10(r) ayzek/Shutterstock; p10(l) ChunkySoup, Wikimedia, https://commons.wikimedia.org/wiki/File:Zoom_elite_2.png, Public domain; p11 Album/Alamy Stock Photo; p12 pictures@lmkmedia.com/LANDMARK MEDIA/Alamy Stock Photo; p13 Patti McConville/Alamy Stock Photo; p17 NurPhoto SRL/Alamy Stock Photo; p20 ArtFamily/Shutterstock; p26 Arthimedes/ Shutterstock; p27 Hulinska Yevheniia/Shutterstock; p28 Boris15/Shutterstock; p29 Courtesy of Zoe Sugg YouTube Channel; p31 Lionel Hahn/Abaca Press/Alamy Stock Photo; p33 Barry Barnes/Alamy Stock Photo; p39 Courtesy of Attitude; p45(t) iQoncept/Shutterstock; p45(b) astel design/Shutterstock; p46 Courtesy of YouGov; p47 quinky/Shutterstock; p52 Michael Tubi/Alamy Live News/ Alamy Stock Photo; p59 BBC/BFI/LES FILMS DU FLEUVE/ SIXTEEN FILMS/WHY NOT PROD/WILD/Album/Alamy; p60 ESB Professional/Shutterstock; p62 Jacek Wojnarowski/ Shutterstock.com; p64(all) Courtesy Isabella Miles-Hardt, Peter Symonds College; p65 Courtesy Isabella Miles-Hardt, Peter Symonds College; p66 Monkey Business Images/ Shutterstock; p70 Nigel J. Harris/Shutterstock.com; p71(t) Antiques & Collectables/Alamy Stock Photo; p71(m) Retro AdArchives/Alamy Stock Photo; p71(b) f8 archive/Alamy Stock Photo; p74 Retro AdArchives/Alamy Stock Photo; p75(both) Courtesy Channel 4; p76 Retro AdArchives/Alamy Stock Photo; p77(l) Cinematic Collection/Alamy Stock Photo; p77(r) BFA/Alamy Stock Photo; p78 BFA/Alamy Stock Photo; p79 Pictorial Press Ltd/Alamy Stock Photo; p81(t) Ground Picture/Shutterstock; p81(b) Neil Baylis/Alamy Stock Photo; p83 Courtesy Oxfam; p85 Everett Collection, Inc / Alamy Stock Photo; p86(t) Virrage Images/Shutterstock; p86(b) Christine Chew/UPI/Alamy Stock Photo; p88 Rommel Canlas/Shutterstock; p89 Masheter Movie Archive/ Alamy Stock Photo; p90 MORA/Everett Collection/Alamy Live News; p91(both) Courtesy Sony; p93(all) Courtesy Sony; p94 Brian Friedman/Shutterstock.com; p95 Creative Lab/Shutterstock.com; p97 Billion Photos/Shutterstock; p101(t) Procyk Radek/Shutterstock.com; p101(b) Ground Picture/Shutterstock; p102 Everett Collection/Shutterstock; p103 Courtesy of Bauer Media; p104 McLittle Stock/ Shutterstock; p105 Hadrian/Shutterstock; p107 Squirrell/ Shutterstock.com; p108 Tero Vesalainen/Shutterstock; p109 G-Stock Studio/Shutterstock; p111 BigTunaOnline/ Shutterstock; p112 Sarunyu L/Shutterstock; p113 Courtesy BFI; p114 Kevin Hayes/Alamy Stock Photo; p117 BBC/ BFI/LES FILMS DU FLEUVE/SIXTEEN FILMS/WHY NOT PROD/WILD/Album/Alamy Stock Photo; p119 1000 Words/ Shutterstock.com; p121 Featureflash Photo Agency/ Shutterstock.com; p126 PAMCo; p128 insta_photos/ Shutterstock; p129 Antonio Guillem/Shutterstock; p130 Trinet Uzun/Shutterstock; p131 BAKOUNINE/Shutterstock.com; p132(t) London Entertainment/Alamy Stock Photo; p132(m) Shawn Goldberg/Shutterstock.com; p132(b) Featureflash Photo Agency/Shutterstock.com; p134 Shawshots/Alamy Stock Photo; p135(t) INTERFOTO/Alamy Stock Photo; p135(b) LightField Studios/Shutterstock; p138(both) Courtesy Channel 4; p139(both) Courtesy Channel 4; p140 charnsitr/Shutterstock.com; p141(t) Lenscap Photography/Shutterstock.com; p141(m) vesna cvorovic/Shutterstock; p141(b) CreativeAngela/Shutterstock.com; p142 Courtesy ESA; p143 adriaticfoto/Shutterstock; p144 Diego Thomazini/Shutterstock.com; p145 Tinxi/ Shutterstock.com; p146 TinoFotografie/Shutterstock.com; p147 Amir Ridhwan/Shutterstock; p150 panitanphoto/ Shutterstock; p154 Moviestore Collection Ltd/Alamy Stock Photo; p155 Album/Alamy Stock Photo; p156 Jean-Claude Lother/Photo12/Haut et Court/Canal+/Alamy Stock Photo; p157 Everett Collection/Alamy Stock Photo; p158(l) Pictorial Press Ltd/Alamy Stock Photo; p158(r) Marvel Studios/The Hollywood Archive/Alamy Stock Photo; p160 LANDMARK MEDIA/Alamy Stock Photo; p161 Pictorial Press Ltd/Alamy Stock Photo; p163 PictureLux/The Hollywood Archive/ Alamy Stock Photo; p173 Alan D West/EMPICS/Alamy Live News; p185 Courtesy lyncglightman; p190 Courtesy Huck/TCO; p191 Courtesy Adbusters; p192 Courtesy Adbusters; p193 Courtesy Huck/TCO; p194(both) Courtesy The Big Issue; p197 Courtesy The Big Issue; p200 Ovidiu Hrubaru/Shutterstock.com; p201 Loredana Sangiuliano/ Shutterstock.com; p202 Courtesy Arabia Felix; p203 Courtesy The Big Issue; p206(t) Courtesy TCO; p206(b) Courtesy The Big Issue Foundation; p208 (both) Courtesy The Big Issue; p212(t) Courtesy The Big Issue; p212(b2) Courtesy Geoff McFetridge; p214 Courtesy The Big Issue; p217 JuliusKielaltis/Shutterstock.com; p218(t) Envato.com/Shutterstock; p218(b) Lambros Kazan/Shutterstock; p220 Courtesy gal-dem; p221 PA Images/Alamy Stock Photo; p222 RomeoLu/Shutterstock; p224 Courtesy Stream Publishing; p225 Courtesy gal-dem; p226 Courtesy gal-dem/ Mathushaa Sagthidas; p228(t) Courtesy Attitude; p228(b) Courtesy Stream Publishing; p234 Courtesy Attitude; p235 Courtesy Shoury Sinha; p241 Kzenon/Shutterstock.com; p242 aria Symchych/Shutterstock; p243 Mila Basenko/ Shutterstock; p245 Haider Y. Abdulla/Shutterstock; p246 PA Images/Alamy Stock Photo; p250(t) Courtesy The Big Issue; p250(m) Namphon2U/Shutterstock; p250(b) sungong/ Shutterstock; p251(t) Nice Vector Wow/Shutterstock; p251(m) Tero Vesalainen/Shutterstock; p251(b) Mark Poprocki/Shutterstock; p252(both) Courtesy Mati Grancia; p283 Courtsy Mati Grancia; p253(t&m) Courtesy Rachel Wells, Heaton Manor School; p253(b) Courtesy Sophie Johnston, Varndean College; p254 Courtesy Sophie Johnston, Varndean College; p255(t) Courtesy Scott Maxwell, Keswick School; p261 ISxMaster/Shutterstock; p262 Alones/Shutterstock; p263(both) Courtesy Kelly Joves, Peter Symonds College; p264(both) Courtesy Kelly Joves, Peter Symonds College; p268 BFA/Alamy Stock Photo; p269 Monkey Business Images/Shutterstock; p272(both) Courtesy Sophie Burman, St Cyres School; p275(t) Gorodenkoff/ Shutterstock; p275(b3) Courtesy of Sony; p276 Courtesy of Rolling Stone UK; p277 Courtesy of Rolling Stone UK; p278 kudla/Shutterstock; p279(t3) Courtesy of George Francis, Peter Symonds College; p279(b5) Courtesy of Amber Bishop, Peter Symonds College; p280(all) Courtesy of Diana Zaletova, Peter Symonds College; p281(both) Courtesy of Michael Shenton, Oldham Sixth Form College; p282(t2) Courtesy of Michael Shenton, Oldham Sixth Form College; p282(all) Courtesy of Michael Shenton, Oldham Sixth Form College; p284 afotostock/Shutterstock; p285 Monkey Business Images/Shutterstock; p287(t) Ground Picture/Shutterstock; p287(b) fizkes/Shutterstock; p295 PictureLux/The Hollywood Archive/Alamy Stock Photo; p296 Photographee.eu/Shutterstock; p303 Tom Wang/ Shutterstock; p305 Licensed under the Creative Commons Attribution-Share Alike 2.0 General licence/Tzvetan Todorov no Fronteiras do Pensamento Porto Alegre 2012; p307(t) Licensed under the Creative Commons Attribution-Share Alike 4.0 International license. Alex Lozupone (Tduk); p307(b) Made available under the Creative Commons CC0 1.0 Universal Public Domain/Judith Butler; p308 GNU Free Documentation License, Version 1.2 /Joe Mabel; p309(t) Creative Commons Attribution-Share Alike 4.0 International license/bandura@stanford.edu; p309(b) Creative Commons CC0 1.0 Universal Public Domain; p310(t) Creative Commons Attribution 2.0 Generic license; p310(b) Creative Commons Attribution 2.0 Generic/https://commons.wikimedia.org/wiki/File:Etech05_Clay2.jpg/James Duncan Davidson